Broadman Comments

52 User-Friendly Bible Study Lessons

Based on the International Sunday School Lessons

Broadman Comments

52 User-Friendly Bible Study Lessons

Based on the International Sunday School Lessons

Robert J. Dean

Frank R. Lewis

James E. Taulman

Nashville, Tennessee

ISBN: 0-8054-1296-4

The Scripture used is in the King James Version.

Dewey Decimal Classification: 268.61
Subject Heading: SUNDAY SCHOOL LESSONS—COMMENTARIES

ISSN: 0068-2721

POSTMASTER: Send address change to *Broadman Comments,*
Customer Service Center, 127 Ninth Avenue, North
Nashville, Tennessee 37234

Printed in the United States of America

WRITERS

STUDYING THE BIBLE

Robert J. Dean continues the theological traditions of *Broadman Comments* while adding his own fresh insights. Dean is retired from the Baptist Sunday School Board (now LifeWay Christian Resources) and is a Th.D. graduate of New Orleans Seminary.

APPLYING THE BIBLE

Frank R. Lewis is senior pastor of the First Baptist Church, Nashville, Tennessee.

TEACHING THE BIBLE

James E. Taulman is a freelance writer in Nashville, Tennessee. Prior to that, Taulman was an editor of adult Sunday school materials for the Baptist Sunday School Board (now LifeWay Christian Resources).

Contents

FIRST QUARTER
From Slavery to Promised Land

SECOND QUARTER
Studies in Matthew

THIRD QUARTER
Helping a Church Face Crisis

FOURTH QUARTER
New Life in Christ

From Slavery to Promised Land

INTRODUCTION

This quarter covers two periods of Old Testament history—the Exodus and the Conquest. It begins with the Israelites as slaves in Egypt and ends with them in control of the Promised Land. The biblical material is from the Books of Exodus, Leviticus, Numbers, Deuteronomy, and Joshua.

Unit I, "Liberation and Covenant," surveys the deliverance from Egypt and the covenant at Mount Sinai. The four lessons focus on the call of Moses, the deliverance at the Red Sea, the making of the covenant at Mount Sinai, and the tabernacle and God's call to obedience.

Unit II, "Wilderness Wanderings," has five lessons that focus on God's leadership in the cloud and fire, the people's refusal to enter the Promised Land, years of wandering in the wilderness until the adult generation died, the commandment to love God wholeheartedly, and the warning about forgetting the Lord when the people prospered in Canaan.

Unit III, "Entering the Land," has four lessons that focus on passing the leadership from Moses to Joshua, crossing the Jordan River, the destruction of Jericho, and Joshua's calling the people to choose to serve the Lord.

Bible Books Covering Periods of Exodus and Conquest

Exodus is the book of redemption. It tells of the deliverance by God of His people from Egyptian slavery. Moses was the human instrument, but the deliverance was wrought by God. The deliverance had two phases: deliverance from Egypt because of the ten plagues and rescue from Pharaoh's pursuing army at the Red Sea. The book also describes the covenant that God made with Israel at Mount Sinai, highlighted by the Ten Commandments; the golden calf; the renewal of the covenant; and the building of the tabernacle.

Leviticus takes its name from Levi, the priestly tribe of Israel. It is a book of rituals and ceremonial laws having to do with priests, sacrifices, and the tabernacle. However, Leviticus has a twofold purpose: (1) to provide a way for sinful humankind to be able to worship the holy God and (2) to define the holiness to which the holy God calls His people. Jesus quoted Leviticus 19:18 as the second commandment of the law.

Numbers is named for two censuses or numberings in the book. The book describes the wilderness experiences of the Israelites. At the center of the book is the tragic account of the refusal of the Israelites to enter Canaan at Kadesh-Barnea. As a result, God condemned the adult generation to wander and die in the wilderness without seeing the Promised Land. The final chapters tell how the Israelites conquered enemies east of the Jordan.

September

October

November

1999

Deuteronomy means "second law." The book is a series of addresses given by Moses as the people prepared to enter Canaan. Moses reminded the people of what God had done for them. He called them to love the one Lord with all their being. He warned them about forgetting the Lord amidst the prosperity of the land of promise. He told them that obedience would lead to life, but disobedience would lead to death. Deuteronomy closes with the death of Moses after he had seen the Promised Land from a distance.

Joshua tells of the conquest of the Promised Land under the leadership of Joshua. God performed miraculous signs by enabling the Israelites to cross the flooded Jordan River and to capture the walled city of Jericho. Near the beginning of the conquest and after it, Joshua led the people to reaffirm their covenant with the Lord. The book closes with Joshua's final plea to choose to serve the Lord and then with his death.

Cycle of 1998 – 2004

1998–1999	1999–2000	2000–2001	2001–2002	2002–2003	2003–2004
Old Testament Survey	Exodus Leviticus Numbers Deuteronomy Joshua	Judges 1, 2 Samuel 1 Chronicles 1 Kings 1–11 2 Chronicles 1–9	Parables Miracles Sermon on the Mount	2 Kings 18–25 2 Chronicles 29–36 Jeremiah Lamentations Ezekiel Habakkuk Zephaniah	James 1, 2 Peter 1, 2, 3 John Jude
New Testament Survey	Matthew	Luke	Isaiah 9; 11; 40–66 Ruth Jonah Nahum	Personalities of the NT	Christmas Esther Job Ecclesiastes Song of Solomon
John	1, 2 Corinthians	Acts	Romans Galatians	Mark	The Cross 1, 2 Thessalonians Revelation
Genesis	Ephesians Philippians Colossians Philemon	1 Kings 12–2 Kings 17 2 Chronicles 10–28 Isaiah 1–39 Amos Hosea Micah	Psalms Proverbs	Ezra Nehemiah Daniel Joel Obadiah Haggai Zechariah Malachi	Hebrews 1, 2 Timothy Titus

God Calls Moses

September

5

1999

Background Passage: Exodus 3:1–22
Focal Passage: Exodus 3:1–12

God is the main person in all the Bible, but the sovereign God has often chosen to work through people to accomplish His work. Think of some of the people in the Bible whom God called for special tasks: Abraham, Moses, Samuel, Amos, Isaiah, Jeremiah, Ezekiel, Saul of Tarsus. This lesson focuses on God's call to Moses.

Study Aim: *To describe how God called Moses and how Moses responded.*

STUDYING THE BIBLE

OUTLINE AND SUMMARY

I. God Speaks to Moses (Exod. 3:1–6)
- **1. The burning bush (3:1–3)**
- **2. The holy God (3:4–6)**

II. God Reveals His Plans (Exod. 3:7–10)
- **1. God's plans for Israel (3:7–9)**
- **2. God's plans for Moses (3:10)**

III. God Answers Moses' Questions (Exod. 3:11–22)
- **1. Who am I? (3:11–12)**
- **2. Who are you? (3:13–22)**

God got Moses' attention with a burning bush (3:1–3). When the holy God spoke to Moses, he responded with submissiveness and reverence (3:4–6). God announced His plans to deliver Israel from Egypt and to give them the Promised Land (3:7–9). God called Moses to be the human leader (3:10). When Moses asked who he was to be given such a task, God promised to be with him (3:11–12). When Moses asked God His name, the Lord told him and gave him instructions and promised to announce to Israel (3:13–22).

I. God Speaks to Moses (Exod. 3:1–6)

1. The burning bush (3:1–3)

1 Now Moses kept the flock of Jethro his father in law, the priest of Midian: and he led the flock to the backside of the desert, and came to the mountain of God, even to Horeb.

You may want to review Exodus 1–2 to see how Moses happened to be a shepherd in Midian. Jethro was a Midianite, one of the descendants of Abraham through Keturah (Gen. 25:1–2). He was a priest who seems to have continued Abraham's faith in one God.

Finding water and grass in that region of the Sinai peninsula led Moses into an area called Mount Horeb (Sinai). This mountain became the mountain of God when God later made His covenant with Israel there, but it may already have had a reputation as a special place for encountering God.

2 And the angel of the LORD appeared unto him in a flame of fire out of the midst of a bush: and he looked, and, behold, the bush burned with fire, and the bush was not consumed.

3 And Moses said, I will now turn aside, and see this great sight, why the bush is not burnt.

God used the miracle of the burning bush to get Moses' attention and prepare him for the special revelation that followed. Moses was not surprised to notice a bush burning; he was surprised that the bush just kept burning and was not destroyed by the fire.

Verse 2 says that the angel of the Lord appeared to him in this burning bush. The word *angel* means "messenger." This special angel is mentioned several times in the Old Testament. Sometimes he appeared in bodily form. Here he appeared in a burning bush. This angel is so closely identified with the Lord that when the angel spoke, the Old Testament refers to the voice as the voice of God.

2. The holy God (3:4–6)

4 And when the LORD saw that he turned aside to see, God called unto him out of the midst of the bush, and said, Moses, Moses. And he said, Here am I.

5 And he said, Draw not nigh hither: put off thy shoes from off thy feet, for the place whereon thou standest is holy ground.

6 Moreover he said, I am the God of thy father, the God of Abraham, the God of Isaac, and the God of Jacob. And Moses hid his face; for he was afraid to look upon God.

Many important truths are revealed in the encounter of God and Moses:

1. *God takes the initiative.* Moses did not seek and discover God; instead God revealed Himself to Moses. The Bible does not tell how people discover God, but how God reveals Himself.

2. *The divine-human encounter is personal.* God called Moses by name. Both God and Moses used "I." God revealed Himself as the God of Moses' father and his ancestors; but for God to be real, He had to become the God of Moses.

3. *God is holy; yet He reveals Himself to sinful humans.* "Holy" means "set apart." It refers to the majestic glory of the infinite Creator and King of the universe in contrast to the frail humanity of one of His creatures. It also refers to the white-hot purity, goodness, and righteousness of God in contrast to sinful mortals.

4. *The appropriate human response to the holy God is reverence and submission.* Taking off one's shoes was a sign of submission, as a slave to a master. Moses also showed his reverence by hiding his face from the face of God. His words "Here am I" imply a humble submissiveness. His words remind us of young Samuel's response when God called him, "Speak; for thy servant heareth" (1 Sam. 3:10).

5. *The God who reveals Himself is the God who is working in human history.* Encounters with God are personal, but God is not the exclusive God of any person. God identified Himself to Moses as the God of Abra-

ham, Isaac, and Jacob. Centuries had passed since the time of the patriarchs, but people of true faith remembered and kept the faith of their forefathers. The Book of Genesis ends with Joseph's death in Egypt and with his promise that God would bring the Israelites back to the Promised Land (Gen. 50:24–26).

II. God Reveals His Plans (Exod. 3:7–10)

1. God's plans for Israel (3:7–9)

7 And the LORD said, I have surely seen the affliction of my people which are in Egypt, and have heard their cry by reason of their taskmasters; for I know their sorrows;

8 And I am come down to deliver them out of the hand of the Egyptians, and to bring them up out of that land unto a good land and a large, unto a land flowing with milk and honey; unto the place of the Canaanites, and the Hittites, and the Amorites, and the Perizzites, and the Hivites, and the Jebusites.

9 Now therefore, behold, the cry of the children of Israel is come unto me: and I have also seen the oppression wherewith the Egyptians oppress them.

When Genesis closed, the Israelites were favored guests in the land where Joseph served as the second in command. However, during the intervening centuries, the Egyptians came to see the Hebrews as a threat. Therefore, they made slaves of them. For centuries the Israelites had lived as slaves. Many of them forgot the promises of God to their forefathers. Those who remembered the promises were tempted to wonder if God had forgotten them and His promises. Did He know and did He care about their plight? If so, why had He not heard their cries and heeded their prayers?

Exodus 2:23–25 announces that God heard the cry of His oppressed people, remembered His promises, and cared about the people. Exodus 3:7–9 records what God announced to Moses, which he in turn was to announce to the people. Notice the strong verbs that describe God's actions. God had seen their affliction and had heard their cries of distress. He knew and cared about them.

Therefore, God announced that He was going to fulfill His promises to Abraham, Isaac, and Jacob. First, God was going to deliver the Israelites from a slavery imposed by the most powerful nation on earth. Then God was going to bring His people into a large, good land. "Milk and honey" describes a land of good crops and plenty of everything, even the sweet honey. At the time, the Promised Land was inhabited by a number of groups of pagan people; but God was going to give that land to Israel.

2. God's plans for Moses (3:10)

10 Come now therefore, and I will send thee unto Pharaoh, that thou mayest bring forth my people the children of Israel out of Egypt.

God had said that He would bring Israel out of Egypt. Now suddenly, God used the same words to describe what Moses was going to do. Moses could not escape the obvious conclusion that God wanted him to be an instrument of the Lord in accomplishing His purpose for His people.

God—who needs nothing or no one—often chooses to do His work through people. All of those whom God called in the Bible were called to be used of God in some great task. None of them was given a more daunting task than Moses. The Israelites were helpless slaves under the iron grip of Egyptian power. Moses was a wanted criminal, whose one attempt to help his people had met with rebuff. They had lost much sense of community, and many had lost their faith. How was this helpless group of slaves to be delivered, much less be able to overcome the powerful groups that inhabited Canaan? God had said that He would do it, and He had called Moses to be the human leader of this seemingly impossible undertaking.

III. God Answers Moses' Questions (Exod. 3:11–22)

1. Who am I? (3:11, 12)

11 And Moses said unto God, Who am I, that I should go unto Pharaoh, and that I should bring forth the children of Israel out of Egypt?

Moses was aware not only of the helpless plight of the children of Israel but also of his own lack of qualifications for this task. Thus he asked, "Who am I" to undertake such a task? Moses had lived long enough to have a pretty clear idea of who he was—or at least who he thought he was. He saw himself as a shepherd and a family man living a quiet life many miles away from the grandeur and terror of Egypt. In Egypt he was a wanted criminal, who had murdered an Egyptian. Among the Israelites, Moses' lack of confidence grew out of how he had been rebuffed in his youthful attempt to help an Israelite (Exod. 2:11–15).

God was calling him to confront Pharaoh and to lead the Israelites out of slavery. Moses wanted to know what God knew about him that he himself did not know. What made God think that this seemingly unqualified shepherd was the person to do this great work?

12 And he said, Certainly I will be with thee; and this shall be a token unto thee, that I have sent thee: When thou hast brought forth the people out of Egypt, ye shall serve God upon this mountain.

God did not give Moses a road map to the future. He simply assured Moses, "Certainly, I will be with thee." God promised to give Moses a sign, but the sign itself was dependent on God delivering Israel and bringing them to Mount Sinai. Moses asked for certainty, and God offered only a promise of His presence. This required Moses to launch out with nothing more than the promise of God. Isn't that all that Abraham had when he answered the call of God? We live by faith, not sight.

For people of true faith, that promise is enough. As we move forward, we find confirmations of that promise. Thus based on experience, people of faith say with Paul, "I can do all things through Christ which strengtheneth me" (Phil. 4:13).

2. Who are you? (3:13–22)

Moses then asked the Lord how he was to answer the Israelites when they asked the name of the God in whose name he came (3:13). God told Moses His name (3:14). The Hebrews considered the personal name of their God so sacred that they would not speak or write it. Scholars debate the exact meaning. The name of the God of Israel is sometimes translated as Jehovah or Yahweh; it appears as "the LORD" in many English translations. The name emphasizes God as the One who is, was, and will be—the eternal God who fulfills His purpose.

God commanded Moses to tell the Israelites God's personal name (3:15) and to announce that the Lord would deliver them (3:16, 17). God told Moses that the Israelite elders would listen and go with him to confront Pharaoh (3:18). God said that Pharaoh would not hear him, and that God would smite Egypt until Pharaoh was forced to let the Israelites go (3:19, 20). God also promised that the Egyptians would give their treasures to the Israelites (3:21,22).

PRONUNCIATION GUIDE

Amorites	[AM uh rights]
Canaanites	[KAY nuhn ights]
Hittites	[HIT tights]
Hivites	[HIGH vights]
Horeb	[HOH reb]
Jebusites	[JEB yoo sights]
Jethro	[JETH roh]
Keturah	[keh TYOO ruh]
Midian	[MID ih uhn]
Perizzites	[PER ih zights]
Sinai	[SIGH nay igh]

SUMMARY OF BIBLE TRUTHS

1. God has a long-range plan for His people and for each person.
2. God knows and cares for His people even when they think He has forgotten them.
3. God is holy; yet He reveals Himself to sinful humans and calls us personally.
4. We should respond to God with reverence and submissiveness.
5. God uses people as instruments to work out His will.
6. God promises to be with us and to supply all we need to do His will.

APPLYING THE BIBLE

1. Seeing the unusual. Unusual things get our attention. Recently a hand grenade was discovered in a nursing home. Apparently, a veteran of World War II brought it in with him when he moved into the facility years ago. It was in a memory box tucked neatly away in the back of his sock drawer. Members of the man's family discovered the grenade in his personal effects following his death, and the authorities were summoned. As you can imagine, this discovery got lots of attention. Moses saw a bush that burned yet was not consumed. It was an unusual sight, and it caused Moses to do things he wouldn't have done under ordinary circumstances. What did Moses do when he saw the fire on his horizon?

- Moses turned aside from where he normally went.
- He drew near, which means he had to draw away from the ordinary.
- Moses observed; he carefully examined the unusual sight before him.
- He listened to the voice of God, forgetting the tasks of herding sheep.
- When instructed, Moses removed his shoes.
- Throughout the encounter, Moses inventoried his life and found it humbling that God would choose to use him.

When God allows a fire to burn on our horizon, would we be willing to turn from the distractions of life and experience him?

2. Learning to listen to God. In an article entitled "How to Be a Better Listener," Vinita Hampton Wright offers several principles that are intended to help sharpen our listening skills. Notice how the principles she suggests apply to Moses' experience at the burning bush.

- *Be aware of body language* (Moses took off his shoes to express his reverence for God).
- *Identify with others' emotions* (God was burdened for His people and Moses needed to be).
- *Be sensitive to the Spirit* (we'll never know what Moses' devotional life was like on the backside of the desert, but he must have remembered and practiced everything his mother taught him).
- *Ask questions to clarify* (Moses asked, "Who am I and who are you?").
- *Listen more than you speak* (the text shows God speaking more than Moses).

It may be that if we would learn to practice these principles of listening, we might hear God more clearly in worship.

3. Breaking out of a rut. Everyone falls into a rut once in a while. It would seem to the critical observer that Moses was in a forty-year rut. He had settled into a comfortable routine in the back side of the desert serving his father-in-law. Yes, God was preparing him for a greater role in the wilderness, but face it, Moses was in a rut and was not looking for a God-sized challenge.

Business leaders offer all kinds of advice for those who are in a rut. Moses could have had the same list in his hip pocket or, had he been like many of us, near the front of his organizer. He may have turned to it often. This list of "rut busters" may be helpful to you:

- Rediscover your passion.
- Rewrite your top five priorities from what they are to what they ought to be.
- Abandon the nonessentials.

- Improve your resumé (take a class, attend a seminar, develop a new skill).
- Find a way to connect with the person who inspires you as "best in your field" and see what makes them tick.
- Reconnect with a valued support system from your past.
- Network with a group of folks who are not in your circle of influence.
- Reach down to help someone as you think about reaching up to better yourself.
- Take some new risk, but do so wisely.
- Remember that it's always too soon to quit.

God's call from the burning bush was a gracious call to leave the rut behind.

4. A God-sized challenge. Winds howl with hurricane force. Exposed skin is threatened by near-instant frostbite. The air is so thin you need 10 breaths to take a single step. Judgment goes to pot. One woozy misstep can mean death.[1]

So writes a reporter describing the challenges that await the individual who faces one of the adventures of a lifetime—climbing Mount Everest, the highest mountain in the world. More than 700 people have made it to the top since the first ascent by Sir Edmund Hillary and Tenzing Norgay in 1953, and 154 have died trying.

Tom Whittaker, a college outdoor education professor with an artificial leg, hopes to become the first disabled climber to reach the top. Imagine that!

At the burning bush, Moses had to decide if he was willing to accept a God-sized challenge. His "Everest Adventure" would be leading the Israelites from Egypt through the wilderness. His only option was to stay on the back side of the wilderness and take care of his father-in-law's sheep.

Can you imagine what would happen in your church if only 10 percent of your congregation decided to accept the God-sized challenge that awaits them? Can you imagine what would happen in your life if you were one of those 10 percent?

Moses' dilemma is yours too. Are you content to stay on the backside of the desert, or will you accept a God-sized challenge today?

TEACHING THE BIBLE

- *Main Idea:* Moses responded to God's call.
- *Suggested Teaching Aim:* God's call to Moses reminds us that He still uses people to accomplish His will.

A TEACHING OUTLINE

1. *God Speaks to Moses (Exod. 3:1–6)*
2. *God Reveals His Plans (Exod. 3:7–10)*
3. *God Answers Moses' Questions (Exod. 3:11–22)*

Introduce the Bible Study

Share: Floyd was herding cattle in West Texas. It was a hot, dusty job. He was startled one day when he saw a fountain of water spewing up in the middle of a dry, arid plain. He had been by the area yesterday, and the fountain was not there. He rode over and got off his horse to look at it. He heard a voice calling, "Floyd, Floyd." Immediately, Floyd . . . Let members suggest Floyd's response.

Ask, What would you think if Floyd had told you this? Say, Moses was as surprised to see the burning bush as Floyd was the fountain. Point out that God wanted to get Moses' attention so God could assign Moses the task of delivering His people.

Search for Biblical Truth

On a chalkboard, write: *1. God Speaks to Moses (Exod. 3:1–6).* Ask a volunteer to read verses 1–6. On a map locate Mount Sinai and point out that it is the same as Mount Horeb. Lecture briefly (or **IN ADVANCE** enlist a member to do so) on Jethro's ancestry.

Explain: (1) The purpose of the flaming bush; (2) the "angel of the Lord"; (3) how knowing this was the same God who had revealed Himself to his ancestors helped Moses.

Relate the five important truths revealed in this encounter. (Or write these on five strips of paper and give to five members to read.) After reading each statement, ask the corresponding question: (1) Why do you think the Bible does not tell us how people discover God, but how God reveals Himself? (2) How does God become real to us? (3) How do you relate to God's holiness? (4) What is an appropriate response to God's holiness? (5) What evidence do you have that God is still working in human history?

Write on the chalkboard: *2. God Reveals His Plans (Exod. 3:7–10).* Ask members to read verses 7–10 silently and identify at least three words that show God's involvement in His people's lives. (Seen, heard, know; v. 7.) Ask, What obstacles did Moses face?

Write on the chalkboard: *3. God Answers Moses' Questions (Exod. 3:11–22).* Ask members to read these verses silently and answer: How did Moses' estimation of himself and God's estimation of him differ? What did God know about Moses that Moses did not know about himself? What did Moses ask God to give him? What did Moses get? **IN ADVANCE,** make a poster with these words on it: *Moses asked for certainty, and God offered him only a promise of His presence.* Ask, Has God done this with you? Why do you think God does this? Why doesn't God reveal the future more clearly for us?

Ask the following based on the "Summary of Bible Truths": (1) Do you believe God has a long-range plan for His people and for each person? Why? (2) What evidence can you cite to show that God knows and cares for His people even when they think He has forgotten them? (3) Why does a holy God still reveal Himself to sinful humans? (4) How can we respond to God with reverence and submissiveness? (5) What evidence can you cite that God uses people as instruments to work out His will? (6) How can you show the validity of God's promise to be with us and supply all we need to do His will?

Give the Truth a Personal Focus

Ask, How does God's call to Moses remind us that God still uses people to accomplish His will? (God has no one else to do His work other than His people; God plus the *weakest* but *willing* person is sufficient.) List ways as members respond. Distribute paper and pencils and ask members to write a faith-promise based on one of these statements that they will claim for some project to which they believe God is calling them.

---

1. Tim Klass, The Associated Press.

September

12

1999

Crossing the Red Sea

Background Passage: Exodus 13:17–14:31
Focal Passages: Exodus 13:17–22; 14:26–31

The exodus from Egypt was not an escape achieved by Moses and the children of Israel; it was a divine deliverance wrought by God. This deliverance was in two phases: (1) breaking the will of a defiant Pharaoh by means of the ten plagues, which led to the Israelites leaving Egypt (Exod. 5:1–13:16) and (2) the deliverance of Israel from Pharaoh's pursuing chariots and the waters of the Red Sea. This lesson focuses on the second phase.

Study Aim: *To cite evidences that the deliverance of Israel was the work of the Lord.*

STUDYING THE BIBLE

OUTLINE AND SUMMARY

I. God Led His People from Egypt (Exod. 13:17–22)
  1. God as Leader (13:17, 18)
  2. Remembering past promises (13:19)
  3. God's presence with them (13:20, 22)

II. God Promised to Deliver from Pursuit (Exod. 14:1–18)
  1. Pursued by Pharaoh (14:1–9)
  2. Israel's unbelief (14:10–12)
  3. God's promise to save them from Pharaoh (14:13–18)

III. God Delivered Israel at the Red Sea (Exod. 14:19–31)
  1. Israel's safe passage through the sea bed (14:19–22)
  2. Destruction of the Egyptians (14:23–29)
  3. Salvation and faith (14:30, 31)

God led Israel as they left Egypt (13:17, 18). Moses took the body of Joseph with them (13:19). God led them in a pillar of cloud by day and a pillar of fire by night (13:20–22). Pharaoh decided to pursue them (14:1–9). The Israelites reacted to the pursuit with unbelief (14:10–12). God promised to save them (14:13–18). God parted the waters of the Red Sea for the Israelites to pass through (14:19–22). Then God allowed the waters to destroy the pursuing Egyptians (14:23–29). As a result, the Israelites saw that the Lord had saved them, and they believed Him (14:30, 31).

I. God Led His People from Egypt (Exod. 13:17–22)

1. God as Leader (13:17, 18)

17 And it came to pass, when Pharaoh had let the people go, that God led them not through the way of the land of the Philistines, although that was near; for God said, Lest peradven-

ture the people repent when they see war, and they return to Egypt:

18 But God led the people about, through the way of the wilderness of the Red sea: and the children of Israel went up harnessed out of the land of Egypt.

The key words in these verses are repeated in both verses: "God led." Just as God had been their deliverer from Egypt, so He became the One who led them as they went on their way.

Verse 17 says that "Pharaoh had let the people go." This had been the ultimatum from God to Pharaoh at the beginning of the contest of wills between God and Pharaoh (5:1). When Pharaoh defied the Lord (5:2), God told Moses that He would smite Egypt so that Pharaoh would not only let them go but drive them out of the land (6:1). After the terrible plague of the death of the firstborn, Pharaoh finally did order the Israelites to leave (12:31, 32).

The shortest route to Canaan lay along the coast of the Mediterranean Sea. This led through a fortified part of Egypt and to the coastal plain settled by the warlike Philistines. God knew the people were not ready for warfare. Although they left Egypt armed (the meaning of "harnessed"), they were unprepared to face determined enemies. God knew that the fickle Israelites would quickly become discouraged and want to return to Egypt.

Therefore, God led them by a route that headed for the Red Sea and the wilderness. He had at least two reasons for this: (1) God was setting up the final phase of deliverance by moving them toward the Red Sea. (2) God planned to lead them to Mount Sinai in order to make a covenant with them there (3:12).

2. Remembering past promises (13:19)

19 And Moses took the bones of Joseph with him: for he had straitly sworn the children of Israel, saying, God will surely visit you; and ye shall carry up my bones away hence with you.

When Joseph was dying, he promised that the Lord would eventually lead the Israelites back to Canaan; and he made them promise to take his body with them and bury him in the Promised Land (Gen. 50:24–26). Joseph had been dead for centuries before God delivered Israel from Egypt, but Moses remembered the promise made by his ancestors to Joseph. Taking the body of Joseph with them not only kept a promise to Joseph but also testified to confidence that God was about to fulfill His promise of leading them to Canaan.

3. God's presence with them (13:20–22)

20 And they took their journey from Succoth, and encamped in Etham, in the edge of the wilderness.

21 And the LORD went before them by day in a pillar of a cloud, to lead them the way; and by night in a pillar of fire, to give them light; to go by day and night:

22 He took not away the pillar of the cloud by day, nor the pillar of fire by night, from before the people.

This is the first of many references to the Lord's presence in the pillar of cloud by day and the pillar of fire by night. The emphasis in verse 21 is on this as the means by which God led Israel (see Num. 9:15–23). The two pillars provided guidance for travel at night as well as by day. The pillar of fire lighted their way through the dark. Exodus 14:19–20 gives an example of how the two pillars also protected Israel from the pursuing Egyptians.

Verse 13:22 emphasizes another aspect of the two pillars. One of them was always visible. This was a constant reminder to the Israelites that the Lord had not forsaken them; His presence was with them. Thus, the two pillars provided: (1) assurance of God's abiding presence with them, (2) a way by which God led and guided them, and (3) protection from their enemies.

II. God Promised to Deliver from Pursuit (Exod. 14:1–18)

1. Pursued by Pharaoh (14:1–9)

During the plagues, Pharaoh had repeatedly changed his mind. Now after driving the Israelites out, he decided to go after them. He was lured into this fatal decision because he thought they were entangled in the wilderness (14:1–4). Pharaoh sent six hundred swift chariots to pursue and overtake the Israelites (14:5–9).

2. Israel's unbelief (14:10–12)

The Israelites complained that God and Moses had led them into the wilderness to die. They said it would have been better to die as slaves in Egypt.

3. God's promise to save them from Pharaoh (14:13–18)

Moses told them to stand still and see God's salvation. God would fight for them (14:13, 14). God told Moses to tell the people to go forward. God promised that when Moses stretched out his hand and rod over the water, He would enable the Israelites to cross over on dry ground (14:15, 16). God predicted that the Egyptians would follow them into the sea bed and be destroyed, causing all concerned to know that the Lord was God (14:17, 18).

III. God Delivered Israel at the Red Sea (Exod. 14:19–31)

1. Israel's safe passage through the sea bed (14:19–22)

The pillar of cloud went before them to light their way and behind them to darken the way of the Egyptians (14:19, 20). When Moses stretched out his hand, the waters parted and the Israelites passed through on dry ground (14:21, 22).

2. Destruction of the Egyptians (14:23–29)

26 And the LORD said unto Moses, Stretch out thine hand over the sea, that the waters may come again upon the Egyptians, upon their chariots, and upon their horsemen.

27 And Moses stretched forth his hand over the sea, and the sea returned to its strength when the morning appeared; and

the Egyptians fled against it; and the LORD overthrew the Egyptians in the midst of the sea.

28 And the waters returned, and covered the chariots, and the horsemen, and all the host of Pharaoh that came into the sea after them; there remained not so much as one of them.

29 But the children of Israel walked upon dry land in the midst of the sea; and the waters were a wall unto them on their right hand, and on their left.

When the Israelites moved through the walls of water safely, the chariots of Pharaoh followed (14:23). Although the Israelites had walked on dry ground through the sea bed, mud began to mire the wheels of the chariots so that they drove heavily. This, of course, was the Lord's work (14:24). Eventually, the Egyptians realized this and exclaimed, "Let us flee from the face of Israel; for the LORD fighteth for them against the Egyptians" (14:25).

The Lord commanded Moses to stretch out his hand a second time over the sea. The first time the sea had parted for the Israelites to pass through. The second time the sea walls collapsed and the rushing waters flowed back to their place. The word *strength* in verse 27 has been translated in various ways. It may mean "normal state" (NASB).

Verse 29 reviews the earlier action described in verse 22. This reminds us that this second phase of divine deliverance from Egypt, crossing the Red Sea, included two stages: (1) the safe passage of all the Israelites on a dry sea bed, and (2) the destruction of all the Egyptians who pursued them into the sea bed.

3. Salvation and faith (14:30, 31)

30 Thus the LORD saved Israel that day out of the hand of the Egyptians; and Israel saw the Egyptians dead upon the sea shore.

31 And Israel saw that great work which the LORD did upon the Egyptians: and the people feared the LORD, and believed the LORD, and his servant Moses.

Verse 30 is the first time in the Bible where the Bible uses "the LORD" as the subject of "saved." This combination is a key concept in both the Old and New Testaments. The Lord saved Israel from the hand of Pharaoh in such a way that no one could doubt that He did it, or that the salvation was thorough and complete. As the Israelites stood on the opposite bank of the sea, they looked around and realized that all of them had safely crossed over. Only God could have held back the waters until they made their way through the walls of water on either side. And only God could have made the sea bed like dry ground for them.

They had seen the chariots become mired in the mud that had been dry ground for their feet. They had seen Moses stretch out his hand at the Lord's command and watched as the walls of water rushed in on the pursuing Egyptians. They now saw the bodies of dead Egyptians floating toward the seashore. They realized that the pursuing army they had so feared had been utterly destroyed. The Egyptians had intended to "overtake" the Israelites (14:9). Instead, the Lord "overthrew" the Egyptians (14:27).

The first part of verse 31 emphasizes that the Israelites realized this "great work" was done by the Lord, not by them or by Moses. God had delivered them from Egypt through signs and wonders; now He had delivered them from the pursuing Egyptians at the Red Sea.

They responded in two ways: (1) "The people feared the LORD." (2) They "believed the LORD, and his servant Moses." They had a new sense of reverent awe and godly fear of the power of their God. And they finally believed not only the Lord but His spokesman Moses. You and I may say, "It's about time after all that the Lord had done for them!" They had been slow to believe. More often than not they responded with unbelief toward God and God's word through Moses. Some have referred to this as Israel's "conversion." That may be too strong a word, since many setbacks lay ahead; however, this was a significant turning point for Israel.

The word *believed* is the same word used in Genesis 15:6, Abraham "believed in the LORD." The meaning is similar to the Greek word used so often in the New Testament to describe the appropriate human response to God's saving acts on our behalf through the work of God in Christ.

PRONUNCIATION GUIDE

Etham	[EE tham]
Philistines	[fih LISS teens]
Succoth	[SUHK ahth]

SUMMARY OF BIBLE TRUTHS

1. Neither we nor our leaders can save us; only God can.
2. Only God can guide us in the way we should go.
3. God's presence provides assurance, guidance, and protection.
4. God can win the victory over all the evil forces that threaten His people and seek to thwart His saving purpose.
5. The Lord's great works of salvation on our behalf should lead to reverent faith in Him.

APPLYING THE BIBLE

1. A sleeping judge. When a California judge was caught napping in the midst of a murder trial, the case was dismissed and a mistrial declared. The judge actually fell asleep on the bench as a witness was giving testimony. The judge attributed his behavior to medication that he was taking for his back.

The presence of God as realized in the cloud and the fire reminded Israel that God never ceased having them in mind. He did not fall asleep. Instead, for the entire time that the Israelites were in the wilderness, all forty years, God kept watch over them to protect and guide them. His presence is just as real in your life today as well.

2. Quotes on deliverance:

"From all blindness of heart, from pride, vainglory, and hypocrisy; from envy, hatred, and malice, and all uncharitableness, Good Lord, deliver us" *(The Book of Common Prayer)*.

"An object in possession seldom retains the same charm that it had in pursuit" (Pliny the Younger).

3. Being in bondage. When faced with what looked like a no-way-out situation, the Israelites became frightened and were ready to return to Egypt as slaves. They had never known freedom. Mohandas Gandhi said, "It is not a shame to be a slave; it is a shame to own a slave."

4. Injustice of slavery. The House of Slaves located on the west coast of Africa is a solemn reminder of the injustice of slavery carried on three hundred years ago. Tourists come to view the place where African children as young as four years old were sold into slavery, never seeing their family or their native Africa again. Ndiaye, tour guide for the House of Slaves, is a proud historian. He has placed a small sign in the foyer for everyone to see with these words printed in his own handwriting: "There is no people without memory and the future of a people can only be enlightening if based on the past."[1]

Exodus begins with the story of a Pharaoh who did not know Joseph. But the Israelites knew him. At least Moses did. The fact that they took his bones out of Egypt points to the hope of exodus that they never forgot. One day, the God who promised to deliver them would keep His promise.

The Lord is not slow in keeping His promise as some understand slowness. He is patient with us, not wanting anyone to perish, but everyone to come to repentance.

5. The resolve to remain free. "The time is now near at hand which must probably determine whether Americans are to be freemen or slaves; whether they are to have any property they can call their own; whether their houses and farms are to be pillaged and destroyed, and themselves consigned to a state of wretchedness from which no human efforts will deliver them. The fate of unborn millions will now depend, under God, on the courage and conduct of this army. Our cruel and unrelenting enemy leaves us only the choice of brave resistance, or the most abject submission. We have, therefore, to resolve to conquer or die" (George Washington, address to the Continental Army before the Battle of Long Island, August 27, 1776).

6. New—for a price. Everything old is new again, but a bit more pricey. Schwinn has released one of its most popular bicycles from the fifties. The roadmaster of bikes cost $120 when it sold forty years ago. Today you can buy a replica of it for $3,500.00. Plymouth has just released a roadster that resembles a fifties hot rod, which can be yours, if you can find one, for only $35,000. In a showroom near you, the Beetle has just been released by Volkswagen. Refined and rejuvenated, the sporty little icon of the American road can be yours for only $17,000, which is only about $15,000 more than you would have paid for a new one in 1970.

People know that our memory is marketable. We will hold onto our memories of yesterday and try to reclaim them. Unfortunately, it is always an expensive proposition.

Try reclaiming a culture that knows not Christ. Try reclaiming a culture where pre-pubescent assassins attack our children during a fire drill, where disputes in the classroom over a girlfriend are settled behind a gym three days before graduation with multiple gunshots leaving one student dead and the other incarcerated for life.

We lament the loss of innocence, the loss of what we knew years ago. It is reclaimable. It won't be cheap. We'll have to do some costly things to get it back. It will cost us more than it would have had we never lost it to begin with, but it is not impossible.

7. God will make a way. It may seem as though God is unable to make a way when our backs are against the wall. Yet a quick survey through Scripture shows just the opposite. When things were bleak and hopeless, God always had a way of coming through for His people.

- A father seeking a miracle for his twelve-year-old daughter was told "your daughter is dead." But Jesus said, "she is only sleeping," and she lived again.
- Mary and Martha were brokenhearted at their brother's death, but Lazarus was called to come out of the tomb.
- "Lord, we are going to perish in this storm!" cried one of the disciples, but they didn't.
- The wages of sin is death, but . . . the gift of God is eternal life through Christ Jesus.

TEACHING THE BIBLE

- *Main Idea:* God delivered the Israelites from Egypt.
- *Suggested Teaching Aim:* To identify ways God delivered the Israelites and us from danger.

A TEACHING OUTLINE

1. *God Led His People from Egypt (Exod. 13:17–22)*
2. *God Promised to Deliver from Pursuit (Exod. 14:1–18)*
3. *God Delivered Israel at the Red Sea (Exod. 14:19–31)*

Introduce the Bible Study

As members enter, give each member a sheet of paper and a pencil. Ask members to write a description of the way God has delivered them from some great difficulty. Ask members to share their experiences if they would like.

Search for Biblical Truth

IN ADVANCE, enlist two readers to overview the lesson by reading alternately the nine summary statements following the "Outline and Summary." **IN ADVANCE,** enlist a member to read the Scripture. Call for Exodus 13:17–22 to be read. On a map of the Exodus, show the possible location of the crossing. Point out the "way of . . . the Philistines" and explain why God did not lead the Israelites that way. Ask, What key phrase in verses 17 and 18 explains all that had happened and would happen? (God led.) Ask, Why do you think God led them through the Red Sea? (Final deliverance from Egypt, and God was going to take them to Sinai to make a covenant.)

Ask, What was significant about the Hebrews taking Joseph's body with them? On the map, locate Succoth. Explain that God led the Israelites by using a pillar of fire at night and a dark cloud by day. Ask, What did these two pillars provide? (See "Studying the Bible.")

Briefly summarize the material in "Studying the Bible" in "2. God Promised to Deliver from Pursuit (Exod. 14:1–18)."

Call for the reader to read Exodus 14:26–31. On a chalkboard, write the following. Ask members to compare and contrast the way the two groups crossed the sea. (Your members may have other suggestions.)

Israelites	Egyptians
Crossed on dry ground	Crossed in mud
Crossed at God's command	Crossed at their own command
Cloud led them	
Crossing led to freedom	Crossing led to death

Ask members to search verses 30 and 31 to find the people's reactions to what the Lord had done (feared and believed). Ask, How do you think this experience influenced the Israelites in later months and years? How did they use it to help them?

Ask, What did it mean that "the people . . . believed the Lord, and his servant Moses" (v. 31)? Explain that the word *believed* is the same word used in Genesis 15:6 (Abraham "believed in the Lord"). Point out that the meaning is similar to the word used in the New Testament to describe the appropriate human response to God's saving acts on our behalf through the work of God in Christ. Ask, How long did this "belief" last? Why did it not last indefinitely?

Read the five "Summary of Bible Truths" statements to summarize the session.

Give the Truth a Personal Focus

Ask members to think back to the experiences they shared earlier. Ask, Is God past delivering His people from bondage? Why? Ask members to write at the bottom of the sheet they received when they entered one area of their lives in which they will trust God to deliver them from some bondage they are now facing. Close in prayer for strength and commitment to follow God's leading.

---

1. Roger Simon for *AOL News*.

September

19

1999

The Covenant

Background Passage: Exodus 19:1–20:21

Focal Passages: Exodus 19:4–6; 20:2–4, 7, 8, 12–17

The Christian Bible's two main parts are the Old Testament and the New Testament. The word *testament* is from a Greek word that was used to translate the Hebrew word for "covenant." Thus, the Old Testament is actually the old covenant. Although the Old Testament contains many covenants, the old covenant was the covenant of God with Israel—the subject of this lesson.

Study Aim: *To name the Ten Commandments and to identify the basic truth about God or humans that each commandment is designed to protect.*

STUDYING THE BIBLE

OUTLINE AND SUMMARY

I. God's Covenant with Israel (Exod. 19:1–25)

1. Terms of the covenant (19:1–6)

2. Israel's preparations for God's revelation (19:7–25)

II. The Ten Commandments (Exod. 20:1–21)

1. Preamble (20:1, 2)

2. Relationship with God (20:3–11)

3. Relationships with others (20:12–17)

4. Moses as God's spokesman (20:18–21)

The terms of God's covenant with Israel dealt with His deliverance of them, His expectations of them, and their relation with Him (19:1–6). God told Moses to prepare the people for His revelation by sanctifying themselves (19:7–25). God began the Ten Commandments by declaring who He was and what He had done in delivering them (20:1, 2). The first four commandments have to do with our relationship with God (20:3–11). The last six have to do with human relationships (20:12–17). Moses agreed to the people's plea that he continue to hear and deliver God's message (20:18–21).

I. God's Covenant with Israel (Exod. 19:1–25)

1. Terms of the covenant (19:1–6)

4 Ye have seen what I did unto the Egyptians, and how I bare you on eagles' wings, and brought you unto myself.

5 Now therefore, if ye will obey my voice indeed, and keep my covenant, then ye shall be a peculiar treasure unto me above all people: for all the earth is mine:

6 And ye shall be unto me a kingdom of priests, and an holy nation. These are the words which thou shalt speak unto the children of Israel.

Three months after leaving Egypt the children of Israel camped at the foot of Mount Sinai (19:1, 2). God gave Moses the words to speak to Israel (19:3).

The deliverance from the Egyptians was the basis for the covenant (19:4). The Lord reminded Israel of what He had done to the Egyptians in the two-phased deliverance from Egypt. More positively, the deliverance was like God bearing up Israel as adult eagles do their young (Deut. 32:11). God's purpose was to bring them into a new relationship with Him.

God's expectations for His people were summed up in two commands. The word *obey* can also be translated "hear." However, for the Hebrews, to hear God's word carried with it the expectation of heeding that word. "Keep" has a variety of similar meanings: take care of, have charge of, fulfill one's obligations to. The word *covenant* describes a contract or agreement between two parties. The Old Testament contains examples of covenants between two equal parties; however, a covenant with God is unique. He takes the initiative in offering it and stating its terms.

God described Israel's new relation with God in three ways. "A peculiar treasure" translates a word used to refer to a king's treasure. "Peculiar" here means "special," not strange. "A kingdom of priests" may mean that each Israelite was to be a priest, but more likely it means that Israel as a whole was to fulfill a priest's role to other nations. "Holy nation" refers to a people set apart by and for God. Unlike pagan religions, whose gods made no moral demands on their followers, the religion of Israel combined worship of one God with moral demands.

All three descriptions refer to Israel as a nation specially chosen by God. This choice of Israel did not mean that God was ignoring other nations, for the whole earth was His. It meant that Israel's choice was not only a privilege but also a responsibility to fulfill God's purpose for all nations.

2. Israel's preparations for God's revelation (19:7–25)

The Israelites promised to obey all that God spoke to them (19:7, 8). Because God was about to reveal Himself, God told Moses to sanctify the people (19:9, 10). Because He was coming down on Sinai, Moses was to set barriers around the mountain to ensure that no Israelite touched the mountain and died (19:11–13). The people were to wash their clothes and refrain from sexual relations during God's revelation (19:14, 15). The Lord's coming was announced with thunder, lightning, a trumpet sound, smoke, and an earthquake (19:16–19). God repeated the warning against anyone coming too close and again called the people to sanctify themselves (19:20–23). Moses went down to deliver these messages (19:24, 25).

II. The Ten Commandments (Exod. 20:1–21)

1. Preamble (20:1, 2)

2 I am the LORD thy God, which have brought thee out of the land of Egypt, out of the house of bondage.

The Ten Commandments were spoken by God (20:1). The God who spoke was the Lord (personal name of God revealed to Moses in Exod. 3:14) who had delivered Israel. Thus, the Ten Commandments are not just some basic moral principles that people developed. They are basic moral demands of the God who redeems. The moral and social demands of the Bible have a spiritual foundation and motivation.

2. Relationship with God (20:3–11)

3 Thou shalt have no other gods before me.

4 Thou shalt not make unto thee any graven image, or any likeness of any thing that is in heaven above, or that is in the earth beneath, or that is in the water under the earth.

The first four commandments deal with people's relationship with God. These commandments protect and enhance four aspects of God: nature, character, name, and worship. The first commandment deals with God's nature as the one true God. Thus, the Israelites were not to mimic their pagan neighbors, most of whom worshiped many gods.

The second commandment deals with the character of God. The invisible and infinite God reveals Himself in His own way. When people make images to represent God, the images always distort and belittle God. This is true whether the images are metal images or mental images of what God is like. Another danger of images of God is that those who create images seek to control their images to get what they want. Verses 5–6 show the seriousness of the sin of making images of God.

7 Thou shalt not take the name of the LORD thy God in vain; for the LORD will not hold him guiltless that taketh his name in vain.

The third commandment protects the name or reputation of God. Names in the Bible meant more than names do today. A name represented the person who bore the name. Thus, the name of God meant God and who He was. "In vain" means "emptily." The warning is against speaking or claiming the name of God in some way that robs the name of its true character and worth. This can be done by profane language or profane living in the name of God. It can be done by trying to use God's name in prayer for selfish purposes or by merely going through the motions of worship.

8 Remember the sabbath day, to keep it holy.

"Holy" means "set apart." The Israelites were to set aside the seventh day as a day of rest. By setting aside one day, the Israelites testified that all days belong to the Lord. Nothing is said here about worship, but later laws made the Sabbath not only a day of rest but also of worship.

This commandment freed humanity from the tyranny of ceaseless toil. Employers, masters, and fathers were commanded not to work or to force their employees, slaves, or children to work all seven days (20:10). The cycle of rest and work is inherent in the nature of God and in the nature of those made in God's image (20:11). At the same time, the commandment to work six days shows that work was one of the parts of God's good creation.

3. Relationships with others (20:12–17)

12 Honour thy father and thy mother: that thy days may be long upon the land which the LORD thy God giveth thee.

13 Thou shalt not kill.

14 Thou shalt not commit adultery.

15 Thou shalt not steal.

16 Thou shalt not bear false witness against thy neighbour.

17 Thou shalt not covet thy neighbour's house, thou shalt not covet thy neighbour's wife, nor his manservant, nor his maidservant, nor his ox, nor his ass, nor any thing that is thy neighbour's.

The last six commandments have to do with relationships with other people. These are inseparable from the first four. In the Bible, our relationship with God calls for right relationships with others. We cannot have right relationships with other people without a right relationship with God. The last six commandments are designed to protect some basic God-given human rights: respect, life, marriage sanctity, property, reputation, and security.

Two of these deal with basic ideals of family life: respect for parents and the sanctity of marriage. The family is the basic building block of society and the basic area of human relationships. Marriage must be built on a one-flesh union of husband and wife. This involves trust and faithfulness. Adultery undermines that trust and disrupts the fabric of marriage.

Parents are cocreators with God of human life. Parents owe their children protection, nurture, and care. Children owe their parents obedience when they are growing up and respect all their lives. When children cease to respect their parents, they are tampering with something basic to who they are and what God intends for them and for others. God promised long life in the land to those who honor their parents. Respect for parents is basic to the stability and health of individuals, families, and society as a whole.

The sixth commandment prohibits murder. Human life is precious because it is a one-time gift of God and, once taken, cannot be restored—at least not by human power. Human life is precious because each person bears the image of the Creator and is capable of fellowship with God (Gen. 9:6).

All of us have a God-given right to have something of our own. Having something of your own frees you from control of the state or others. Having something of your own enables you to have the means to care for the needs of loved ones (1 Tim. 5:8) and the needs of others (Eph. 4:28). Thus, stealing is taking more than someone's money and possessions. It is taking his independence, his ability to care for his family, and his opportunity to give to the needy.

The ninth commandment speaks directly to a courtroom setting, but it applies also to gossip in daily life. When truth is replaced with lies and slanders, untold damage is done to everyone. Innocent people are convicted of crimes they did not commit while the guilty go free.

Reputations are ruined forever. Sometimes issues of life and death depend on telling the truth. The New Testament calls for speaking the truth in love (Eph. 4:15). Human relationships must be built on trust, and truth is the guarantee of that trust.

The tenth commandment is most like what Jesus said about the importance of the inner attitude as well as the outward action (Matt. 5:21, 22, 27, 28). This commandment deals with an inner attitude. Coveting goes one step beyond envy, for the covetous person not only envies what someone has but also wants it for himself. Ahab's coveting Naboth's vineyard led to bearing false witness, to legalized murder, to stealing (1 Kings 21).

4. Moses as God's spokesman (20:18–21)

The people were terrified by the manifestations of God's presence and pleaded with Moses to continue to be the only one who approached God (20:18, 19). Moses calmed them and then went to hear more of the word of the Lord (20:20, 21).

SUMMARY OF BIBLE TRUTHS

1. God's covenant is based on who He is and what He has done to deliver His people.
2. The one true God has spiritual, moral, and social expectations of His people.
3. Being chosen by God is both a privilege and a responsibility.
4. A right relationship with God and right relationships with others are inseparable.
5. God's commandments are designed to protect the nature, character, name, and worship of God.
6. God's commandments also protect the God-given rights to people of respect, life, sanctity of marriage, property, reputation, and security.

APPLYING THE BIBLE

1. A culture that dislikes the commandments. Two years ago a survey of 1,200 people aged fifteen to thirty-five found that most of those polled could name no more than two of the Ten Commandments, and they weren't too happy about some of the others when they were told about them.[1] Until our society is willing to put aside their dislike in exchange for grief at having gone so far from the law (as Israel did in 2 Kings 22), we will never experience revival or awakening again. America has not only forgotten God, she has forgotten how to respond to a sovereign.

2. Updating the commandments. When people were asked about "updating" the Ten Commandments, the following suggestions were made: "Thou shalt not drink and drive" and "Thou shalt care for the environment."[2] The first falls under the commandment prohibiting murder, and the second could remind us of our relationship to God as stewards of the earth. However, both suggestions show the consequences that a culture realizes from having put aside the commandments in the first place.

We begin treating symptoms and ignoring the disease. The disease we have is stubborn independence. Man wants to be on the throne, and in his effort to sit as sovereign he is faced with innumerable fires to put out.

3. Rewriting the Ten Commandments. When the survey respondents were given a list of nonreligious figures and asked who might be entrusted with the task of drawing up a new list of commandments, the person receiving the most support was Oprah Winfrey.[3] No explanation was given, but I would assume her name rises to the top because of the ability she possesses to identify and sympathize with the underdog. Her television program reflects her deep ability to show compassion. I take this as good news, and she is to be commended. God gave the commandments to us because He is a compassionate God who cares for His people. The restrictions are for our good. The admonitions and directions, are to benefit us, not harm us. Unfortunately, people have rejected the compassionate nature of God and tuned in to other sources of comfort.

4. Commanding our attention:

- Test them if you like, ignore them if you will, but the results are always the same.[4]
- Support is growing among various factions of institutionalized religions to have the Ten Commandments revised to better reflect modern times.[5]
- We never outgrow the Ten Commandments because we never outgrow God.[6]

5. God's character. Good secular advice may say, "Vote for the man who promises least. He'll be the least disappointing."[7] But this is not true when it comes to the promises and the character of God. What He promises, He delivers. The Ten Commandments are evidence that God not only is able to deliver His people, but that He intends to have a growing relationship with us. They reveal the character of the promise-making God, as the One who keeps His promises.

6. Peculiar treasure. Shakespeare wrote, "The purest treasure mortal times afford is spotless reputation."[8] As God's peculiar treasure, the Ten Commandments are the standard for our character. While Christ alone makes us spotless, obedience and awareness of the moral compass provided by the commandments identifies us as His.

TEACHING THE BIBLE

- *Main Idea:* The Ten Commandments identify and protect basic truths about God and humans.
- *Suggested Teaching Aim:* To identify ways basic truths about God and human life portrayed in the Ten Commandments influence our daily lives.

A TEACHING OUTLINE

1. *God's Covenant with Israel (Exod. 19:1–25)*
2. *The Ten Commandments (Exod. 20:1–21)*

Introduce the Bible Study

IN ADVANCE, copy each of the Ten Commandments on large strips of paper and place them randomly around the room or on a large table. As members enter, ask them to arrange the commandments in order without consulting their Bibles. Point out that the order is not as important as obeying these commandments. (Do not rearrange at this time if they are not in order.)

Search for Biblical Truth

Lecture briefly, explaining the following: (1) three months after leaving Egypt, the Israelites arrived at Sinai (locate Sinai on a map); (2) the deliverance was the basis for God's covenant; (3) Israel's part of the covenant was to *obey* and *keep;* (4) God's part was to make Israel (a) a special *treasure*, (b) *a kingdom of priests,* which may mean as individuals or more likely as a nation, and (c) a *holy nation,* meaning that Israel would be set apart by and for God. On a chalkboard write: ***Privilege* = *Responsibility.*** Suggest that Israel's choice was not only a privilege but also a responsibility.

IN ADVANCE, make two strip posters: *Relationship with God* and *Relationships with Others.* Place the first poster on the focal wall. Place the first and second commandments under it. **IN ADVANCE,** enlist a member to read the commandments aloud. Ask for the first two to be read at this time. Ask: What kind of idols of God can we make? (Carved or mental.) What is wrong with making images of God—either metal or mental? (See "Studying the Bible.")

Place the third and fourth commandments under the first two. Ask, How do we keep God's name holy? His day?

Place the *Relationships with Others* poster on the wall. Place the fifth and seventh commandments under it, leaving room for the sixth. Ask the reader to read these. Point out that these two commandments have to do with the basic ideals of family life: respect for parents and the sanctity of marriage. Ask: What do parents owe their children? What do children owe their parents? What do spouses owe each other? Place the sixth commandment on the wall. Ask, Why is murder wrong? (We are made in God's image.) Place the eighth commandment on the wall and ask for it to be read aloud. Ask, Why is stealing wrong? (Takes away our independence, and our ability to care for our families and to give to the needy.)

Place the ninth commandment on the wall and ask for it to be read aloud. Ask: What damage can violating this commandment do in the court room? in personal relationships? What new emphasis does Ephesians 4:15 add to this commandment? (Speak the truth in love.)

Place the tenth commandment on the wall and ask for it to be read aloud. Ask half of the members to turn to Matthew 5:21, 22 and the other half to Matthew 5:27, 28. Ask: What light do these verses shed on the tenth commandment? Can you think of examples where coveting led to other sins? (Naboth, 1 Kings 20:18–21 and David, 2 Sam. 11–12.)

Give the Truth a Personal Focus

Ask, How do the basic truths about God and human life portrayed in the Ten Commandments influence our daily lives? Copy and distribute the six "Summary of Bible Truths" to the six groups you have formed. Ask each group to write one principle that will help them to apply the commandments to their daily lives. Ask groups to read the summary statement and then to read their principle. Close in prayer for courage to obey.

---

1. Cullen Murphy, "Broken Covenant?: The Time to Revise the Ten Commandments, Some Say, Draws Nigh," *The Atlantic Monthly,* Nov. 1996, 22.
2. Ibid.
3. Ibid.
4. James M. Wall, "Immutable Truths: Inescapable Commandments," *The Christian Century,* Nov. 6, 1996, 1059.
5. Murphy, 22.
6. Roy Honeycutt, *These Ten Words* (Nashville: Broadman Press, 1966), 7.
7. Bernard Baruch (1870-1965), American financier, *Bartlett's Familiar Quotations* (Little, Brown and Company, Inc., 1980).
8. William Shakespeare, "King Richard the Second," act 1, scene 1, line 177.

September

26

1999

The Tabernacle and Obedience

Background Passages: Exodus 40:1–33; Leviticus 26:1–46
Focal Passages: Exodus 40:1–9; Leviticus 26:2–6, 11–13

Some people who set out to read the Bible through get bogged down in the last part of Exodus or in Leviticus. Some Sunday school teachers dread lessons on these portions of the Bible. Genesis and the first half of Exodus are filled with stories of people and events; but much of the last part of Exodus deals with the tabernacle, and much of Leviticus deals with priests and sacrifices. The tabernacle ceased to exist centuries ago; just a few stones are all that remain of its successor—the temple. Besides, all these things have been fulfilled in Jesus Christ—our High Priest and once-for-all, all-sufficient sacrifice. However, these neglected passages were important to the Hebrews. They contain lasting principles, and they also provide a greater appreciation for what we have in Christ.

Study Aim: *To describe the tabernacle and what was in it and to explain the importance of obedience.*

STUDYING THE BIBLE

OUTLINE AND SUMMARY

I. Setting Up and Sanctifying the Tabernacle (Exod. 40:1–33)

1. **Instructions for setting up the tabernacle (Exod. 40:1–8)**
2. **Instructions for sanctifying the tabernacle (Exod. 40:9–15)**
3. **Following instructions (Exod. 40:16–33)**

II. Importance of Obedience (Lev. 26:1–46)

1. **Acknowledging God through reverent worship (Lev. 26:1, 2)**
2. **Blessings of obedience (Lev. 26:3–10)**
3. **Lord's deliverance and presence (Lev. 26:11–13)**
4. **Consequences of disobedience (Lev. 26:14–39)**
5. **Confession and hope (Lev. 26:40–46)**

God gave Israel instructions for setting up (Exod. 40:1–8) and sanctifying the tabernacle (Exod. 40:9–15). Moses saw that these instructions were followed exactly (Exod. 40:16–33). Israel was to acknowledge the holy God through reverent worship (Lev. 26:1, 2). If they obeyed God, He promised wonderful blessings (Lev. 26:3–10). The best blessings were His presence and the freedom and dignity that came with being God's free people (Lev. 26:11–13). If Israel disobeyed God's commandments, they would reap terrible consequences (Lev.

26:14–39). However, if they confessed their sins, God would forgive and restore them (Lev. 26:40–46).

I. Setting Up and Sanctifying the Tabernacle (Exod. 40:1–33)

1. Instructions for setting up the tabernacle (Exod. 40:1–8)

1 And the LORD spake unto Moses, saying,

2 On the first day of the first month shalt thou set up the tabernacle of the tent of the congregation.

3 And thou shalt put therein the ark of the testimony, and cover the ark with the veil.

4 And thou shalt bring in the table, and set in order the things that are to be set in order upon it; and thou shalt bring in the candlestick, and light the lamps thereof.

5 And thou shalt set the altar of gold for the incense before the ark of the testimony, and put the hanging of the door to the tabernacle.

6 And thou shalt set the altar of the burnt offering before the door of the tabernacle of the congregation.

7 And thou shalt set the laver between the tent of the congregation and the altar, and shalt put water therein.

8 And thou shalt set up the court round about, and hang up the hanging at the court gate.

You may wonder why Exodus 40:1–8 is so concise. This is just one of the final stages in the Bible passages about the tabernacle. In order to understand Exodus 40, we need to read Exodus 25–31; 35–39. Exodus 25–31 describes the plans for the tabernacle, its furnishings, and the priests and their garments. Exodus 35–39 describes the construction of the parts. These chapters also describe how diligently the people gave and worked.

Exodus 40:1–8 gives instructions about how to set up the tabernacle and its furnishings. "Tabernacle" translates a Hebrew word that has the basic meaning of "dwelling place." The tabernacle was the place where God's presence dwelt during this phase of Israel's life (Exod. 25:8). "Tent of the congregation," literally "tent of meeting," was another name for the tabernacle.

In the innermost part of the tabernacle was the "ark of the testimony," sometimes called "ark of the covenant," "ark of the Lord," or simply "the ark." "The testimony" is another name for the two tables of the Ten Commandments, which were placed in the ark (for more information, see Exod. 25:10–22; 40:20). The mercy seat and two cherubim were on top of the ark. The ark was located in the most holy place or holy of holies, which was separated from the holy place by a veil (Exod. 26:31–37).

In the holy place (the outer part of the tabernacle) were "the altar of incense," "the table" and "candlestick" (actually, "lampstands"). The altar of incense stood right outside the veil. Like most things in the tabernacle, it was covered with gold (Exod. 27:1–8). The table had "shewbread" placed on it (Exod. 25:23–30). The lampstand had seven lamps, a central one and three on each side. It stood across from the table of the shewbread (Exod. 25:31–39). The entrance to the holy place of the tabernacle was covered with a hanging cloth that served as a door.

The tabernacle was actually a tent within a courtyard surrounded with a covered wall and entered by a door made of hanging cloth (27:9–21). In the court was "the altar of the burnt offering," where sacrifices were made and parts of some sacrifices were burned (Exod. 30:1–10). Nearby was "the laver" filled with water for cleansing the priests (Exod. 30:17–21). A door made of cloth covered the entrance to the courtyard.

2. Instructions for sanctifying the tabernacle (Exod. 40:9–15)

9 And thou shalt take the anointing oil, and anoint the tabernacle, and all that is therein, and shalt hallow it, and all the vessels thereof: and it shall be holy.

Before they used the tabernacle, the Lord instructed the people to "hallow" it and everything in it. The word *hallow* is from the same root as the word *holy*. It can be translated "sanctify" or "consecrate." Its basic meaning is "set apart as holy."

The anointing oil was a special mixture designed for this purpose. The base was olive oil, but it contained other things also (Exod. 30:23–25). Not only the tent but also the furnishings were to receive the anointing oil. This was in preparation for the presence of the holy God and for the holy purpose of this place.

The altar and laver in the court were also to be set apart as holy by using the anointing oil (Exod. 40:10, 11). The priests were first to be cleansed with water. Then they and their garments were also to be anointed (Exod. 40:12–15).

3. Following instructions (Exod. 40:16–33)

Moses was careful to follow all the Lord's instructions (Exod. 40:16). As you read verses 17–32, you will see much repetition from earlier verses. The repetition shows how carefully Moses followed the instructions given in verses 1–15. The passage ends by emphasizing that Moses finished the task (40:33).

II. The Importance of Obedience (Lev. 26:1–46)

1. Acknowledging God through reverent worship (Lev. 26:1, 2)

2 Ye shall keep my sabbaths, and reverence my sanctuary: I am the LORD.

Leviticus has as its theme: the holy God is due holy worship and holy living. Verses 1, 2 are a kind of summary of the first four of the Ten Commandments looked at from the perspective of this theme. The people were to worship only God and not worship idols or graven images (Lev. 26:1).

One of the statements that recurs in Leviticus is the reminder, "I am the LORD." This was the word of the Lord God of Israel, who had delivered them from Egypt, brought them unto Himself, and called them to keep His covenant as His holy people (see Exod. 19:4–6; Lev. 26:11–13).

Verse 2 focuses on keeping the Lord's sabbaths and showing reverence for His sanctuary. "Sanctuary" is another word from the root of the Hebrew word meaning "holy." It means "place set apart as holy." The Israelites knew that God's presence could not be confined to His special days or to special places, however holy they might be. Solomon acknowledged this in his prayer of dedication for the temple (1 Kings 8:27). However, the Israelites knew that remembering God at special times and places was the best way also to meet Him at any time or place.

2. Blessings of obedience (Lev. 26:3–10)

3 If ye walk in my statutes, and keep my commandments, and do them;

4 Then I will give you rain in due season, and the land shall yield her increase, and the trees of the field shall yield their fruit.

5 And your threshing shall reach unto the vintage, and the vintage shall reach unto sowing time: and ye shall eat your bread to the full, and dwell in your land safely.

6 And I will give you peace in the land, and ye shall lie down, and none shall make you afraid: and I will rid evil beasts out of the land, neither shall the sword go through your land.

The overall theme of Leviticus 26 is the blessings of obedience and the evil consequences of disobedience (see also Exod. 23:20–23; Deut. 28). The Lord promised great things to the Israelites if they walked in His statutes and kept His commandments. He promised rain and good crops. The rich harvests would feed them with plenty and provide an abundance of seed for the next sowing season. They would not only have plenty to eat, but they would also dwell in the land securely.

Many people today go to bed hungry and afraid. God promised an obedient Israel that He would give them the kind of peace and security that enabled them to lie down without fear of what might happen during the night. What a blessing! God promised to rid the land of wild beasts, to give victory over enemies, and to provide for all their needs (Lev. 26:7–10).

3. The Lord's deliverance and presence (Lev. 26:11–13)

11 And I will set my tabernacle among you: and my soul shall not abhor you.

12 And I will walk among you, and will be your God, and ye shall be my people.

13 I am the LORD your God, which brought you forth out of the land of Egypt, that ye should not be their bondmen; and I have broken the bands of your yoke, and made you go upright.

God saved the greatest blessing for last. He promised to dwell with them, to walk among them, and to be their God—if they acted in ways that showed they were His people. If they walked in His ways, He would walk with them.

The first part of verse 13 is an expansion of the "I am the LORD" of verse 2. It is a repetition of the formula at the beginning of the Ten

Commandments (Exod. 20:2). The people were to live in light of the fact that the Lord had delivered them from slavery in Egypt.

Along with freedom went a new sense of dignity and meaning for the liberated slaves. The word translated "upright" is not the usual Hebrew word that is so translated. The word in verse 13 does not mean "righteous" but "erect." The picture is that of a person who can walk erect with head up and shoulders back. Part of the reason is that his back is no longer stooped with the heavy burdens of the yoke of slavery, but part of it is the new sense of worth that God gives to His freed people.

4. Consequences of disobedience (Lev. 26:14–39)

The opposite kind of consequences would come to the children of Israel if they forgot the Lord and disobeyed His commandments. They would suffer fear, hunger, defeat, humiliation, and end up as slaves in a foreign land as their ancestors had been before the Lord delivered them.

5. Confession and hope (Lev. 26:40–46)

God did hold out a ray of hope. If they disobeyed but repented and confessed their sins, God would be gracious to them. He would remember His covenant and restore them.

SUMMARY OF BIBLE TRUTHS

1. We acknowledge God through reverent worship.
2. Special days and places enable us to acknowledge God on every day and in every place.
3. We acknowledge God by holy, obedient living.
4. God blesses obedient living.
5. God's greatest blessing is His presence.
6. Those whom God has delivered from slavery receive freedom and a new sense of personal dignity and worth.

APPLYING THE BIBLE

1. Symbol of loss. Between February 1864 and May 1865, more than 35,000 Union prisoners were crammed inside the stockade walls of a camp originally intended to hold 10,000. One hundred prisoners died each day at Camp Sumter, the formal name of the prison camp at Andersonville. Andersonville has been chosen as the site to commemorate those who were captured by the enemy and endured the hardships that followed. At the dedicatory address of the National Prisoner of War Museum, Senator John McCain (R-Ariz.), said that those who were able to walk away from Andersonville left with a "dignity . . . more alive, more powerful for the afflictions they endured than the dignity of those who had been the agents of their suffering."

This is the dignity that God says belongs to those who obey and worship Him. We may experience difficult times, but freedom will be our reward one day, and with freedom in Christ comes the dignity of being out from under the weight of sin's oppression.

2. Symbol of extravagance. Attending the dedication of the National Prisoner of War Museum, retired Army master sergeant Jim Petty said, "It's something we can leave our kids and grandkids and the country. We need to let them know that all this freedom we have isn't free. It costs a whole bunch." The brazen altar is a symbol of the cost required to atone for sin. It would one day cost "a whole bunch" in Petty's words. The brazen altar reminds us of the death of Christ.

3. Freedom. In an impassioned speech regarding freedom of the press, Zechariah Chafee Jr. argued, "Freedom from something is not enough. It should also be freedom for something. Freedom is not safety but opportunity."[1]

The freedom that God offers is freedom from the bondage of sin and a freedom to walk in newness of life. It is a complete freedom. Christian worshipers are reminded of their freedom in the symbol of our faith, the cross of Christ.

4. Symbol of victory. Winston Churchill motivated all of England and inspired much of war-torn Europe by holding two fingers in the air, giving birth to the symbol V for Victory. He explained the symbol by saying, "The V sign is the symbol of the unconquerable will of the occupied territories, and a portent of the fate awaiting the Nazi tyranny."[2]

The symbol had incredible value to the heart and soul of a nation that was near defeat. It was a symbol that was literally in the hand of every son and daughter of Europe. It became the symbol of liberation and a symbol that spelled the defeat of the Third Reich.

The symbols of the Tabernacle had a similar effect. When people thought about them, they were reminded of the promises of the God who delivered them. Faith was strengthened because of the symbols and what they taught about Israel's relationship to God.

5. Quotes on peace:

"First keep the peace within yourself, then you can also bring peace to others" (Thomas à Kempis, *Imitation of Christ,* Book II, ch. 3 [1420]).

"No more wars, no more bloodshed. Peace unto you. Shalom, salaam, forever" (Menachem Begin, on signing the Egyptian-Israeli peace treaty, Washington, D.C. [March 26, 1979]).

TEACHING THE BIBLE

- *Main Idea:* God's people are to obey His directions about worship and obedience.
- *Suggested Teaching Aim:* To lead adults to describe the significance of the tabernacle and explain the importance of obedience.

A TEACHING OUTLINE

1. Setting Up and Sanctifying the Tabernacle (Exod. 40:1–33)
2. Importance of Obedience (Lev. 26:1–46)

Introduce the Bible Study

Ask, Where do you worship best? Why? List reasons on a chalkboard or on a sheet of paper. You will use them later. Point to the theme of Leviticus which you have written on a poster **IN ADVANCE:** *The holy God is due holy worship and holy living.*

Search for Biblical Truth

Copy the seven summary statements in "Outline and Summary" on small pieces of paper and give them to members to read aloud to overview the lesson.

IN ADVANCE, enlist a member to read the article "Tabernacle" from a Bible dictionary and share highlights of the article with the class. Display an enlarged drawing of the tabernacle. Use the drawing to place the different elements in the tabernacle: ark of the covenant, Ten Commandments, mercy seat, altar of incense, the shewbread table, the lampstands, the altar for the burnt offerings, and the laver. Point out that while many of these items have been replaced by Jesus' coming, the purpose of all of them was to provide a place for the Israelites to worship.

Read the first of the "Summary of Bible Truths" statements and ask members if this statement applies to our worship today. If so, how? Read the second statement. Ask, Do special worship services planned on special days such as Christmas and Easter help you to worship and acknowledge God on every day and in every place?

Ask members to suggest some *if–then* events. (*If* you do A, *then* B will happen.) Such cause-and-effect events are common in our lives. (*If* children disobey parents, *then* they will be punished; *if* you are caught speeding, *then* you will get a ticket.) Ask members to open their Bibles to Leviticus 26:3–10 and find the cause-and-effect statement in these verses. On a chalkboard write *If* and *Then.* Ask members to identify the *If* elements (walk, keep, do) and the *Then* elements (generous harvest, peace, security). Write these on the chalkboard under the appropriate words. Ask them to look at 26:11–13 and identify the *Then* statements (set my tabernacle, not abhor, walk among you, be your God). Use "Studying the Bible" to explain "upright" in verse 13.

Read the third "Summary of Bible Truths" statement. Ask, If we do not live holy and obedient lives, do we believe God is holy? Why? Read the fourth statement. Ask, Does God always bless obedient living? Read the fifth statement. Ask, Would you agree or disagree that God's greatest blessing is His presence? Why? Read the sixth statement. Ask, How has God delivered you from slavery and given you a new sense of personal dignity and worth?

Give the Truth a Personal Focus

God's people are to obey His directions about worship and obedience. Ask, Where do you worship best? Why? List reasons on a chalkboard or on a sheet of paper.

Read the list of places where members said they worship best. Ask: If you worship best in this place, do you go there often enough? What can you gain from regular worship? Read this statement: *If* we walk in God's ways, *then* He will walk with us. Close in prayer.

---

1. Zechariah Chafee Jr., "The Press Under Pressure," *Nieman Reports* (April 1948).

2. Message to the people of Europe on launching the V for Victory propaganda campaign, July 20, 1941.

The Cloud and the Fire

Background Passages: Exodus 40:34–38; Numbers 9:15–23

Focal Passages: Exodus 40:34–38; Numbers 9:15–19, 22, 23

In the preceding unit of four lessons, we looked at how God delivered Israel from Egypt and how He made a covenant with them. The cloud and the pillar performed a threefold function during those days: (1) assured Israel of God's presence with them, (2) protected them from their enemies, and (3) guided them (see comments on Exod. 13:21). This new unit deals with the time from Sinai to the Promised Land. The cloud and the fire dwelt in or over the tabernacle to continue to perform these three functions.

Study Aim: *To identify what the cloud and the fire reveal about God and about the people's responses to God.*

STUDYING THE BIBLE

OUTLINE AND SUMMARY

I. God's Presence (Exod. 40:34–38)
  1. Gracious presence (Exod. 40:34)
  2. Glorious presence (Exod. 40:35)
  3. Guiding presence (Exod. 40:36–38)

II. People's Responses (Num. 9:15–23)
  1. Abiding with the God who abides (Num. 9:15–18)
  2. Waiting on the God who tarries (Num. 9:19–22)
  3. Obeying the God who commands (Num. 9:23)

God's glory filled the tabernacle after it was finished (Exod. 40:34). His glory made it impossible for Moses to enter (Exod. 40:35). God's presence in the cloud by day and the fire by night either stopped over the tabernacle or moved, thus showing the people when and where to move (Exod. 40:36–38). When God's cloud hovered over the tabernacle, the people stopped and stayed in their tents (Num. 9:15–18). The people were commanded to tarry there for as long as the cloud tarried—no matter how long (Num. 9:19–22). The people faithfully kept the Lord's charge by obeying the commandments of the Lord delivered through Moses (Num. 9:23).

I. God's Presence (Exod. 40:34–38)

1. Gracious presence (Exod. 40:34)

34 Then a cloud covered the tent of the congregation, and the glory of the LORD filled the tabernacle.

Exodus 40:34–38 is the climax of the passage studied in the preceding lesson. After Moses and the people had constructed and set up the tabernacle according to the Lord's instructions (Exod. 40:1–33), the cloud covered the tabernacle.

The same action also involved the glory of the Lord filling the tabernacle. The Hebrew word for "glory" signified "weight" or "heaviness," and thus came to stand for a weighty person or thing in the figurative sense. When used of God's glory, the word describes the majesty, holiness, and worth of the Lord.

This action by the Lord signified His acceptance of the tabernacle, but Exodus 32–34 reminds us that the cloud was not a reward to faithful Israel but an expression of grace to unfaithful Israel. These chapters record the sad spectacle of the Israelites making a golden calf while Moses was on Mount Sinai. When Moses had punished the evildoers, he began to intercede with God not to leave the unfaithful people. God promised that His presence would go with them (33:14, 15). Moses then prayed to see God's glory (33:18). The Lord revealed His name as a Lord of justice but also of mercy and grace toward repentant sinners (34:6, 7).

2. Glorious presence (Exod. 40:35)

35 And Moses was not able to enter into the tent of the congregation, because the cloud abode thereon, and the glory of the LORD filled the tabernacle.

Earlier when Moses asked the Lord to show Moses His glory, the Lord told him that no man could see His face and live. Therefore, God hid Moses in the cleft of the rock and allowed Moses to see God only after He passed by and proclaimed His name (Exod. 33:19–23). In the same way, even Moses wasn't allowed to enter the tabernacle when it was filled with the Lord's glory. This initial complete filling of the tabernacle was a special sign of the Lord's holy presence with His people. The cloud remained on or near the tabernacle, but Moses and the priests were later allowed to enter. The presence of the Lord was in the holy of holies, into which only the high priest could go on the Day of Atonement.

At the end of Moses' life, he was described as a man "whom the LORD knew face to face" (Deut. 34:10). This was a way of describing the close relationship of Moses with the Lord; but it did not mean that even Moses ever looked directly on the full glory of the Lord.

The Old Testament revealed the paradox of God coming to people and inviting them to Him, yet warning them to come with fear and trembling. When Moses first encountered the Lord, God used a burning bush to attract him; however, when Moses drew near, he was told to take off his shoes for he was standing on holy ground (Exod. 3:2–5). Yet God then proceeded to reveal Himself (Exod. 3:6–22).

Even the New Testament invites us to God but warns us of the need to come with reverence and awe. Based on the access which God opened to Himself through the death of His Son, God invites believers to come boldly to God's throne of grace (Heb. 4:16). Yet the same book warns that "it is a fearful thing to fall into the hands of the living God" (Heb. 10:31).

3. Guiding presence (Exod. 40:36–38)

36 And when the cloud was taken up from over the tabernacle, the children of Israel went onward in all their journeys:

37 But if the cloud were not taken up, then they journeyed not till the day that it was taken up.

38 For the cloud of the LORD was upon the tabernacle by day, and fire was on it by night, in the sight of all the house of Israel, throughout all their journeys.

As the Lord had guided the people by the cloud before the tabernacle was built, now He did the same by means of the cloud's position with regard to the tabernacle. When the cloud was taken up, the people followed by moving the tabernacle and the camp wherever the cloud led them. When the cloud stopped, the people stopped and set up the tabernacle and the camp there.

Notice the repetition of "the cloud taken up." Also notice some form of "journey" is found three times: "in all their journeys," "then they journeyed," and "throughout all their journeys." Israel's God was not a God confined to one place; He was a God of all places. He was a God with a purpose for His people; therefore, He was God on the move. As He moved, He did it in such a way as to guide His people to go with Him. For their part, they were a pilgrim people who did not stand still, but were sensitive to the Lord's leadership (see Heb. 11:13–16).

II. People's Responses (Num. 9:15–23)

1. Abiding with the God who abides (Num. 9:15–18)

15 And on the day that the tabernacle was reared up the cloud covered the tabernacle, namely, the tent of the testimony: and at even there was upon the tabernacle as it were the appearance of fire, until the morning.

16 So it was alway: the cloud covered it by day, and the appearance of fire by night.

17 And when the cloud was taken up from the tabernacle, then after that the children of Israel journeyed: and in the place where the cloud abode, there the children of Israel pitched their tents.

18 At the commandment of the LORD the children of Israel journeyed, and at the commandment of the LORD they pitched: as long as the cloud abode upon the tabernacle they rested in their tents.

Numbers 9:15 begins at the same point and uses almost the same language as Exodus 40:34. "On the day" refers to the day when God's presence first filled the newly completed tabernacle. Throughout the two passages are similar terminology and similar messages.

One of the messages both passages have in common is this: God's presence was visible by day and by night. At times the phenomena are called a pillar of cloud and a pillar of fire. The references to the "appearance of fire" may mean that at night the cloud that they saw during the day was lit up with the appearance of fire at night. Or there may have been two separate pillars. In either case, the Lord provided assurance of His presence, protection, and guidance by day and by night.

Two things in the holy place of the tabernacle symbolized the cloud and the fire. The altar of incense created a cloud of incense. The seven lamps of the lampstand kept the fire burning.

When the cloud "abode," the people "pitched their tents." That is, wherever the Lord chose to abide, they abided with Him. This brings to mind the Lord Jesus' words about abiding in Him (John 15:1–8). They tried to go with the Lord as He moved, to stop when and where He stopped, and thus to continue to abide with Him.

2. Waiting on the God who tarries (Num. 9:18–22)

> **19 And when the cloud tarried long upon the tabernacle many days, then the children of Israel kept the charge of the LORD, and journeyed not.**
>
> **22 Or whether it were two days, or a month, or a year, that the cloud tarried upon the tabernacle, remaining thereon, the children of Israel abode in their tents, and journeyed not: but when it was taken up, they journeyed.**

It is somewhat arbitrary to emphasize God's revelation in Exodus 40:34–38 and Israel's responses in Numbers 9:15–23. Both passages begin at the same point with almost the same words, and both passages include both revelations about God and about human responses. However, Numbers 9:15–23 refers several times to "the commandment of the Lord" (9:18, 20, 23) and twice says that the people "kept the charge of the LORD" (9:19, 23).

At times the Lord's cloud stayed in place over the tabernacle for a short time. At other times, it stayed there a long time, sometimes as long as a year. Regardless of how short or how long the cloud stayed, the people were commanded to move when it moved and to stop and stay when it stopped and stayed. These responses are taught consistently throughout the Bible: We are to follow the Lord. In order to do that, we must be sensitive to His leading and to obey His guidance. At times, this requires hard, strenuous, seemingly endless movement or action. At other times, it calls for patiently waiting on the Lord.

Both of these responses present challenges. When we are weary, we want to rest; but the Lord may call us to get up and strike out on some new mission or to persevere in a task already in progress. At other times, waiting on the Lord is harder than actively working for the Lord. God does not operate on our time schedules, but on His.

3. Obeying the God who commands (Num. 9:23)

> **23 At the commandment of the LORD they rested in the tents, and at the commandment of the LORD they journeyed: they kept the charge of the LORD, at the commandment of the LORD by the hand of Moses.**

The Hebrew word for "kept" is the same word in Exodus 19:5, where the Lord told Israel to "keep" His covenant. It means to be a faithful trustee over something entrusted to you or to meet one's obligations in an agreement. The people of Israel had promised to keep God's covenant. This involved obeying His commandments, not only His moral Ten Commandments but His commandments about following His leadership day by day.

"The commandment of the LORD" occurs three times in verse 23. This refers to the commandment of the Lord about following the guidance given to them through the movement of the cloud. This commandment had been the word of the Lord delivered to them by the Lord's human spokesman Moses. Thus, the people had to believe and obey the word of the Lord that Moses spoke, and they had to watch the symbolic means by which the Lord led them—the cloud.

At times believers may envy the Israelites for having such a clearly visible sign of when and where the Lord wanted them to go. We must walk by faith and not by sight. Some of the Lord's commandments and guidelines are clearly spelled out in His written word. At other times, we must be sensitive to whatever means the Lord uses to show us some personal aspect of His will. Proverbs 3:5, 6 assures us that if we trust in Him and not in ourselves, God in His own way and time will show us the way we should take.

SUMMARY OF BIBLE TRUTHS

1. God offers His presence to us because of His grace.
2. God is unapproachable; yet He opens a way for us to come to Him.
3. God guides His people.
4. We are to abide with the God who offers to abide with us.
5. We are to wait on the Lord, no matter how long He tarries.
6. We are to obey the Lord's word and follow where He leads us.

APPLYING THE BIBLE

1. God's house. We often pray words like, "God, thank you for letting us be in Your house today." Someone said long ago, "God does not need a house." Rather, we need God to need a house like ours so we might feel that God is living among us.[1]

2. God just wants to be with us. R. C. Sproul, a philosopher and theologian, was asked, "What, in your opinion, is the greatest spiritual need in the world today?"

Dr. Sproul paused, then replied, "The greatest need in people's lives today is to discover the true identity of God." He pointed out that most nonreligious people do not really understand the God they're rejecting.

Someone then asked the theologian a follow-up question: "What, in your opinion, is the greatest spiritual need in the lives of church people?"

Sproul shot back the very same answer: "To discover the true identity of God. If believers really understood the character and the personality and the nature of God, it would revolutionize their lives."[2]

3. Lessons from cloud gazers. During the wilderness wanderings, the Israelites demonstrated a very important practice for people of faith. They moved when the cloud moved and they stayed put when the cloud didn't move. Throughout our journey of faith, we must know when to follow and when to lag behind the moving of God, nor running ahead of Him.

4. What makes a building a place of worship? G. Campbell Morgan says, "Without God's presence, the tabernacle is just a tent." This is true in our churches today as well. Regardless of how elaborate our buildings seem, God's presence is the feature that makes them special. His presence transforms any location into a place of worship.

5. How do you look at clouds? There are two fundamental rabbinic ideas found when we study the cloud of God's presence. Human beings are under God's protection, care, and providence in this world, just as the Israelites were in the desert sojourn. Yet this world, material possessions and all worldly experience—joy, suffering, prosperity, satisfaction, and sickness—are transient (as temporary as clouds on a cloudy day). Only divine protection transcends this world and endures in the next.[3]

6. The presence that really matters. Our Roman Catholic friends view communion differently than most Protestants. But recent polls suggest that younger members of the Catholic church are beginning to see communion as a symbol of Christ's presence (a Baptist view), not the reality of His presence (transubstantiation, a Catholic view). Roman Catholic theologian the late Edward Kilmartin suggests that the central issue of eucharistic theology is not "How does Christ become present to us?" but "How do we become present to Christ?"[4]

7. Where is God? Archbishop Desmond Tutu was awarded the Nobel Peace Prize in 1984 for his leadership in the struggle to end his country's system of apartheid. He tells the story about a Jew in a concentration camp who was made to clean out toilets. His Nazi guard taunted him, "Where is your God now?" The Jewish man replied, "He is right here with me, in the muck."[5]

8. How does God know? Children often provide a fresh perspective on our faith. A ten-year-old named Sheila wrote a quick inquiry to God as follows: "Dear God, I read somewhere that you know what we are going to do before we do it. How much advance notice do you get?"[6]

TEACHING THE BIBLE

- *Main Idea:* God used the cloud and the fire to assure, protect, and guide Israel.
- *Suggested Teaching Aim:* To lead adults to identify ways God assures, protects, and guides us.

A TEACHING OUTLINE

1. *God's Presence (Exod. 40:34–38)*
2. *People's Responses (Num. 9:15–23)*

Introduce the Bible Study

Copy the three statements about the cloud and pillar's function on three small strips of paper and give them to three members to read. Call for the first statement to be read and see if members can identify to what the statement refers. Continue with the other two statements. Point out that the pillar and cloud will play a significant role in the events that happen to Israel in our study this month.

Search for Biblical Truth

On a chalkboard write: *1. God's Presence.* Read aloud Exodus 40:34–36. Using "Studying the Bible," lecture briefly describing: (1) the same cloud that had guided Israel across the sea covered the tabernacle after Moses and the people had followed God's requirements in setting it up; (2) the meaning of the word *glory;* (3) how the pillar indicated God's acceptance of the tabernacle; (4) the cloud and/or pillar remained over the tabernacle; (5) the initial complete filling of the tabernacle was a special sign of the Lord's presence; (6) even Moses never saw the full glory of God; (7) God's presence guided the Israelites as they journeyed.

Form three groups, and make these assignments:

Group 1: "God's Gracious Presence" (Exod. 40:34)

Group 2: "God's Glorious Presence" (Exod. 40:35)

Group 3: "God's Guiding Presence" (Exod. 40:36–38)

Ask each group to read the Scripture assigned to them and to identify as many principles as possible that would help us understand God's assurance of His presence, His protection, and His guidance. Allow four to five minutes for study and then call for reports.

Write on the chalkboard: *2. People's Responses*. Read aloud Numbers 9:15–19, 22–23. Using "Studying the Bible," lecture briefly, covering these points: (1) God's presence was visible night and day; (2) in the tabernacle, the altar of incense and the lampstand symbolized the cloud and the fire; (3) the Israelites "abode" with God even as Christians abide in Jesus; (4) at times the cloud stayed for a short time and at other times it stayed a long time; (5) Israel obeyed the "commandment of the Lord by the hand of Moses" (Num. 9:23)—a way of saying they obeyed the commandments of God but were dependent on Moses to instruct them as to what those commandments were.

Make the following assignments to the original three groups:

Group 1: "Abiding with the God who abides" (Num. 9:15–18)

Group 2: "Waiting on the God who tarries" (Num. 9:19, 22)

Group 3: "Obeying the God who commands" (Num. 9:23)

Ask each of the groups to read their Scriptures and list principles we can use to guide our lives.

Give the Truth a Personal Focus

Read the six statements in "Summary of Bible Truths" and ask: Which one of these means the most to you? Why? Which statement is the most difficult for you to accept? Why? Close in prayer that all will know God's presence, protection, and guidance.

---

1. Gerardus van der Leeuw, quoted in "Learning from Laon," *America,* August 26, 1995, 6.
2. Bill Hybels, *The God You're Looking For* (Nashville: Thomas Nelson Publishers, 1997).
3. Jeffrey L. Rubenstein, "The Symbolism of the Sukka, Part 2," *Judaism: A Quarterly Journal of Jewish Life and Thought,* Fall 1996, 387.
4. S. J. Edward Kilmartin, "The Catholic Tradition of Eucharistic Theology: Towards the Third Millennium," *Theological Studies,* 55 (1994).
5. Desmond Tutu, quoted in "The Face of God," *Life,* Dec. 1990, 47.
6. David Heller, "Dear God, What Religion Were the Dinosaurs? (children's letters to God)," *Redbook,* Jan. 1990, 52.

October

10

1999

The People Rebel

Background Passage: Numbers 12:1–14:25

Focal Passages: Numbers 13:1–3, 32–14:4, 20–24

The refusal of Israel to enter the Promised Land is the most important event between the deliverance from Egypt and the crossing of the Jordan River into Canaan. This rebellion doomed most of the adult generation that had come out of Egypt to perish during forty years of wandering in the wilderness.

Study Aim: *To explain how all the spies saw the same things but reached such different conclusions.*

STUDYING THE BIBLE

OUTLINE AND SUMMARY

I. Rebellion of Miriam and Aaron (Num. 12:1–16)

II. Rebellion of Israel (Num. 13:1–14:25)

1. **Sending out twelve spies (13:1–20)**
2. **A mixed report (13:21–33)**
3. **Israel's rebellion (14:1–4)**
4. **Responses of Moses, Aaron, Joshua, and Caleb (14:5–10a)**
5. **God's responses (14:10b–23)**
6. **Caleb's reward (14:24, 25)**

Miriam and Aaron complained that Moses was not the only worthy leader (12:1–16). Israel sent out twelve spies to bring back a report of Canaan (13:1–20). All agreed on certain things, but ten said that the Israelites could never defeat the powerful people of the land (13:21–33). The people blamed Moses and God (14:1–4). Moses, Aaron, Joshua, and Caleb mourned; and the two spies tried unsuccessfully to change the people's mind (14:5–10a). Moses' prayer for the people led God not to destroy them, but He said that the rebels would never see Canaan (14:10b–23). God said that faithful Caleb would enter the Promised Land (14:24, 25).

I. Rebellion of Miriam and Aaron (Num. 12:1–16)

Miriam and Aaron used as their pretext the issue of Moses' marriage, but the real problem was jealousy of Moses (12:1, 2). The Lord summoned all three to the tabernacle (12:3–5), where He vindicated Moses as His spokesman (12:6–8). God's wrath left Miriam a leper (12:9, 10). Aaron repented and prayed for Miriam (12:11, 12). Moses prayed for her to be healed (12:13). The Lord healed her but made her live outside the camp for seven days (12:14–16).

II. Rebellion of Israel (Num. 13:1–14:25)

1. Sending out twelve spies (13:1–20)

1 And the LORD spake unto Moses, saying,

2 Send thou men, that they may search the land of Canaan, which I give unto the children of Israel: of every tribe of their fathers shall ye send a man, every one a ruler among them.

3 And Moses by the commandment of the LORD sent them from the wilderness of Paran: all those men were heads of the children of Israel.

They had been camped in the wilderness of Paran (10:12; 13:3). Later the place is called Kadesh (Num. 13:26) and Kadesh-Barnea (Deut. 1:19), which apparently was within the larger area called Paran. This was not too far south of Canaan.

The twelve representatives of Israel's twelve tribes (13:4–16) were to move throughout the country from south to north and to bring back a report. They were to report on the land, whether it was rich or poor; on the people, whether they were few or many, weak or strong; and on the cities, whether they were camps or fortified fortresses. They also were to bring back fruit from the land (13:17–25).

2. A mixed report (13:21–33)

All twelve spies agreed on what they had seen. They reported that Canaan was indeed a land flowing with milk and honey. They brought back a huge cluster of grapes as evidence (13:26, 27). They all agreed that the people were large enough to be called giants and that the cities were walled and fortified. Groups from many warlike people lived in various parts of Canaan (13:28, 29).

The last part of the report must have set the people murmuring; because when Caleb spoke, he had to quiet the people. Because of the Lord's past actions, he said, "Let us go up at once, for we are well able to overcome it" (13:30). Ten of the spies, however, set the crowd buzzing again by contradicting Caleb. They complained, "We be not able to go up against the people; for they are stronger than we" (13:31).

32 And they brought up an evil report of the land which they had searched unto the children of Israel, saying, The land, through which we have gone to search it, is a land that eateth up the inhabitants thereof; and all the people that we saw in it are men of a great stature.

33 And there we saw the giants, the sons of Anak, which come of the giants: and we were in our own sight as grasshoppers, and so we were in their sight.

This report was "evil" because it was stated in such a way as to bring out the worst in the rest of the Israelites. For example, they said that the land "eateth up the inhabitants thereof." This ambiguous description was highly volatile and negative in its impact. We cannot be sure exactly how they meant that the land devoured the inhabitants. It could have meant that the land was not as fertile as it appeared to be. It could have meant that the land was so fertile that it was a constant battleground. It could have meant that the land of life was really a land of death.

They claimed that "all the people" they saw were huge people. They no doubt saw some large people, but surely this was an exaggeration to say that everyone was "of a great stature." No one denied that there were giants in the land. The word translated "giants" is the Hebrew word *nephilim,* which is also used to describe the giants in Genesis 6:4. The name *Anak* means "long-necked" or "strong-necked." During the later conquest of Canaan, the descendants of Anak lived in the hill country of Hebron (Josh. 11:21).

When the ten faint-hearted spies saw these giants, they saw themselves as grasshoppers. Because of their weak self-image, they assumed that the giants also saw them as grasshoppers. As you contrast the counsel of the ten spies with that of Joshua and Caleb, notice the difference that faith makes in how people respond to the same challenges.

3. Israel's rebellion (14:1–4)

> **1 And all the congregation lifted up their voice, and cried; and the people wept that night.**
>
> **2 And all the children of Israel murmured against Moses and against Aaron: and the whole congregation said unto them, Would God that we had died in the land of Egypt! or would God we had died in this wilderness!**
>
> **3 And wherefore hath the LORD brought us unto this land, to fall by the sword, that our wives and our children should be a prey? were it not better for us to return into Egypt?**
>
> **4 And they said one to another, Let us make a captain, and let us return into Egypt.**

Notice that "all the congregation" ("all the children of Israel," "the whole congregation") became like a mob that had been stirred up into a frenzy. They "cried," "wept," and "murmured." Moses had been listening to this familiar refrain from the early days in Egypt. They murmured first at the human leaders Moses and Aaron; in verse 3 they even blasphemed God Himself.

They exclaimed that they would have been better off to have died in Egypt or even in the wilderness than to perish fighting the hopeless odds against them in Canaan. They blasphemed God by blaming Him for bringing them to Canaan to die by the sword and to see their wives and children as prey for the people of Canaan.

They asked one another if they would not be better off if they turned around and went back to Egypt. Often in the past they had expressed a preference for slavery in Egypt compared to the dangers and privations of following the Lord. They decided to appoint a new leader who would lead them back to Egypt.

4. Responses of Moses, Aaron, Joshua, and Caleb (14:5–10a)

Moses and Aaron fell on their faces before the Lord. They were aware of the terrible blasphemy of which the people were guilty (14:5). Joshua and Caleb tore their clothes in grief (14:6). Then they tried in vain to make the mob listen. The land was a good land, just as the Lord had said that it was (14:7). He so loved His people that He had promised to give them this land of milk and honey (14:8). Joshua and Caleb pleaded with the people not to rebel against the Lord or to fear the people of Canaan. They said, "They are bread for us: their defence is departed from them, and the LORD is with us: fear them not" (14:9).

However, their pleas were to no avail; for the people began to gather stones to kill these men of faith and courage (14:10a).

5. God's responses (14:10b–23)

The Lord got everyone's attention as His glory filled the tabernacle (14:10b). Addressing Himself to Moses, the Lord asked two questions: "How long will this people provoke me? and how long will it be ere they believe me, for all the signs which I have shewed among them?" (14:11). God announced that He planned to destroy the Israelites and to make of Moses a new nation (14:12).

Moses prayed for the people (14:13–16). Moses then asked the Lord to show His power (14:17) and the kind of mercy He had revealed when He told Moses His name (14:18; Exod. 34:6, 7). Moses boldly asked the Lord to pardon His sinful people as He had in the past (14:19).

20 And the LORD said, I have pardoned according to thy word:

21 But as truly as I live, all the earth shall be filled with the glory of the LORD.

22 Because all those men which have seen my glory, and my miracles, which I did in Egypt and in the wilderness, and have tempted me now these ten times, and have not hearkened to my voice:

23 Surely they shall not see the land which I sware unto their fathers, neither shall any of them that provoked me see it.

God told Moses that He had pardoned the people "according to thy word." We cannot understand the mysteries of intercessory prayer, but God uses it to work out His will. "Pardoned" did not mean that He would not punish them. Instead, He meant: (1) He would not destroy them then and there, and (2) He would not give up on Israel.

Verse 21 states one solid certainty and then uses it as the basis for a vow about another certainty: (1) The first certainty is that some day the glory of the Lord will fill all the earth, (2) As surely as the first promise is true, God vowed that none of the rebels would see the Promised Land. Everyone over twenty would perish in the wilderness during forty years of wandering (Num. 14:26–35). God killed the ten evil spies right then (14:36, 37).

God was amazed that these were the very people who had witnessed the miracles in Egypt and in the wilderness. They also had put God to the test ten times. (The rabbis listed these as the ten: Exod. 14:11; Ps. 106:7; Exod. 15:23, 24; 17:2; 16:3, 20, 27; Num. 11:4; Exod. 32; Num. 13:25–14:10.) How could people who had witnessed so many of God's mighty deliverances be so unbelieving and disobedient?

6. Caleb's reward (14:24, 25)

24 But my servant Caleb, because he had another spirit with him, and hath followed me fully, him will I bring into the land whereinto he went; and his seed shall possess it.

By contrast, God rewarded the faith and courage of Caleb. God said that Caleb had followed the Lord completely when most others were turning from Him. He promised that Caleb would live to enter the Promised Land and that his descendants would possess it. Joshua also is mentioned in the same way in 14:38. Perhaps Caleb is mentioned first because he was the first of the two to speak up (13:30). Later both Joshua and Caleb spoke with courage (14:6–9). They were the only two adults who left Egypt who would be allowed to enter the Promised Land. Joshua became Moses's successor and led the conquest of Canaan. Caleb claimed his right to take part of the land promised to his descendants (Josh. 14:6–15).

Moses was told to head toward the wilderness (14:25).

PRONUNCIATION GUIDE

Aaron	[AIR'n]
Anak	[AY nak]
Caleb	[KAY luhb]
Hebron	[HEE bruhn]
Kadesh-Barnea	[KAY desh-BAHR nee uh]
Miriam	[MIR ih uhm]
Paran	[PAY ruhn]

SUMMARY OF BIBLE TRUTHS

1. People can draw different conclusions from seeing the same things.
2. Unbelief can be contagious.
3. Some people refuse to trust God, in spite of all He has done.
4. God uses intercessory prayer to work out His will.
5. Unbelief excludes people from the blessings of God.
6. God rewards courageous faith.

APPLYING THE BIBLE

1. A call for leaders. Top CEOs are skilled at developing "chains of followership," observes Ronald Frank, vice president of Mercer Management Consulting. Frank identifies six conditions that must be present for followers to be effective. They must:

- know what to do,
- know how to do it,
- understand why they're doing it,
- want to do it,
- have the right resources, and
- believe they have the proper leadership.

Great CEOs, he says, make sure these conditions exist.[1]

In God's economy, all was in place. Moses was undeniably "God's man" and with the miraculous deliverance that God orchestrated, we find it hard to believe that the Israelites would not resonate with an assurance that the other five conditions were present as well. Still they rebelled. The reminder is simple: a negative, fear-filled report can spread like a cancer in the ranks of God's people influencing and hindering them from experiencing God's very best.

2. Vision casting. Vision casting requires at least two things from leaders: (1) envisioning a future and (2) communicating that vision so others see it and want it. Most visions die because of communication breakdown. When people say no to God, it may be the result of their inability to picture themselves in a bright future with the blessings of God on their lives.

3. Vision and direction. I heard Dr. Warren Wiersbe preach a message from this text in Numbers. He said, "Tell me what you are looking at, and I'll show you where you are going." It was a one-point sermon that stuck with me. If you look at the obstacles, the giants, the potential for defeat, you'll probably be defeated. If you look at the land of promise and see the God who promised to give it to you, it will soon become reality.

4. Saying no to God. Negative reports come from negative people. The nature of the negative report in today's lesson is identical to the negative reports we hear (and possibly believe) in churches today. Negative reports have the following characteristics:

- compare the incomparable,
- exaggerate the challenges,
- criticize,
- they are contagious,
- invite complaints,
- long for that which is no longer an option,
- become depressing,
- question what God has made obvious,
- rationalize and involve others,
- would prefer bondage rather than risk failure, and
- fashion a leader with same weaknesses.

5. Caleb leaders. Churches need men and women who are willing to be "Caleb leaders." A Caleb leader is:

- one willing to stand in contrast to the majority,
- one who belongs to/is possessed by God,
- one who is a servant,
- one who understands what it is to be loyal,
- one who refuses to blend in and bend over,
- one who is a breath of fresh air (Hebrew word for *spirit* is used here; Caleb is a different or fresh spirit to God), and
- one who knows how to follow fully (literally "filled after me"; God showed him the line, and Caleb continually walked it with intention).

6. Quotes on leadership:

"But the bravest are surely those who have the clearest vision of what is before them, glory and danger alike, and yet notwithstanding go out to meet it" (Thucydides).

"Vision is the art of seeing things invisible" (Jonathan Swift).

"Above all he [John F. Kennedy] gave the world for an imperishable moment the vision of a leader who greatly understood the terror and the hope, the diversity and the possibility, of life on this planet and who made people look beyond nation and race to the future of humanity" (Arthur Schlesinger Jr., *A Thousand Days,* 1965).

"To be a leader of men one must turn one's back on men" (Havelock Ellis).

"Keep your fears to yourself, but share your courage with others" (Robert Louis Stevenson).

TEACHING THE BIBLE

- *Main Idea:* The Israelites rebelled against God's command to possess the land.
- *Suggested Teaching Aim:* To lead adults to trust God to guide them in overcoming some barrier.

A TEACHING OUTLINE

1. *Rebellion of Miriam and Aaron (Num. 12:1–16)*
2. *Rebellion of Israel (Num. 13:1–14:25)*

Introduce the Bible Study

Share: Filmmakers who make horror films often use oversized animals or insects in their movies. Filmmakers enlarge film of animals, insects, and bugs and superimpose them on film with humans, making the insects look like they are larger than humans. The secret is to take something that is ordinary and enlarge it so it becomes frightening. Everything depends on one's perspective.

The twelve spies who were supposed to spy out Canaan had a false perspective. They saw themselves as mere grasshoppers compared to the inhabitants. What they saw scared them, and they rebelled.

Search for Biblical Truth

Say, Today's lesson tells of two examples of rebellion. The first example came from Miriam and Aaron, Moses' sister and brother. **IN ADVANCE,** enlist someone to read the material in "Studying the Bible" about *1. Rebellion of Miriam and Aaron* at this time.

The second example of rebellion was disastrous for the whole nation. On a map locate the wilderness of Paran or Kadesh-Barnea and show the relation to southern Canaan. Briefly explain that Moses appointed twelve representatives from the twelve tribes to spy out the land of Canaan. The spies were to report on the land, whether it was rich or poor; on the people, whether they were few or many, weak or strong; and on the cities, whether they were camps or fortified fortresses. They were also to bring back fruit from the land (13:17–27).

When the spies returned, they agreed on some things and disagreed on others. On a chalkboard write *Agree* and *Disagree*. Ask members to search Numbers 13:21–33 to find things on which the spies agreed and disagreed. Ask half the class to look for matters on which they agreed and the other to look for matters on which they disagreed. (They all agreed on everything except whether they could occupy the land.)

Ask members to read silently Numbers 14:1–4 to find four reactions of the people to the majority report of the spies (lifted, cried, wept, murmured). Ask, What was the people's reasoning? (Better to have died slaves in Egypt than to be killed as free people in the wilderness.) What did they decide to do? (Choose a new leader and return to Egypt.)

Briefly summarize the comments in "Studying the Bible" in *4. Responses of Moses, Aaron, Joshua, and Caleb (14:5–10a).* Point out that the people were ready to stone these four leaders who stood in their way when God's glory came and stood over the tabernacle.

Ask members to read silently 14:10b–19 to find what God proposed and Moses' reaction to the proposal. (God proposed wiping them off the face of the earth; Moses interceded for the people and urged God to pardon His people.) Ask, What argument did Moses use in asking God not to kill the people? (People will say God wasn't powerful enough to bring the people into the promised land.)

Ask a volunteer to read aloud 14:20–23. Ask, Although God pardoned the people because of Moses' request, what punishment did God give the people? (All disbelievers would die in the wilderness.) Who of the leaders would be able to enter the promised land? (Only Joshua and Caleb.)

Give the Truth a Personal Focus

IN ADVANCE, copy the six "Summary of Bible Truths" statements on small strips of paper. Organize members into six groups (if you have fewer than six members, choose the statements most applicable to your class). Give each group one of the statements and ask them to read the statement and write a case study that would relate the statement to their daily lives. Let the groups share their statements with the class. Close in prayer that members will be able to trust God to guide them in overcoming some barrier they face.

---

1. "The Stuff of Leadership: Management Gurus Suggest Other Common Qualities of Successful Leaders," *Industry Week,* August 18, 1997, 100.

October

17

1999

The Desert Years

Background Passage: Deuteronomy 1:41–2:25
Focal Passages: Deuteronomy 1:41–44; 2:1–7, 16–18

The setting for Deuteronomy was across the Jordan River from Canaan (1:1–5). Moses delivered a series of sermons or addresses as the Israelites prepared to go into the Promised Land. The first address in Deuteronomy 1:6–4:43 is a review of God's leadership from Egypt to Canaan. Deuteronomy 1:41–2:25 covers the beginning and end of the forty years in the wilderness or desert.

➧**Study Aim:** *To identify reasons for the failure to take Canaan from Kadesh-Barnea and promises God kept during the years in the desert.*

(**Note:** You may have as the focal passage Deuteronomy 1:41–2:8 instead of the passages listed in the lesson heading. Because of this, all verses in both focal passages will be explained; although only those in the heading will be printed.)

STUDYING THE BIBLE

OUTLINE AND SUMMARY

I. Further Sins in Trying to Take Canaan (Deut. 1:41–2:1)
   1. **False repentance (1:41)**
   2. **Presumptuous disobedience (1:42, 43)**
   3. **Inevitable defeat (1:44, 45)**
   4. **Predictable punishment (1:46–2:1)**

II. Promises Kept (Deut. 2:2–25)
   1. **Heading toward Canaan (2:2, 3)**
   2. **God's provisions for the people (2:4–8)**
   3. **Punishment for the rebels (2:9–23)**
   4. **Preparing for battle (2:24, 25)**

After God pronounced punishment on the rebels, they said that they had sinned (1:41). God warned them that if they went into Canaan, they would go without Him (1:42, 43). When they attacked Canaan on their own, they suffered defeat (1:44, 45). They spent many years in the desert (1:46–2:1). Finally, God told them to head north toward Canaan (2:2, 3). During the years in the desert, God provided for their needs (2:4–8). All the rebels died during the years in the desert (2:9–23). As they headed toward their first enemy, the Lord told them to prepare for battle (2:24, 25).

I. Further Sins in Trying to Take Canaan (Deut. 1:41–2:1)

1. False repentance (1:41)

41 Then ye answered and said unto me, We have sinned against the LORD, we will go up and fight, according to all that the LORD our God commanded us. And when ye had

girded on every man his weapons of war, ye were ready to go up into the hill.

Those who spoke in verse 41 were the same people who had blasphemed God and planned to return to Egypt (Num. 14:40–45). Only after God announced their punishment did they say, "We have sinned." Just saying these words does not guarantee genuine repentance. The rebels were only sorry they faced punishment.

They were brazen enough even to say that they were now going to act "according to all that the LORD our God commanded us." This was the same Lord whose commands they had spurned and whom they had blasphemed. The word translated "were ready" can also mean "to be easy." They had not believed that the Lord could overcome the Canaanites. Now they said that it would be easy for them to do it.

2. Presumptuous disobedience (1:42, 43)

42 And the LORD said unto me, Say unto them, Go not up, neither fight; for I am not among you; lest ye be smitten before your enemies.

43 So I spake unto you; and ye would not hear, but rebelled against the commandment of the LORD, and went presumptuously up into the hill.

Moses delivered to the rebels a clear warning from God. He ordered them not to go up on their own. He made clear that God had withdrawn His earlier promise to be with His people. God warned that He was not going to be with them if they entered Canaan against His orders. They had missed their opportunity.

However, the people once again deliberately disobeyed the Lord. They had rebelled when He told them to enter with His help; now they again rebelled by presumptuously going on their own.

3. Inevitable defeat (1:44, 45)

44 And the Amorites, which dwelt in that mountain, came out against you, and chased you, as bees do, and destroyed you in Seir, even unto Hormah.

The results of their presumptuous attack were inevitable. The powerful Amorites easily overcame the rebels who attacked without the Lord's presence. Their defeat was humiliating. The rebels fled like people with a swarm of angry bees after them. Seir is the name of the mountain range south of Canaan in Edom.

The survivors of this defeat returned to camp and "wept before the LORD," apparently going through the motions of repentance and prayer. But just as they earlier had paid no heed to the Lord, now He ignored their cries (1:45).

4. Predictable punishment (1:46–2:1)

1 Then we turned, and took our journey into the wilderness by the way of the Red sea, as the LORD spake unto me: and we compassed mount Seir many days.

After pronouncing judgment on the rebels, God had told Moses to head into the desert toward the Red Sea (Num. 14:25; Deut. 1:40). Before they did this, however, the people stayed at Kadesh "many days"

(1:46). Then they turned and journeyed into the wilderness as the Lord had commanded. The route they took was southeast from Kadesh, the opposite direction from the Promised Land.

These two verses seem to summarize the years until the rebels died. The word translated "wilderness" means a desolate place without much vegetation; thus, "desert" may be a more accurate description. This desert lay north of the Red Sea, east of Sinai, and south of Canaan. No doubt the Israelites moved many times during those years; but 1:46 says that they stayed "many days" at Kadesh; and 2:1 says they spent "many days" near Mount Seir.

The only thing we know for sure about the amount of time is that forty years was the time in the desert (Num. 14:33; Deut. 2:7). Deuteronomy 2:14 says that thirty-eight years elapsed from the time they left Kadesh-Barnea until all the rebels had died. This departure from Kadesh probably refers to the time when the rebels launched their disastrous attack toward Canaan. The thirty-eight years apparently assumes that two years elapsed from the time they left Egypt until the failed attack from Kadesh. This would make a total of forty years.

II. Promises Kept (Deut. 2:2–25)

1. Heading toward Canaan (2:2, 3)

2 And the LORD spake unto me, saying,

3 Ye have compassed this mountain long enough: turn you northward.

After journeying away from the Promised Land (2:1), they were told by the Lord to head north toward the Promised Land. They were not allowed to make a beeline for it; but they began moving in the right general direction to eventually bring them there.

2. God's provisions for the people (2:4–8)

4 And command thou the people, saying, Ye are to pass through the coast of your brethren the children of Esau, which dwell in Seir; and they shall be afraid of you: take ye good heed unto yourselves therefore;

5 Meddle not with them; for I will not give you of their land, no, not so much as a foot breadth; because I have given mount Seir unto Esau for a possession.

6 Ye shall buy meat of them for money, that ye may eat; and ye shall also buy water of them for money, that ye may drink.

7 For the LORD thy God hath blessed thee in all the works of thy hand: he knoweth thy walking through this great wilderness: these forty years the LORD thy God hath been with thee; thou hast lacked nothing.

Between the southern desert and Canaan's eastern borders lay Edom, Moab, and Ammon. The Lord wanted the Israelites to pass peacefully either through or around these nations, who had some claim on Israel's good will. These nations were not part of Canaan, and the Lord had not promised any of these lands to Israel. In fact, He had given the lands to their present occupants.

God commanded the Israelites to avoid any conflict with the people of Edom. The Edomites were descendants of Esau, the brother of Jacob. This explains why the Lord said they were "brethren." God had given Esau and his descendants the land of Edom (Gen. 36:1–8). Since the Edomites were naturally uneasy about this large multitude of people tramping across their land, the Israelites were told to try to go around Edom. The word translated "coast" means "border." We use "coast" of a border of land and a body of water, but the Hebrew word can refer to any kind of border.

The Israelites were to bend over backwards to avoid provoking a conflict of any kind. They were to go out of their way to be polite and friendly. Rather than foraging, stealing, or looting for what they needed, the Israelites were to pay for all they needed. Notice that in such dry country, water had to be purchased.

Moses reminded the Israelites that the Lord had cared for their needs during all those years in the wilderness. When they left Egypt, the Egyptians gave their treasures to the Israelites (Exod. 12:35, 36). Later, Moses used even more graphic language to describe what the Lord said about how He cared for the people's needs in the desert years: "I have led you forty years in the wilderness: your clothes are not waxen old upon you, and thy shoe is not waxen old upon thy foot" (Deut. 29:5).

Verse 8 summarizes the route the Israelites took to go around Edom. They journeyed along the eastern border of Edom along a road that connected Moab with Elath and the Gulf of Aqaba.

3. Punishment for the rebels (2:9–23)

As the Israelites approached Moab, the Lord commanded them not to harass or provoke the Moabites, who were descendants of Lot, Abraham's nephew. Just as God had given Edom to the descendants of Esau, so had He given Moab to Lot's descendants (Gen. 19:37). God told Israel that He had not given them any of Moab (2:9).

God had driven out the earlier inhabitants of Moab in order to give the land to Lot (2:10–13), just as He had driven out the earlier inhabitants of Edom in order to give it to Esau (2:14).

16 So it came to pass, when all the men of war were consumed and dead from among the people,

17 That the LORD spake unto me, saying,

18 Thou art to pass over through Ar, the coast of Moab, this day.

Verses 14–16 are crucial verses because they mark the fulfillment of the Lord's punishment of those who rebelled at Kadesh. The Lord had said that every one of the rebellious adult generation (people over twenty) would die during forty years in the desert. Only Moses, Joshua, and Caleb would live to see it; and even Moses only viewed it from across the Jordan River but never entered in.

Deuteronomy 2:14–16 announces that the last of the rebels died. Several words are used to describe their demise as more than just the natural process of aging and death. Verse 14 says that "the men of war were wasted out from among the host." Verse 15 spells it out: "The hand of the LORD was against them, to destroy them."

The generation that crossed into Moab, therefore, was the new generation that would have the task of conquering Canaan. Ar is either a city in Moab or another name for Moab. Earlier God had told Israel to avoid trouble with the Moabites. Verse 18 is the command to move through or around Moab.

As they approached Ammon, the Israelites once again were told to avoid any conflict. Like Moab, Ammon had been given by the Lord to the descendants of Lot. God had not promised any of it to Israel (2:19). God had driven the earlier inhabitants out of Ammon as He had done in Edom (2:21–23).

4. Preparing for battle (2:24, 25)

Some of the people to be conquered by Israel were on the east side of the Jordan River. As the Israelites approached the first of the enemy, they were told to prepare for battle. The Lord promised to give this first enemy king into their hands (2:24). He also predicted that the fear of the approaching Israelites would set the stage for victory (2:25).

PRONUNCIATION GUIDE

Ammon	[AM uhn]
Amorites	[AM uh rights]
Aqaba	[AK uh buh]
Ar	[AHR]
Edom	[EE duhm]
Elath	[EE lath]
Kadesh-Barnea	[KAY desh-BAHR nee uh]
Moab	[MOH ab]
Seir	[SEE ur]

SUMMARY OF BIBLE TRUTHS

1. True repentance involves more than saying, "I have sinned."
2. Trying to live without God's presence and blessing is presumption, not faith.
3. God doesn't hear the prayers of those who persistently fail to trust and obey Him.
4. God supplies all we need to do what He calls us to do.
5. Sinners eventually reap what they sow.

APPLYING THE BIBLE

1. Unbelief. "Unbelief wastes time, an eleven-day journey turned into 40 years of wandering and death."[1]

2. Repentance. The Israelites went through the motions of repentance, but they did not repent. They were bothered by God's judgement and offered half-hearted regret. A French philosopher once said, "Our repentance is not so much regret for the ill we have done as fear of the ill that may happen to us in consequence."[2]

3. Sorry enough to stop. Real repentance is defined as being sorry enough about your sin to stop. It involves the change of one's mind, and because of that, one's behavior. Regret differs from repentance in that it is little more than an emotional response to getting caught doing something wrong.

4. Regrets. Webster's dictionary defines regret as "a note politely declining an invitation."[3] When we are confronted with sin, it is in effect an invitation to practice repentance and experience forgiving grace. We have become a nation that is so casual with God that we seem to offer regrets when we are invited to confess and repent of sin.

5. Heart disease. Adults are encouraged to have regular physical checkups to prevent the damage caused by heart disease. The author of Hebrews refers to the rebellion of the Israelites in Hebrews 3:7–12 and teaches a lesson about the condition of our hearts. Some hearts are hard, some are evil, and some hearts drift.

6. Danger signs for spiritual heart disease. The signs of spiritual heart disease can be detected and corrected. The following checklist could be used to identify the signs of a hardening or wandering heart:

- Sensitivity to spiritual things is weak.
- Fruit of the Spirit seems nonexistent.
- Spiritual passion is weak or nonoperative.
- Intimacy with God is at an all-time low.
- Sin is gaining new or renewed territory.

7. Keeping your heart tender:

- Examine the heart.
- Make the changes necessary for spiritual health, including diet (God's Word) and exercise (walking with God and practicing your faith).
- Begin obeying God in the "little things" of life.
- Learn to listen for God's will in the "bigger things" of life.

8. Life in the desert. "How often life is a wilderness way. As we journey, there seems to be no map, no plan, no timetable. God is not only accompanying us on the march, He goes before us and selects the places of our pausing. The places we pitch our tents are chosen by God" (G. Campbell Morgan).

9. Destiny. The Israelites thought too little of God. As a result, fear took over, hearts grew hard, and an inheritance was forfeited by an entire generation. The story of the spies and Israel's rebellion are underscored by the admonition written by Frank Outlaw.

Watch your thoughts; they become words.
Watch your words; they become actions.
Watch your actions; they become habits.
Watch your habits; they become character.
Watch your character; it becomes your destiny.[4]

10. Monotony. Monotony is the constant companion of the believer who fails to trust God for the spiritual adventure God has planned.

TEACHING THE BIBLE

- *Main Idea:* Israel was unfaithful and disobedient, but God kept His promises.
- *Suggested Teaching Aim:* To lead adults to affirm that God is faithful even if they are not.

A TEACHING OUTLINE

1. *Further Sins in Trying to Take Canaan (Deut. 1:41–2:1)*
2. *Promises Kept (Deut. 2:2–25)*

Introduce the Bible Study

Share this case study: Martha had trouble doing what she said she would do. She often would promise to do something and then not do it. One day she told a friend, "Nobody keeps promises. Everybody breaks them. You just can't trust anyone." Ask, What relationship exists between Martha's inability to keep her promises and her belief that everybody else breaks promises?

Israel broke their part of the covenant they had made with God, and they assumed that God would act as they had done and break His part of the bargain. However, God kept His promises for thirty-eight years in the wilderness.

Search for Biblical Truth

Explain that the Book of Deuteronomy is a retelling of Israel's struggles in escaping Egypt and entering into the Promised Land. On a map of the wilderness wanderings, locate Kadesh-Barnea and identify it as the place where Israel sinned by refusing to obey God and continued to sin by trying to take Canaan on their own. On a chalkboard write: *Further Sins in Trying to Take Canaan*. Ask members to open their Bibles to Deuteronomy 1:41–2:1. Ask members to read silently these verses and answer these questions: (1) Why did God not accept Israel's statement that they had sinned? (2) Why do you think the people ignored Moses' warning from God not to attack Canaan? What happened to the Israelites immediately because they had consistently disobeyed God? What was the long-term effect?

DISCUSS: Is it ever too late to confess our sins and receive the Lord's full blessings?

Write on the chalkboard: *Promises Kept.* On a map of the conquest, trace Israel's route up through Edom and Moab and across from Jericho.

Ask members to read silently 2:2–7, 16–18 and answer these questions: (1) Why did the Lord direct Israel around Edom, Moab, and Ammon? Trace the ancestry of Edomites (Esau), Moabites (Lot), and Ammonites (Lot). (2) How were the Israelites to get water and other supplies from these people? (3) What had the Lord done to provide for the people's needs? (4) What was the event that prompted God to begin the move toward Canaan?

DISCUSS: What evidence can you cite to show that God has kept His promises to you?

Give the Truth a Personal Focus

IN ADVANCE, write out the five statements in "Summary of Bible Truths" and give them to five different members before class. Ask them to listen during the lesson for two or three ideas that support their statement and be prepared to read their statement and to share their ideas with the class.

DISCUSS: Do you think that God is faithful to you even if you are not faithful to Him? Why?

---

1. Warren Wiersbe, *With the Word* (Nashville: Oliver Nelson, 1991), 107.
2. François, Duc de La Rochefoucauld, *Reflections; or, Sentences and Moral Maxims.*
3. *Merriam-Webster's Collegiate Dictionary,* 10th Ed., 1993.
4. Frank Outlaw, *Bits and Pieces,* vol. R. (Fairfield, N.J.: The Economic Press, Inc.), 7.

The Great Commandment

Background Passage: Deuteronomy 6:1–25
Focal Passages: Deuteronomy 6:1–9, 20–24

Deuteronomy 6:4–5 has played an important role in the faith of the Old Testament people of God. These verses, along with some others, are still recited by many Jews as the heart of their faith. They call this the Shema, from the Hebrew word for "hear." These verses are crucial for Christians because Jesus quoted them as the greatest commandment of the law (Matt. 22:34–39; Mark 12:28–31; Luke 10:25–28).

Study Aim: *To cite reasons why both the Old and the New Testament consider Deuteronomy 6:4, 5 to be important.*

STUDYING THE BIBLE

OUTLINE AND SUMMARY

- **I. General Principles (Deut. 6:1–3)**
- **II. Foundational Realities (Deut. 6:4–9)**
  1. **Faith in one God (6:4)**
  2. **Wholehearted love for God (6:5)**
  3. **Keeping and sharing the faith (6:6–9)**
- **III. Future Applications (Deut. 6:10–25)**
  1. **Don't forget the Lord (6:10–15)**
  2. **Don't test the Lord (6:16–19)**
  3. **Remember what God did and what He expects (6:20–25)**

God called Israel to hear and obey His commandments (6:1–3). They believed in one God, the Lord (6:4). He expects wholehearted love (6:5). God's words are to be memorized, taught, and practiced at all times and in all ways (6:6–9). When Israel entered Canaan, they were warned not to forget the Lord (6:10–15). They were not to test the Lord as their forefathers had (6:16–19). When their children asked about their religion, parents were to testify to God's mighty acts of deliverance as the basis of His commandments (6:20–25).

I. General Principles (Deut. 6:1–3)

1 Now these are the commandments, the statutes, and the judgments, which the LORD your God commanded to teach you, that ye might do them in the land whither ye go to possess it:

2 That thou mightest fear the LORD thy God, to keep all his statutes and his commandments, which I command thee, thou, and thy son, and thy son's son, all the days of thy life; and that thy days may be prolonged.

3 Hear therefore, O Israel, and observe to do it; that it may be well with thee, and that ye may increase mightily, as the LORD God of thy fathers hath promised thee, in the land that floweth with milk and honey.

Commandments, statutes, and judgments refer to the specific stipulations of the law that God was about to give Moses (5:31). God delivered these words to Moses, who in turn was to teach the people. Probably these refer to the specific stipulations in Deuteronomy 12–26. Notice the various words that describe obedience to these commandments: "do," "keep," "observe."

Deuteronomy 6:1–3 is one of many Old Testament passages that called on the Israelites to fear the Lord. This is not cringing terror that flees from God but reverent awe that is expressed in obedience to God's words and commands. The word for "hear" appears often in the Bible. The assumption always is that anyone who hears the word of God will obey it.

These laws were for the current generation and for their sons and for their grandchildren. This is one of three verses in Deuteronomy 6 that speaks of the need to share the faith with each succeeding generation (6:7, 20).

These laws were not arbitrary rules and restrictions given by God just to prove He was God; instead, they were moral and spiritual expectations that were for the good of humanity. God told the Israelites that He gave them these "that it may be well with thee" (6:3; see also 6:24).

II. Foundational Realities (Deut. 6:4–9)

1. Faith in one God (6:4)

4 Hear, O Israel: the LORD our God is one LORD.

The faith of Israel stood in marked contrast to that of pagan people in two significant ways. Sometimes the faith of Israel is called ethical monotheism. They believed in one God, as opposed to the many gods of other people; and the one God called them to be holy as He is holy.

Jesus and His earliest followers were all Jews. The New Testament clearly affirms faith in one God; however, "one" is not defined in some limited, restricted way. Even in the Old Testament, the one God was viewed as above and beyond humanity; yet He appeared as the angel of the Lord; and His Spirit moved in human lives. Christians believe in one God; but we believe that the one God has revealed Himself and we have experienced Him as Father to whom we pray, Son who became incarnate, and Spirit who abides within us (Eph. 2:18).

2. Wholehearted love for God (6:5)

5 And thou shalt love the LORD thy God with all thine heart, and with all thy soul, and with all thy might.

Verses 4 and 5 go together. People who worship many gods must spread their love and devotion around. Only as we believe in one God can we focus all our love and devotion on Him. At the same time, wholehearted love is the only way to respond to the one true God. He fits in only one place in human hearts—the first place reserved for God.

The word *all* appears three times. People of real faith in God give Him all that they have and are. "Heart," "soul," and "might" are not separate compartments of a person. They are ways of saying that all that I am is to be directed in obedient love to God.

Ordinarily, the Old Testament uses other words to describe how humans are to respond to God: fear, trust, obey, praise, and so forth. "Love" is a warmer word that implies a personal relationship like that of a family. Our love for God is motivated by God's love for us. Deuteronomy is one of the few Old Testament books to refer to God's love for His people and their love for Him (7:7, 9).

3. Keeping and sharing the faith (6:6–9)

> **6 And these words, which I command thee this day, shall be in thine heart.**
>
> **7 And thou shalt teach them diligently unto thy children, and shalt talk of them when thou sittest in thine house, and when thou walkest by the way, and when thou liest down, and when thou risest up.**
>
> **8 And thou shalt bind them for a sign upon thine hand, and they shall be as frontlets between thine eyes.**
>
> **9 And thou shalt write them upon the posts of thy house, and on thy gates.**

What did it mean to have these words in their hearts? At the very least, it meant to memorize them; but it probably also meant to integrate these words into their attitudes and actions. "Thy word have I hid in mine heart, that I might not sin against thee" (Ps. 119:11).

Parents were to teach their children to give wholehearted love to the one God. The instruction was to be informal as well as formal. The parents were to talk of these things in conversation in the home and as they went from place to place. These words were to be part of their routine day and night.

Were verses 8, 9 intended to be taken literally or figuratively? In later years, many Jews took them literally. They put Scripture verses in boxes that were worn on their forearms and on their foreheads. The words were literally inscribed on the doorposts or placed in boxes near the door. Whether taken literally or not, the verses obviously were intended to be taken seriously. People of faith in the one God are to keep their faith and their devotion to Him constantly before them and others.

III. Future Applications (Deut. 6:10–25)

1. Don't forget the Lord (6:10–15)

When they arrived in Canaan, God would give the people all the good things He had promised that they would find in the land (6:10, 11). Their prosperity would tempt them to forget the Lord, who had brought them out of Egyptian slavery into that good land. In words soon to be repeated in Deuteronomy 8, they were warned not to forget the Lord (6:12). They were to fear God and not be drawn away to serve other gods because such a heinous sin would bring terrible judgment on them (6:13–15).

2. Don't test the Lord (6:16–19)

One of the besetting sins of Israel was to put God to the test. They were warned not to commit this sin of their forefathers (6:16; see Num. 14:22). Instead, they were diligently to keep His commandments and to do what is right and good in His sight (6:17, 18). This would be necessary if the Lord was to cast out their enemies from Canaan and give the land to them (6:19).

3. Remember what God did and what He expects (6:20–25)

20 And when thy son asketh thee in time to come, saying, What mean the testimonies, and the statutes, and the judgments, which the LORD our God hath commanded you?

21 Then thou shalt say unto thy son, We were Pharaoh's bondmen in Egypt; and the LORD brought us out of Egypt with a mighty hand:

22 And the LORD shewed signs and wonders, great and sore, upon Egypt, upon Pharaoh, and upon all his household, before our eyes:

23 And he brought us out from thence, that he might bring us in, to give us the land which he sware unto our fathers.

24 And the LORD commanded us to do all these statutes, to fear the LORD our God, for our good always, that he might preserve us alive, as it is at this day.

Verse 20 is the third reference in Deuteronomy 6 to teaching children the faith (6:3, 7). The setting is years in the future. A son, observing the actions of his parents and becoming aware of the commandments by which they lived, might ask the meaning of these statutes. Fathers were told to welcome such a question and to use the opportunity to testify and teach the younger generation the basics of their faith: what God had done for them (6:21–23) as the reason for His covenant relationship and expectations (6:24, 25).

One purpose of the Passover was to provoke children to ask similar questions (Exod. 13:14). The same was true of the stone markers set up after the Israelites crossed the Jordan River into the Promised Land (Josh. 4:21). Parents should welcome questions from their children as teaching opportunities. These are teachable moments, indeed.

The faith of the Israelites was based on God's mighty acts of deliverance on their behalf. Verses 21–23 is one of many such summaries of their confession and testimony of faith. Notice they said, "We were," not just "our forefathers were." Each generation of Israelites remembered and relived (as if they were there) what God had done in delivering the Israelite slaves from the power of Pharaoh and the Egyptians.

As we saw in our study of Exodus, this was a divine deliverance that could have been accomplished only by the mighty hand of the Lord. God smote Pharaoh and his household with such great and painful signs and wonders that the formerly defiant Pharaoh begged the Israelites to leave Egypt. God then brought them out of Egypt and after many other miracles brought them into the land that He had promised to give them. As we shall see in studying the conquest of Canaan, the conquest was as much the work of the Lord as was the deliverance from Egypt.

These divine acts for Israel served for Old Testament people of faith the same role as the cross and resurrection do for Christians. These acts of divine deliverance are the historical basis for our faith. On the basis of these acts of deliverance, God called the Israelites into a covenant relationship with Him. The promises of the covenant also were grounded in what God had done for them in the past. The point in verses 20–24 is that His commandments grow out of the covenant relationship, which in turn was made possible by His mighty acts on their behalf. Righteousness was living in light of what God had done by obeying the commandments of the God who had acted on their behalf (6:25).

SUMMARY OF BIBLE TRUTHS

1. Hearing God's commandments calls for obedience.
2. Faith in one God calls for a response of wholehearted love.
3. Parents should teach their children what God has done and what He expects.
4. They are to use every opportunity and method to do this.
5. God's words are to be memorized, talked about, and lived daily.
6. God's saving acts provide the historical basis for our relationship with Him and His expectations of us.

APPLYING THE BIBLE

1. Parental tips. Parents are expected to share and model the essential elements of faith with their children. John Maxwell offers seven tips to parents who are willing to take this Old Testament commission to heart in what he calls "Getting to Know God . . . with Your Children."

- *Be an example.* Albert Schweitzer said, "Example is not the main thing in influencing others . . . it is the only thing." Never underestimate the power of our example for our children.
- *Keep it simple.* Don't be intimidated when talking about God and praying with children. Take what you know and think of ways to communicate simply and clearly to your children.
- *Be sensitive.* Listen to the concerns, fears, and thoughts of your children. Jesus did this often with His disciples.
- *Make it exciting.* Use creativity. Watch and discuss Christian videos. Use games.
- *Be consistent.* Balance flexibility with consistency.
- *Be transparent with them.* We are all sinners saved by grace. We are all real people with fears and faults. Don't pretend to be something you are not—your kids will see right through you.
- *Begin today.* The time spent with your children getting to know God doesn't need to be perfect . . . it just needs to happen.

2. What society sees. Eleanor L. Doan said, "Education is the mirror of society." For Christians, the education we give our children through our influence in the home and our insistence upon their training through our church provides a countercultural mirror for our society.

3. What a child becomes. We should consider not so much what the child is today as what he may become tomorrow.

4. Quotes on influencing a child:

"Today's unchurched child is tomorrow's criminal."

"Our children are the only earthly possessions we can take with us to glory."

"Child by child, we build our nation."

"The kind of person your child is going to be, he is already becoming."

5. The Heart of a Child

Whatever you write on the heart of a child,
No water can wash away.
The sand may be shifted when billows are wild,
And the efforts of time may decay.
Some stories may perish. Some songs be forgot,
But this graven record—time changes it not.
Whatever you write on the heart of a child,
A story of gladness or care
That heaven has blessed or earth has defiled,
Will linger unchangeably there.

—Author unknown

TEACHING THE BIBLE

- *Main Idea:* The Great Commandment should be obeyed and taught.
- *Suggested Teaching Aim:* To lead adults to affirm their desire to obey and teach the Great Commandment.

A TEACHING OUTLINE

1. *General Principles (Deut. 6:1–3)*
2. *Foundational Realities (Deut. 6:4–9)*
3. *Future Applications (Deut. 6:10–25)*

Introduce the Bible Study

Read the following from a list of "Really Important Stuff Kids Have Taught Me":

- Even if you've been fishing for 3 hours and haven't gotten anything except poison ivy and a sunburn, you're still better off than the worm.
- It doesn't matter who started it.
- Ask for sprinkles. Sometimes you have to take the test before you've finished studying.
- There is no good reason why clothes have to match.
- Even Popeye didn't eat his spinach until he absolutely had to.
- Toads aren't ugly; they're just toads.

- If you stand on tiptoe to be measured this year, you'll have to stand on tiptoe for the rest of your life.

Suggest that children learn a lot of important beliefs early in their lives; that is why God commanded parents to teach them about Him.

Search for Biblical Truth

To overview the lesson, copy the seven summary statements in the "Outline and Summary" section on large strips of paper. Tape these at random around the room. Read Deuteronomy 6:1–3 and ask members to identify the summary statement that best describes these verses. Do this with the rest of these references: 6:4; 6:5; 6:6–9; 6:10–15; 6:16–19; 6:20–25.

On a chalkboard write: **ActionPrincipleResult**

Ask members to open their Bibles to Deuteronomy 6:1–3. Ask a third of the class to find the actions God wanted the Israelites to do (do, fear, keep, hear, observe); a third to find the principles God wanted them to obey (commandments, statutes, judgments); a third to find the result the Israelites would experience if they did this (prolonged days, increase mightily).

DISCUSS: Why did God establish these rules? What were the reasons behind them?

Ask members to open their Bibles to Deuteronomy 6:4–9. Ask a third of the class to find the actions God wanted the Israelites to do (hear, love); a third to find the principles God wanted them to obey (words); a third to find the result the Israelites would experience if they did this (not sin; see Ps. 119:11).

DISCUSS: How does memorizing Scripture help us? How can we teach Scripture to our children?

Ask members to open their Bibles to Deuteronomy 6:10–25. Ask a third of the class to find the actions God wanted the Israelites to do (say, do); a third to find the principles God wanted them to obey (testimonies, statutes, judgments); a third to find the result the Israelites would experience if they did this (our good always, preserve us alive).

DISCUSS: How can we use elements in our worship services to teach about our faith? What blessing of God can you share with others that will encourage them and strengthen you?

Give the Truth a Personal Focus

IN ADVANCE, copy the six "Summary of Bible Truths" on sheets of paper for each member. (Or write them on one large sheet and give members blank sheets of paper.) Read the *Suggested Teaching Aim:* "To lead adults to affirm their desire to obey and teach the Great Commandment." Ask the members to read the summary statements silently and then choose one statement to make into a promise to God in light of the Teaching Aim. (For example, the first statement could be rephrased something like this: "I promise that I will obey God's commands in the area of ____.") Let volunteers read their promises if they wish. Close in prayer.

A Warning

Background Passage: Deuteronomy 8:1–20
Focal Passage: Deuteronomy 8:7–20

Two terms with similar meanings sum up the theme of Deuteronomy, especially chapter 8. The words are "remember" and "forget not." Moses called the Israelites to remember what God had done for them and the lessons He had taught them. This was especially true as they prepared to enter the Promised Land, where they would face a new temptation—prosperity. They were warned against the deadly results of forgetting the Lord.

Study Aim: *To explain how prosperity tempts people to forget the Lord and how remembering God is expressed.*

STUDYING THE BIBLE

OUTLINE AND SUMMARY

I. Remember God and the Lessons of the Past (Deut. 8:1–6)
II. Bless God for His Blessings (Deut. 8:7–10)
III. Forget Not God in Prosperity (Deut. 8:11–20)
1. Beware forgetting the Lord (8:11–13)
2. Beware taking credit for what God has done (8:14–17)
3. Remember the source of all blessings (8:18)
4. Forgetting God leads to ruin (8:19, 20)

Moses called Israel to remember what God did for them and taught them in the desert (8:1–6). When they enjoyed the good land God was giving them, they should bless the Lord (8:7–10). They were to beware forgetting God when they experienced prosperity (8:11–13). Forgetting God could lead them to take credit for what God alone had done (8:14–17). Remembering God includes remembering that He alone gives power to make wealth (8:18). If Israel forgot God and turned to false gods, Israel would go the way of the idolatrous nations that were about to be driven out of Canaan (8:19, 20).

I. Remember God and the Lessons of the Past (Deut. 8:1–6)

Earlier Moses called Israel to remember how God had delivered them from Egypt (5:15). Deuteronomy 8:1–6 was a call to remember the wilderness years and the lessons God taught them. God used the hard years in the wilderness to humble Israel and to teach them obedience (8:1, 2). By feeding them manna, God was trying to teach them that they lived not only through physical sustenance but also through God and His Word (8:3). God not only fed them but provided clothes and shoes that lasted (8:4). He chastened them to teach them obedience (8:5, 6).

II. Bless God for His Blessings (Deut. 8:7–10)

7 For the LORD thy God bringeth thee into a good land, a land of brooks of water, of fountains and depths that spring out of valleys and hills;

8 A land of wheat, and barley, and vines, and fig trees, and pomegranates; a land of oil olive, and honey;

9 A land wherein thou shalt eat bread without scarceness, that shalt not lack any thing in it; a land whose stones are iron, and out of whose hills thou mayest dig brass.

10 When thou hast eaten and art full, then thou shalt bless the LORD thy God for the good land which he hath given thee.

Having reminded the Israelites of the wilderness years and of God's deliverances and leadership, Moses pointed ahead to the good days that lay ahead when they claimed God's promises in the Promised Land. The word *land* occurs seven times in verses 6–10, twice as the "good land." The adjective "good" occurs over twenty times in Deuteronomy, usually in reference to the good land that the Lord was giving to them.

Verses 6–9 describe various aspects of the goodness of the land, and verse 10 called the Israelites to make a proper response to such blessings. After forty years in the desert, nothing sounded so good as an abundance of water. Moses promised a land of brooks, fountains, and springs. In addition, the hills had rich mineral deposits of iron and copper.

All kind of crops would grow in that good land. These included not only staples like wheat, barley, grapes, and figs but also special treats like pomegranates and honey. Olive oil was used for cooking, lighting, and medicine. Seldom had they known full stomachs during the hard wilderness years; but in Canaan, they would seldom know anything but full stomachs.

When they entered the good land and were enjoying all these good gifts of God, they were admonished by Moses to bless the Lord. He was the giver of the good land and all its good things (James 1:17). Praise and gratitude ought to be the responses from those who have received the good gifts from God.

III. Forget Not God in Prosperity (Deut. 8:11–20)

1. Beware forgetting the Lord (8:11–13)

11 Beware that thou forget not the LORD thy God, in not keeping his commandments, and his judgments, and his statutes, which I command thee this day:

12 Lest when thou hast eaten and art full, and has built goodly houses, and dwelt therein;

13 And when thy herds and thy flocks multiply, and thy silver and thy gold is multiplied, and all that thou hast is multiplied.

Moses appealed to them to keep God's commandments. He feared that the prosperity of Canaan would lure many of them away from God and His commandments. The words "this day" referred to the day on which Moses was speaking to them (see also "as it is this day" in 8:18). Past, present, and future came together in many of his exhortations. He reminded them of the past deliverances and leadership of God and of the lessons He had taught them. He pointed ahead to their future in the Promised Land. And he appealed to them that day to renew their covenant with God.

Verses 7–10 describe how people should respond to prosperity. Verses 11–20 warn against how not to respond to prosperity. These verses are a sad reminder that in every generation, wealth can be at least as powerful a temptation as poverty.

The words "forget" and "forget not" appear repeatedly throughout Deuteronomy. They are found in Deuteronomy 8:11, 14, 19. "Forget" is the opposite of "remember." Moses did not use either word purely of the mental processes of remembering or forgetting. He was speaking of people who live as if they remember or as if they have forgotten God and the lessons He has taught them.

The Israelites faced many temptations during the terrible years in Egypt and during the hard years in the desert. However, Moses knew that they soon would face more subtle but powerful temptations when their stomachs were full, when their herds and flocks were many, when they lived in nice houses, when their silver and gold were multiplied, and—in fact—when everything multiplied into abundance and wealth.

2. Beware taking credit for what God has done (8:14–17)

14 Then thine heart be lifted up, and thou forget the LORD thy God, which brought thee forth out of the land of Egypt, from the house of bondage;

15 Who led thee through that great and terrible wilderness, wherein were fiery serpents, and scorpions, and drought, where there was no water; who brought thee forth water out of the rock of flint;

16 Who fed thee in the wilderness with manna, which thy fathers knew not, that he might humble thee, and that he might prove thee, to do thee good at thy latter end;

17 And thou say in thine heart, My power and the might of mine hand hath gotten me this wealth.

Moses feared two things: (1) They would forget the Lord and the lessons He had taught them, and (2) their hearts would be lifted in pride. These two, of course, go together.

Verses 14b–16 reminded the Israelites once again of the realities of their heritage that they must not forget. The Israelites must never forget that the Lord delivered them from Egypt. They must never forget how He led them and supplied their needs in the hard wilderness years. They must never forget that the land of Canaan was a gift from God and that their prosperity in the Promised Land was made possible by God.

The last part of verse 16 is a reminder of the biblical doctrine of divine providence. That is, God has a good purpose at work for His people. At times, especially during hard times, we may wonder if this is true; however, God's ultimate purpose is to do good for His people (Rom. 8:28).

Verse 17 states a timeless truth. Moses applied it directly to the Israelites as they entered Canaan, but it is as true now as it ever was. When the Israelites got into Canaan and began to enjoy the good land and its blessings, they were in danger of gradually forgetting that these blessings came from God. When that happened, they were in danger of beginning to take personal credit for their prosperity. They were tempted to think and to say, "My skill, intelligence, strength, and hard work explain my prosperity."

3. Remember the source of all blessings (8:18)

18 But thou shalt remember the LORD thy God: for it is he that giveth thee power to get wealth, that he may establish his covenant which he sware unto thy fathers, as it is this day.

"Remember" is the positive antidote against forgetting the Lord and all the accompanying sins. This word occurs fourteen times in Deuteronomy, including twice in chapter 8 (vv. 2, 18). Remembering God is more than a mental exercise, although it does begin with mentally remembering what God has done for His people in the past as well as what He has done for each person individually.

At the heart of remembering God is renewing our personal relationship with Him. The last part of verse 18 reminded the Israelites that remembering the Lord was bound up in their covenant with the Lord. God gives us good things, but He Himself is the best gift. Accepting His gifts of love but rejecting or forgetting Him is a serious sin. Remembering God involves remembering the lessons He has taught us and living out of that wisdom.

A key lesson is stated in Deuteronomy 6:3. Jesus quoted this when Satan tempted Him to turn stones into bread (Matt. 4:1–4; Luke 4:1–4). This was a temptation not so much for Jesus to feed Himself but a temptation to become a Messiah who would meet only human physical needs. People need bread to live physically, but they need God and His word of life if they would truly live.

Anyone who remembers God will never be such a fool as to say what the person said in verse 17. How can I claim credit for any good thing since God is the giver of every gift? But someone may say, "I did the planning and the work." Don't forget that everything involved in such a claim is among God's good gifts—the gift of life, health, strength, skills, and so on. We take God's blessings for granted until one of them is threatened.

4. Forgetting God leads to ruin (8:19, 20)

19 And it shall be, if thou do at all forget the LORD thy God, and walk after other gods, and serve them, and worship them, I testify against you this day that ye shall surely perish.

20 As the nations which the LORD destroyeth before your face, so shall ye perish; because ye would not be obedient unto the voice of the LORD your God.

Forgetting God leads inevitably to substituting gods for the true and living God. In many cases, one of these gods—probably the main false god—is oneself (8:17); but other gods also soon fill the spiritual vacuum when God is left out of His rightful place—the only place into which He fits—first place (Deut. 6:5).

Moses warned of the terrible consequences of forgetting God and turning to false gods. If the Israelites did this, they would end up on the scrap heap of history with all nations which made that mistake. God was about to drive out of Canaan people steeped in idolatry and all its abominations. If Israel eventually committed the same sins, Israel would suffer the same fate.

What happens when people forget God? This chapter mentions or implies four sins that flow from this basic sin: (1) not thanking God for His blessings (8:10), (2) beginning to disobey God's commandments (8:1, 6, 11), (3) pride that takes credit for what God has done (8:14, 17), and (4) turning to other gods (8:19).

SUMMARY OF BIBLE TRUTHS

1. God's purpose for His people is ultimately for our good.
2. We should bless God for His blessings to us.
3. Prosperity tempts people to forget God.
4. Forgetting God involves taking credit for what God has done.
5. Remember God and the lessons He has taught.
6. Forgetting God leads ultimately to judgment.

APPLYING THE BIBLE

1. Living in the nation that wants to forget God. William F. Buckley was visiting lecturer at Old Dominion University, Norfolk, Virginia. Following a discussion session with fifteen honor students, one student was to be photographed with the speaker.

Posing them on either side of the large college seal, the photographer, an elderly woman, focused her camera. Pausing, she pointed to the student, who was dressed in denims and an open-collared shirt. She called attention to a tiny cross on a silver chain around his neck and asked, "Would you please tuck the cross inside your shirt?"

Mr. Buckley asked the photographer, "Why have you asked him to hide his cross?"

Frazzled by the question, she said, "Well, you know, there are a lot of people who'll be seeing this picture and a lot of them aren't Christians."

The speaker pointed to the student and said, "So what? He is a Christian, and he wants to wear his cross."

"Well, you know," the lady mumbled. "It's—you have no idea the sensitivity of people. I mean, if somebody has a drink in his hand I have to say, 'Please put down your drink.' Of if they have a cigarette, I have to say, 'Please put that away.'"[1]

So there you have it. Christianity is now as offensive as cigarettes and alcohol, at least in the opinion of this photojournalist. The real reason is more personal than this. The cross was offensive to the photographer. It is easier to live in a society with no crosses, no remembrances of a God who judges sin. It's far easier to get along in the midst of our possessions without a God who demands a moral standard from His people.

2. Memory. Memory is the receptacle and sheath of all knowledge.

3. Remembering God in past, present, and future:

Yesterday is history.
Tomorrow a mystery.
Today is a gift . . . that's why it's called the present!

4. Remembering not to forget. Dr. W. C. F. Powell, pastor of First Baptist Church, Nashville (1926–1955), would often remind his congregation to remember and forget not with these words: "The past is prologue; the present is unparalleled; the future is as great as our faith in God."

5. The value of memory in changing times. The transitions in our lives are those events—or nonevents—that alter our roles, relationships, routines, and assumptions.[2] They include:

- Anticipated transitions: the major life events we usually expect to be a part of adult life, such as marrying, becoming a parent, starting a first job, or retiring.
- Unanticipated transitions: the often-disruptive events that occur unexpectedly, such as major surgery, a serious car accident, a surprise promotion, or a factory closing.
- Nonevent transitions: the expected events that fail to occur, such as not getting married, not having a baby, or living longer than expected.

Change and transition face us every single day of life. God's call to remember and forget not is in reality a gracious call. In the midst of change, we have to remember who we are and who God is.

6. Who remembers better? It has been said that "creditors have betters memories than debtors." In reality, this is good news. We are debtors in the hands of God. We are instructed to remember and forget not from the One who will never forget about us.

TEACHING THE BIBLE

- *Main Idea:* God warned that prosperity often tempts people to forget Him and rely on their own strength.
- *Suggested Teaching Aim:* To lead adults to identify ways they can remember the Lord to keep prosperity from destroying them.

A TEACHING OUTLINE

1. *Remember God and the Lessons of the Past (Deut. 8:1–6)*
2. *Bless God for His Blessings (Deut. 8:7–10)*
3. *Do Not Forget God in Prosperity (Deut. 8:11–20)*

Introduce the Bible Study

Read the following bumper sticker: "God, let me prove that winning the lottery won't ruin me." Say, An owner of a cable television company recently gave away over a billion dollars. He said he did not want his family to be extremely rich. Ask, What dangers do you think his family would face? Say, A study showed that those who won the lottery were destroyed by their win, and in the end they were in worse shape than before they won.

Search for Biblical Truth

On a chalkboard write: *God's Blessings for Israel.* Ask members to open their Bibles to Deuteronomy 8:7–13 and identify the blessings God had given Israel when He gave them the "good land." List these on the chalkboard as members suggest them.

Ask members to read silently Deuteronomy 8:14–20. Ask, According to these verses, what did God do for Israel? (Delivered them from Egypt, led them in the wilderness, provided water from rock, fed them with manna.) What was Moses afraid would happen when they became prosperous? (See 8:17.)

Ask, If God is the source of all blessings (8:18), why do God's people think they have earned their blessings? **IN ADVANCE,** make a poster with these words and place it on the focal wall: *God gives us good things, but He Himself is the best gift.*

DISCUSS: What does it mean to "remember" God? How does remembering God keep us from claiming that we have earned our wealth in our own strength and might?

Ask, What did God promise would happen to Israel if they forgot Him? (God would destroy them like He was going to destroy the other nations that He would drive out of Canaan.) **IN ADVANCE,** copy on large strips of paper (or write on a chalkboard) the following four sins that result in forgetting God: (1) not thanking God for His blessings (8:10); (2) beginning to disobey God's commandments (8:1, 6, 11); (3) pride that takes credit for what God has done (8:14, 17), and (4) turning to other gods (8:19).

Give the Truth a Personal Focus

Read this case study: Bill and Dorothy had met at a church function during their college years. They married and launched their careers. Bill was a doctor and Dorothy was a lawyer. Both worked night and day to get established in their careers. At first, they really made an effort to attend church and be active, but gradually they found it so much easier to sleep in on Sunday or to go to work. They found it good for business to join certain clubs and organizations. When they had time, they attended these instead of church. Of course, Bill's schedule often demanded that he work on Sunday. As they became more established in their professions, they built a new home and bought larger cars. Shortly after they had built their dream house, they were involved in an automobile accident. Dorothy was killed, and Bill was disabled and told he would never be able to practice medicine again. Their pastor went to see Bill, and in his bitterness, Bill lashed out at God: "Why did God do this to us?" The pastor replied . . . . Ask several members to suggest what the pastor may have said.

Ask, What can we do to remember the Lord to keep prosperity from destroying us? List ideas on a chalkboard. Challenge members to remember that it really is God who gives us the "power to get wealth." Point to the poster and challenge members to claim the best gift—God!

---

1. William F. Buckley, Jr., "The New Scarlett Letter (Crosses Become a Target of Political Correctness," *National Review,* Oct. 27, 1997, 63.

2. Nancy K. Schlossberg, "Taking the Mystery Out of Change," *Psychology Today,* May 1987, 74.

November

7

1999

Joshua Succeeds Moses

Background Passages: Deuteronomy 31:1–8; 34:1–12
Focal Passages: Deuteronomy 31:1–8; 34:5–8a, 9

As we noted in the lesson on the call of Moses (Sept. 5), God often chooses to do His work through human beings. He called and worked through Moses in delivering Israel, making His covenant with Israel, and leading them in the desert years. Now Moses was about to die. God chose Joshua as his successor, and Moses commissioned Joshua as the new leader.

Study Aim: *To identify the steps in the transfer of human leadership from Moses to Joshua.*

STUDYING THE BIBLE

OUTLINE AND SUMMARY

I. Moses' Challenges to Israel and Joshua (Deut. 31:1–8)
1. **Moses, the old leader (31:1–2)**
2. **God the leader and His plans for Joshua (31:3–5)**
3. **Challenge to Israel (31:6)**
4. **Challenge to Joshua (31:7, 8)**

II. Death of Moses (Deut. 34:1–12)
1. **Moses' view of the land of promise (34:1–4)**
2. **Moses' death and burial (34:5–7)**
3. **Mourning for Moses; obedience to Joshua (34:8, 9)**
4. **Final tribute to Moses (34:10–12)**

Moses was 120 years old when he last spoke to Israel (31:1, 2). God promised to work through Joshua to lead the people (31:3–5). God challenged Israel (31:6) and Joshua (31:7, 8) to have courage because He was with them (31:7, 8). God enabled Moses to view Canaan from a high mountain (34:1–4). When Moses died, God buried him (34:5–7). After mourning Moses, Israel obeyed Joshua (34:8, 9). Moses had a close relationship to the Lord and was mightily used by Him (34:10–12).

I. Moses' Challenges to Israel and Joshua (Deut. 31:1–8)

1. Moses, the old leader (31:1, 2)

1 And Moses went and spake these words unto all Israel.

2 And he said unto them, I am an hundred and twenty years old this day; I can no more go out and come in: also the LORD hath said unto me, Thou shalt not go over this Jordan.

Verse 1 introduces the final section of Deuteronomy, in which the dominant theme is the transfer of leadership to Joshua. Moses gave two reasons why he could no longer serve as the human leader of Israel. For one thing, he was 120 years old. He was 40 when he left Egypt for Midian, and he was 80 when he led the Israelites out of Egypt (Acts 7:2, 3;

Deut. 2:7). He was no longer able to "go out and come in." This apparently means that he no longer had the strength to lead the people, especially to lead them into battle (see 34:7).

The second reason that Moses had to relinquish leadership was that the Lord had told him that he could not enter the Promised Land. Numbers 20:1–13 records the incident in which Moses sinned and was punished by being forbidden from entering the land. Later Moses pleaded with the Lord to allow him to enter, but the Lord said no. However, the Lord did promise to show Moses the land from the east side of the Jordan (Deut. 3:23–29).

2. God the leader and His plans for Joshua (31:3–5)

3 The LORD thy God, he will go over before thee, and he will destroy these nations from before thee, and thou shalt possess them: and Joshua, he shall go over before thee, as the LORD hath said.

4 And the LORD shall do unto them as he did to Sihon and to Og, kings of the Amorites, and unto the land of them, whom he destroyed.

5 And the LORD shall give them up before your face, that ye may do unto them according unto all the commandments which I have commanded you.

Throughout all that had happened while Moses had been the human leader of Israel, the Lord had been the people's true leader and deliverer. Moses had been only His instrument. The same would be true when Joshua become their leader. Just as it was the Lord, not Moses, who had delivered Israel from Egypt, so it would be the Lord, not Joshua, who would lead them to conquer Canaan.

"Go over before" meant to lead by taking the point position. God took the ultimate point position. Notice that the same words are used to describe Joshua. As God's leader, Joshua would lead them to take the Promised Land. This was to be done because God chose Joshua to do this (Deut. 3:28).

Notice also that destroying the pagan nations of Canaan was to be done by the Lord, but Israel was to be His instrument in doing this. God would destroy them as He had already done the Amorites of the east side of the Jordan (Deut. 2:26–3:11). God had commanded the Israelites to utterly wipe out the pagan Canaanites, lest their evil ways corrupt Israel (Deut. 7:2). But God Himself would be the One who would give the enemies up into the hands of the Israelites; and He thus was the One who would give them the land, fulfilling His promise to the patriarchs and repeated to them. God was giving them the land; they needed only to go in and possess it.

3. Challenge to Israel (31:6)

6 Be strong and of a good courage, fear not, nor be afraid of them: for the LORD thy God, he it is that doth go with thee; he will not fail thee, nor forsake thee.

Based on the promises of verses 3-5, the Lord challenged the Israelites to be strong and courageous. These qualities are the opposite of the fear that kept their fathers from entering the land a generation earlier (Num. 13–14). The Lord did not want the younger generation to be paralyzed by such fear. Instead, they needed strength and courage that grows out of the assurance that the Lord would go over before them and would never leave nor forsake them.

4. Challenge to Joshua (31:7, 8)

> **7 And Moses called unto Joshua, and said unto him in the sight of all Israel, Be strong and of a good courage: for thou must go with this people unto the land which the LORD hath sworn unto their fathers to give them; and thou shalt cause them to inherit it.**
>
> **8 And the LORD, he it is that doth go before thee; he will be with thee, he will not fail thee, neither forsake thee: fear not, neither be dismayed.**

When we review earlier references to Joshua, we see that he was the obvious one for God to select to lead Israel into Canaan. Shortly after leaving Egypt, Joshua appears as the leader of the fighting men against the Amalekites (Exod. 17:8–16). Joshua went part of the way up Mount Sinai with Moses (Exod. 24:12, 13) and came down with Moses and assisted Moses after the golden calf episode (Exod. 32:17; 33:11). He, along with Caleb, stood against the ten spies who rebelled and refused to enter Canaan (Num. 13:16; 14:6–10).

Notice that Moses delivered the challenge of verses 7, 8 to Joshua "in the sight of all Israel." Moses did everything possible to publicly appoint and commission Joshua to be his successor. He did not want any power struggle to result from unclear instructions on this matter. Numbers 27:18–23 tells of a public commissioning service in which Moses laid his hands on Joshua and gave him the charge that God had told Moses to give to Joshua.

Also notice how similar were the challenges to Israel as a whole in verse 6 and to Joshua their leader in verses 7, 8. Almost the same words were used in both challenges. Joshua was told to be strong and courageous. Joshua was assured that although he was the human leader, the Lord would go before him as leader and would go with him. Thus, he was told not to be afraid or dismayed. This message of challenge and assurance was given to Joshua again after the death of Moses (Josh. 1:6–9) and repeated at crucial points during the conquest of Canaan (Josh. 8:1; 10:25). God spoke similar words to later leaders (Jer. 1:8; Ezek. 2:6).

Both Joshua and the people were reminded that the Lord had promised to give this land to the patriarchs, and He had repeated this promise to their fathers when they were called out of Egypt. God keeps His promises.

However, Joshua could not assume a purely passive role. Moses reminded Joshua that he was the one appointed by God "to cause them to inherit" the Promised Land. God was the Leader and power, but He needed a human being who would lead and fight to fulfill God's promises.

II. Death of Moses (Deut. 34:1–12)

1. Moses' view of the land of promise (34:1–4)

Moses had been speaking to the Israelites on the plains of Moab, just east of southern Canaan. Moses climbed up Mount Nebo, or Pisgah, which was across the Jordan Valley from Jericho (34:1a). From that high place, the Lord enabled Moses to see across the Jordan River and to see the Promised Land. He saw from Gilead at the southern end of eastern Canaan to Dan in the north (34:1b). Moses even saw western Canaan from Naphtali in the north though Ephraim and Manasseh in central Canaan as far as the sea in the distant west (34:2). Then Moses looked to the south across the Jordan Valley to Zoar (34:3). The Lord told Moses that although he was not allowed to enter, he had at least seen the land God had promised to Abraham, Isaac, and Jacob (34:4).

2. Moses' death and burial (34:5–7)

> **5 So Moses the servant of the LORD died there in the land of Moab, according to the word of the LORD.**
>
> **6 And he buried him in a valley in the land of Moab, over against Beth-peor: but no man knoweth of his sepulchre unto this day.**
>
> **7 And Moses was an hundred and twenty years old when he died: his eye was not dim, nor his natural force abated.**

After looking over into the Promised Land, Moses died, just as the Lord had said. He had seen the land from a distance, but he was not allowed to set foot in Canaan. The first "he" in verse 6 must refer to the Lord. This conclusion is confirmed by the last part of verse 6. The fact that no man knew where Moses was buried shows that the Lord buried Moses.

Verse 7 gives Moses' age as 120 and adds that "his eye was not dim." This clear vision was demonstrated in Moses' ability to see all of Canaan from many miles away. Also his strength was not abated. Although Deuteronomy 31:2 indicates that Moses did not have his former strength, he was still a vigorous man for his age.

3. Mourning for Moses; obedience to Joshua (34:8, 9)

> **8 And the children of Israel wept for Moses in the plains of Moab thirty days: so the days of weeping and mourning for Moses were ended.**
>
> **9 And Joshua the son of Nun was full of the spirit of wisdom; for Moses had laid his hands upon him: and the children of Israel hearkened unto him, and did as the LORD commanded Moses.**

When the Israelites realized Moses was dead, they mourned their great leader for thirty days. Some of what they said may be included in the glowing tribute in verses 10–12. Then they obeyed the command that the Lord had given them concerning Joshua. Moses had done all he could to make plain that the Lord had chosen Joshua to lead Israel into the Promised Land. Apparently the new generation had learned the bitter lesson of disobedience by watching their rebellious fathers perish in the desert. Never did Joshua face the kind of constant bickering that Moses endured during the time he tried to lead the people of Israel.

The transition to the new leader went smoothly, and the people obeyed Joshua. They recognized that the Lord had given Joshua the kind of wisdom and discernment so essential for God's leader.

4. Final tribute to Moses (34:10–12)

Deuteronomy closes with an appropriate tribute to Moses. At the time this tribute was written, no prophet had arisen in Israel who was like Moses. He had a unique relationship with the Lord that brought him into as intimate fellowship with God as was possible for any human (34:10). The Lord used Moses in all the signs and wonders by which He delivered Israel from Egyptian slavery (34:11). In fact, all the signs that Israel witnessed in those days were wrought through Moses as God's human instrument (34:12).

PRONUNCIATION GUIDE

Amalekites	[AM uh lek ights]
Amorites	[AM uh rights]
Beth-peor	[beth-PEE awr]
Ephraim	[EE frih uhm]
Gilead	[GILL ih uhd]
Manasseh	[muh NASS uh]
Moab	[MOH ab]
Naphtali	[NAF tuh ligh]
Nebo	[NEE boh]
Og	[AHG]
Pisgah	[PIZ guh]
Sihon	[SIGH hahn]
Zoar	[ZOH ur]

SUMMARY OF BIBLE TRUTHS

1. God leads His people, but often does so through human leaders.
2. Human leaders live and die, but God continues His work.
3. God challenges His people to follow Him and God-chosen leaders.
4. God keeps His promises.
5. God promises His power and presence to His leaders.
6. God challenges them to be courageous as they do His will.

APPLYING THE BIBLE

1. Transitions in leadership. Moses paved the way for a smooth leadership transition by being a good encourager. Warren Wiersbe says Moses encouraged in at least three ways:

- He encouraged the people as they began a new life in a new land with a new leader.
- He encouraged Joshua to be bold and courageous.
- He encouraged the Levites to protect and proclaim the Word of God.[1]

2. Leadership. It is time for a new generation of leadership, to cope with new problems and new opportunities. For there is a new world to be won.[2]

3. Two aspects of a leader's ministry. "The quality of your ministry will be determined by your knowledge of and relationship to Jesus Christ. The security of your ministry will be determined by your understanding and acceptance of Christ's assignment in service."[3]

4. Looking for leaders. In 1987, *Time* magazine's cover story entitled "Who's in Charge?" contained the following somber quote: "The nation calls for leadership and there is no one home." It was during this same time period that the television evangelist scandals were in the news every day. What a shame that when culture cried out for a leader, the Christian community seemed paralyzed by shame and disgrace.

Similarly, a University of Michigan study several years ago asked survey respondents to list the top ten greatest dangers to society. Nuclear war was the first danger, followed closely by epidemic. The third danger to society was the quality of leadership in America.

5. Top 12 qualities of a leader:

- Has a mission that matters
- Is a big thinker
- Has high ethics
- Change master
- Is sensitive
- Risk taker
- Decision maker
- Uses power wisely
- Communicates effectively
- Is a team builder
- Is courageous
- Is committed.

—Sheila Murray Bethel

6. Church leaders. If the church is to make a difference in the world, every one of its members must begin to act and think like leaders.

7. Leadership is hard to define. As Warren Bennis points out in his book *On Becoming a Leader* (1989), leadership still remains the most studied and least understood topic in all the social sciences. Leadership is all too often still "like beauty, or love, we know it when we see it but cannot easily define or produce it on demand."[4]

8. A letter to future leaders. Leighton Ford, brother-in-law of Billy Graham, wrote a letter (published in *Christianity Today*) to two future leaders in which he verbalized his prayer for them. This is an encouraging prayer list that you may want to voice for your spiritual leaders and for those who are being called out as leaders from your congregation. Dr. Ford said:

I pray that you will be "hopers."

I pray that you will be world Christians.

I pray that you will be visionaries like Jesus.

I pray that you will be kingdom and not empire builders.

I pray that you will model the inclusiveness of Jesus.
I pray that you will have a pioneering spirit for the gospel.
I pray that you will stay attuned to the Holy Spirit.
I pray that you will seek a heart for God.

TEACHING THE BIBLE

- *Main Idea:* God chose Joshua to succeed Moses as Israel's leader.
- *Suggested Teaching Aim:* To lead adults to be encouraged by the transfer of leadership from Moses to Joshua and to seek to follow God's leadership in their lives.

A TEACHING OUTLINE

1. *Moses' Challenges to Israel and Joshua (Deut. 31:1–8)*
2. *Death of Moses (Deut. 34:1–12)*

Introduce the Bible Study

During the Crimean War in 1854, an English army officer mistakenly ordered the Light Cavalry consisting of 673 soldiers to charge the Russian army consisting of 12,000 men plus heavy artillery. The men did not question what appeared to be a senseless order, but charged to their death. Alfred Lord Tennyson immortalized their faithfulness in his poem, "The Charge of the Light Brigade."

Theirs not to make reply,
Theirs not to reason why,
Theirs but to do and die:
Into the valley of Death
Rode the six hundred.[5]

Say, When it came time for Moses to give up his leadership, the Israelites accepted Joshua without question. They, like the six hundred, followed Joshua into battle. However, as long as they followed the Lord's leadership, they were successful.

Search for Biblical Truth

On a chalkboard or a large sheet of paper write: *Transferring the Leadership.* **IN ADVANCE,** enlist a member to read the eight sentences in the "Outline and Summary" section to overview the lesson. Ask members to open their Bibles to Deuteronomy 31:1, 2 and read these verses silently while they look for steps in the transferring of power from Moses to Joshua. Using the material in "Studying the Bible," add appropriate information about these suggestions. (Members may find additional steps but consider these: [1] Moses told them he was too old; [2] God refused to let Moses enter the promised land.) Write members' suggestions under the heading on the chalkboard.

DISCUSS: How do we know when a person is too old to provide leadership?

Ask members to read silently 31:3–5 and identify the steps taken to transfer power. ([3] Moses assured the people of God's leadership;

[4] Moses assured the people that God had chosen Joshua; [5] Moses assured the people they would defeat the Canaanites.)

DISCUSS: How does God choose people today to do His tasks?

Ask members to read silently 31:6–8 and identify the steps. ([6] Moses encouraged Israel to be strong; [7] God assured the people He would go into battle before them; [8] Moses visibly passed leadership to Joshua.)

DISCUSS: How does the Lord give us strength and courage today?

Ask members to read silently 34:5–9 and identify the steps. ([9] God removed Moses' body so it would not become an object of worship; [10] Moses laid his hands on Joshua as a visible transference of leadership.)

DISCUSS: How can we know when God has chosen a leader for us to follow?

Give the Truth a Personal Focus

Distribute paper and pencils to all members. Read the first of the six "Summary of Bible Truths" statements. Ask members to write a sentence based on this statement that would be applicable to your church. (For example, God has revealed to us His leadership by giving us people like Mary Hutchinson and Bill Green.) Do this for each summary statement. Close in prayer.

---

1. Warren Wiersbe, *With the Word* (Nashville: Oliver Nelson, 1991), 123.
2. John Fitzgerald Kennedy, television address, July 4, 1960.
3. Cecil Sims, graduation speech, Golden Gate Baptist Theological Seminary, Mill Valley, California.
4. Charles Handy, *The Age of Unreason* (Boston: Harvard Business School Press, 1990), 133.
5. *The Oxford Dictionary of Quotations,* 2nd ed. (London: Oxford University Press, 1955), 528.

November

14

1999

Israel Crosses the Jordan River

Background Passage: Joshua 3:1–17

Focal Passage: Joshua 3:7–17

Although miracles occur throughout the Bible, most of them fall into three key stages in divine revelation and deliverance: the periods of exodus and conquest, the Baal crisis during the times of Elijah and Elisha, and the work of Christ and the apostles. During this quarter, we are looking at the first of these. Already we have seen the many divine signs connected with the deliverance from Egypt and the years in the desert. In this and the next lesson, we will be looking at two notable miracles of the period of the conquest: crossing the Jordan River and taking Jericho.

Study Aim: *To identify similarities and differences between crossing the Red Sea and crossing the Jordan River.*

STUDYING THE BIBLE

OUTLINE AND SUMMARY

I. Instructions About Crossing the Jordan (Josh. 3:1–6)

II. Promises About Crossing the Jordan (Josh. 3:7–13)

1. Magnify Joshua as leader (3:7, 8)

2. Reveal God as living and universal (3:9–13)

III. Crossing the Jordan (Josh. 3:14–17)

1. Stopping the waters (3:14–16)

2. Crossing the river (3:17)

Joshua and his officers instructed people and priests about crossing the Jordan River (3:1–6). God promised to magnify Joshua as leader in the eyes of the people (3:7, 8). God's purpose was to reveal Himself as living and as Lord of all the earth (3:9–13). When the priests' feet touched the water, the waters were stopped (3:14–16). While the priests and ark stood in the middle of the river bed, the people passed over safely (3:17).

I. Instructions About Crossing the Jordan (Josh. 3:1–6)

The main task that God gave Joshua was to lead Israel into Canaan and conquer the land (Josh. 1:2). Joshua led the people to camp just east of the Jordan River (3:1). After three days, officers went throughout the camp to instruct the people (3:2). The officers told them to follow the ark of the covenant, but to allow space so they could see where the ark led them (3:3, 4). Joshua ordered the people to sanctify themselves (3:5). Joshua also told the priests to carry the ark and go over in front of the people (3:6).

II. Promises About Crossing the Jordan (Josh. 3:7–13)

1. Magnify Joshua as leader (3:7, 8)

7 And the LORD said unto Joshua, This day will I begin to magnify thee in the sight of all Israel, that they may know that, as I was with Moses, so I will be with thee.

8 And thou shalt command the priests that bear the ark of the covenant, saying, When ye are come to the brink of the water of Jordan, ye shall stand still in Jordan.

One of God's purposes in parting the Jordan River was to validate His choice of Joshua as the new leader of Israel. No one had challenged Joshua's right to command, but this miracle at the beginning of his new role as Moses' successor would clearly show the people that Joshua was God's chosen leader. This would reassure the people that the Lord was with Joshua and would work through him as He had done in Moses' lifetime as leader.

The ark of the covenant is prominent throughout the Book of Joshua. This sacred ark from the holy of holies signified the presence of the Lord with His people. As the ark was carried forward by the priests, this signified that the Lord was fulfilling His promise to go before the people into the Promised Land.

Many obstacles lay ahead for the Israelites to conquer Canaan. The first obstacle was a natural barrier—the Jordan River at flood stage. At many times of the year, the river would not have been a barrier. Often it was shallow enough to be forded at certain points; however, during harvest time (April), it had overflowed its banks and thus was too deep to ford (see Josh. 3:15).

2. Reveal God as living and universal (3:9–13)

9 And Joshua said unto the children of Israel, Come hither, and hear the words of the LORD your God.

10 And Joshua said, Hereby ye shall know that the living God is among you, and that he will without fail drive out from before you the Canaanites, and the Hittites, and the Hivites, and the Perizzites, and the Girgashites, and the Amorites, and the Jebusites.

11 Behold, the ark of the covenant of the Lord of all the earth passeth over before you into Jordan.

12 Now therefore take you twelve men out of the tribes of Israel, out of every tribe a man.

13 And it shall come to pass, as soon as the soles of the feet of the priests that bear the ark of the LORD, the Lord of all the earth, shall rest in the waters of Jordan, that the waters of Jordan shall be cut off from the waters that come down from above; and they shall stand upon an heap.

Joshua told the Israelites that God was preparing to give them a sign that He would fulfill His promise to drive out the pagan people of Canaan. The sign is stated in verse 11. The Lord would go before them as signified by the ark of the covenant leading them into the Jordan River. Verse 13 explains what the Lord intended to do by having the priests march into the flooded Jordan River. He was going to stop the waters of the river. God did not explain how He was going to do that, but He promised that He would.

These words reminded the people of what had happened a generation earlier at the crossing of the Red Sea. There are some similarities and some differences between these two mighty acts of God on behalf of His people. Both miracles involved a body of water that stood in the way of advance by God's people. Both miracles involved parting the waters to allow the Israelites to cross over safely. Both miracles revealed the presence and power of God.

The Lord, speaking through Joshua, emphasized two aspects of His being that He would reveal by enabling the Israelites to cross the flooded Jordan River. For one thing, they would clearly see that He is the "living God." This means that He was a real God who was active on behalf of His people, not one of the false deities that pagans worshiped. Second, the personal "LORD" of the Israelites would show Himself to be also "the Lord of all the earth."

Many people of that day thought of each nation having its own god, more or less confined to them and their land. Although God had chosen to work at this stage of redemptive history through the people of Israel, He was Lord of all people, places, and things. He had showed His power over the nonexistent gods of Egypt. Now He was about to part the waters of a river in the land of Canaan.

One of the differences was that Moses had been the leader at the Red Sea. Now Joshua was the leader. At the Red Sea, the Israelites were a frightened mass of slaves. The new generation about to enter Canaan had been tested and trained during the years in the desert. They had more faith and more ability than their unbelieving fathers. Moses had taken more of a direct role in the Red Sea miracle than Joshua did at the Jordan. He delivered God's commands, but the priests played a crucial role in this miracle. At the Red Sea, Moses stretched out his hand and rod. At the Jordan River, the priests acted in faith by marching into the flooded river.

At the Red Sea, their enemies had been the pursuing Egyptian army trying to trap the Hebrews with their backs to the impassable Red Sea. At the Jordan, the enemies of the Israelites were in their fortified cities throughout the land of Canaan. Joshua listed seven of the main groups that lived in Canaan. At that time, Canaan was not one united nation but a land of many city-states controlled by various groups of people. This lack of unity worked to the advantage of the invading Israelites; but as the twelve spies had reported a generation earlier, many of these groups were formidable enemies; and many lived in fortified cities.

Verse 12 makes sense only as we read what the twelve men were to do and why (Josh. 4:1–9). They each carried a stone across the river to form a monument, which was to remind future generations of what God had done for Israel at the Jordan River. This is another similarity to the Red Sea miracle. Both were woven together with other acts of God during the Exodus and the Conquest to form the historical basis for Israel's confession of faith in the Lord.

Joshua 4:12 suggests another purpose of the twelve men, one from each tribe. The Israelites had already conquered the Amorites on the east side of the Jordan. This conquered territory had already been apportioned among three of Israel's tribes. Moses feared that the fighting men of the families who settled the east bank would not help conquer the rest of Canaan. He exacted from them a solemn oath that they would fulfill their duty (Num. 32). Joshua 3:12 and 4:12 show that they kept that promise to Moses and the Lord.

III. Crossing the Jordan (Josh. 3:14–17)

1. Stopping the waters (3:14–16)

14 And it came to pass, when the people removed from their tents, to pass over Jordan, and the priests bearing the ark of the covenant before the people;

15 And as they that bare the ark were come unto Jordan, and the feet of the priests that bare the ark were dipped in the brim of the water, (for Jordan overfloweth all his banks all the time of harvest,)

16 That the waters which came down from above stood and rose up upon an heap very far from the city Adam, that is beside Zaretan: and those that came down toward the sea of the plain, even the salt sea, failed, and were cut off: and the people passed over right against Jericho.

The biblical account has built suspense by mentioning several times the movement of the priests and the ark into the flooded river (3:6, 8, 11, 13). The people have been told to follow the ark (3:3, 4). However, the actual advance of the priests and people is not described until verses 14–16.

These verses need to be read together. Verses 14, 15 describe the obedient faith of the priests, but only verse 16 tells what happened when they stepped into the flooded river. The waters stopped only when their feet actually stepped into the water. God made this miracle dependent on the willingness of the priests to act in faith that God would keep His promise. This is another difference from the crossing of the Red Sea. God parted the waters before the people started across. At the Jordan River, God stopped the waters only when the feet of the priests touched the water.

The Jordan River had its sources at Mount Hermon in the north. The elevation there is more than one thousand feet above sea level. It flowed south until it emptied into the Dead Sea, which is over thirteen hundred feet below sea level. The Israelites crossed the river about even with the city of Jericho, which is near the end of the river. Thus, the description in verse 16 means that at some point upstream the waters were stopped and piled up and that the waters below that point rushed downstream, leaving the river bed open for crossing.

2. Crossing the river (3:17)

17 And the priests that bare the ark of the covenant of the LORD stood firm on dry ground in the midst of Jordan, and all the Israelites passed over on dry ground, until all the people were passed clean over Jordan.

The Hebrew word translated "passed over" occurs twenty-two times in these two chapters. The miracle at the Jordan River enabled the Israelites to pass over the flood-swelled river.

The priests and to some degree the people acted with considerable faith and courage. The Jordan River had several banks, and the water was out of all its banks. The priests had to step into that flood with no assurance other than God's promise. Then they stood in the middle of the riverbed while all the Israelites passed them and marched to safety. During all this time, they had only God's promise that the waters upstream might not suddenly be released.

Joshua 4:10, which describes the same crossing, uses the word "hasted" to describe the speed with which the people crossed the river. They moved quickly. Even so, with so many to cross, this must have taken some time. During all that time, the priests were standing in the middle of the river bed.

PRONUNCIATION GUIDE

Amorites	[AM uh rights]
Girgasites	[GUR guh sights]
Hittites	[HIT tights]
Hivites	[HIGH vites]
Jebusites	[JEB yoo sights]
Perizzites	[PEE riz ights]
Zaretan	[ZER uh tan]

SUMMARY OF BIBLE TRUTHS

1. God validates the calling of those whom He calls.
2. God is actively working on behalf of His people.
3. God is Lord of all the earth.
4. God enables His people to cross barriers to His work.
5. God makes some of His promises conditional on our faith.

APPLYING THE BIBLE

1. Obstacles. "A problem is a chance for you to do your best" (Duke Ellington).

2. Facing problems. "I have yet to see any problem, however complicated, which, when you looked at it in the right way, did not become still more complicated" (Paul Anderson).

3. Faith in the face of obstacles. The major obstacle of the Christian's entrance into the rest-land of a victorious, abiding life is that which appears to be the impossible factor in his life. But the bigger the obstacle the greater the manifestation of God's might. God requires faith in the face of the obstacle, but He will always go before.[1]

4. Miracles. How do you explain the miracle of the Jordan stopping and "heaping up" at one end in the midst of flood season? You don't. As one theologian said: "For those who believe in God no explanation is needed; for those who do not believe in God no explanation is possible."[2]

5. Cross over times. John Huffman uses the phrase "cross over times" in describing the events of the third chapter of Joshua.[3] While cross over times are the times of change and transition, the Hebrew verb *'abar* indicates the decisive nature or the intentional choice in crossing over the Jordan.

6. Five characteristics of "cross over times":

- Cross over times follow wilderness experiences, those growing, testing times of discipline.
- Cross over times require a step of faith.
- Cross over times require determination, for it is impossible to accidentally step over the Jordan.
- The threshold to a cross over time is usually an obstacle or a seemingly impossible challenge.
- Cross over times are gateways to promised blessing that will never be ours from a distance.

7. Thinking like "cross over people." The Hebrew word *'abar* is not used to describe the crossing of the Red Sea, for a different mindset is required now that was not required then. As the Israelites "cross over," they have to do so by determining the kind of people they will be in a new land with new challenges. Think about the "cross over times" that may be facing your church or members of your class. What are some of the decisive elements that must accompany the choices you are facing?

8. The cost of "crossing over." J. Sidlow Baxter says that the experience at the Jordan is a crisis of faith. "To be 'brought out of Egypt' was one thing; but it was another thing altogether to 'go over this Jordan' and thus become committed, without possibility of retreat, to the struggle against the powers of Canaan . . . To the natural eye it was to hazard everything on the chance of battle, to have no retreat, and to run the risk of losing everything."[4]

TEACHING THE BIBLE

- *Main Idea:* The Israelites trusted God to lead them across the Jordan River.
- *Suggested Teaching Aim:* To lead adults to trust God's miraculous power to work a miracle in their lives.

A TEACHING OUTLINE

1. *Instructions About Crossing the Jordan (Josh. 3:1–6)*
2. *Promises About Crossing the Jordan (Josh. 3:7–13)*
3. *Crossing the Jordan (Josh. 3:14–17)*

Introduce the Bible Study

As members enter, give them paper and a pencil. Ask them to write what they think is the greatest miracle in the Bible without discussing this with other members. Assure members there is no right or wrong answer; ask volunteers to share their choice and why they chose it. Point out that although miracles occur throughout the Bible, most of them fall into three stages: (1) the periods of the Exodus and Conquest, (2) the Baal crisis during the time of Elijah and Elisha, and (3) the work of Christ and the apostles.

Search for Biblical Truth

Explain that today's lesson will compare and contrast two great miracles of the first period: crossing the Red Sea and the Jordan River. Ask half of the class to suggest ways the crossings were similar and the other half to suggest ways the crossings were different.

Briefly summarize the material in "Studying the Bible" under "1. Instructions About Crossing the Jordan (Josh. 3:1–6)." Ask members to look at 3:7–13. Lecture briefly, covering these points: (1) crossing the Jordan validated Joshua's leadership role; (2) the ark of the covenant verified God's presence with Israel; (3) the Jordan was out of its banks; (4) the miraculous crossing was a sign of encouragement to Israel; (5) the priests exercised great faith in stepping into the flooded waters; (6) the miracle showed God was active and Lord over all the earth; (7) Joshua chose twelve men to carry twelve stones from the Jordan to make a monument to memorialize the crossing.

On a chalkboard or large sheet of paper write: *Similarities* and *Differences*. Ask each of the groups to suggest ways the crossing was similar to and different from the crossing of the Red Sea. (See "Studying the Bible" for some suggestions; however, your members may suggest other ideas that are also correct.) Write their suggestions under the appropriate heading.

Ask members to look at Joshua 3:14–16. Lecture briefly, covering these points: (1) the water did not stop until the priests stepped into the water; (2) the priests' actions showed they trusted God; (3) the river from the point the priests entered south to the Dead Sea had no water in it; (4) the people crossed quickly, but with so many it still took a long time; (5) the priests stood in the middle of the dry river bed while all the Israelites crossed.

Ask each of the groups to suggest ways the crossing was similar to and different from the crossing of the Red Sea.

Give the Truth a Personal Focus

Read each of the five "Summary of Bible Truths" and then rephrase them as a question: (1) How does God validate the calling of those He calls? (2) How do you see God actively working on behalf of His people? (3) What evidence can you cite to show God is Lord of all the earth? (4) What barriers has God enabled you to cross to do His work? (5) Which of God's promises to you are conditional on your faith? Ask members to turn their paper over and take one minute to think about some miracle they want God to work in their lives. Ask them to write the miracle on the piece of paper and keep it until God answers in one way or another.

---

1. Irving Jensen, "Joshua, Rest-land Won," *Everyman's Commentary* (Chicago: Moody Press, 1966), 48.

2. Father John Lafarge, *The Concise Columbia Dictionary of Quotations* (Columbia University Press, 1990).

3. John Huffman, *The Communicator's Commentary,* Lloyd J. Ogilvie, gen. ed. (Waco: Word Books Publisher, 1986), 70f.

4. J. Sidlow Baxter, *Explore the Book* (Grand Rapids: Zondervan Publishing House), 256.

November

21

1999

The Destruction of Jericho

Background Passage: Joshua 6:1–27

Focal Passages: Joshua 6:1–5, 15–20

The fall of Jericho was the second miraculous sign that the Lord gave Israel as they began the conquest of the Promised Land. Crossing the Jordan River enabled them to pass safely over the first natural barrier. Causing the walls of Jericho to fall enabled Israel to continue the advance through the first man-made barrier. Both were miracles wrought by God, although each required faith and obedience by the Israelites.

Study Aim: *To identify what God promised and what He commanded at Jericho.*

STUDYING THE BIBLE

OUTLINE AND SUMMARY

I. Promises and Obedience (Josh. 6:1–16)
   1. **Jericho—a formidable barrier (6:1)**
   2. **God's plan and promises (6:2–5)**
   3. **Israel's faith and obedience (6:6–16)**

II. Destruction and Deliverance (Josh. 6:17–27)
   1. **Destruction and deliverance commanded (6:17–19)**
   2. **Destruction of the city (6:20, 21)**
   3. **Deliverance of Rahab (6:22–27)**

The walled city of Jericho closed its gates tightly as the Israelites approached (6:1). The Lord told Joshua the plan of attack and promised to give Israel Jericho by causing its walls to fall (6:2–5). The people responded to God's commands and promises with faith and obedience (6:6–16). Everyone and everything in Jericho was to be destroyed, except for delivering Rahab and her family and placing the metal things in the Lord's treasury (6:17–19). When the people shouted, the walls fell, the soldiers advanced, and the city was taken and destroyed (6:20, 21). Rahab and her family were delivered (6:22–27).

I. Promises and Obedience (Josh. 6:1–16)

1. Jericho—a formidable barrier (6:1)

1 Now Jericho was straitly shut up because of the children of Israel: none went out, and none came in.

Jericho blocked the advance of any invader from the east. It was one of the walled and well-fortified cities of Canaan that struck fear into the fathers of the invading Israelites (Num. 13:28). The walls are not mentioned in verse 1, but only walls could enable the city to be "shut up" so that "none went out, and none came in."

Ordinarily, a city under attack sent out patrols to attack the enemy or forage for provisions. However, the people of Jericho had shut themselves in tightly. God had promised that the advance of the Israelites would strike fear into the Canaanites (Deut. 2:25). Rahab's words to the two spies confirmed that such fear was real in Jericho as the Israelites approached (Josh. 2:9–11).

2. God's plan and promises (6:2–5)

2 And the LORD said unto Joshua, See, I have given into thine hand Jericho, and the king thereof, and the mighty men of valour.

3 And ye shall compass the city, all ye men of war, and go round about the city once. Thus shalt thou do six days.

4 And seven priests shall bear before the ark seven trumpets of rams' horns: and the seventh day ye shall compass the city seven times, and the priests shall blow with the trumpets.

5 And it shall come to pass, that when they make a long blast with the ram's horn, and when ye hear the sound of the trumpet, all the people shall shout with a great shout; and the wall of the city shall fall down flat, and the people shall ascend up every man straight before him.

When the Lord spoke to Joshua, the Lord said, "I have given into thine hand Jericho." He did not say, "I will give you Jericho," but "I have given . . . Jericho." He used language that spoke of a future event as if it had already taken place. God's promises are that sure. Earlier, God had promised to give Canaan to Israel. By giving them Jericho at the beginning of the conquest, the Lord would signify that He could keep His promise to give them the entire land.

Walls were the major protection of cities of that day. The king and "mighty men of valour" (6:2) could withstand a powerful invading force as long as they were safe behind their walls. Taking a walled city ordinarily called for one or more of the following strategies: (1) a siege that starved a city into submission, (2) ladders and powerful soldiers to scale the walls, (3) smashing a hole in the gates or walls, (4) building a ramp, (5) digging a tunnel under the walls, or (6) using trickery as the Greeks did with the Trojan horse. The Israelites did not use any of the usual strategies.

God's plan called for seven days of marching around the city. Seven priests were to go in front of the ark of the covenant and blow rams' horns, which were not metal trumpets but signal horns. The "men of war" were to go with them, but not the women and children. Verse 13 shows that some of the fighting men went ahead and some went behind the ark. On each of six days they were to march around Jericho with the seven priests blowing their horns, but with no shouting from the people until the seventh day. On that day, they were to march seven times around the city; then when the horns blew, the people were to shout.

When that happened, the Lord promised that the walls of Jericho would fall flat. Then each Israelite soldier was to attack straight across the ruins of the fallen wall. The fallen wall was a miracle of God, but

God expected the army to do its part in conquering the city. This combination of divine power and human obedience runs throughout the story.

3. Israel's faith and obedience (6:6–16)

15 And it came to pass on the seventh day, that they rose early about the dawning of the day, and compassed the city after the same manner seven times: only on that day they compassed the city seven times.

16 And it came to pass at the seventh time, when the priests blew with the trumpets, Joshua said unto the people, Shout; for the LORD hath given you the city.

Verses 6, 7 record Joshua passing along God's word to the priests and the people. Verses 8–14 describe how carefully the priests and people carried out the Lord's plan for six days. On the seventh day, they got up early as they had the other days. The people of Jericho, watching from behind their walls, noticed something different. The Israelites did not just march around once and then return to their camp. Instead they kept going around the city until they had done this seven times.

Then the Israelites did something else for the first time at Jericho. The people of Jericho had become accustomed to the loud blasts of the rams' horns, but they had wondered at the total silence of the soldiers. All that changed after the seventh circuit on the seventh day. They heard Joshua cry out. Joshua repeated to the Israelites what the Lord had told him. He shouted, "Shout, the LORD hath given you the city."

In the roll call of faith in Hebrews 11, we read, "By faith the walls of Jericho fell down, after they were compassed about seven days" (v. 30). The people of Israel had no basis for expecting this to happen other than the promise of God; however, unlike their unbelieving fathers, they trusted and obeyed the Lord.

II. Destruction and Deliverance (Josh. 6:17–27)

1. Destruction and deliverance commanded (6:17–19)

17 And the city shall be accursed, even it, and all that are therein, to the LORD: only Rahab the harlot shall live, she and all that are with her in the house, because she hid the messengers that we sent.

18 And ye, in any wise keep yourselves from the accursed thing, lest ye make yourselves accursed, when ye take of the accursed thing, and make the camp of Israel a curse, and trouble it.

19 But all the silver, and gold, and vessels of brass and iron, are consecrated unto the LORD: they shall come into the treasury of the LORD.

These are the hardest verses for us to understand and explain. First of all, there is the challenge of understanding what these verses mean. The key word is translated "accursed" or "accursed thing." The word is hard to translate. It refers to an ancient practice of irrevocably giving over things and people to the Lord, usually by destroying them. By the standards of that day, this was considered an act of religious devotion. Notice "to the LORD" in verse 17 and "consecrated unto the LORD" in verse 19. "Accursed" can be translated "under the ban."

Even harder to explain is how this practice can be reconciled with New Testament teachings about loving our enemies (Matt. 5:38–47; Rom. 12:17–21). Two facts may help us as we struggle with this issue. First of all, the people of Canaan were despicably wicked. In Abraham's time, it was said, "The iniquity of the Amorites is not yet full" (Gen. 15:16). It was many centuries later when the Israelites invaded Canaan. For these wicked people to remain would have been a tremendous influence on the Israelites.

Second, Rahab and her family were delivered. The emphasis given to her deliverance in Joshua shows that this is significant. Her inclusion in the genealogy of Jesus is another indication of the importance of Rahab's faith and salvation (Matt. 1:5). When Joshua sent two spies into Jericho before the Israelites entered Canaan, Rahab risked her life to hide them from the king's men. She did this because she had come to believe in the Lord God of Israel. When she asked that the Israelites spare her and her family, the spies promised they would if she hung a red thread from her window (Josh. 2). When Joshua gave final instructions to the Israelites, he delivered the Lord's commands to utterly destroy everything in Jericho except Rahab and her family.

The gold, silver, and metal vessels were to be saved, but they were to be consecrated to the Lord and placed in His treasury. This signified their total dedication to the Lord. The Lord through Joshua gave a solemn warning to the Israelites about keeping for themselves anything from Jericho. Joshua told them that if they disobeyed this warning, that would make themselves accursed and bring a curse and trouble on Israel.

Joshua 7 tells the sad story of Israel's defeat at Ai because one man, Achan, disobeyed this warning. When he came before Joshua, Achan said that he saw some garments and some silver and gold. He coveted and took these things for himself. As a result, all Israel was defeated in battle; and Achan and his family were executed.

2. Destruction of the city (6:20, 21)

20 So the people shouted when the priests blew with the trumpets: and it came to pass, when the people heard the sound of the trumpet, and the people shouted with a great shout, that the wall fell down flat, so that the people went up into the city, every man straight before him, and they took the city.

The shout of verse 20 followed Joshua's command in verse 16. What a terrifying sound that must have been to the ears of the people of Jericho!

When the people shouted, the Lord kept His promise. The sturdy walls of Jericho fell down flat, crumbled by the power of God. Then each Israelite attacked straight ahead as they had been instructed to do. Because the Israelites had been marching around the city, the soldiers of Jericho who survived the collapse of the walls saw Israelites charging from all directions at once. The Israelites thus took the city. And after the city was taken, all the people and animals were destroyed (6:21).

3. Deliverance of Rahab (6:22–27)

Rahab and her family were delivered as promised. Joshua sent the two messengers, who knew where Rahab lived, to rescue her (6:22). They rescued her and her family (6:23). The city was burned; and the gold, silver, and metal vessels were placed in the Lord's treasury (6:24). Verse 25 repeats the assurance that Rahab and her family were delivered. Joshua pronounced a curse on anyone who tried to rebuild Jericho (6:26, 27).

PRONUNCIATION GUIDE

Achan	[AY kuhn]
Ai	[AY igh]
Amorites	[AM uh rights]
Rahab	[RAY hab]

SUMMARY OF BIBLE TRUTHS

1. Walls of various kinds hinder the advance of God's people.
2. God promises to break down such walls.
3. Trusting God to do so calls for faith.
4. Faith results in obedience.
5. God keeps His promises.
6. God judges persistent sinners but saves those who trust in Him.

APPLYING THE BIBLE

1. When God leads. "On the plains of hesitation bleach the bones of countless millions who at the dawn of victory, sat down to wait and waiting died" (George Cecil).

2. What really happened at Jericho? God didn't need the Israelites' help in conquering Jericho. He could have spoken the word and the walls would have crumbled. However, God was busy developing people who would make good citizens in the land of promise. These citizens would:

- do what God expects even when it makes no sense,
- humbly prefer His will to their own,
- choose to love Him for who He is, and
- grow through trials that lead to victory.

He is determined to make us more than conquerors (Rom. 8:31f).

3. Recognizing the real battle. The real battle is not with Jericho; it is in the hearts and minds of the Israelites. This is true for us today. You are not through with this lesson until you ask yourself, "What battle is the Lord interested in winning in my life today?"

4. Trust

How often we trust each other,
And only doubt the Lord.
We take the word of mortals
And yet distrust His word;
But, oh, what light and glory

Would shine o'er all our days,
If we always would remember
God means just what He says.
—A. B. Simpson

5. Trust and obey even if it makes little sense. John Sammis understood this. That's why we still sing the hymn "Trust and Obey." "When we walk with the Lord in the light of His word" describes the experience of Joshua and the Israelites at Jericho. They didn't understand everything, but they trusted and did what they understood God was telling them to do. They walked.

TEACHING THE BIBLE

- *Main Idea:* God provided a miracle at Jericho to encourage Israel at the beginning of their possession of Canaan.
- *Suggested Teaching Aim:* To lead adults to identify miracles God has provided to encourage them.

A TEACHING OUTLINE

1. *Promises and Obedience (Josh. 6:1–16)*
2. *Destruction and Deliverance (Josh. 6:17–27)*

Introduce the Bible Study

Share this: A cartoon shows a man sitting behind a stone desk with scrolls in jars and on the desk. Behind him on the wall are the words: "Fertile Crescent Construction Company." Another man stands in the doorway. Both men are dressed in biblical outfits. The man in the doorway is saying to the man behind the desk, "The mayor of Jericho is here, and boy is he mad!" Point out that the destruction of the walls of Jericho was a divine miracle that also served as food for faith for the Israelites.

Search for Biblical Truth

IN ADVANCE, ask two members to be prepared to read the Scripture by alternately reading the verses when called on. Ask them to read Joshua 6:1–5 at this time.

Ask: (1) What was there in God's language to Joshua that indicated that the destruction of Jericho was a certain event? (2) Why do you think God chose this way to destroy the city rather than helping Israel defeat them in a traditional battle as He had done when they defeated the Amalekites (Exod. 17:8–16)? (3) What was God's part in this battle? (4) What was Israel's part in this battle?

Ask the enlisted members to read Joshua 6:15, 16. Ask, (1) What is unusual about this battle? List members' suggestions on a chalkboard or a large sheet of paper. (Consider these: marched in silence, destroyed all instead of keeping loot for themselves, saved a prostitute.)

Distribute paper and pencils and ask half the class to write an article for the *Jericho Gazette* that describes the siege and battle from Israel's perspective and half to write from the perspective of a resident of Jericho.

This can be from the perspective of a soldier, man, woman, child. It could be an interview with someone. Let volunteers read their articles.

Ask the enlisted readers to read Joshua 6:17–19. Lecture briefly, and explain (1) the concept of "accursed" (6:17) and why this was important at this stage of the conquest; (2) why God destroyed the people of Canaan; and (3) why God chose to save a prostitute; relate Rahab's actions before the battle and her place in Israel after the battle.

IN ADVANCE, enlist two people to portray Rahab and a television reporter. Ask the reporter to interview Rahab after the battle. Let them devise their own questions, but suggest these as a starting point: Why were you and your family the only ones saved in the whole city? What made you hide the spies? What are your feelings about the destruction of the whole city, including your friends and neighbors? What are your plans for the future? Do you plan to change your occupation now? Do you think it will be hard to begin a new life with a new nation and culture?

Give the Truth a Personal Focus

Use these questions based on the six "Summary of Bible Truths": (1) What walls or barriers have hindered you? (2) Do you believe God can break down these walls? (3) Has God broken down some walls in the past that would help you trust Him to do so in the future? (4) Is your faith strong enough to encourage you to obey God's commands? (5) Do you believe God will keep His promises to you? (6) What evidence can you cite that God judges persistent sinners but saves those who trust in Him? Close in prayer that members will have strength to let God continue to work His miracles through them.

Choosing to Serve the Lord

Background Passage: Joshua 24:1–33

Focal Passages: Joshua 24:1, 2a, 14–22, 25

During these three months, we have studied the periods of the Exodus and the Conquest. We began with the call of Moses. We close with the challenge of the aged Joshua for the people to choose to follow the Lord. These two great men served as human leaders during two significant periods of Old Testament history.

Study Aim: *To describe how God called Israel to choose the Lord and how the people responded.*

STUDYING THE BIBLE

OUTLINE AND SUMMARY

- **I. Call to Remember and Choose (Josh. 24:1–15)**
  - **1. Call to remember (24:1–13)**
  - **2. Call to choose (24:14, 15)**
- **II. Decision and Covenant (Josh. 24:16–28)**
  - **1. Israel's profession (24:16–18)**
  - **2. Joshua's warning (24:19, 20)**
  - **3. Israel's reaffirmation (24:21–24)**
  - **4. Covenant with Israel (24:25–28)**
- **III. Three Burials (Josh. 24:29–33)**

Joshua called Israel to Shechem and reminded them of what the Lord had done (24:1–13). Then he called them to choose to serve the Lord and testified that he had so chosen (24:14, 15). The people promised to serve the Lord and forsake other gods (24:16–18). Joshua warned of dire consequences if they didn't (24:19, 20). Israel reaffirmed their promise and accepted the role of witnesses (24:21–24). Joshua declared that the ceremony constituted a covenant (24:25–28). Joshua and Eleazer died and were buried, and the bones of Joseph were buried in the Promised Land (24:29–33).

I. Call to Remember and Choose (Josh. 24:1–15)

1. Call to remember (24:1–13)

1 And Joshua gathered all the tribes of Israel to Shechem, and called for the elders of Israel, and for their heads, and for their judges, and for their officers; and they presented themselves before God.

2 And Joshua said unto all the people.

Shechem was where Abraham first stopped in Canaan and built an altar to the Lord (Gen. 12:6, 7). It was where Jacob settled when he returned after twenty years away from Canaan (Gen. 33:18, 19). Shechem was located in the north central hill country. It was built on the shoulder of Mount Ebal and faced Mount Gerizim. Early in the campaign to conquer Canaan, Joshua had called the people together at these two mountains in accordance with the command of God through Moses (Josh. 8:30–35; Deut. 27:12, 13). On that occasion, Israel renewed its covenant with the Lord. Now after the conquest was completed, Joshua called them together again for a covenant renewal.

Notice that Joshua invited not only all levels of leaders but also "all the people." Then Joshua delivered to them the word of the Lord, which called Israel to remember what God had done for them in the past. He had called Abraham to leave his home from beyond the Euphrates River and to leave also the gods his ancestors had served (24:2b, 3). God chose Isaac and Jacob to inherit His promise to Abraham, but Jacob went down into Egypt (24:4). God sent Moses, sent plagues on Egypt, saved Israel at the Red Sea, and led them during the wilderness years (24:5–7). God gave them victory over the Amorites and thwarted Balak's schemes to use Balaam to curse Israel (24:8–10). God led Israel to capture Jericho and to defeat the many national groups in Canaan (24:11–13).

2. Call to choose (24:14, 15)

> **14 Now therefore fear the LORD, and serve him in sincerity and in truth: and put away the gods which your fathers served on the other side of the flood, and in Egypt; and serve ye the LORD.**
>
> **15 And if it seem evil unto you to serve the LORD, choose you this day whom ye will serve; whether the gods which your fathers served that were on the other side of the flood, or the gods of the Amorites, in whose land ye dwell: but as for me and my house, we will serve the LORD.**

"Therefore" shows that Joshua was applying the lessons from remembering what God had done for them. "Fear the LORD" is a familiar Old Testament refrain. It did not mean to cringe in terror but to worship reverently and to obey completely the commands of the Lord. It involved serving the Lord totally and faithfully. The word translated "sincerity" means totally or perfectly. The word translated "truth" was ordinarily applied to God's faithfulness to Israel (Exod. 34:6), but it was also used of the faithfulness that God expected of Israel. Relationships are built on trust and trustworthiness, and our relationship with God is no exception.

Such a relationship with the one true God demanded that the Israelites worship and serve God exclusively. Therefore, the negative side of Joshua's call was to put away other gods. They could not serve the Lord and also serve other gods; therefore, they must choose whom they would serve.

Israel's history had been a history of serving other gods. Their forefathers had worshiped other gods in the lands beyond the Euphrates River ("beyond the flood"). During the years in Egypt, many Israelites worshiped the gods of Egypt. Now they had come into the land of the Amorites, whose religion was to prove especially attractive to many Israelites. The religions of Canaan promised fertile lands, good crops, and prosperity; in addition, their rites of worship often included sexual immorality.

The Lord had chosen Israel to be His people, but this did not automatically ensure that each Israelite accepted the Lord. God gave them a choice. They were free to serve Him, but they were also free to choose to serve other gods.

Joshua left no doubt about his own choice and that of his family. He was an old man, and the people knew that Joshua had lived up to what he said when he testified, "As for me and my house, we will serve the LORD."

II. Decision and Covenant (Josh. 24:16–28)

1. Israel's profession (24:16–18)

16 And the people answered and said, God forbid that we should forsake the LORD, to serve other gods;

17 For the LORD our God, he it is that brought us up and our fathers out of the land of Egypt, from the house of bondage, and which did those great signs in our sight, and preserved us in all the way wherein we went, and among all the people through whom we passed:

18 And the LORD drave out from before us all the people, even the Amorites which dwelt in the land: therefore will we also serve the LORD; for he is our God.

The Israelites immediately responded to Joshua's twofold call. They denied that they would forsake the Lord to serve other gods. They professed their intention to serve the Lord as their God.

They based this profession on what God had done for them. Some of them had been old enough to witness what God had done through mighty signs in delivering Israel from Egypt. They had seen how He had led them during the wilderness years. They had just seen how the Lord had driven out the Amorites and given them the land of Canaan. They realized that all of these things had been wrought by the power of God acting on their behalf.

2. Joshua's warning (24:19, 20)

19 And Joshua said unto the people, Ye cannot serve the LORD: for he is an holy God; he is a jealous God; he will not forgive your transgressions nor your sins.

20 If ye forsake the LORD, and serve strange gods, then he will turn and do you hurt, and consume you, after that he hath done you good.

Joshua apparently had some reason to doubt the people's profession to forsake other gods and serve the Lord. Perhaps he thought they answered without thinking of the commitment they were making. Perhaps he knew the subtle power of the new temptations that they soon would face. Perhaps he suspected that they were trusting too much in their own ability to remain true. Perhaps he felt that too many of them saw no contradiction between worshiping the Lord and dabbling in other religions. At any rate, he questioned their ability to live up to their profession.

He cited as one factor the twofold nature of God as holy and jealous. "Holy" has the basic meaning of being set apart and different. God is the infinite Creator of all things, the Lord who redeemed them. "Holy" also came to mean perfectly righteous and pure. Sinful man cannot fully please the holy God, especially when he relies on his own strength. God is "jealous" in that He will not tolerate any rival god in the affections of His people. He is like a groom who will regard any such act as comparable to unfaithfulness to the vow that bound Israel to the Lord.

Joshua warned that if the people did forsake the Lord for other gods, they would not receive the good He intended for His faithful people. Instead they would receive evil. We know from many places in the Old Testament that the Lord forgave His people when they repented (Exod. 34:6, 7); yet we also know that God will not and cannot forgive people who persist in sin and refuse to repent.

3. Israel's reaffirmation (24:21–24)

> **21 And the people said unto Joshua, Nay; but we will serve the LORD.**
>
> **22 And Joshua said unto the people, Ye are witnesses against yourselves that ye have chosen you the LORD, to serve him. And they said, We are witnesses.**

The people were disturbed at Joshua's charge that they would not actually serve the Lord. They strongly denied his charge and with equal force they reaffirmed that they would serve the Lord.

Acting like an official in a law court, Joshua swore in the people as witnesses to the promise they had just made. He solemnly told them that they were witnesses who some day might have to bear testimony against themselves if they ever went back on this commitment. They quickly accepted this role as witnesses.

Once again Joshua challenged them to act by putting away other gods and inclining their hearts toward the Lord (24:23). They repeated, "The LORD our God will we serve, and his voice will we obey" (24:24).

4. Covenant with Israel (24:25–28)

> **25 So Joshua made a covenant with the people that day, and set them a statute and an ordinance in Shechem.**

In one sense, this was a renewal of the covenant from Mount Sinai; and in another sense it was a new covenant. It was made in a new setting under a new human leader. At this critical stage in their history, Joshua addressed those who were about to settle into a daily routine of living in the Promised Land. They would soon face new opportunities and new temptations. They needed to face these with an up-to-date and personal commitment to the Lord.

Each new generation needs to make its own covenant with the Lord in the sense of claiming the Lord for themselves. And each person and generation needs times of individual and public reaffirmation of that covenant.

The covenant at Shechem was sealed with a written form of the agreement (24:26). A huge rock was inscribed as a lasting reminder of the occasion (24:27). Then the people returned to the part of Canaan they had inherited (24:28).

III. Three Burials (Josh. 24:29–33)

Joshua, the servant of the Lord, died at 110 and was buried. His influence for good was so strong that at least two generations remained true to the Lord (24:29–31). The body of Joseph at long last was buried in the land of promise, just as he had requested (24:32; Gen. 50:25; Exod. 13:19). And Eleazer, the priest who succeeded Aaron, died and was buried (24:33).

PRONUNCIATION GUIDE

Amorites	[AM uh rights]
Balaam	[BAY luhm]
Balak	[BAY lak]
Ebal	[EE buhl]
Eleazer	[EL-ih AY zur]
Euphrates	[yoo FRAY teez]
Gerizim	[GER ih zim]
Shechem	[SHEK uhm]

SUMMARY OF BIBLE TRUTHS

1. God must be given total and faithful devotion.
2. Temptations to give Him less are strong and subtle.
3. God gives us freedom to serve Him or not to serve Him.
4. One person's bold stand for God influences others.
5. Covenants with the Lord need to be renewed.

APPLYING THE BIBLE

1. The decision to serve. Jacob J. Chestnut, known to friends as "J. J.," was looking forward to retirement. After eighteen years in the capitol police force, he gave his life to stop a gunman who barged into the U.S. capitol and opened fire Friday, July 24, 1998.

Neighbors, friends, and lawmakers described Chestnut as a "wonderful and cheerful man." His pastor called him committed.

"He took his job seriously," said Jack Marcom, pastor of Fort Washington Baptist Church in Fort Washington, Maryland, where Chestnut was a member. "He was a very fine man, committed to his family and his community," Marcom added.

Chestnut was also a *mentor* to the younger officers on the police force. "He was 'Daddy' to a lot of those young men," the pastor said. "He always had a kind word of advice. He was known for saying, 'Well, you've got some options here.'"

"More than anything, he was a servant," Marcom added. "He didn't need to be the greatest, he just needed to serve."[1]

Jacob Chestnut was buried Friday, July 31, in Arlington National Cemetery. His repeated words to young men, "you've got some options here," became the bridge for his witness and testimony. He is a model for what it means to claim the words of Joshua, "As for me and my house, we will serve the Lord."

2. What matters is how you live your life:

I read of a man who stood to speak
At the funeral of a friend.
He referred to the dates on her tombstone
From the beginning . . . to the end.
He noted that first came the date of her birth
And spoke of the following date with tears,
But he said what mattered most of all
Was the dash between those years.
For that dash represents all the time
That she spent alive on earth . . .
And now only those who loved her
Know what that little line is worth.
For it matters not how much we own:
The cars . . . the house . . . the cash.
What matters is how we live and love
And how we spend our dash.
So think about this long and hard:
Are there things you'd like to change?
For you never know how much time is left.
(You could be at "dash mid-range.")
If we could just slow down enough
To consider what's true and real,
And always try to understand
The way other people feel.
And be less quick to anger,
And show appreciation more
And love the people in our lives
Like we've never loved before.
If we treat each other with respect,
And more often wear a smile,
Remembering that this special dash
Might only last a little while.
So, when your eulogy's being read
With your life's actions to rehash . . .
Would you be proud of the things they say
About how you spent your dash?

—Author unknown

3. Service. What we can do for Christ is the test of service. What we can suffer for Him is the test of love.

4. As for me and my house. You do not do God a favor by serving Him. He honors you by allowing you to serve Him.

TEACHING THE BIBLE

- *Main Idea:* Joshua's challenge to Israel to follow God also challenges us to do the same.
- *Suggested Teaching Aim:* To lead adults to decide to follow God.

A TEACHING OUTLINE

1. *Call to Remember and Choose (Josh. 24:1–15)*
2. *Decision and Covenant (Josh. 24:16–28)*
3. *Three Burials (Josh. 24:29–33)*

Introduce the Bible Study

IN ADVANCE, make three or four posters that ask: "Have you made your decision?" and place them around the room. Ask members to list choices they have made today. (This can include when to get up, what to wear, what to eat, and so forth.) Suggest that our lives are filled with choices but that the greatest choice is whether we will serve God, because this determines how we live in this life and for eternity.

Search for Biblical Truth

IN ADVANCE, number and print the six summary statements in "Outline and Summary" on large strips of paper and tape them to the backs of members' chairs. Ask members to read them and tape them in order to the focal wall.

On a map of the Conquest, locate Shechem. Ask a volunteer to read Joshua 24:1–2. Summarize the material in "Studying the Bible" for these verses.

Ask a volunteer to read Joshua 24:14–15. In a brief lecture, do the following: (1) define: "therefore," "fear the Lord," "sincerity," and "truth"; (2) explain that Joshua's challenge had a positive side (choosing God) and a negative side (putting away other gods); (3) relate Israel's history of idolatry (beyond the Euphrates, in Egypt, and the golden calf in the wilderness); (4) Joshua called on each of them to make the same decision he had made to follow God.

Ask half the class (Group 1) to open their Bibles to 24:16–18 and the other half (Group 2) to open theirs to 24:19–20. Ask Group 1 to answer: (1) what the people declared; and (2) on what they based their decision. Ask Group 2 to answer: (1) why Joshua had some doubts that the people would serve the Lord; and (2) what would happen if they did forsake the Lord.

Ask a volunteer to read 24:21–22, 25. Ask: What other covenants had God made with Israel? (At Sinai.) How was this covenant similar and different from that made at Sinai? How was this covenant sealed? (See "Studying the Bible.")

Briefly relate the material in "3. Three Burials."

Give the Truth a Personal Focus

Ask members to list some actions God has performed in their lives in the past. Write these on a chalkboard. Point to the questions around the room and ask, Have you made your decision to follow God? Read the five "Summary of Bible Truths" statements. Challenge members who have not chosen to follow God to do so today. Challenge those who have made that decision earlier to renew their covenant with the Lord. **IN ADVANCE,** make a covenant for each person:

My Covenant

On this 28th day of November, 1999, I hereby affirm the following decision:

____ I will choose this day to follow God.

____ I will reaffirm the covenant I made with God earlier in my life.

(Signed) ___________________________ (Date) _____________

Ask members to spend a few moments in making their decision and then close in prayer. Suggest that you will be available after class to talk with anyone about their decision.

---

1. Lynne Jones, Baptist Press.

Studies in Matthew

December

January

February

1999—2000

INTRODUCTION

This study of Matthew's Gospel focuses on the life and ministry of Jesus. Most lessons depict a certain aspect of His ministry and how He was received by those to whom He ministered.

Unit I, "Beginnings: Birth and Ministry," is a four-lesson unit. The first lesson presents the preaching of John the Baptist and the baptism of Jesus. The second lesson looks at the temptations of Jesus and the beginning of His ministry. The third lesson is Matthew's account of the birth of Jesus, for the Sunday just before Christmas. The fourth lesson focuses on the coming of the wise men.

Unit II, "Jesus' Teachings and Ministry," is a five-lesson unit. Lessons include the calling and mission of the twelve disciples, teachings on prayer from the Sermon on the Mount, examples of Jesus' miracles of compassion, growing opposition to Jesus, and the parable of laborers in the vineyard.

Unit III, "Fulfillment of Jesus' Mission," is a four-lesson unit. These lessons focus on Jesus' royal entry and cleansing the temple, being ready for Christ's return, the death of Jesus, and the risen Lord's commission to His followers.

Cycle of 1998–2004

1998–1999	1999–2000	2000–2001	2001–2002	2002–2003	2003–2004
Old Testament Survey	Exodus Leviticus Numbers Deuteronomy Joshua	Judges 1, 2 Samuel 1 Chronicles 1 Kings 1–11 2 Chronicles 1–9	Parables Miracles Sermon on the Mount	2 Kings 18–25 2 Chronicles 29–36 Jeremiah Lamentations Ezekiel Habakkuk Zephaniah	James 1, 2 Peter 1, 2, 3 John Jude
New Testament Survey	Matthew	Luke	Isaiah 9; 11; 40–66 Ruth Jonah Nahum	Personalities of the NT	Christmas Esther Job Ecclesiastes Song of Solomon
John	1, 2 Corinthians	Acts	Romans Galatians	Mark	The Cross 1, 2 Thessalonians Revelation
Genesis	Ephesians Philippians Colossians Philemon	1 Kings 12– 2 Kings 17 2 Chronicles 10–28 Isaiah 1–39 Amos Hosea Micah	Psalms Proverbs	Ezra Nehemiah Daniel Joel Obadiah Haggai Zechariah Malachi	Hebrews 1, 2 Timothy Titus

THE GOSPEL ACCORDING TO MATTHEW

I. Beginnings: Birth and Ministry (Matt. 1:1–4:25)
1. **Genealogy and Birth of Jesus (1:1–25)**
2. **Wise Men and Herod (2:1–23)**
3. **John the Baptist and Jesus' Baptism (3:1–17)**
4. **Temptations and Beginning of Ministry (4:1–25)**

II. Ministry of the King-Messiah (Matt. 5:1–16:12)
1. **Sermon on the Mount (5:1–7:29)**
2. **Miracles of Compassion and Power (8:1–9:34)**
3. **Mission of the Twelve Disciples (9:35–11:1)**
4. **Jesus Misunderstood and Rejected (11:2–12:50)**
5. **Parables of the Kingdom (13:1–52)**
6. **Mixed Responses to Jesus (14:1–16:12)**

III. Mission of the Son of Man (Matt. 16:13–25:46)
1. **Revelation of the Way of the Cross (16:13–28)**
2. **On and Off the Mount of Transfiguration (17:1–27)**
3. **Teachings About Human Relationships (18:1–19:15)**
5. **Royal Entry and Cleansing the Temple (21:1–22)**
6. **Teachings in the Temple (21:23–23:39)**

IV. Death and Resurrection of Jesus (Matt. 26:1–28:20)
1. **The Last Supper and Gethsemane (26:1–46)**
2. **Betrayed, Arrested, Tried, Condemned (26:47–27:26)**
3. **Crucified, Dead, and Buried (27:27–66)**
4. **Great Commission of the Risen Lord (28:1–20)**

King's Herald and Baptism

December

5

1999

Background Passage: Matthew 3:1–17

Focal Passages: Matthew 3:1–8, 11–17

Matthew 1–4 deals with "Beginnings: Birth and Ministry." Our "Studies in Matthew" will begin with the beginnings of Jesus' ministry, thus postponing studying the birth and the coming of the wise men for the Sundays before and after Christmas. This lesson deals with John the Baptist and with Jesus' baptism by John in Matthew 3.

Study Aim: *To explain the significance of John the Baptist's preaching and Jesus' baptism.*

STUDYING THE BIBLE

OUTLINE AND SUMMARY

I. John the Baptist (Matt. 3:1–12)

1. **John preached repentance (3:1–6)**
2. **John condemned religious leaders (3:7–10)**
3. **John predicted baptism with the Spirit (3:11, 12)**

II. Baptism of Jesus (Matt. 3:13–17)

1. **Jesus explained why He was baptized (3:13–15)**
2. **God showed His approval of His Son (3:16, 17)**

John the Baptist preached repentance and baptized those who confessed their sins (vv. 1–6). He condemned the religious leaders for their dangerous hypocrisy (vv. 7–10). He predicted the coming of One who would baptize with the Spirit (vv. 11, 12). Jesus explained that His baptism was to fulfill all righteousness (vv. 13–15). The Father showed and spoke words that approved His Son's commitment to a mission as Suffering Servant (vv. 16, 17).

I. John the Baptist (Matt. 3:1–12)

1. John preached repentance (vv. 1–6)

1 In those days came John the Baptist, preaching in the wilderness of Judaea,

2 And saying, Repent ye: for the kingdom of heaven is at hand.

3 For this is he that was spoken of by the prophet Esaias, saying, The voice of one crying in the wilderness, Prepare ye the way of the Lord, make his paths straight.

4 And the same John had his raiment of camel's hair, and a leathern girdle about his loins; and his meat was locusts and wild honey.

5 Then went out to him Jerusalem, and all Judaea, and all the region round about Jordan.

6 And were baptized of him in Jordan, confessing their sins.

These verses tell us the *who, when, where,* and *what* of the preaching of John the Baptist.

Who? By the time the Gospel of Matthew was written, the name and work of John the Baptist were so well-known that Matthew mentioned him with no introduction. His name came from his baptizing. The Jews had an immersion as one entry requirement for Gentiles who became Jews; however, John demanded that all needed to repent—Jews as well as Gentiles—as they confessed their sins.

The Jews had been expecting Elijah or a prophet like Elijah to precede the Messiah's coming (Mal. 4:5). When John emerged dressed in camel's hair and a leather girdle, they immediately thought of Elijah (2 Kings 1:8).

Matthew quoted Isaiah 40:3 as fulfilled in John the Baptist. John was the voice of the herald crying, "Prepare ye the way of the Lord." The symbolic picture of his work in verse 3 describes how special people went before a king announcing his coming and calling for the road to be made ready for him.

When? Unlike Luke, who gave the year in human history when John began his preaching (Luke 3:1), Matthew made only a vague reference to "those days." Matthew emphasized the time in God's epochs of His dealings with humanity, "The kingdom of heaven is at hand." Most Bible students recognize that "the kingdom of heaven" is the same as the "kingdom of God." The Jews, who had such great reverence for God's name that they wouldn't say it, often used "heaven" to refer to God. "Kingdom" here refers to the reign of God.

Jesus (Mark 1:14, 15) declared that the kingdom had arrived; but Jesus also taught His followers to pray, "Thy kingdom come" (Matt. 6:10). God has always been the Sovereign of all His creation, but people in their sins rejected His rule in their lives. The coming, life, death, and resurrection of Jesus declared the reality of that divine kingship and called people to accept God as King in their lives. For those who do, the kingdom becomes a reality in which we live by faith; but we also await the consummation of God's plan, when every knee will bow.

Where? John did his preaching "in the wilderness of Judaea." Strictly speaking, this is the barren area to the east of the Dead Sea; however, since John baptized people in the Jordan River, his area of ministry extended to the banks of the Jordan. The description in verse 5 has people coming to hear John from Jerusalem, Judea, and the region around the Jordan. Since John later got into trouble with Herod Antipas, who reigned over Perea (west of Jordan) and Galilee, John apparently at times preached on both the east and west sides of the Jordan River.

What? The preaching of John was basically a call to repent. The Greek word meant "to change one's mind," but actions as well as thoughts are changed in true repentance. To repent is to turn around and go in the other direction. (See Luke 3:10–14 for examples of specific changes that John called on people to make.)

A prominent feature in repentance is sincere confession of one's sins. Matthew does not emphasize John's baptism except as a call to and an occasion for confessing sins. Nowhere is there any hint that the waters of the Jordan washed away sins. God forgave sins as people confessed and forsook their sins (Ps. 32:5).

John the Baptist attracted a lot of attention for many reasons. People flocked out of Jerusalem, the farms and villages of Judea, and the regions all around the Jordan River. Some of them heeded his call and were baptized by John, confessing their sins.

2. John condemned religious leaders (vv. 7–10)

7 But when he saw many of the Pharisees and Sadducees come to his baptism, he said unto them, O generation of vipers, who hath warned you to flee from the wrath to come?

8 Bring forth therefore fruits meet for repentance.

Verse 7 introduces the Pharisees and Sadducees. They are listed together because members of these two major religious-political parties formed the Sanhedrin, the highest Jewish court in the land. Usually fierce enemies, these two groups formed a deadly alliance when anything threatened both of them.

John the Baptist saw these leaders among the crowd listening to his preaching. He knew they had not come to confess their sins. John the Baptist, like the Old Testament prophets, was never timid about condemning sin. Later his bold denunciation of Herod and Herodias led to his imprisonment and death (Mark 6:14–29). Jesus paid tribute to John as a courageous prophet (Matt. 11:7–15).

John called these self-important religious leaders a "generation of vipers." Like snakes, they dug their poisonous fangs into people. The religious leaders apparently at first tried to appear as part of the multitude of sincere seekers who came to escape divine wrath by confessing and forsaking their sin. John unmasked them. If they truly had come to repent of their sins, the fruits of sincere repentance were deeds of true righteousness. John knew that the leaders were trusting in their ancestry as descendants of Abraham, not in the transforming power of God (v. 9). The ax of divine judgment had already made its cutting mark on them; eventually God's wrath would fall (v. 10).

3. John predicted baptism with the Spirit (vv. 11, 12)

11 I indeed baptize you with water unto repentance: but he that cometh after me is mightier than I, whose shoes I am not worthy to bear: he shall baptize you with the Holy Ghost, and with fire:

12 Whose fan is in his hand, and he will throughly purge his floor, and gather his wheat into the garner; but he will burn up the chaff with unquenchable fire.

John contrasted his water baptism with the Spirit baptism of the One whose coming he preceded. Pentecost was the one-time historical fulfillment of the coming of the Spirit with power after the completion of Jesus' mission (Acts 1:5). The new birth when the Spirit comes into the life of a believer is its fulfillment in each Christian (John 3:1–8; Rom. 8:9).

John pictured himself as an unworthy servant compared to the Lord Jesus. He was not worthy even to carry His sandals. He was the Savior of penitent sinners and Judge of the impenitent. Verse 12 pictures the Lord as a farmer who separates the wheat from the useless chaff.

II. Baptism of Jesus (Matt. 3:13–17)

1. Jesus explained why He was baptized (vv. 13–15)

13 Then cometh Jesus from Galilee to Jordan unto John, to be baptized of him.

14 But John forbad him, saying, I have need to be baptized of thee, and comest thou to me?

15 And Jesus answering said unto him, Suffer it to be so now: for thus it becometh us to fulfil all righteousness. Then he suffered him.

When Jesus came from his native Galilee, this was His first public appearance in preparation for launching His ministry. He asked to be baptized. However, John apparently recognized Jesus as the sinless One for whose coming he had been preparing the people. John, therefore, objected to baptizing Jesus. Instead, Jesus the sinless One should be baptizing John the unworthy servant.

Jesus' answer to John in verse 15, along with God's words from heaven in verse 17, are our best clues to why Jesus wanted to be baptized. Jesus had no sins to confess. Why then did He insist that John baptize Him?

For one thing, Jesus set an example for all who would later follow the Lord in the obedience of baptism. One meaning of "fulfilling righteousness" means to do the right thing by obeying God. Jesus obeyed the Father and was baptized; so do His followers obey the Father by being baptized as He commanded.

When taken with verse 17, verse 15 also pointed ahead to how Jesus would fulfill divine righteousness through His death and resurrection. Baptism depicts death and resurrection. At the beginning of His ministry, Jesus signified His commitment to a mission that would culminate in His death and resurrection. He was not one of the sinners who confessed their sins as John baptized them, but Jesus publicly identified Himself with these sinners, whom He had come to save.

2. God showed His approval of His Son (vv. 16, 17)

16 And Jesus, when he was baptized, went up straightway out of the water: and lo, the heavens were opened unto him, and he saw the Spirit of God descending like a dove, and lighting upon him:

17 And lo a voice from heaven, saying, This is my beloved Son, in whom I am well pleased.

Matthew emphasized that Jesus saw the Spirit descend on Him like a dove. Jesus was committing Himself to the mission given Him by the Father. The vision of the dove was the Father's assurance that the full power of His Spirit rested on Jesus.

The heavenly voice quoted parts of two important strands of Old Testament prophecy about the mission of the Messiah. The first part was from Psalm 2:7, which pictured the anointed One who would fulfill the royal role of Son of David and Son of God. The latter part was from Isaiah 42:1, one of Isaiah's Servant passages. The most explicit Servant passage is Isaiah 53—the Suffering Servant.

First-century Jews were looking for the Messiah-King, whom they expected to restore the power of Israel as it was in David's time. Few of them thought of Isaiah 53 as a prophecy of the Messiah. Jesus, however, saw the two as inseparable. He could become King only by way of the cross. He was committing Himself to this kind of mission. God's sign of the dove and the twofold reference to Psalm 2:7 and Isaiah 42:1 were the Father's stamp of approval on Jesus' commitment to a mission of salvation that involved suffering, death, and resurrection.

PRONUNCIATION GUIDE

Antipas	[AN tih puhs]
Esaias	[ih ZAY uhs]
Herod	[HAIR uhd]
Herodias	[hih ROH dih uhs]
Pentecost	[PEN tih kawst]
Perea	[puh REE uh]
Pharisees	[FER uh seez]
Sadducees	[SAD yoo seez]
Sanhedrin	[SAN he drihn]

SUMMARY OF BIBLE TRUTHS

1. All people need to confess their sins and turn from sin to God.
2. God's kingdom was revealed when Jesus came, but its consummation is still in the future.
3. Baptism with the Spirit took place historically at Pentecost and occurs personally when people experience the new birth.
4. Jesus committed Himself to a mission of death and resurrection.
5. At Jesus' baptism, God showed that this was the mission He had given His Son.
6. All believers should follow the Lord in baptism.

APPLYING THE BIBLE

1. How casually we use His name. We have come a long way from the days when God's name was revered. From the days of the Old Testament to the days when the Gospels were written, Jews went out of their way to avoid speaking the name of God for fear they would profane His holy name with human lips. They chose "kingdom of heaven" instead of "kingdom of God," "Adoni" or "LORD" instead of "Jehovah."

For many years we have lived in a culture that pairs the name of God with profanity and thinks nothing of it. Our conversation is marked like a pothole-scarred highway with casual expressions using God's name, slang expressions of Jesus, or the use of the word *holy* in ways that are anything but holy. It is a shameful loss of innocence that no one seems to notice.

2. Baptism as symbol. A young man made his profession of faith in our mission church in Nevada years ago. He was absolutely "broken" due to the regret of his wasted life. After talking with him about repentance and forgiveness, I felt he was ready for baptism. Just as we were about to enter the sanctuary, he turned to me and said, "Pastor, be sure to hold me under water just a little longer than usual. I've got lots of sin that has to be washed away."

What a comfort to remind him that the moment he asked Jesus to come into his life, all of his sin was washed away. We couldn't begin to stay underwater long enough to come up righteous, but thanks be to God, He has made us new creatures!

3. First impressions. We have often heard the phrase, "You only have one chance to make a good first impression." This causes us to develop a strong handshake, dress for success, read books on influencing others, strive for an impressive resume, act strong, give in to perfectionism, and often put on false airs that are intended to put us in enviable light in front of our peers.

Jesus made His first impressions in a totally different way. His earthly parents were humble, hard-working commoners. His birthplace was a stable. His first visitors were shepherds. Now, in His first public appearance beginning His ministry, Jesus identified with the outcast, the broken, the blind, the lost, those who were repentant and in need of a new beginning. He went to His cousin for baptism.This first impression of baptism marked the ministry of the Suffering Servant, born to die that we might die to live.

4. Baptism and obedience. If Jesus was willing to walk the estimated twenty-plus miles in the dangerous and difficult wilderness for a baptism that identifies Him with us (He who knew no sin with us who were lost and condemned in sin), what excuse can we possibly offer that justifies our disobedience?

5. Identifying an impostor. With the use of expensive, high-tech electronics and computer systems, security companies now have the ability to decrease the possibility of fraudulent access to high security areas they seek to protect. Body language takes on a whole new meaning these days. Fingerprinting software can correct or "heal" the intentionally altered imprint on the hands of a criminal. A machine that scans palm prints looks at two square inches in the center of the palm, and boasts a one-percent false reject and 0.00025-percent false acceptance rate. Machines that scan the human eye map the retina in a microsecond and can give positive identification with virtually no error.[1]

John the Baptist looked at the Pharisees and Sadducees, the religious leaders of the day, and spotted spiritual impostors immediately. Knowing they had not come to confess sin, he rejected them on sight, labeling them a "generation of vipers." Imagine how thoroughly God interprets the scan of our hearts.

6. Servant leadership. Jesus identified with John's ministry and man's need in His baptism. He modeled the role of Isaiah's Suffering

Servant and set the standard for those who would become His followers. Robert K. Greenleaf set the standard for servant leadership in business following his retirement when he wrote extensively on the subject. His ideas arose from his strong Quaker ethic.Walter Kiechel summarizes Greenleaf's philosophy with "The Five Things Every Servant Leader Does."[2]

- He takes people and their work seriously.
- He listens and takes his lead from the troops.
- He heals ("grief-work" is the new buzz word in consulting firms).
- He is self-effacing.
- He sees himself as a steward.

TEACHING THE BIBLE

- *Main Idea:* John's preaching and Jesus' baptism were evidences that God's kingdom had broken in on humans.
- *Suggested Teaching Aim:* To lead class members to identify how John's preaching and Jesus' baptism show how God broke through into human history.

A TEACHING OUTLINE

1. John the Baptist (Matt. 3:1–12)
2. Baptism of Jesus (Matt. 3:13–17)

Introduce the Bible Study

Use number 1, "How Casually We Use His Name," in "Applying the Bible" to introduce the lesson. Point out that Jesus and John took God's name seriously. Read aloud the "Main Idea" of the lesson and state that the lesson will help class members to identify why John's preaching and Jesus' baptism were significant.

Search for Biblical Truth

IN ADVANCE, enlist two people to read aloud the Scripture passages alternately—either every other verse or every other section.

To briefly overview the Scripture, write the five Scripture references of the background Scripture on a chalkboard or a large sheet of paper. Distribute paper and pencils and ask members to write a one-sentence summary for each reference. You could ask members to form five small groups of one or more persons and let each group write one summary or all members could write all five of the summaries.

Call on the members to read their summary of Matthew 3:1–6. On a chalkboard or a large sheet of paper, write: *Who? When? Where? What?* Ask members to open their Bibles to Matthew 3:1–12. Ask:

- Who is the subject of verses 1–6? (Write "John" opposite the word *Who?*)

- When did John begin his ministry? (Write "those days" opposite the word *When?* and use the information in "Study the Bible" to explain when "those days" were.)
- Where did John's preaching take place? (Write "wilderness of Judaea" opposite *Where?* Locate the area on a map showing Jesus' ministry.)
- What was the basic thrust of John's preaching? (Write "call to repent" opposite *What?)*

Call on the members to read their summary of Matthew 3:7–10. Ask members to suggest one-word descriptions of John's preaching. Ask, What two religious groups came to investigate John's preaching? (Pharisees and Sadducees.) What term did John use to refer to the religious leaders? (Vipers.) Why do you think this was an accurate term? What evidence of true repentance did John demand?

Call on the members to read their summary of Matthew 3:11, 12. Ask members to describe:

- John's attitude toward the Messiah;
- John's attitude toward himself; and
- What image John used to describe the way God was going to separate the evil from the righteous.

Call on the members to read their summary of Matthew 3:13–15. Using a map, locate Galilee and the approximate place on the Jordan River where John was baptizing (near Aenon—John 3:23). Using the material in "Studying the Bible," explain why Jesus insisted that John baptize Him.

Call on the members to read their summary of Matthew 3:16–17. Ask, What do you think the dove symbolized? Identify the two Old Testament Scriptures that the heavenly voice used. (Ps. 2:7 and Isa. 42:1.) Why do you think the heavenly voice quoted these?

Give the Truth a Personal Focus

IN ADVANCE, copy the six "Summary of Bible Truths" on six strips of paper and tape these to a focal wall. Ask members to explain how John's preaching and Jesus' baptism show how God broke through into human history. Ask members to suggest which statement applies most to them. Close in prayer.

---

1. Timothy O. Bakke, "Body-Language Security Systems," *Popular Science,* June 1996, 76.

2. Walter Kiechel III, "The Leader as Servant," *Fortune,* May 4, 1992, 121.

Temptations and Ministry

December

12

1999

Background Passage: Matthew 4:1–17

Focal Passage: Matthew 4:1–14

Two events involving Jesus Himself preceded the beginning of His public ministry: His baptism and His temptations. In our last study we focused on the preaching of John the Baptist, which led up to Jesus' baptism. In this lesson, we focus on the temptations of Jesus, which led to the opening part of His public ministry.

Study Aim: *To identify characteristics of temptation and ways to overcome temptation.*

STUDYING THE BIBLE

OUTLINE AND SUMMARY

I. Temptations of Jesus (Matt. 4:1–11)

1. **Tested and tempted (4:1)**
2. **Meeting physical needs (4:2–4)**
3. **Using holy things (4:5–7)**
4. **Achieving goals (4:8–10)**
5. **Victory over temptation (4:11)**

II. Beginning the Galilean Ministry (Matt. 4:12–17)

Jesus was led by the Spirit into the wilderness, where He was tempted by the devil (v. 1). The tempter tried to get Jesus to use His power to meet physical needs (vv. 2–4). Jesus was tempted to rely on Psalm 91:11, 12 to save Him from harm (vv. 5–7). Then Satan tempted Jesus to achieve His goals without going to the cross (vv. 8–10). Jesus overcame temptation (v. 11). Jesus began His ministry where the people in darkness needed light (vv. 12–17).

I. Temptations of Jesus (Matt. 4:1–11)

1. Tested and tempted (v. 1)

1 Then was Jesus led up of the spirit into the wilderness to be tempted of the devil.

Temptation often strikes soon after a time of spiritual exaltation. "Then" shows that the wilderness experience came on the heels of the high moment for Jesus when the Spirit descended and the Father spoke His approval.

The Spirit led Jesus into the wilderness to be tempted by the devil. James 1:13–15 denies that God is tempted by evil or that God ever tempts anyone to do evil. The same Greek word can mean either "test" or "tempt." God leads us into situations in which our faith is tested, but His purpose is that our faith be strengthened. The devil, however, seeks to use such tests as temptations to do evil.

Hebrews 4:15 makes plain that Jesus was tempted as we are. Otherwise, He would not have been human as well as divine. Only as He faced and overcame real temptations was He enabled to be the sacrifice for our sins and to help us when we are tempted.

2. Meeting physical needs (vv. 2–4)

2 And when he had fasted forty days and forty nights, he was afterward an hungered.

3 And when the tempter came to him, he said, If thou be the Son of God, command that these stones be made bread.

4 But he answered and said, It is written, Man shall not live by bread alone, but by every word that proceedeth out of the mouth of God.

One of the purposes for fasting in Bible times was to prepare for some special mission or experience (Exod. 34:28). As Jesus prepared to launch His public ministry, He went without food. Because Jesus had not eaten for so long, He was hungry. The devil, here called "the tempter," attacked at this point of meeting physical needs.

The form of the clause in Greek indicates that the word *if* meant "since." The tempter was not casting doubt on who Jesus was; he was challenging the Son of God to use His divine power to turn stones into loaves of bread. This was a temptation for Jesus on two levels. On a personal level, Jesus was tempted to use His power to perform a miracle to satisfy His own hunger. On another level, the devil was implying that Jesus could use His divine power to feed the starving people of the world.

He quoted Deuteronomy 8:3, which summarizes what God tried to teach the Israelites during their forty years in the wilderness (Deut. 8:2). As important as bread is to meet our bodies' needs for physical life, the Word of God is essential for the kind of deeper life that comes through faith in God.

People do not live by bread alone, but they do need bread. He taught us to pray for daily bread (Matt. 6:11). He taught us to feed hungry people (Matt. 25:31–46). At times Jesus did use His powers to feed hungry people (Matt. 14:13–21). However, because many of the Jewish people were expecting just such a messiah, when Jesus out of compassion fed five thousand people, they tried to make Him their kind of king (John 6:15). Jesus refused to be the kind of messiah they wanted (John 6:22–71).

Notice that Jesus quoted Scripture to turn aside the temptations. He practiced Psalm 119:11, "Thy word have I hid in mine heart, that I might not sin against thee."

3. Using holy things (vv. 5–7)

5 Then the devil taketh him up into the holy city, and setteth him on a pinnacle of the temple,

6 And saith unto him, If thou be the Son of God, cast thyself down: for it is written, He shall give his angels charge concerning thee: and in their hands they shall bear thee up, lest at any time thou dash thy foot against a stone.

7 Jesus said unto him, It is written again, Thou shalt not tempt the Lord thy God.

In the second temptation, Satan moved from the mundane to the holy. He took Jesus to the holy city and to the highest point on the holy temple. Then he quoted the holy Scriptures to Jesus to call on the holy God.

In rejecting the devil's temptation to turn stones into bread, Jesus had quoted holy Scriptures and even used a text that emphasized the Word of God. Picking up on that, the devil quoted Psalm 91:11, 12 as a basis for doing what he then asked Jesus to do. The devil implied: "All right, you want to obey the Holy Scriptures; Psalm 91:11, 12 is God's Word. It says to step out in bold faith and God will send His angels to deliver you. If that applied to any believer, how much more does it apply to You—since You are the Son of God?"

Like the first temptation, this was a temptation on two levels. On a personal level, the devil tempted Jesus to give God an opportunity to prove what He had said at Jesus' baptism. Words are one thing, the devil implied; but actions are another. By rescuing you from this fall, God will show beyond a shadow of a doubt that Jesus is His Son. On another level, Jesus was tempted to do something spectacular that would impress the people and gain Him a following immediately.

Jesus rejected the devil's interpretation of Psalm 91:11, 12. He saw that doing what the devil suggested would not be showing trust in God but putting God to the test. Thus, Jesus quoted Deuteronomy 6:16. God wants us to trust Him to care for our needs; and at times, God challenges us to launch out boldly on His Word alone. Testing is when we try to use God for our own purposes.

Jesus often used signs and wonders, but never to impress people and to gain an easy following from the fickle crowds. He resisted all demands for a sign to convince people (Matt. 12:38–42). He knew that people could see obvious signs and still refuse to believe (see Luke 16:29–31; John 11:44–53).

4. Achieving goals (vv. 8–10)

8 Again, the devil taketh him up into an exceeding high mountain, and sheweth him all the kingdoms of the world, and the glory of them;

9 And saith unto him, All these things will I give thee, if thou wilt fall down and worship me.

10 Then saith Jesus unto him, Get thee hence, Satan: for it is written, Thou shalt worship the Lord thy God, and him only shalt thou serve.

On the surface, this appears the most brazen temptation of all; but it was probably done more deceptively than it sounds. What kind of glory would tempt Jesus? He was not the kind of person who seeks worldly fame or pleasure. Jesus had been promised glory and the allegiance of the nations, but only after fulfilling His mission of suffering and death. Satan was probably offering Jesus a shortcut to achieving His mission. Satan suggested that he knew ways Jesus could accomplish His goals without all the suffering and without dying for sin.

The disciples often argued among themselves about human success and greatness. Jesus had to keep reminding them that His way involves humble, self-giving service—of which His death was to be the ultimate expression (Mark 10:35–45). People worship the devil when they adopt his methods of achieving their goals. People give in to the tempter's suggestion that the good end justifies whatever is necessary to achieve it. Those who look for the quick, easy way to achieve goals often are unknowingly bowing before the devil, whose first commandment is, "The end justifies the means."

5. Victory over temptation (v. 11)

11 Then the devil leaveth him, and, behold, angels came and ministered unto him.

The devil left him, but passages like Matthew 16:23; 26:36–46 show that Satan continued to tempt Jesus. However, Jesus had won a crucial victory over temptation. When the devil left, the angels came and ministered to Jesus. As in the case of Elijah, the ministry probably included feeding Jesus (1 Kings 19:5–8).

Jesus' victory shows several facts about temptation and how to overcome it. Being tempted is not the same thing as sinning. Jesus was tempted as we are; yet Jesus did not sin.

Temptation can be overcome. The devil could not force Jesus to sin. He cannot force any of us. He can tempt, but the one who yields to sin cannot blame Satan—as Eve tried to do (Gen. 3:13; see James 1:13–15).

God always provides a way to escape when we are tempted (1 Cor. 10:13). The resources that sustained Jesus are still available—the Word of God and the power of God's Spirit. In our case, the Spirit is the Spirit of the Lord Jesus, who knows what it is to be tempted as we are and who comes to encourage and empower us to overcome as He did (Heb. 2:17, 18; 4:14–16).

II. Beginning the Galilean Ministry (Matt. 4:12–17)

12 Now when Jesus had heard that John was cast into prison, he departed into Galilee;

13 And leaving Nazareth, he came and dwelt in Capernaum, which is upon the sea coast, in the borders of Zabulon and Nephthalim:

14 That it might be fulfilled which was spoken by Esaias the prophet.

John the Baptist's arrest, imprisonment, and execution are recounted later in Matthew (11:2; 14:1–12). Jesus had been brought up in the little town of Nazareth, which was in the larger area of Galilee. One of the key cities of Galilee was Capernaum, which was located on the northwest coast of the Sea of Galilee. Galilee was in the area of Canaan originally given to the tribes of Zebulun and Naphtali.

Focusing His ministry in Galilee fulfilled Scripture. John 7:41, 42 shows that most Judean Jews denied that the Messiah would come from Galilee. They no doubt were thinking of Micah's prophecy of the Messiah's birth in Bethlehem in Judea (Mic. 5:2; Matt. 2:5, 6). Matthew quotes Isaiah 9:1, 2 as being fulfilled in the ministry of Jesus in Galilee (4:15, 16).

The quotation shows why Jesus focused on Galilee. "Galilee of the Gentiles" (4:15) had more Gentiles than any other of the Jewish territories. Also the Galilean Jews were not well thought of by the more pious Jews of Judea, who lived nearer the holy city of Jerusalem. Jesus occasionally went to Judea. John's Gospel emphasizes His ministry in Judea and Jerusalem, but Matthew emphasizes His work in this area of moral and spiritual darkness. He brought light to the Jews of Galilee during His earthly ministry, but His ministry in Galilee foreshadowed the worldwide scope of the gospel after Pentecost.

Jesus began preaching the same message that John the Baptist preached (compare 4:17 and 3:2).

PRONUNCIATION GUIDE

Capernaum	[kuh PURR nay uhm]
Esaias	[ih ZAY uhs]
Galilee	[GAL ih lee]
Nazareth	[NAZ uh reth]
Nephthalim	[NEF thuh lim]; same as Naphtali [NAF tuh ligh]
Zebulun	[zeb YOO luhn]; same as Zabulon

SUMMARY OF BIBLE TRUTHS

1. God allows us to be tested, but the devil tempts us to do evil.
2. Because Jesus was tempted as we are, yet without sinning, He is able to help us overcome temptations.
3. The devil uses every trick in his trade, including quoting Scripture.
4. Jesus relied on the Scriptures and the Spirit to overcome temptation.
5. The devil can tempt us, but each of us is responsible if we yield to temptation and sin.
6. Jesus shines His light where moral and spiritual darkness are greatest.

APPLYING THE BIBLE

1. Spiritual challenges and temptation. In a recent survey of *Discipleship Journal,* readers ranked areas of greatest spiritual challenge to them:

- materialism,
- pride,
- self-centeredness,
- laziness,
- anger/bitterness,
- sexual lust,
- envy,
- gluttony, and
- lying.

Survey respondents noted temptations were more potent when they had neglected their time with God (81 percent) and when they were physically tired (57 percent). Resisting temptation was accomplished by prayer (84 percent), avoiding compromising situations (76 percent), Bible study (66 percent), and being accountable to someone (52 percent).

2. Repeated battles. "You may have to fight a battle more than once to win it" (Margaret Thatcher).

3. Excuses. We live in a society where excuses for immoral behavior abound. Think of the Old Testament character, Joseph. When Potiphar's wife invited him to become her "lover," Joseph could have offered any one of the following excuses to rationalize his sin. He could have said:

- "It's only natural to do this. After all, God gave me the physical desire."
- "I'm lonely, and this is a way to satisfy a God-given need that I have."
- "I've had a hard life of rejection from my family, and I owe this to myself."
- "I'm different from others; this won't affect me or my walk with God in the long run."
- "It's not all my fault. I'm just a slave. I have to do what she says."
- "The palace is empty. I can do this and no one will ever know about it."

Yes, Joseph could have offered any one of these excuses. But he didn't. The appeals were many. Going to bed with Potiphar's unfaithful wife probably appealed to Joseph physically, mentally, emotionally, and even spiritually. ("Where was God when I was sold into slavery?" Joseph could have asked.) In the end, he demonstrated the best way for us to avoid sin in the midst of temptation. He ran the other way! (See Gen. 39:1–12.)

4. The character of temptation. Temptation can be explained by making an acrostic from the word to teach significant truths from today's lesson. One acrostic may include the following phrases.

T	Temptation is an invitation to sin, but it is not a sin to be tempted.
E	Temptation often says, "The end justifies the means."
M	Temptation causes us to mistrust in the provision and promises of God.
P	Temptation appeals to the passions you cultivate in your life. (If you have a problem with lust, quit watching explicit material on TV and memorize Job 31:1.)
T	The timing of temptation often follows periods of spiritual growth.
A	God is faithful and always provides a way of escape.
T	Tests and trials are the very fabric of faith.
I	Temptation is an invitation to grow stronger or weaker spiritually, depending on our response.
O	Overcoming temptation requires discipline.
N	No one is immune to being tempted. No one.

5. What would you do? F. B. Meyer is credited with saying, "When we see a brother or sister in sin, there are two things we do not know: First, we do not know how hard he or she tried not to sin. And second, we do not know the power of the forces that assailed him or her."

Stephen Brown adds, "We also do not know what we would have done in the same circumstances" (Stephen Brown, *Christianity Today,* April 5, 1993, 17).

6. Avoid the temptation. This poem speaks to the human nature of putting ourselves in the path of temptation. It ends by reminding us how to avoid temptation traps in the future.

There's a Hole in My Sidewalk

I walk down the street.
There is a deep hole in the sidewalk.
I fall in.
I am lost . . . I am helpless, it isn't my fault.
It takes forever to find a way out.
I walk down the same street.
There is a deep hole in the sidewalk.
I pretend I don't see it.
I fall in, again.
I can't believe I am in the same place.
But, it isn't my fault.
I walk down the same street.
There is a deep hole in the sidewalk.
I see it there.
I still fall in . . . it's a habit . . . but I know where I am.
It is my fault.
I get out immediately.
I walk down the same street.
There is a deep hole in the sidewalk.
I walk around it. I walk down another street.

—Portia Nelson

TEACHING THE BIBLE

- *Main Idea:* Jesus used Scripture and His relationship with God to overcome temptation.
- *Suggested Teaching Aim:* To lead adults to identify ways Jesus overcame temptation.

A TEACHING OUTLINE

1. *Temptations of Jesus (Matt. 4:1–11)*
2. *Beginning the Galilean Ministry (Matt. 4:12–17)*

Introduce the Bible Study

Use number 1, "Spiritual Challenges and Temptation," in "Applying the Bible" to introduce the lesson.

Search for Biblical Truth

IN ADVANCE, number the summary statements in "Outline and Summary" and copy them on six small strips of paper. Give the statements to six different members. Ask the person with the first strip to read it aloud and read Matthew 4:1. Briefly lecture concerning the following points:

- Temptation often strikes soon after a time of spiritual exaltation.
- Locate the "wilderness" on a map of Jesus' ministry.
- The role of the devil and the Spirit in the temptation.

DISCUSS: Why do you think that temptation often strikes so close to times of spiritual high?

Ask the person with the second summary strip to read it aloud and then read Matthew 4:2–4. Ask: What did the tempter ask Jesus to do in these verses? Why do you think this was a real temptation for Jesus? What were the two levels of temptation for Jesus? How did Jesus respond?

DISCUSS: Why, when we have power to provide bread for hungry people, are we tempted to keep it for ourselves?

Ask the person with the third summary statement to read it aloud and to read Matthew 4:5–7. Ask: What did the tempter ask Jesus to do in these verses? Why do you think this was a real temptation for Jesus? What were the two levels of temptation for Jesus? How did the tempter misquote Scripture? How did Jesus respond?

DISCUSS: What are some examples today of people who are still trying to appeal to the spectacular by performing signs and wonders?

Ask the person with the fourth summary statement to read it aloud and to read Matthew 4:8–10. Ask: What did the tempter ask Jesus to do in these verses? What was the likely meaning of this temptation for Jesus? Why do you think this was a real temptation for Jesus? How did Jesus respond?

DISCUSS: What are some ways we give in to this temptation today?

Ask the person with the fifth summary statement to read it and Matthew 4:11 aloud. Read the three statements in "Studying the Bible" in the commentary on verse 11. Ask members if they agree or disagree with the following statements:

- "Being tempted is not the same thing as sinning."
- The devil "can tempt, but the one who yields to sin cannot blame Satan—as Eve tried to do."
- "God always provides a way to escape when we are tempted."

Ask the person with the sixth summary statement to read it and Matthew 4:12–17. Locate Galilee on the map and show where Jesus went when John was arrested.

DISCUSS: How would you compare and contrast Jesus' preaching with John the Baptist's preaching?

Give the Truth a Personal Focus

Use the summary statements to present a brief lecture summarizing the truths of the lesson. Close in prayer.

Birth of Jesus

December

19

1999

Background Passage: Matthew 1:1–25
Focal Passages: Matthew 1:1–6, 18–25

Matthew 1–2 and Luke 1–2 describe the events related to the birth of Jesus. John 1:1–18 provides a theological perspective. Jesus is the focus in all these Gospels; however, Matthew tells the story from Joseph's point of view, and Luke, from Mary's. Matthew 1 tells of the genealogy of Jesus and of the announcement of His birth to Joseph.

Study Aim: *To testify to what Matthew 1 says about who Jesus is and what He came to do.*

STUDYING THE BIBLE

OUTLINE AND SUMMARY

I. Genealogy of Jesus (Matt. 1:1–17)

II. Announcement of the Birth of Jesus (Matt. 1:18–25)

1. Joseph and Mary (1:18, 19)

2. Jesus Immanuel (1:20–23)

3. Joseph's trust and obedience (1:24, 25)

The genealogy of Jesus presents Jesus as the Messiah-King who fulfilled God's promises to David and as One who came for all people (vv. 1–17). Jesus is central, but God chose two people of genuine faith to raise Him (vv. 18, 19). Jesus is the incarnate Son of God and Savior from sin, who came into the world by means of a miraculous conception to a virgin (vv. 20–23). Joseph acted with complete trust and obedience to the Lord (vv. 24, 25).

I. Genealogy of Jesus (Matt. 1:1–17)

1 The book of the generation of Jesus Christ, the son of David, the son of Abraham.

2 Abraham begat Isaac; and Isaac begat Jacob; and Jacob begat Judas and his brethren;

3 And Judas begat Phares and Zara of Thamar; and Phares begat Esrom; and Esrom begat Aram;

4 And Aram begat Aminadab; and Aminadab begat Naasson; and Naasson begat Salmon;

5 And Salmon begat Booz of Rachab; and Booz begat Obed of Ruth; and Obed begat Jesse;

6 And Jesse begat David the king; and David the king begat Solomon of her that had been the wife of Urias.

Beginning a book with a long genealogy seems strange to us today; however, genealogies are a familiar feature in the Old Testament; and this particular genealogy reveals much about who Jesus is and what He came to do.

Jesus was the fulfillment of Old Testament promises. "The book of the generation" reminds us of similar words that separate the divisions of the

Book of Genesis (see for example, Gen. 2:4; 5:1; 6:9; and so on). The name or title "Christ" means "Anointed One" and refers to the Messiah-King for whom the Jews looked, based on God's covenant with David (2 Sam. 7:11b–16). Thus Jesus (Savior, see 1:21) Christ was the son of David. The arrangement of the names in the genealogy emphasizes Jesus as the son of David. Verses 2–6 go from Abraham to David; verses 7–11 go from David to the exile, which seemed the end of David's line of kings; however, 12–16 go from the exile and show that Jesus was the true King.

Jesus also was the son of Abraham. He fulfilled God's promises to Abraham (Gen. 12:1–3), which were renewed with the other patriarchs Isaac and Jacob. Jacob predicted that the Promised One would come from the tribe of Judah, David's tribe (sometimes spelled "Judas"; Gen. 49:10).

The unusual feature of this genealogy is the mention of five women: Tamar (Thamar), Rahab (Rachab), Ruth, wife of Uriah (Bathsheba), and Mary. Tamar was the daughter-in-law of Judah, whose husband had died before she bore children; therefore, she disguised herself as a prostitute in order to have a child by Judah (Gen. 38). Rahab was the prostitute of Jericho whose family was spared because she hid the Israelite spies (Josh. 2). We are more familiar with the other three. Why did Matthew depart from custom by adding the names of these women?

As far as the first four are concerned, they were probably added to remind readers of the inclusiveness of Jesus' mission. He came for women as well as men. He came for Gentiles as well as Jews (Rahab and Ruth were foreigners). He came to save sinners. Tamar, Rahab, and Bathsheba were involved in sexual sins. If we are looking for sinners, we can also find many among the male ancestors of Jesus, including David himself. The most notorious sinner in the list was King Manasseh (v. 10).

Mary is included because she was the mother of Jesus. Although the genealogy was based on the line of Matthew, verse 17 sets the stage for the description of the miracle of Jesus' conception by the Holy Spirit (v. 20) and His birth to a virgin (vv. 22, 23).

II. Announcement of the Birth of Jesus (Matt. 1:18–25)

1. Joseph and Mary (vv. 18, 19)

18 Now the birth of Jesus Christ was on this wise: When as his mother Mary was espoused to Joseph, before they came together, she was found with child of the Holy Ghost.

19 Then Joseph her husband, being a just man, and not willing to make her a publick example, was minded to put her away privily.

Although the focus in Matthew 1 is on Jesus, some attention is given to the kind of people God chose to raise Him. Luke 1:26–38 tells of the angel's announcement of Jesus' birth to Mary, a dedicated, obedient, pure young woman of simple yet profound faith and trust in God. She and Joseph were engaged but not yet married. First-century Jewish engagements were more binding than modern engagements. A formal agreement or contract bound them to become married. This relationship could be broken only by a divorce.

In those days, as should be true in every generation, the engaged couple did not engage in sex. That came only after they were married. Although Joseph is called Mary's "husband," the word *espoused* refers to being engaged; and the words *before they came together* emphasize that they were not living together as husband and wife.

During this period, Joseph became aware that Mary was expecting a child. The Bible does not tell us whether Mary had told Joseph of the unique manner of the child's conception. My own feeling is that she had not told him. For one thing, Mary was a person of trust, and she probably trusted God to inform Joseph in His own way and time. In addition, the actions of Joseph strongly imply that he did not know she was pregnant until it became apparent that she was.

The custom of the day was for the man to subject his unfaithful fiancee to divorce and public humiliation. Joseph chose not to do this. He is described as "a just (righteous) man." He did not want a wife who was guilty of adultery, but he was not a vindictive man. Mercy tempered his sense of doing what was right. Therefore, he made plans to divorce Mary but to do so as quietly as possible. He felt this would be best for all concerned—himself, Mary, and the child.

2. Jesus Immanuel (vv. 20–23)

20 But while he thought on these things, behold, the angel of the Lord appeared unto him in a dream, saying, Joseph, thou son of David, fear not to take unto thee Mary thy wife: for that which is conceived in her is of the Holy Ghost.

21 And she shall bring forth a son, and thou shalt call his name JESUS: for he shall save his people from their sins.

22 Now all this was done, that it might be fulfilled which was spoken of the Lord by the prophet, saying,

23 Behold, a virgin shall be with child, and shall bring forth a son, and they shall call his name Emmanuel, which being interpreted is, God with us.

Mary's confident trust in God was justified. God sent an angel to speak to Joseph in a dream and to tell him what an angel had told her months before. Mary was not guilty of adultery; the child was miraculously conceived by the Holy Spirit. Neither in this announcement to Joseph nor in the announcement to Mary is this miracle described in sensual terms, like the pagan myths of gods who cohabited with humans. Yet it was a miracle involving conception without a human father.

Joseph and Mary were both told to name the child Jesus. Joseph was told why. Names in those days had great significance. The name *Jesus* means "the Lord (Yahweh or Jehovah) is Savior." The mission of Jesus was to save people from their sins. This reinforces the implication of including the names of sinners in the genealogy.

The miraculous conception of the Savior fulfilled Old Testament prophecy. Matthew quoted Isaiah 7:14, which foretold the virgin birth of One called Immanuel (Emmanuel). Matthew explained to any non-Jewish readers that this name means "God with us." What more appropriate way for the incarnate Son of God to enter the world on His mission as Savior?

The miraculous conception of Jesus is only one of a number of events that point to this great miracle of incarnation. The doctrine of incarnation emphasizes that the eternal Word or Son of God became "flesh" (a real human being; see John 1:1, 2, 14). The events described in Matthew 1–2 and Luke 1–2, which we tell and retell each Christmas, emphasize both the human and the divine in the coming of the Savior. It was as if heaven came down and touched earth in this mixture of the heavenly and the earthly.

The earthly is seen in such things as shepherds tending their flocks, a young woman giving birth in humble surroundings, wise men searching the heavens for a sign. The heavenly is seen in the sudden appearance of angels to announce a special birth to the shepherds. It is seen in the miraculous conception of the child; although the birth was real enough in physical terms, the young mother was a virgin. It is seen in a miraculous star that led the wise men to where the young child was in order that they might worship Him.

The miracle of Jesus' conception fits the entire miracle of all the events of His coming, His ministry, His death, His resurrection, and His continuing work through the Spirit. Anyone who believes in the God of creation and redemption believes in a God who has acted in ways beyond human understanding to bring sinners to Himself.

3. Joseph's trust and obedience (vv. 24, 25)

24 Then Joseph being raised from sleep did as the angel of the Lord had bidden him, and took unto him his wife:

25 And knew her not till she had brought forth her firstborn son: and he called his name JESUS.

We honor Mary for her trust and obedience. Joseph showed the same kind of trust and obedience. He did not question the angel's unusual (to say the least) explanation for Mary's pregnancy, nor did he delay in obeying what the Lord told him to do. Instead of divorcing Mary, he married her. However, he carefully refrained from any sexual relations with her until after she had borne her firstborn son. When the child was born, Joseph named Him Jesus—as the angel had told him to do.

Luke 2:1–7 tells more details of the events connected with the actual birth. Matthew 1:25 simply tells us that this incarnate Savior was born to the virgin Mary.

Those who know Jesus Christ as Lord and Savior are able to show the kind of trust and obedience seen in Joseph and Mary—and thus to experience the true meaning and joy of celebrating Christmas.

PRONUNCIATION GUIDE

Aminadab	[uh MIN uh dab]
Aram	[AY ram] same as Ram
Booz	[BOH ahz] same as Boaz
Esrom	[ES ruhm]
Naasson	[nay ASS uhn]
Phares	[FAY reez] same as Perez
Rachab	[RAY kab] same as Rahab
Thamar	[THAY mar] same as Tamar
Zera	[ZEE ruh] same as Zerah

SUMMARY OF BIBLE TRUTHS

1. Jesus is the Messiah promised in the Old Testament.
2. He came as Savior for all kinds of people.
3. God chose two people of genuine faith to raise His Son.
4. Jesus is the One whom God sent to save people from their sins.
5. His conception by the Holy Spirit and His birth to a virgin are consistent with the total miracle of salvation.
6. Only those who know Jesus as personal Savior and Lord can understand the real meaning and joy of Christmas.

APPLYING THE BIBLE

1. A child's complete Christmas. A young girl slipped a piece of paper into her pastor's hand just as he was entering the sanctuary for the Christmas Eve service. As he sat down, he unfolded the paper and read the precious words that express the true joy of Christmas written in her simple handwriting.

Katherine Hall's Complete Christmas Recipe[1]

½	cup of joy
4 ½	cups of peace
2	cups of love
3 ⅓	cups of praise
7	cups of Christ
5 ¾	teaspoons of giving

Stir gently for 1 minute.
Share with others the true Christmas.

2. Gifts of Christmas:

God's gift:	Jesus
Joseph and Mary's gift:	obedience
The shepherds' gift:	wonder
The wise men's gift:	excellence
Jesus' gift:	peace

3. The gift goes on, but only if delivered. Margaret Taylor died three weeks before Christmas without getting a chance to mail the Christmas cards and wrapped presents that sat on a table in her home. But the police officer who found the 77-year-old woman's body made sure the gifts and cards were sent. Officer Aisha Perry stamped the cards and mailed them along with the packages, including a note telling Ms. Taylor's friends that she had died.

Since then, ten people have written the officer to thank her for the cards and tell her stories about their old friend. The gifts brought joy to those for whom they were intended and to the one committed to seeing that they were delivered.

The message of Christmas is a gift that keeps on giving, too, but it has to be delivered. Jesus is the source of joy, and those who know Him can't help but share the message with those who don't.

4. Joy. Joy shared is joy doubled.

5. No presents, but a wonderful gift. In the classic tale *Little Women* (1868), Louisa May Alcott brought the story of her past to life. Facing the hardship of a nation rebuilding following the Civil War, she wrote, "Christmas won't be Christmas without any presents."

But God has given the greatest gift through His Son Jesus. There will always be a gift available to us because of what Christ accomplished on our behalf.

6. The greatest gift:

GOD: the greatest Lover
SO LOVED: the greatest degree
THAT HE GAVE: the greatest act
HIS ONLY BEGOTTEN SON: the greatest gift
THAT WHOSOEVER: the greatest opportunity
BELIEVETH: the greatest simplicity
IN HIM: the greatest attraction
SHOULD NOT PERISH: the greatest promise
BUT: the greatest difference
HAVE: the greatest certainty
EVERLASTING LIFE: the greatest possession.

7. Letters to Santa. We often read "Letters to Santa" from children. Adults have been known to write them, too:

> Dear Santa,
> Christmas Eve I'll be 46. I'm in great need of eyeglasses. I cannot see to read any more. I live in the hills of Appalachia and with no work here, there's no money for such things. If you could find me glasses, I'd be ever grateful.
>
> Shirley, from Kentucky[2]

Jesus did not come to be the world's Santa, but He did come to be the Light of the world. Those walking in darkness, the prophets cried, upon them a light will fall. Until all the Shirleys in the world have their spiritual sight restored—our task in sharing the gift of Christmas—the message of Christ is not complete.

TEACHING THE BIBLE

- *Main Idea:* Jesus is God's Son and came to save the world from sin.
- *Suggested Teaching Aim:* To lead adults to demonstrate the same kind of trust and obedience seen in Joseph and Mary.

A TEACHING OUTLINE

1. *Genealogy of Jesus (Matt. 1:1–17)*
2. *Announcement of the Birth of Jesus (Matt. 1:18–25)*

Introduce the Bible Study

Use No. 3, "The Gift Goes On," in "Applying the Bible" to introduce the lesson. Point out that Jesus' birth was God's eternal and everlasting gift to the world.

Search for Biblical Truth

On a chalkboard write in two columns: *Known* and *Unknown.* Ask members to open their Bibles to Matthew 1:1–6 and identify people in Jesus' genealogy whom they know. List these under *Known.* List all the others under *Unknown.* Now ask members to identify the women in Jesus' genealogy. (Tamar, Rahab, Ruth, and Bathsheba.) Ask: Why was it unusual to include women in a genealogy? What is unusual about these women that would link them all together? (They were either foreigners [Ruth, Rahab] or had sexual sin in their background [Rahab, Tamar, Bathsheba] or both [Rahab].)

IN ADVANCE, assign someone a three- to four-minute report on the four women in Jesus' genealogy. Call for the report at this time. Ask: Why do you think Matthew included these particular four women in his listing of Jesus' ancestors? Let members share their answers. Include the following: Jesus came for women as well as men; He came for Gentiles as well as Jews; He came to save sinners.

DISCUSS: What does Jesus' genealogy say to us about our ancestry?

On a chalkboard write *Joseph* and *Mary.* Ask members to locate Matthew 1:18–19 and list characteristics of these two people whom God had chosen to raise His Son. Use the material in "Studying the Bible" to explain first-century engagement/marriage customs.

Ask members to look at Matthew 1:20–23 and answer these questions: What were Mary and Joseph to name the child? Why did Jesus come? What prophet did Matthew cite who had predicted Jesus' birth? What name did Isaiah give the child?

Point out that Jesus' birth was a mixture of the heavenly and the earthly. On the chalkboard, write *Heavenly* and *Earthly.* Ask members to suggest the heavenly events associated with Jesus' birth. (Your members may think of others but consider: angels, miraculous conception, and miraculous star.) Now ask members to suggest earthly events. (Shepherds, young woman giving birth, wise men.)

Ask members to look at Matthew 1:24–25. Ask, How did Joseph display trust and obedience? (Did not question angel; married Mary immediately; named the Baby Jesus.)

Give the Truth a Personal Focus

Write the six "Summary of Bible Truths" statements on small strips of paper. Distribute these and ask members to: (1) read aloud the statement and (2) suggest one way that truth will apply to their life this coming week.

IN ADVANCE, copy the following quotation on a large poster and display it at this time: "Those who know Jesus Christ as Lord and Savior are able to show the kind of trust and obedience seen in Joseph and Mary—and thus to experience the true meaning and joy of celebrating."

---

1. Katherine Hall, First Baptist Church, Nashville, Tennessee, Christmas Eve 1997.
2. *Good Housekeeping,* Dec. 1994, 74.

Coming of the Wise Men

Background Passage: Matthew 2:1–23

Focal Passage: Matthew 2:1–12

Matthew 2 tells of two kinds of people who both claimed to want to worship Jesus. The wise men sought Him sincerely. Herod sought Him insincerely. The wise men, on whom this lesson focuses, found Jesus and worshiped Him. God delivered Jesus from the evil, deceitful Herod; and God even used the wise men to help thwart the evil plans of Herod.

Study Aim: *To recognize the significance of the coming of the wise men.*

STUDYING THE BIBLE

OUTLINE AND SUMMARY

I. Seeking Jesus to Worship Him (Matt. 2:1–8)
- **1. Sincere seeking of the wise men (2:1, 2)**
- **2. Insincere seeking of Herod (2:3–8)**

II. Wise Men's Search Rewarded (Matt. 2:9–11)
- **1. Guided to joy (2:9, 10)**
- **2. Worshiping Jesus (2:11)**

III. Herod's Search Thwarted (Matt. 2:12–23)
- **1. The wise men's part in thwarting Herod (2:12)**
- **2. Divine deliverance of Jesus (2:13–23)**

The wise men sought the King of the Jews in order to worship Him (vv. 1, 2). Although Herod told the wise men that he intended to worship Jesus, he was lying (vv. 3–8). The wise men rejoiced when the star led them to the King (vv. 9, 10). They worshiped Jesus by bowing and offering Him treasures (v. 11). They obeyed God and left Judea without letting Herod know (v. 12). God delivered Jesus from the murderous intentions of Herod (vv. 13–23).

I. Seeking Jesus to Worship Him (Matt. 2:1–8)

1. Sincere seeking of the wise men (vv. 1, 2)

1 Now when Jesus was born in Bethlehem of Judaea in the days of Herod the king, behold, there came wise men from the east to Jerusalem,

2 Saying, Where is he that is born King of the Jews? for we have seen his star in the east, and are come to worship him.

The three main people in the drama of Matthew 2 are introduced in verse 1. Although Jesus was a child who played only a passive role in this drama, Jesus is the main person. God was actively at work throughout the drama to achieve His long-range purpose in His Son. Jesus is the King of the Jews whom the wise men sought and eventually found. He is the One whom Herod correctly saw as a threat to him, although not for the reasons he thought at the time. Although Jesus was the newborn

King, He had no aspirations for Herod's paltry kind of reign or evil power.

The wise men play a key role in our annual retelling of the Christmas story; and although they appear only in Matthew 2:1–12, they played a key role in the biblical account of the coming of Jesus. Their role is somewhat like that of the shepherds in Luke 2. The first group to see the newborn King were the lowly shepherds. The wise men were probably the first to see the sign of His birth in the star; and although they did not arrive on the night of Jesus' birth, they were the first group in Matthew's account to worship Jesus.

The shepherds show that Christ came for the lowly, common people of the world. The wise men show that Jesus came for Gentiles, although high-born people, yet pagans by biblical standards. They were not kings, but a cross between astronomers and astrologers. Astronomy by our standards is a valid science of studying the universe. Astrology is an ancient superstition, consistently condemned in the Bible, that assumes our lives are governed by our astrological signs and predictions. Thus, by biblical standards, the wise men were pagan Gentiles.

Yet God used a star (of all things) to lead these pagan Gentiles to the Jewish King, who was destined also to be Savior of the world. They came from the east, probably Persia. When they spoke of seeing the star "in the east," they meant that they were to the east of Jerusalem when they saw it. They went to Jerusalem, which was the natural place to go in seeking a newborn King of the Jews. When they arrived, they announced to the current king of the Jews who they were, where they were from, and why they had come.

2. Insincere seeking of Herod (vv. 3–8)

> **3 When Herod the king had heard these things, he was troubled, and all Jerusalem with him.**

The words of the wise men shocked the city of Jerusalem. These foreigners did not know that Herod had spent much of his reign killing people whom he suspected of aspiring to be king of the Jews, and most of those Herod killed were members of his own family. However, the people of Jerusalem knew what Herod was like; and they were troubled because the coming of the wise men probably meant a new blood bath.

> **4 And when he had gathered all the chief priests and scribes of the people together, he demanded of them where Christ should be born.**
>
> **5 And they said unto him, In Bethlehem of Judaea: for thus it is written by the prophet,**
>
> **6 And thou Bethlehem, in the land of Juda, art not the least among the princes of Juda: for out of thee shall come a Governor, that shall rule my people Israel.**

Herod was only half-Jewish, and he was far from being a religious man; but he knew enough about Jewish religion to recognize "King of the Jews" as the title of the long-awaited Messiah of the Jews. Therefore, he called in the biblical scholars to tell him where the Messiah or Christ was to be born. They quickly quoted to Herod the well-known prophecy of Micah 5:2, which named Bethlehem.

7 Then Herod, when he had privily called the wise men, enquired of them diligently what time the star appeared.

8 And he sent them to Bethlehem, and said, Go and search diligently for the young child; and when ye have found him, bring me word again, that I may come and worship him also.

Herod had a private meeting with the unsuspecting wise men. Herod was a wily man who knew how to use deceit to get what he wanted. He had found out where the Messiah was to be born. Then he pumped the wise men for information about when they first saw the star, thinking this would give him information needed to determine when the King was born. Since Herod later killed male babies under two years of age, two years represents the outer limits of what the wise men told Herod about when they saw the star.

Herod then told them to go to Bethlehem, a village only a few miles from Jerusalem. Herod apparently told them of Micah's prophecy. Using his polished skills at deception, Herod asked the wise men to send him word when they had found Jesus so that Herod could follow the wise men's example and worship the young child. Notice that Herod called Jesus "young child" (see also v. 11).

II. Wise Men's Search Rewarded (Matt. 2:9–11)

1. Guided to joy (vv. 9, 10)

9 When they had heard the king, they departed; and, lo, the star, which they saw in the east, went before them, till it came and stood over where the young child was.

10 When they saw the star, they rejoiced with exceeding great joy.

Some facts about the star are clear, but much remains a mystery. One fact is that the wise men saw the star while they were in the east, and they concluded that it heralded the birth of the King of the Jews (v. 2). Verses 9, 10 reveal these additional facts: The star led them as they left Jerusalem, it stopped over where Jesus was, and they felt great joy as a result. What is not clear is where the star was when they went to Jerusalem. Either the star had not been visible since they first saw it, or it had been stationary over Judea. At any rate, it now led them to the place in Bethlehem where Jesus was.

Their joy was not in the star, but in the One to whom it led them. When the star led them to where Jesus was, they knew that their long pilgrimage from the east was about to be rewarded.

2. Worshiping Jesus (v. 11)

11 And when they were come into the house, they saw the young child with Mary his mother, and fell down, and worshipped him: and when they had opened their treasures, they presented unto him gifts; gold, and frankincense, and myrrh.

The words *house* and *young child* show that the wise men did not arrive on the night of Jesus' birth. Their worship of the King illustrates some of the marks of true worship: joy, reverence, and offerings. Worship is an act of veneration. These men fell down in reverence, awe, submission, and gratitude before the King.

Their offerings were called "treasures," which shows they were valuable. Gold is renowned for its value. Frankincense and myrrh were valuable spices and perfumes. The word *gifts* reminds us that offerings must be given voluntarily from among those things that God has blessed us with. (The Bible never tells us how many wise men came to worship Jesus. The number three probably was based on the assumption that each wise man brought an individual gift.)

III. Herod's Search Thwarted (Matt. 2:12–23)

1. The wise men's part in thwarting Herod (v. 12)

12 And being warned of God in a dream that they should not return to Herod, they departed into their own country another way.

The wise men apparently had been completely fooled by Herod. Therefore, they were probably about to send word to him as he had requested or perhaps even to stop in Jerusalem on their way home and tell him personally. However, God spoke to them in a dream and warned them about Herod. God told them not to let Herod know they had found Jesus.

These men were sensitive enough to God that they took this revelation as being from God. Therefore, they obeyed God's word and hid from Herod the information he had asked them to send him. Their act of faith and courage was the first part of God's plan to thwart the murderous intentions of Herod.

When the wise men left Bethlehem, they avoided going back the way they had come—through Jerusalem. If they had traveled through Jerusalem, Herod might have heard and had them apprehended. Even going another way was risky. Herod could have had someone following them. They were acting with courage in defying Herod's request. They were in danger as long as they were in lands ruled by Herod.

Matthew 2:12 is the last mention in the Bible of the wise men. Yet later—in the Book of Acts—we read how the good news was preached to all people. The wise men's coming to Jesus when He was only a young child foreshadowed the vast multitudes of non-Jews who would later come to Jesus as Savior of the world.

2. Divine deliverance of Jesus (vv. 13–23)

Joseph was a key human figure in God's deliverance of His Son. Joseph immediately obeyed the divine warning to flee Bethlehem by taking Jesus and Mary to Egypt (vv. 13–15). When Herod realized that he had been outwitted by the wise men, his murderous rage was vented by ordering the slaughter of Bethlehem's boys of two and under (vv. 16–18). After Joseph heard that Herod was dead, he also learned that Herod's evil son Archelaus reigned in Judea. A dream led him to go to Nazareth in Galilee (vv. 19–23).

Although God delivered Jesus as a young child from the murderous grasp of Herod, the Father allowed His Son later to place Himself in the hands of those who wanted to kill Him. In this way, divine deliverance from sin and death was offered to all the lowly shepherds and pagan wise men of the world.

PRONUNCIATION GUIDE

Archelaus [ahr kih LAY uhs]

SUMMARY OF BIBLE TRUTHS

1. Some seek Jesus sincerely in order to worship Him.
2. Some who claim to want to worship Jesus are insincere.
3. Those who sincerely seek Jesus find Him.
4. God often uses the most unlikely people to achieve His purpose.
5. Real worship includes joy; reverence; and generous, voluntary offerings.
6. God offers salvation to all people.

APPLYING THE BIBLE

1. What's a camel doing here? It could have happened in Bethlehem 2,000 years ago. But it happened in Maryland in 1998. On a cold, winter night, men dressed in the regal robes of wise men dragged the carcass of an Arabian camel off the highway.

The camel had been one of the star attractions in a live nativity scene. While his handlers were changing into their outfits, the camel broke free of his tether and ran for the highway.

Vinit Mody could not avoid the collision with the animal. He got out of the car and said, "What in the world is a camel doing on Route 50 in the United States of America? You only see a camel in the zoo."

One of the signs that we live in an increasingly secular society is that we no longer recognize the symbols of faith's most incredible story. More than a camel died on the highway that night. So did the sense of awe at what God did 2,000 years ago.

2. Worship defined. Seeing what God is worth, and then giving Him what He is worth.[1]

3. Worship anything you choose. "Satan doesn't care what we worship, so long as we don't worship God" (D. L. Moody).

4. Benefits of worship. The person who bows the lowest in the presence of God stands the straightest in the presence of sin.

5. Wise men and worship. Worship is the first step to wisdom.

6. We don't want to offend anyone. To avoid offending anybody, the schools dropped religion altogether and started singing about the weather. At my son's school, they now hold the winter program in February and sing increasingly nonmemorable songs such as "Winter Wonderland," "Frosty the Snowman," and—this is a real song—"Suzy Snowflake," all of which is pretty funny because we live in Miami. A visitor from another planet would assume that the children belonged to the Church of Meteorology.[2]

All this is a far cry from the reality of the anthem, "Joy to the world, the Lord is come, let earth receive her King!" And we are the poorer for it.

TEACHING THE BIBLE

- *Main Idea:* The wise men symbolize that Jesus came for Gentiles as well as Jews.
- *Suggested Teaching Aim:* To lead adults to list ways to worship Jesus sincerely.

A TEACHING OUTLINE

1. *Seeking Jesus to Worship Him (Matt. 2:1–8)*
2. *Wise Men's Search Rewarded (Matt 2:9–11)*
3. *Herod's Search Thwarted (Matt. 2:12–13)*

Introduce the Bible Study

Use number 1, "What's a Camel Doing Here?" in "Applying the Bible" to introduce the lesson.

Search for Biblical Truth

Organize the class into four groups. Ask each group to listen for one of the following:

- How the wise men followed God's will.
- How the wise men worshiped Jesus.
- How the wise men demonstrated great faith in the face of danger.
- How the wise men are examples for us.

Ask the groups to listen for ways the wise men accomplished their assigned function. Members will be asked to share their observations later. You might distribute paper and pencils.

IN ADVANCE, enlist two members to read aloud the Scripture. Ask them to read every other verse. Call for them to read Matthew 2:1–2 at this time. Ask members to share what they know about the wise men. **IN ADVANCE,** write the following chart on a large sheet of paper:

Compare and Contrast the Wise Men and the Shepherds

	Wise Men	Shepherds
Who were they?		
Where were they from?		
How did they learn of Jesus?		
How did they respond?		
How long did it take them to respond?		
How long did it take them to get to Jesus?		
Why do you think God revealed Jesus' birth to them?		

Ask the readers to read Matthew 2:3–8. Ask: Why was Jerusalem troubled when Herod heard about Jesus' birth? What approach did Herod take to the wise men's question? How did the chief priests and the scribes know where the Messiah was going to be born? (Locate Bethlehem and Jerusalem on a map showing Jesus' ministry.) What did Herod ask the wise men to do? What in Herod's response may indicate that the wise men came some time after Jesus' birth?

Ask the readers to read Matthew 2:9–10. Ask, What do we know about the star? (See "Studying the Bible.")

Before the reader reads Matthew 2:11, ask members to listen for marks of true worship in the wise men's adoration of Jesus and ask members to share their responses.

Ask the reader to read Matthew 2:12. Ask, What made the wise men's actions so dangerous?

Call for groups to share their responses to their assignments.

Give the Truth a Personal Focus

Read the six "Summary of Bible Truths" statements to summarize the lesson. Then read each statement again and ask members how that statement applies to their lives. Ask: What action do you need to take today to worship Jesus sincerely? Do you need to give Him a gift? Do you need to let Him use you to achieve His purpose? Do you need to accept His salvation? Challenge each member to respond in accordance with their individual needs.

---

1. Tim Keller, "What It Takes to Worship Well," *Leadership Journal,* Spring 1994, 19.
2. Dave Barry, "Notes on Western Civilization," *Chicago Tribune Magazine,* July 28, 1991.

The Disciples of Jesus

Background Passages: Matthew 4:18–22; 9:9–12; 10:1–4
Focal Passages: Matthew 4:18–22; 9:9–12; 10:1–4

In referring to "disciples" of Jesus, Matthew and the other New Testament writers sometimes meant a special group of twelve disciples and at times meant followers of Jesus other than the Twelve. The twelve disciples had a unique calling, relationship to Jesus, and mission; however, because they formed the nucleus of the church, we also learn from them some lessons about all disciples.

Study Aim: *To name the unique characteristics of the twelve disciples and the basic lessons from them for all disciples.*

STUDYING THE BIBLE

OUTLINE AND SUMMARY

I. Called to Follow Jesus (Matt. 4:18–22)
II. Befriending Sinners in Jesus' Name (Matt. 9:9–12)
  1. Matthew the tax collector (9:9)
  2. Friend of sinners (9:10, 11)
  3. Physician for sinners (9:12)
III. Sent Forth with Jesus' Authority (Matt. 10:1–4)

Jesus called four fishermen to follow Him and become fishers of men (4:18–22). Jesus called Matthew the tax collector (9:9). The Pharisees asked the disciples why Jesus ate with tax collectors and sinners (9:10, 11). Jesus compared Himself to a physician for people diseased by sin (9:12). Jesus sent the twelve apostles after giving them authority to heal and cast out evil spirits (10:1–4).

I. Called to Follow Jesus (Matt. 4:18–22)

18 And Jesus walking by the sea of Galilee, saw two brethren, Simon called Peter, and Andrew his brother, casting a net into the sea: for they were fishers.

19 And he saith unto them, Follow me, and I will make you fishers of men.

20 And they straightway left their nets, and followed him.

21 And going on from thence, he saw other two brethren, James the son of Zebedee, and John his brother, in a ship with Zebedee their father, mending their nets; and he called them.

22 And they immediately left the ship and their father, and followed him.

Early in Jesus' ministry in Galilee (Matt. 4:12–17), He called two pairs of brothers to be disciples. John 1:35–42 tells us of an earlier encounter with Andrew and Peter, and also probably with John. Matthew 4:18–22 describes how Jesus called Peter, Andrew, James, and John to full discipleship.

Although the word *disciples* is not used in Matthew 4:18–22, the call to "follow me" was a call to be disciples (Matt. 10:1). "Follow me" was an invitation of Jesus for people to commit themselves totally to Him, to learn from Him, to become like Him, and to be sent forth on mission for Him. Following Jesus in this way is what it means to be a disciple of His.

"Disciples" was a familiar term to describe pupils who attached themselves to a special teacher, often as live-in students. John the Baptist, for example, had disciples (Matt. 11:2). Thus, the Twelve were not the only followers of Jesus called "disciples." He had many other disciples during His public ministry (Matt. 8:21). The Book of Acts uses *disciples* as one of the terms to describe all who followed Jesus (Acts 11:26).

The Twelve were disciples in some special ways. They were chosen to be with Him during His incarnate ministry and later to tell of His teachings and be witnesses of His resurrection to all nations. Mark 3:13–17 says that Jesus called many to Himself, but He appointed twelve to be with Him, to be sent forth to preach, and to be given authority to heal the sick and cast out demons. Luke 6:12–16 calls these twelve "disciples" and "apostles."

In those days, a person ordinarily became a disciple by seeking out a teacher and joining his school. By contrast, Jesus took the initiative in seeking and calling His disciples. They did not choose Him; He chose them (John 15:16). This was true of the Twelve, and it is true of all His followers.

Jesus demands total commitment to Him. He said, "Follow me." Of course, people have a choice about whether to follow Him. In the case of the four fishermen, they immediately left everything and followed Jesus. People who were not willing to accept Jesus on His own terms could not become true disciples (Luke 9:57–62). In some cases, those called "disciples" proved false disciples by being unwilling to let Jesus fulfill His mission in His own way (John 6:66–69).

Jesus called the four fishermen to be "fishers of men." This showed that they were not just to be with Him and to learn from Him as pupils, but they were also to persuade others to become followers of Christ (see 10:1–4).

Parallelism is a characteristic of Hebrew poetry and of Hebrew thought in general. The Hebrews often emphasized something by repeating the same idea in slightly different words. In this case, the calls of James and John in verses 21, 22 have many parallels: two brothers, fishermen on the Sea of Galilee, called by Jesus, immediate obedience, left all, followed Jesus. By repeating these facts, Matthew emphasized the importance of being called as a disciple of Jesus.

II. Befriending Sinners in Jesus' Name (Matt. 9:9–12)

1. Matthew the tax collector (v. 9)

9 And as Jesus passed forth from thence, he saw a man, named Matthew, sitting at the receipt of custom: and he saith unto him, Follow me. And he arose, and followed him.

Matthew is sometimes called Levi (Mark 2:14). Like Simon Peter, Matthew Levi had two names. He collected customs fees, probably on goods passing along one of the roads near Capernaum. Tax collectors were hated by all the people because many of them used their positions of authority to demand more taxes than were due. They were hated by patriotic Jews because they collaborated with the Roman government, who controlled their lands. They were hated by pious groups like the Pharisees because the tax collectors became ceremonially unclean by associating with unclean people and things.

Significantly, Jesus chose as one of His disciples one of these hated "sinners." Matthew, like the four fishermen, was sought out and called by Jesus; and like them, he followed Jesus.

2. Friend of sinners (vv. 10, 11)

10 And it came to pass, as Jesus sat at meat in the house, behold, many publicans and sinners came and sat down with him and his disciples.

11 And when the Pharisees saw it, they said unto his disciples, Why eateth your Master with publicans and sinners?

Luke 5:29 indicates that Matthew Levi gave this feast and invited not only Jesus and His disciples but also some of his fellow tax collectors. The Pharisees were offended by this would-be rabbi eating with such people. The Pharisees defined just about everyone except Pharisees as "sinners" in the sense of not taking seriously the distinctions between clean and unclean things. However, among these "sinners" were some who were considered sinners even by Jesus (see, for example, Luke 7:37–48).

Jesus Himself often broke the Pharisees' rigid rules about what was unclean. Having table fellowship with unclean people was a flagrant abuse of their rules. To the Pharisees, one of Jesus' "sins" was that He was a friend of sinners (Luke 15:1, 2).

3. Physician for sinners (v. 12)

12 But when Jesus heard that, he said unto them, They that be whole need not a physician, but they that are sick.

Jesus and the Pharisees had totally different strategies of evangelism. Because the Pharisees feared contamination, they avoided any close contact with sinners. They would accept repentant sinners if they came to the Pharisees, confessed their sins, and began to live by Pharisaic standards of righteousness. By contrast, Jesus sought out sinners, befriended them, and showed them God's love in order to lead them to repent (Luke 15:3–32; 19:10).

He illustrated this with the simple analogy of a physician going to the sick, not to healthy people. Jesus was not necessarily conceding that the Pharisees were truly righteous (see Matt. 5:20; Luke 18:9–14). He was simply accepting their basic premise that Jesus was eating with sinners. Jesus replied that since He had come to heal those who were diseased by sin, He obviously needed to spend time with those who were sick.

III. Sent Forth with Jesus' Authority (Matt. 10:1–4)

1 And when he had called unto him his twelve disciples, he gave them power against unclean spirits, to cast them out, and to heal all manner of sickness and all manner of disease.

2 Now the names of the twelve apostles are these; The first, Simon, who is called Peter, and Andrew his brother; James the son of Zebedee, and John his brother;

3 Philip, and Bartholomew; Thomas, and Matthew the publican; James the son of Alphaeus, and Lebbaeus, whose surname was Thaddaeus;

4 Simon the Canaanite, and Judas Iscariot, who also betrayed him.

Verse 1 assumes that Jesus called twelve disciples. Mark 3:13–19 and Luke 6:12–16 describe His appointment of the Twelve. Each of these passages lists the Twelve by name. Matthew lists the Twelve by name after describing how He gave them authority to perform miracles in His name. This authority was given as Jesus sent the Twelve out on a mission in His name. All the names in the three lists are not the same. This was because some of them were called by one of their two names. Bartholomew was probably the Nathanael of John 1:45–49. In Luke 6:16, Thaddaeus is called Judas, the brother of James, to distinguish him from Judas Iscariot. Because the Greek text says, Judas of James, some translators assume he was "the son of James" (NASB).

The mission, which is described in the rest of Matthew 10, is implied in Matthew's use of the word *apostles,* which means "those sent out." The mission of the twelve apostles is closely related to Matthew 9:36–38. Verse 36 describes Jesus' compassion for the multitudes, far more than He could personally help in His incarnate form. Thus, Jesus told the disciples that the harvest was far too great for the few harvesters; therefore, to pray that the Lord of the harvest would send forth workers. Matthew 10:5 says, "These twelve Jesus sent forth."

Their mission was primarily to preach (v. 7), but they were also given power or authority to perform miracles as signs of the kingdom whose coming they announced. Jesus Himself was engaged in a ministry of preaching, teaching, and healing (Matt. 4:23). Jesus performed miracles as acts of compassion (see Matt. 9:18–38, in the lesson for Jan. 16). Matthew 28:18–20 records the Great Commission, which Jesus gave to the apostles in a unique way, but which is given to all followers of Jesus in all ages. The emphasis in Matthew 28:18–20 is on Jesus giving His authority and commissioning His followers to make disciples of all nations by going, baptizing, and teaching.

The word *apostles* is occasionally used in the New Testament of missionaries in general, but the word normally was used to refer to this unique group of apostles. An apostle in the unique sense was someone who was a witness of the risen Lord and commissioned by the Lord as a bearer of His message to all the world. The New Testament is the inspired record of the unique testimony and teachings of these apostles. They have no successors; we have them with us as the Spirit of the risen Lord speaks to us through their writings in the New Testament.

PRONUNCIATION GUIDE

Alphaeus	[al FEE uhs]
Bartholomew	[bar THAHL uh myoo]
Capernaum	[kuh PURR nay uhm]
Lebbaeus	[luh BEE uhs]

Thaddaeus [THAD ih uhs]
Zebedee [ZEB uh dee]

SUMMARY OF BIBLE TRUTHS

1. Jesus called twelve disciples to follow Him with total commitment during His earthly ministry.
2. He sent them forth as apostles on a mission that foreshadowed their later mission to the whole world.
3. Although the twelve disciples were unique in some ways, in other ways they had characteristics of all true disciples.
4. Jesus seeks sinners and calls them to salvation and discipleship.
5. All disciples are to walk with the Lord, learn from Him, become like Him, and represent Him in the world.

APPLYING THE BIBLE

1. Cost of discipleship. "When Christ calls a man, he bids him come and die" (Dietrich Bonhoeffer).

2. The Twelve. It has been suggested that the twelve men selected by Jesus to be His disciples would not have made it in today's business environment. A response to Jesus from a business consulting firm in regard to the personality profiles of the Twelve might well have included Tim Hansel's imaginary assessment which reads in part:

"It is the staff opinion that most of your nominees are lacking in background, education and vocational aptitude for the type of enterprise you are undertaking. They do not have the team concept. We would recommend that you continue your search for persons of experience in managerial ability and proven capability.

"Simon Peter is emotionally unstable and given to fits of temper. Andrew has absolutely no qualities of leadership. The two brothers, James and John, the sons of Zebedee, place personal interest above company loyalty. Thomas demonstrates a questioning attitude that would tend to undermine morale. We feel that it is our duty to tell you that Matthew had been blacklisted by the Greater Jerusalem Better Business Bureau; James, the son of Alphaeus, and Thaddaeus definitely have radical leanings, and they both registered a high score on the manic-depressive scale.

"One of the candidates, however, shows great potential. He is a man of ability and resourcefulness, meets people well, has a keen business mind, and has contacts in high places. He is highly motivated, ambitious, and responsible. We recommend Judas Iscariot as your controller and right-hand man."[1]

3. Our friend. Jesus is called the friend of sinners. As His followers, we are supposed to love the things that Jesus loves. It is unthinkable that we would in turn reject the very ones that Christ would have spent His time with when He was on the earth in the flesh. We wear the letters WWJD (What Would Jesus Do?) on bracelets, but few of us have come to the point of abandoning ourselves to the ones Jesus went to.

4. Cost of a cross. Clarence Jordan, author of the "Cotton Patch" New Testament translation and founder of the interracial Koinonia Farm in Americus, Georgia, was getting a red-carpet tour of another minister's church. With pride the minister pointed to the rich, imported pews and luxurious decorations. As they stepped outside, darkness was falling, and a spotlight shone on a huge cross atop the steeple. "That cross alone cost us ten thousand dollars," the minister said with a satisfied smile.

"You got cheated," said Jordan. "Times were when Christians could get them for free."

5. Worth of discipleship. "A religion that gives nothing, costs nothing, and suffers nothing, is worth nothing" (Martin Luther).

6. The question. At the close of life, the question will not be:

- How much have you gotten? but How much have you given?
- How much have you won? but How much have you done?
- How much have you saved? but How much have you sacrificed?
- How much were you honored? but How much have you loved and served? (Nathan C. Schaeffer).

7. Tough training. "It is better to train ten people than to do the work of ten people. But it is harder" (D. L. Moody).

8. What mentors do. Leadership experts would use the term *mentoring* to describe what Jesus did. The following are things mentors do for those whom they mentor:

- set high expectations of performance,
- help build self confidence,
- encourage professional behavior,
- offer friendship,
- confront negative behaviors and attitudes,
- listen to personal problems,
- teach by example,
- provide growth experiences,
- explain how an organization works,
- coach mentorands,
- stand by mentorands in critical situations,
- offer wise counsel,
- inspire mentorands, and
- help with a mentorand's career.[2]

TEACHING THE BIBLE

- *Main Idea:* Jesus called people to follow and minister in His name.
- *Suggested Teaching Aim:* To lead adults to commit themselves to follow Jesus and minister in His name.

A TEACHING OUTLINE

1. *Called to Follow Jesus (Matt. 4:18–22)*
2. *Befriending Sinners in Jesus' Name (Matt. 9:9–12)*
3. *Sent Forth on Mission (Matt. 10:1–4)*

Introduce the Bible Study

Ask, If you had been Jesus, what kind of disciples would you have called? Use number 2, "The Twelve," in "Applying the Bible" to introduce the lesson.

Search for Biblical Truth

Ask members to open their Bibles to Matthew 4:18–22. Write on a chalkboard or a large sheet of paper: *Disciple* and *Apostle.* Ask: What is the difference between a disciple and an apostle? (Basically, there is little difference in the way the New Testament refers to the two; a disciple is a "follower" and an apostle is "one who is sent out.")

Ask if anyone can name all twelve of Jesus' apostles. Ask: Who was the first disciple Jesus called? What did Jesus ask the men He called to do? ("Commit themselves totally to Him, to learn from Him, to become like Him, and to be sent forth on mission for Him.") Ask, Would you agree with this statement from "Applying the Bible": "When Jesus calls a man, He bids him come and die"?

DISCUSS: Does Jesus call followers at a lesser level of commitment today than He did in the first century? Why do you think so? What does that imply about our discipleship?

Ask a volunteer to read Matthew 9:9–11 aloud. Ask, Why would Jesus call a man whose title of office was used as a synonym for a cheat, who was hated by the patriotic Jews for collaborating with Rome, and who was hated by the religious groups because he was ceremonially unclean?

Ask someone to read Luke 5:29. What was one of Matthew's first actions after accepting Jesus' call? Why do you think Matthew did this? Why did the religious leaders object?

DISCUSS: How can we reach out to people who will not come inside a church building?

Ask a volunteer to read aloud Matthew 10:1–4. Ask, Are any of the names of the Twelve unfamiliar to you? Why? (Many likely had two names, like Simon Peter, and one list would list one name and another would list another name.)

Give the Truth a Personal Focus

Explain: Today the term *mentoring* has become quite popular. It means to guide, coach, train, instruct, tutor. A person becomes a mentor to someone else. Read number 8, "What Mentors Do," in "Applying the Bible." Ask: How good a job does our church do in mentoring new Christians? How can we improve?

Lead in prayer that the members will commit themselves to follow Jesus and minister in His name.

---

1. Tim Hansel, *Eating Problems for Breakfast* (Word Publishing, 1988), 194-195.
2. Clinton and Clinton, *The Mentor Handbook* (Altadena, Calif.: Barnabas Publishers, 1991), from the Preface.

January

9

2000

Teachings on Prayer

Background Passage: Matthew 6:1–15

Focal Passage: Matthew 6:1–15

Matthew's Gospel gives special attention to the teachings of Jesus. For example, it contains the Sermon on the Mount (Matt. 5–7). Within that sermon is a section on right motives for religious duties: giving, praying, and fasting. Attached to the verses about right motives about praying are some other teachings about prayer.

Study Aim: *To distinguish what Jesus taught about how not to pray from what He taught about how to pray.*

STUDYING THE BIBLE

OUTLINE AND SUMMARY

I. How Not to Pray (Matt. 6:1–8)

1. Don't pray to get people's attention (6:1–6)

2. Don't pray to get God's attention (6:7, 8)

II. How to Pray (Matt. 6:9–15)

1. Praise God (6:9, 10)

2. Ask God for what you need (6:11–13)

3. Live as you pray (6:14, 15)

Don't pray in such a way as to seek human attention and praise (vv. 1–6). Don't pray as if prayers are necessary to inform God or get Him to care (vv. 7, 8). Praise God our Father and ask Him to glorify His name, complete His work, accomplish His will (vv. 9, 10). Ask God for daily bread, forgiveness, and deliverance from temptation (vv. 11–13). Live as we pray by forgiving others as God has forgiven us (vv. 14, 15).

I. How Not to Pray (Matt. 6:1–8)

1. Don't pray to get people's attention (vv. 1–6)

1 Take heed that ye do not your alms before men, to be seen of them: otherwise ye have no reward of your Father which is in heaven.

2 Therefore when thou doest thine alms, do not sound a trumpet before thee, as the hypocrites do in the synagogues and in the streets, that they may have glory of men. Verily I say unto you, They have their reward.

3 But when thou doest alms, let not thy left hand know what thy right hand doeth:

4 That thine alms may be in secret: and thy Father which seeth in secret himself shall reward thee openly.

The word *alms* in verse 1 is "righteousness" in many ancient copies of Matthew. This is an introductory verse to three examples of religious duties: giving (vv. 2–4), praying (vv. 5, 6), and fasting (vv. 16–18). In between verses 6 and 16 are further teachings about prayer. The point in verse 1 is not that people of faith ought not perform religious duties. The warning is against doing religious duties for the wrong reason: in order to get people's attention and thus their praise.

Giving to the needy is a duty for all people of faith, but giving is not to be done in order to draw attention to the person who is giving. Hypocritical people make a big flourish about their giving in order to win the praise of others. Jesus said that such human praise is the only reward these seekers of human praise will receive.

Verse 3 puzzles many people. Jesus was not saying that we should not be aware of what we give. His point was that we should not take personal pride in our gifts.

5 And when thou prayest, thou shalt not be as the hypocrites are: for they love to pray standing in the synagogues and in the corners of the streets, that they may be seen of men. Verily I say unto you, They have their reward.

6 But thou, when thou prayest, enter into thy closet, and when thou hast shut thy door, pray to thy Father which is in secret; and thy Father which seeth in secret shall reward thee openly.

Jesus was not forbidding praying in public. He was warning against praying in order to be seen and praised by others. If that is our reason for praying, the praise we get will be our only reward. The Bible gives examples of people leading in public praying and of individuals praying in ways that were visible to others, but sincere people of prayer don't pray in order to get the attention and thus win the praise of others.

The foundation for our praying is a time of private communion with God. The description of a specific place implies that such a personal prayer time ought to be part of our daily lives.

2. Don't pray to get God's attention (vv. 7, 8)

7 But when ye pray, use not vain repetitions, as the heathen do: for they think that they shall be heard for their much speaking.

8 Be not ye therefore like unto them: for your Father knoweth what things ye have need of, before ye ask him.

Heathen prayers assume that the gods either don't know or don't care about human needs and can be moved to act when people repeat certain prayer words. Jesus taught that such praying is heathen because it denies trust in the heavenly Father. We do not need to pray in order to inform God of our needs or to convince Him to care enough to do something about our needs. He already knows and cares.

"Much speaking" does not forbid long prayers. The Bible contains some long prayers. For example, Solomon's prayer of dedication for the temple was long (2 Chron. 6).

"Repetitions" does not forbid persistent praying. Jesus taught persistence in praying. Some of Jesus' parables emphasized that true needs are always expressed over and over (Luke 11:5–8; 18:1–8). A superficial reading of these parables might seem to imply that God is reluctant to heed our prayers and must be persuaded by constant praying on our part. However, Jesus' point is that true prayer, by its very nature, is persistent.

The references to God as Father in Matthew 7:9–11; Luke 11:9–13 reinforce the reference to God as our Father in Matthew 6:8.

Someone may ask, "If God already knows and cares, why do we need to pray at all?" Here are four reasons:

- Many of our greatest needs can only be met when we recognize them and ask God for them. God wants to save all people, but He has made salvation conditioned on our prayers of confession and trust.
- Our greatest ongoing need is communion with God, and prayer is primarily communion with God.
- God has ordained that He uses human prayers to work out His will in the world.
- When we pray, we ourselves are transformed.

II. How to Pray (Matt. 6:9–15)

1. Praise God (vv. 9, 10)

9 After this manner therefore pray ye: Our Father which art in heaven, Hallowed be thy name.

10 Thy kingdom come. Thy will be done in earth, as it is in heaven.

Instead of the proud praying of the hypocrites or the vain babblings of the heathen, how should one pray to the Father who already knows and cares? Jesus answered that question by giving the Model Prayer, usually called the Lord's Prayer.

When we say "our Father," we show that we are part of the family of faith that praises and prays to the same Father. The famous Psalm 23 begins, "The LORD is my Shepherd." God is our Father and my Father. He must be real to each of us; however, we realize that He is near to all who know Him. When we add "which art in heaven," we are acknowledging His infinite greatness and His intimate closeness.

The Model Prayer begins with three petitions in a spirit of praise to our heavenly Father. We pray that His name be glorified, that His kingdom come in all its fullness, and that His will be done on earth as in heaven. Notice that these are not prayers that we be able to glorify Him, bring in His kingdom, and do His will. These are all appropriate prayers; but this prayer is addressed to the only One who can bring these things to pass—whether through human instruments or in some other way.

2. Ask God for what you need (vv. 11–13)

11 Give us this day our daily bread.

12 And forgive us our debts, as we forgive our debtors.

13 And lead us not into temptation, but deliver us from evil: For thine is the kingdom, and the power, and the glory, for ever. Amen.

The second group of three petitions focuses on our own needs. Everyone needs bread. In commenting on Jesus' quotation of Deuteronomy 8:3 in Matthew 4:4, we noted that we do not live by bread alone but we do need bread to live physically. When Jesus ate, He said a prayer (Matt. 14:19). So should we. Because we are dependent on God for all our needs, we express our thanks for bread in the past and our dependence on God for future bread. We do this daily. The trust in this prayer is similar to the trust Jesus advocated as an antidote for anxiety (Matt. 6:25–34).

All of us need forgiveness, even people who have trusted Jesus as Savior (1 John 1:9, 10). Unconfessed sin is unforsaken sin, and it stands as a barrier to our joy in the Lord and our usefulness in His kingdom.

Not only do we sin against God, but also sin against one another. Jesus taught us to seek reconciliation whether the sin is ours (Matt. 5:23, 24) or another's against us (Matt. 18:15–20). Thus, whenever we pray to the Father for His forgiveness, we affirm that we have forgiven those who have sinned against us. As we shall see in verses 14, 15, these two are inseparable.

The third petition has two parts. "Lead us not into evil" may imply that God is the author of temptations to do evil. When we studied the temptations, we noted Matthew 4:1, "Then was Jesus led up of the spirit into the wilderness to be tempted of the devil." In commenting on that verse, we distinguished between two meanings of the same Greek word: test and tempt. The Bible denies that God ever tempts anyone to do evil (James 1:13–15). However, God does allow us to be tested in order to mature in our faith and endurance. The devil, however, seeks to turn each situation in which we are tested into a temptation to do evil.

Thus, the first part of verse 13 may be a request that God honor His promise not to allow us to face tests beyond our capacity to endure (1 Cor. 10:13). We know we are weak, and thus we ask the Father not to subject us to great tests.

Some Bible students think that both parts of the verse express the same prayer in different words. In other words, "lead us not into temptation" is another way of saying, "deliver us from evil." This would be consistent with Hebrew parallelism, in which the same idea is repeated in slightly different words. If so, "lead us not into temptation" means "don't let us fall prey to temptation."

The word *evil* can mean "evil thing" or "evil one." Many translators think Jesus had in mind a prayer to be able to overcome the temptations of the devil. The Bible assumes this can be done, but only as we meet Satan in the power of God (James 4:7; 1 Cor. 10:13; Eph. 6:10–18).

3. Live as you pray (vv. 14, 15)

> **14 For if ye forgive men their trespasses, your heavenly Father will also forgive you:**
>
> **15 But if ye forgive not men their trespasses, neither will your Father forgive your trespasses.**

Our lives must be consistent with our prayers. One example of this principle is seen in verses 14 and 15. These verses emphasize that the two kinds of forgiveness in verse 12 are inseparable. Jesus elaborated on this in the parable of the unforgiving servant, which He told after Peter asked about how often to forgive someone (Matt. 18:21–35). Be careful not to misunderstand what Jesus was teaching. He was not teaching that forgiving others is a good work that merits God forgiving our sins.

His point is that forgiveness is not a one-way street, in which the only direction for forgiveness is from God into our hearts and lives. Forgiveness is like a two-way street in which traffic flows in both directions: from God to us and from us to others. The person who closes His heart in either direction closes it in the other. The person whose heart is open to receive God's forgiveness is also a person who freely offers forgiveness to others. A heart that is closed to forgiveness flowing out is closed to forgiveness flowing in.

SUMMARY OF BIBLE TRUTHS

1. Don't pray in order to be seen and praised by others.
2. Don't pray as if God does not know and care about us.
3. Praise the heavenly Father and ask Him to glorify His name, bring in His kingdom, and accomplish His sovereign will.
4. Ask God for daily bread, forgiveness, and deliverance from evil.
5. The heart that is open to receive God's forgiveness is also open for forgiveness to flow out to others.

APPLYING THE BIBLE

1. The greater work. "Prayer does not fit us for the greater works; prayer is the greater work" (Oswald Chambers).

2. Three facets of prayer. While lecturing on the Sermon on the Mount, David Perkins, New Testament professor, New Orleans Baptist Seminary, said forgiveness is like a three-faceted diamond. First, forgiveness is causative. Because we have been forgiven, we must forgive others. Second, forgiveness is comparative. We are asking God to forgive us just as we forgive others. Third, forgiveness is resultative. If we expect God to forgive us, we must not stop forgiving others.

3. God's go-ahead. Pastor Bill Hybels has an insight on prayer that is easy to remember:

- When I am wrong, God says "grow."
- When the timing is wrong, God says "slow."
- When the request is wrong, God says "no."
- But when I am right, the timing is right, and the request is right, God says "go."[1]

4. Friendship with God. Roberta C. Bondi, author and teacher, says intercessory prayer is based upon our friendship with God. This doesn't mean that God wants what we want, but that we want what God wants. If God's deepest longing is for the well-being of the world, then God wants the well-being of war-torn countries, the homeless, the sick and diseased. We intercede in prayer for these things out of friendship with God.[2]

5. Three elements of prayer. Roberta C. Bondi suggests steps for the individual having difficulty "learning to pray," encouraging them to include three elements in their prayer. (1) Read a favorite Scripture passage as a part of your prayer. The Psalms and many of Paul's letters contain wonderful prayers. (2) Remember that prayer is simply conversation with God in which you really speak your mind. (3) Learn to listen, be silent in God's presence without saying anything.[3]

6. Driven to pray. Jean-Paul Kaufmann, a French journalist, was freed by Muslim terrorists in 1988 after three years in captivity. In an interview, he gave this chilling account.

"It was the second or third day, and I was sitting tied to a chair in a dark room. I felt in that solitude that I had no one to speak to but God. I felt very close to Him then, perhaps because there was no one to distract me. I feel further removed from God now that I am back with my family in comfortable surroundings. In that prison, I was face-to-face with God. I almost miss the luxury of that solitude. I have nostalgia for that intimacy with God. I try to find it now in my house in the country, but the intensity cannot be repeated.

"I knew that God was with me in my ordeal. I can't tell you how I knew, I just did. I felt that He would protect me. I avoided the opportunistic trade of favors: I'll do this for you if you do that for me. I just said to Him, 'Let Your will be done.'"

7. Unusual forms of prayer. Laurence A. Wagley, professor of preaching and worship at Saint Paul School of Theology (United Methodist), in Kansas City, Missouri, characterizes prayer in unusual ways.

- **Listening as prayer.** Listening to music, to the wind in the trees, to the noise of the city may be a form of prayer. "Be still and know that I am God."
- **Prayer as remembering.** The central act of the holiest prayer—the eucharistic prayer—is remembering.
- **Prayer when you can't think of anything else.** This is the prayer of crisis, of panic and trouble. "O God, get me out of this!" Children pray, "God, don't let it happen," or "Don't let it have happened."
- **Prayer to go to sleep by.** This would be characterized by a quiet sense of well-being.
- **Prayer during wasted time or during underutilized time.** Prayer while driving, vacuuming, mowing the lawn, waiting—this is a natural turning to God in which we discover that God has been close all the time.
- **Non-discursive prayer.** Practicing the presence of God without words.

TEACHING THE BIBLE

- *Main Idea:* Jesus taught His disciples how to pray.
- *Suggested Teaching Aim:* To lead adults to identify characteristics of prayer Jesus taught.

A TEACHING OUTLINE

1. *How Not to Pray (Matt. 6:1–8)*
2. *How to Pray (Matt. 6:9–15)*

Introduce the Bible Study

Use number 5, "Three Elements of Prayer," in "Applying the Bible" to introduce the lesson.

Search for Biblical Truth

- Write the following on a chalkboard or a large sheet of paper:

When You Pray	
Don't:	Do:

Ask members to open their Bibles to Matthew 6:1–8 and read these verses silently to find Jesus' teachings on how *not* to pray. List these under *Don't.* Ask members to read different translations of verse 3 to clarify what Jesus was *not* saying. Ask, How can we know that in verse 6 Jesus was not forbidding us to pray in public?

Ask members to read silently Matthew 6:7–8. Using the material in "Studying the Bible," explain Jesus' objection to "much speaking" and "vain repetitions."

IN ADVANCE, on four small strips of paper, copy the four reasons why we need to pray if God already knows and cares. Distribute these to four different people and ask them to read the statement and comment on it.

Ask members to add additional *Don'ts* to the list.

Ask members to read silently Matthew 6:9–15 to find how Jesus said we should pray. List these under *Do* on the chart.

Organize members into three groups and give each group one of the following sets of questions. Allow about five minutes for study and then call for responses. (Use these questions with the entire group if your members do not respond well to groups.)

1. Praise God (Matt. 6:9–10)

Based on the above verses:

- What does praying "Our Father" indicate about our relationship with other believers and God's intimate closeness?
- What does "in heaven" indicate about God's infinite greatness?

2. Ask God for What You Need (Matt. 6:11–13)

Based on the above verses:

- What does the request for physical bread indicate about the relationship of the physical and spiritual?
- What happens if believers do not confess their sins?
- Why does God allow us to be tested?
- How can we overcome the temptations of the devil?

3. Live as You Pray (Matt. 6:14–15)

Based on the above verses:

- What is the relationship between forgiving others and receiving forgiveness?
- Why is forgiving others not a good work that merits God's forgiveness of our sins?

- Can a person who has experienced God's wonderful forgiveness of sin harbor an unforgiving spirit toward another person?

Ask members if they can add any additional *Do's* to the list.

Give the Truth a Personal Focus

Distribute paper and pencils. Ask them to look at the list of *Do's* and *Don'ts* and select one statement from each list that they will covenant to work on this week. Close by sharing illustration No. 6, "Driven to Pray," in "Applying the Bible."

---

1. Bill Hybels, *Too Busy Not to Pray.*
2. "Learning to Pray: An Interview with Roberta C. Bondi," *The Christian Century,* March 20, 1996, 326.
3. Ibid.

January

16

2000

Miracles of Compassion

Background Passage: Matthew 9:18–38
Focal Passages: Matthew 9:18–31, 35, 36

Miracles were a prominent feature of Jesus' ministry. Many were acts of compassion designed to help desperate people. Many of these people were not treated with compassion by anyone but Jesus. Because Jesus saw all life as valuable, He acted with compassion toward the dying and their families, toward the chronically ill, toward the unclean, and toward people with disabilities.

Study Aim: *To resolve to act with compassion that affirms the value of all people and human life.*

STUDYING THE BIBLE

OUTLINE AND SUMMARY

I. Miracles That Helped Desperate People (Matt. 9:18–34)

1. A distraught father (9:18, 19)

2. A seriously ill woman 9:20–22)

3. Grieving parents (9:23–26)

4. Two blind men (9:27–31)

5. A demoniac who could not speak (9:32–34)

II. Ministry of Compassion (Matt. 9:35–38)

When a distraught father asked Jesus to come because his daughter was all but dead, Jesus followed him (vv. 18, 19). Jesus healed a seriously ill woman who showed her faith by touching His clothes (vv. 20–22). Jesus called a dead girl back to life (vv. 23–26). He opened the eyes of two blind men in response to their bold faith (vv. 27–31). When Jesus cast a demon out of a man, the man was able to speak (vv. 32–34). Jesus' ministry was motivated by His compassion for people, whom He saw as shepherdless sheep and as a vast harvest field with few harvesters (vv. 35–38).

I. Miracles That Helped Desperate People (Matt. 9:18–34)

1. A distraught father (vv. 18, 19)

18 While he spake these things unto them, behold, there came a certain ruler, and worshipped him, saying, My daughter is even now dead: but come and lay thy hand upon her, and she shall live.

19 And Jesus arose, and followed him, and so did his disciples.

You may want to read Mark 5:21–43 and Luke 8:40–56, the longer accounts of the two miracles of Matthew 9:18–26. From them, we learn that the name of the ruler was Jairus, and that he was a ruler of the synagogue. Only Matthew, however, tells us that the ruler worshiped Jesus as he made his request.

The exact time of the daughter's death is not clear. Our translation of Matthew 9:18 has the ruler tell Jesus, "My daughter is even now dead." But "is even now dead" could be translated "has just come to the point of death." This is similar to "lieth at the point of death" in Mark 5:23. The ruler felt that she was dead or as good as dead. He thus showed great faith in asking Jesus to help someone caught in the clutches of death.

Notice that Matthew uses the word "followed" to describe Jesus' response. This is the same word that Jesus used to call people to become His disciples. Now in response to the desperation and faith of this father, "Jesus arose, and followed him."

2. A seriously ill woman (vv. 20–22)

20 And, behold, a woman, which was diseased with an issue of blood twelve years, came behind him, and touched the hem of his garment:

21 For she said within herself, If I may but touch his garment, I shall be whole.

22 But Jesus turned him about, and when he saw her, he said, Daughter, be of good comfort; thy faith hath made thee whole. And the woman was made whole from that hour.

Matthew tells us that the woman had been losing blood for twelve years. Mark 5:26 adds, she "had suffered many things of many physicians, and had spent all that she had, and was nothing bettered, but rather grew worse." We also know from Leviticus 15:25–27 that her condition made her ceremonially unclean.

When she heard that Jesus was near, she joined the crowd following Him. She was reluctant to get in front of Him and make her request. Therefore, she came up with the plan to touch His garment, hoping that the touch might heal her. The form of her words in verse 21 had more uncertainty than the translation reveals. Yet even so, hers was amazing faith to dare to hope that merely touching His clothes could heal her.

Mark 5:30–34 elaborates on what happened when she touched the hem of His garment. He asked who had touched Him. Jesus had felt power flow from Him. The frightened woman confessed that she had touched Him. Matthew and Mark both tell how Jesus calmed the woman's fears and assured her that her faith had healed her. The healing coincided with the time of her touch of faith.

3. Grieving parents (vv. 23–26)

23 And when Jesus came into the ruler's house, and saw the minstrels and the people making a noise,

24 He said unto them, Give place: for the maid is not dead, but sleepeth. And they laughed him to scorn.

25 But when the people were put forth, he went in, and took her by the hand, and the maid arose.

26 And the fame hereof went abroad into all that land.

Many of Jesus' most important opportunities to help people might have appeared to others to be interruptions. Matthew 9:18 has the ruler coming to Jesus while He was teaching. The woman had interrupted Jesus on His urgent mission to the ruler's house. We can only imagine how Jairus was feeling during this delay in getting to the bedside of his little girl.

As Jesus approached the house, He heard the familiar sounds of a first-century Jewish mourning for the dead. The custom was for the bereaved family to hire flute players, who played sad music, and mourners, who wailed loudly. Even a poor family was expected to hire at least two flute players and one woman wailer. As a prominent person, Jairus probably had more than one professional mourner.

All this sounded like "noise" to Jesus. "Give place" means "leave" or "get out." He told the professional mourners to leave because He claimed the dead girl was not dead, but sleeping. What happened next showed the superficiality of the pretended mourning. They laughed at Jesus and His words. His response was to force them to leave. This is the meaning of the rather mild translation "the people were put forth."

Then Jesus went in and brought the dead child back to life. This was His intended meaning of the words "not dead, but sleepeth." Jesus was not denying that she was really dead, for she was. Neither was He implying anything about the state of the dead as some kind of suspended animation or soul sleep. He was saying that from God's point of view, the condition of the dead is not hopeless and lifeless. The person who is literally asleep will wake up. Jesus was saying that in the same way, He had the power to overcome death and cause the dead to live.

The Gospels give three examples of Jesus recalling dead people to life: Jairus's daughter, the only son of the widow of Nain (Luke 7:11–17), and Lazarus (John 11:1–44). Each of these miracles was a restoration to physical life. These victories over death foreshadowed the unique resurrection of Jesus Himself. Jesus was not just restored to physical life, later to die. He conquered death once and for all. He has dominion over death and is alive forever. And because He lives, those who know Him as Lord and Savior will live also.

4. Two blind men (vv. 27–31)

27 And when Jesus departed thence, two blind men followed him, crying, and saying, Thou Son of David, have mercy on us.

28 And when he was come into the house, the blind men came to him: and Jesus saith unto them, Believe ye that I am able to do this? They said unto him, Yea, Lord.

29 Then touched he their eyes, saying, According to your faith be it unto you.

30 And their eyes were opened; and Jesus straitly charged them, saying, See that no man know it.

31 But they, when they were departed, spread abroad his fame in all that country.

The distraught ruler, his grieving wife, and the seriously ill woman were all in desperate conditions. So were these two blind men. Like the ruler and the woman, these two came to Jesus. As they groped along following Jesus, they cried out loudly for all to hear as they asked Jesus to show mercy on them.

Jesus acted as if He had not heard them. He continued on His way and entered the house. The blind men were made bold by their desperate plight and by their faith. We wonder why Jesus did not stop as soon as they cried out. We cannot fathom the ways of the Lord, but His words to them give two strong clues to His reasons.

1. He asked them if they really believed. Thus, His failure to respond immediately seems to have tested the reality of their faith. After they both assured Jesus, whom they called "Lord," that they truly believed, Jesus touched their eyes. "According to your faith" means "in response to your faith." His healing touch and authoritative word opened the eyes of these two blind men.

2. The other reason for His reluctance is seen in His strong command to the two men not to tell others what had happened. Such commands were common during Jesus' public ministry. These puzzle many people in light of the commands after His resurrection to tell everyone. The most likely explanation for Jesus telling people not to spread the word about His miracles was the distorted expectation of many first-century Jews concerning the Messiah. Many were looking for an earthly king, who would use divine power to establish Himself and restore Israel to its lost glory.

These two men had called Jesus "Son of David," a favorite title for the Messiah and one that often expected the "Son of David" to restore the glory of Israel under David. Jesus did not want to become known primarily as a worker of miracles because it would feed that false expectation. This false expectation made it all the more difficult for Jesus to fulfill His real role as King and Suffering Servant.

5. A demoniac who could not speak (vv. 32–34)

When Jesus cast a demon out of a man who could not speak, the man was able to speak (vv. 32, 33a). The people were amazed, but the Pharisees accused Jesus of performing this miracle with Satan's help (vv. 33b, 34).

II. Ministry of Compassion (Matt. 9:35–38)

35 And Jesus went about all the cities and villages, teaching in their synagogues, and preaching the gospel of the kingdom, and healing every sickness and every disease among the people.

36 But when he saw the multitudes, he was moved with compassion on them, because they fainted, and were scattered abroad, as sheep having no shepherd.

Matthew 9:35 repeats Matthew 4:23. In between are examples of each of three aspects of Jesus' ministry, especially His teachings and His miracles.

Verse 36 is a transition verse. It sums up the motive for what Jesus had done and what He was about to do. "Compassion" means to be so deeply moved with concern for others that one takes action to help. Jesus looked at the crowds and was moved with compassion because they were like sheep without a shepherd. "Fainted" means "harassed," and "scattered abroad" means "helpless." Jesus was concerned because He was the Shepherd from whom they had strayed.

Jesus also compared the spiritual needs of people to a vast harvest field. He challenged the Twelve to pray that the Lord of the harvest would send forth workers into the field (vv. 37, 38).

First-century Gentiles placed little value on human life. Abortion and child exposure, for example, were common. Even Jews often ignored people who were chronically ill, who had disabilities, or who were considered unclean. They offered little real hope for the dying and for the bereaved. By contrast, Jesus, who was moved with compassion toward all people, acted to give love, hope, and help to all. Thus, this is an appropriate lesson for Sanctity of Human Life Sunday.

PRONUNCIATION GUIDE

Jairus	[JIGH ruhs]
Lazarus	[LAZ uh ruhs]

SUMMARY OF BIBLE TRUTHS

1. Affirm the value of all human life by acts of compassion.
2. Help the helpless and hopeless.
3. Show compassion on the dying and their families.
4. Help the bereaved find hope.
5. Take time for the chronically ill.
6. Treat people who have disabilities with respect and love.

APPLYING THE BIBLE

1. The power of compassion. When you think about compassion, you generally think of people who give themselves away to others like obscure missionaries, teachers committed to the inner cities, and relief workers who labor for little in return. No one usually thinks about rock and roll stars. Yet in 1984 at the height of the Ethiopian famine, a British rocker named Bob Geldof was moved to raise nearly 72,000 British pounds ($100,000 in U.S. currency) after watching the evening news. He did this in only a very few months and in the process motivated American musicians to sponsor a similar event. Millions of dollars became available to feed hungry people a world away all because somebody did something.

What motivated Bob Geldof was compassion. He saw a need, and he did what he could to meet it. If today's church would only demonstrate half of the compassion for the lost and hurting of our world as Geldof did, our world would be in much better shape.

2. Funeral customs. Tennessee Williams wrote, "Funerals are pretty compared with death."[1] He may well have considered the funeral customs of Jesus' day. A little girl lay dead, and while nothing was pretty about that, custom demanded that professional mourners be hired. The shallowness of the funeral demonstrates the compassion of Jesus. He saw the meaningless rut we were in and came to change it.

3. Evidence of compassion. One day a student asked anthropologist Margaret Mead for the earliest sign of civilization in a given culture. He expected the answer to be a clay pot or perhaps a fish hook or grinding stone. Her answer was, "A healed femur." Mead explained that no healed femurs are found where the law of the jungle, survival of the fittest, reigns. A healed femur shows that someone cared. Someone had to do that injured person's hunting and gathering until the leg healed. The evidence of compassion is the first sign of civilization.[2]

4. How to cultivate compassion:

- Practice kindness and grace while driving in rush hour this week.
- Become a volunteer in a homeless shelter for one night during the holidays this year.
- Do something compassionate for a family who is watching a loved one die.
- Write a "thinking of you" card on the death anniversary to encourage a widow.
- Adopt a nursing home resident and visit this person once a month for the coming year.
- Start looking for people with disabilities and become a servant to them in some small way.

5. Setting an example:

- Be responsive to the needs of your child. Feeling cared for makes a child feel secure and connected to other people, so that he or she, in turn, can care for others.
- Encourage your child to be helpful to others. When a child helps out and realizes how good she has made others feel, she will feel satisfied and will begin to see herself as a helpful person.
- When your child begins to say or do something mean, explain how these behaviors make others feel, and gently remind him of a time when someone hurt him.
- Make a habit of extending common courtesy and respect to others, strangers included. For instance, let a driver who needs to turn onto the main road pull in front of you, or help an elderly person manage her cart at the supermarket. Let your children see you taking time for others in a non-resentful way.
- Demonstrate a strong sense of honesty. Don't say, "Tell her I'm not here," when the phone is for you.
- Praise good and kind behavior . . . and praise it again.[3]

6. Compassion fatigue. For those who feel they have given too much, there is a trendy new ailment that has been diagnosed. Just when we thought there were no more excuses, someone has coined the phrase "compassion fatigue." Anna Quindlen says, "People sometimes suffer from compassion fatigue when they are overwhelmed at the needs and hurts of people, such as competing tragedies, breast cancer, heart disease, homelessness, hunger, famine, domestic crime, teenage pregnancy, rape, and addicted babies. Compassion fatigue is the result of not knowing who to help first."[4] The danger of compassion fatigue is that soon, overwhelmed by it all, no one will be helped at all.

TEACHING THE BIBLE

- *Main Idea:* Jesus' compassion affirmed the value of all people and human life.
- *Suggested Teaching Aim:* To lead adults to identify persons to whom they can show compassion.

A TEACHING OUTLINE

1. *Miracles that Helped Desperate People (Matt. 9:18–34)*
2. *Ministry of Compassion (Matt. 9:35–38)*

Introduce the Bible Study

Use number 3, "Evidence of Compassion," in "Applying the Bible" to introduce the lesson.

Search for Biblical Truth

IN ADVANCE, on separate strips of paper write each of the following:

How do you think . . .

. . . Jairus felt when he came to Jesus? (1)
. . . Jesus felt about Jairus's request? (2)
. . . the crowd felt when Jesus followed Jairus? (3)
. . . the seriously ill woman felt? (4)
. . . Jairus felt as Jesus delayed to help the woman? (5)
. . . the mourners felt when Jesus told them the girl was sleeping? (6)
. . . Jairus and his wife felt when Jesus gave them their daughter? (7)
. . . the blind men felt when they heard Jesus was coming? (8)
. . . the blind men felt when Jesus ignored them? (9)
. . . the blind men felt when Jesus healed them? (10)
. . . Jesus felt when He went to bed at night and knew there were people still in pain whom His power could have healed? (11)

How do you feel when you encounter a need? (12)

Place the heading on the wall and call on the person you have enlisted **IN ADVANCE** to read all of the Scripture at this point. Place the first question under the heading and ask members to respond. Using the material in "Studying the Bible," explain who Jairus was.

Place the second poster under the first poster. Ask, Do you think Jesus ever got tired of people coming to Him for help?

Place the third poster on the wall. Ask, Was the crowd surprised to see Jesus follow this man?

Place the fourth poster on the wall. Use the material in "Studying the Bible" to explain how isolating this woman's disease was and why she was reluctant to confront Jesus openly for healing.

Place the fifth question on the wall and ask members to respond.

Place the sixth question on the wall. Use the material in "Studying the Bible" to explain the role of professional mourners.

Place the seventh question on the wall and ask members to respond to how Jairus and his wife felt.

Place the eighth poster on the wall and ask members to respond.

Place the ninth poster on the wall and ask members to respond. Use the material in "Studying the Bible" to explain why Jesus may not have responded immediately.

Place the tenth poster on the wall and ask members to respond by using only one word.

Place the eleventh poster on the wall and ask members to respond.

Give the Truth a Personal Focus

Read the six "Summary of Bible Truths" statements. Begin by saying, "This lesson teaches us that we . . . ." Tape the twelfth poster on the wall over the rest of the statements and ask members to respond to that question in light of the lesson. Ask members to identify persons to whom they can show compassion this week.

---

1. Tennessee Williams, *A Streetcar Named Desire,* 1947.
2. R. Wayne Willis, Louisville, Kentucky.
3. Laurie Tarkan, "Teaching Kids Compassion," *Good Housekeeping,* Oct. 1996, 166.
4. Anna Quindlen, *Redbook,* May 1994, 38.

January

23

2000

Opposition to Jesus

Background Passage: Matthew 12:22–45
Focal Passages: Matthew 12:22–32, 38–40

Jesus was moved with compassion when He saw the crowds, but the religious leaders were moved with jealous rage when they saw Jesus. They saw Him as a threat to their positions. They were frustrated by their attempts to discredit Him in the eyes of the people. Therefore, their attacks became more vicious and reckless.

Study Aim: *To describe two examples of opposition to Jesus and how He responded to each.*

STUDYING THE BIBLE

OUTLINE AND SUMMARY

I. Accusing Jesus of Using Satan's Power (Matt. 12:22–37)
1. **Reckless accusation (12:22–24)**
2. **Miracles wrought by the Spirit's power (12:25–29)**
3. **No neutrals in the cosmic struggle (12:30)**
4. **The unpardonable sin (12:31, 32)**
5. **Warning of judgment (12:33–37)**

II. Demanding That Jesus Give Them a Sign (Matt. 12:38–45)
1. **Request for a sign (12:38)**
2. **Sign of Jonah (12:39–42)**
3. **Danger of spiritual emptiness (12:43–45)**

After Jesus performed an exorcism, the Pharisees accused Him of using Satan's power (vv. 22–24). Jesus said that God's Spirit, not Satan, was at war with evil (vv. 25–29). In this cosmic struggle, one is either with Jesus or against Him (v. 30). He warned the Pharisees about a sin for which there is no pardon (vv. 31, 32). Judgment is sure on evil hearts, which overflow with evil fruit and evil words (vv. 33–37). The Pharisees asked Jesus to show them a sign (v. 38). He warned against demanding signs and told them that the only sign would be that of Jonah (vv. 39–42). An empty heart or life will be filled by evil if not by God (vv. 43–45).

I. Accusing Jesus of Using Satan's Power (Matt. 12:22–37)

1. Reckless accusation (vv. 22–24)

22 Then was brought unto him one possessed with a devil, blind, and dumb: and he healed him, insomuch that the blind and dumb both spake and saw.

23 And all the people were amazed, and said, Is not this the son of David?

24 But when the Pharisees heard it, they said, This fellow doth not cast out devils, but by Beelzebub the prince of the devils.

The man's basic problem was that he was possessed by a demon. In his case, this problem was accompanied by the man's inability to see or to hear. When Jesus exorcised the demon, the man was able to speak and see. The astonished people wondered if Jesus might be the Messiah (son of David) for whom they were looking.

The angry Pharisees could not deny that a miracle had taken place; therefore, they made a reckless charge against Jesus in an attempt to discredit Jesus in the eyes of the people. They accused Jesus of casting out the demon by the power of Beelzebub. Explanations for the derivation of the name vary, but the name means "lord of the flies" and became another name for Satan, who was the prince of evil spirits.

2. Miracles wrought by the Spirit's power (vv. 25–29)

25 And Jesus knew their thoughts, and said unto them, Every kingdom divided against itself is brought to desolation; and every city or house divided against itself shall not stand:

26 And if Satan cast out Satan, he is divided against himself; how shall then his kingdom stand?

27 And if I by Beelzebub cast out devils, by whom do your children cast them out? therefore they shall be your judges.

Jesus began His response with an obvious fact of human life and history. When a nation engages in a civil war, the result is the desolation of the country. When a city is divided into warring factions or a family is divided by infighting, the city or the family cannot survive as a healthy functioning unit of society. By the same token, Satan's domain cannot survive if Satan wages war against himself by casting out some of his evil forces. Therefore, the charge that Satan would help Jesus or anyone else cast out demons makes absolutely no sense.

Some of the Pharisees were exorcists who claimed they had power to cast out evil spirits. Jesus asked if they also were using Satan's power to perform exorcisms. If Jesus was casting out demons by Satan's power, it was only logical to assume that all exorcists also relied on the devil's power. The Pharisees certainly were not willing to make such a charge against their own.

28 But if I cast out devils by the Spirit of God, then the kingdom of God is come unto you.

29 Or else how can one enter into a strong man's house, and spoil his goods, except he first bind the strong man? and then he will spoil his house.

Jesus then forced His attackers to face the logical answer to the question, "By what power does Jesus cast out demons?" If Jesus did not rely on Satan for His power, He relied on the power of the Holy Spirit—the true enemy of Satan. If He was casting out demons by the Spirit's power, then this was one of many signs that the kingdom of God had come.

Verse 29 uses a human analogy to reinforce Christ as the victor over Satan. If a strong man's house is robbed while the strong man is at home, the intruder must overcome and render helpless the strong man. In this short illustration, Satan is the strong man; and Jesus is the One who overcomes and binds the strong man.

This passage deals with three important Bible doctrines: the Holy Spirit, Christ's victory over Satan, and the kingdom of God.

1. In earlier lessons in Matthew, we saw the Spirit's work in the miraculous conception (1:20), One who would baptize with the Holy Spirit (3:11), when Jesus was baptized (3:16), and the temptations (4:1). The Spirit was the power by which Jesus cast out demons.

2. Jesus' work is portrayed as a victory over Satan. His victory over temptation was part of this victory (Matt. 4:11). Casting out demons was a sign of His victory. His death and resurrection delivered mortal blows to Satan (John 12:31; Heb. 2:14, 15).

3. The kingdom of God was revealed in Jesus' coming, life, death, and resurrection. Jesus also taught His followers to pray, "Thy kingdom come" (Matt. 6:10). The kingdom of God came in Jesus Christ's victory over Satan, sin, and death; however, the consummation of that kingdom has not yet taken place.

3. No neutrals in the cosmic struggle (v. 30)

30 He that is not with me is against me; and he that gathereth not with me scattereth abroad.

Verses 22–29 make clear that a cosmic struggle was raging during Jesus' ministry. The rest of the New Testament makes clear that the struggle continues. Satan has received a mortal blow that dooms him and all who follow him; but like a mortally wounded animal, he viciously attacks everything in sight (1 Pet. 5:8). In such a cosmic struggle between God and Satan, no one can be neutral. Those who claim to be neutral are actually on Satan's side. This is the point of the strong words of Jesus in verse 30.

In Matthew 9:36–38, Jesus used two analogies to describe His work and that of His followers. He is the Good Shepherd who seeks the lost sheep who are scattered. He calls His followers to pray for workers in a vast harvest field. The words *gathereth* and *scattereth abroad* may reflect either of these. If we are not helping gather in the scattered flock or engaged in gathering in the vast harvest, we are not really with Christ; for these are His priorities. And if we are not with Him, we are against Him.

4. The unpardonable sin (vv. 31, 32)

31 Wherefore I say unto you, All manner of sin and blasphemy shall be forgiven unto men: but the blasphemy against the Holy Ghost shall not be forgiven unto men.

32 And whosoever speaketh a word against the Son of man, it shall be forgiven him: but whosoever speaketh against the Holy Ghost, it shall not be forgiven him, neither in this world, neither in the world to come.

By focusing exclusively on the unpardonable sin in this passage, we often fail to notice the promises of forgiveness of all other sins. Except for this one sin, "all manner of sin and blasphemy shall be forgiven unto men." This includes words spoken against the Son of man. Jesus prayed on the cross for those who crucified Him (Luke 23:34). The heart of God yearns to forgive sinners; only when people make that impossible is God unable to forgive.

Considerable discussion swirls around what Jesus meant by the sin that "shall not be forgiven." Whatever it was, it was committed by people opposed to Jesus, not His followers. It also had to do with rejecting God's revelation in Christ as signified by the power of God's Spirit.

The most narrow interpretation limits the unpardonable sin to attributing the work of the Holy Spirit to Satan. This was how the sin was expressed in this specific situation. However, many people see this as only one expression of a broader sin—that of persistently rejecting God's revelation of Himself in Christ as the Spirit convicts people of sin and seeks to point them to Jesus.

This broader interpretation is consistent with other Bible passages. After all, the work of the Spirit is to glorify Christ, not call attention to Himself (John 16:13, 14). Persistently refusing to believe in Christ in the full light of God's revelation is to choose darkness rather than light (John 3:17–21; 9:37–41). The Pharisees knew that Jesus was God's Son; yet they rejected Him in the full light of that knowledge. Thus, the unpardonable sin is refusing God's offer of pardon.

5. Warning of judgment (vv. 33–37)

The human heart is the source of evil, and those whose hearts are evil bear evil fruit in their lives and speak evil words with their tongues (vv. 33–35). Such evil people will not escape sure judgment for their evil hearts, lives, and words (vv. 36, 37).

II. Demanding That Jesus Give Them a Sign (Matt. 12:38–45)

1. Request for a sign (v. 38)

38 Then certain of the scribes and of the Pharisees answered, saying, Master, we would see a sign from thee.

A "sign" was different from an ordinary miracle. There were a number of miracle workers around, but the Pharisees requested a sure sign from heaven that Jesus was who He claimed to be.

2. Sign of Jonah (vv. 39–42)

39 But he answered and said unto them, An evil and adulterous generation seeketh after a sign; and there shall no sign be given to it, but the sign of the prophet Jonas:

40 For as Jonas was three days and three nights in the whale's belly; so shall the Son of man be three days and three nights in the heart of the earth.

Demanding that Jesus prove Himself by a special sign from heaven is evidence of the arrogant unbelief of the people who make such a demand. Jesus labeled the sign seekers "an evil and adulterous generation." Jesus knew that their hearts were so evil that they would not accept a sign, even if it were given. (For examples, see Luke 16:31; John 11:46–53; Matt. 28:11–15.)

This was in fact the only sign Jesus said they would be given—the sign of Jonah (Jonas). Jesus' reference to Jonah and the great fish foreshadowed the death, burial, and resurrection of Jesus. Sinners today have the word of this good news brought to bear on their hearts by the Spirit. Sadly, many reject as did so many in Jesus' day.

Repentant sinners of earlier generations will condemn those who reject the full revelation of God in Christ. These will include the evil people of pagan Nineveh who repented at the preaching of a reluctant Jonah and the queen of Sheba who came to see the wisdom of Solomon. Jonah and Solomon were pale shadows of the One who is so much greater than any other (vv. 41, 42).

3. Danger of spiritual emptiness (vv. 43–45)

Jesus compared that evil generation to a person who had gotten rid of one evil spirit only to have that spirit return along with seven worse spirits. A person or a nation must do more than get rid of its evils. An empty heart will soon be invaded by old and new evils unless God is allowed into a cleansed heart and life.

PRONUNCIATION GUIDE

Beelzebub	[bee EL zee buhb]
Nineveh	[NIN uh vuh]
Sheba	[SHEE bah]

SUMMARY OF BIBLE TRUTHS

1. Jesus, the Son of God, has power over evil.
2. Casting out demons was one sign of Jesus' victory over Satan.
3. The miracles of Jesus were signs of the coming of God's kingdom.
4. Stubborn resistance to the Spirit makes a person unpardonable.
5. One evidence of a hardened heart is a demand for God to give a special sign.
6. Stubborn unbelief would not be changed even if a sign were given.

APPLYING THE BIBLE

1. Jealousy and jaundice. John Dryden called jealousy the "jaundice of the soul."[1] Those who oppose Jesus do so because they are spiritually jaundiced.

2. Too much self-love. In jealousy there is more self-love than love.[2] The opposition to Jesus comes from those who are drowning in self-love. They oppose Jesus to protect their own interest, not for their love for God.

3. Hardened hearts. In the devotional classic *My Utmost for His Highest* Oswald Chambers says, "Never try to explain God until you have obeyed him." The hardened hearts of the Pharisees were evidence that they had not obeyed God with the matters of the heart. Not only could they not explain Him; they couldn't recognize Him in the person of His Son.

4. Wrong signs. The signs that people want from God are usually spectacular signs, not the signs that speak to the heart about the person of Christ. Woody Allen may well summarize an entire generation of sign seekers when he says, "If only God would give me some clear sign! Like making a large deposit in my name at a Swiss bank."

5. John's seven signs. The Gospel of John records seven signs of Jesus, each one intended to demonstrate something of Jesus' character.

Sign	Demonstration
Changing water into wine	Jesus is the source of our joy
Healing a nobleman's son	Jesus is the source of our hope
Healing a lame man	Jesus is the source of our strength
Feeding 5,000 with a boy's lunch	Jesus is the supplier of our deepest need
Calming a storm	Jesus is the source of our courage
Healing a man born blind	Jesus is the source of our vision
Raising Lazarus from the dead	Jesus is the source of our life

God had given all the signs necessary, especially to those who knew the Hebrew Scriptures, but they refused to believe.

6. Don't miss the signs. When we miss the signs that are intended for our good, three things can happen: (1) We do not arrive at our desired destination; we are lost instead. (2) We are in danger of getting hurt; signs warn us of danger. (3) We will live with regret; missing a sign always has consequences.

TEACHING THE BIBLE

- *Main Idea:* People who did not want to accept Jesus opposed Him.
- *Suggested Teaching Aim:* To lead adults to accept Jesus rather than oppose Him.

A TEACHING OUTLINE

Accusing Jesus of Using Satan's Power (Matt. 12:22–37)
Reckless accusation (vv. 22–24)
Miracles wrought by the Spirit's power (vv. 25–29)
No neutrals in the cosmic struggle (v. 30)
The unpardonable sin (vv. 31–32)
Warning of judgment (vv. 33–37)
Demanding That Jesus Give Them a Sign (Matt. 12:38–45)
Request for a sign (v. 38)
Sign of Jonah (vv. 39–42)
Danger of spiritual emptiness (vv. 43–45)

Introduce the Bible Study

Use number 3, "Hardened Hearts," in "Applying the Bible" to introduce the lesson.

Search for Biblical Truth

IN ADVANCE, enlist a member to read aloud the summary statements in "Outline and Summary" to overview the Scripture passages. Call for the reading now.

Present a lecture, using the material in "Studying the Bible." Copy the above outline on strips of paper or write it on a chalkboard. Place the first point ("I. Accusing Jesus of Using Satan's Power [Matt. 12:22–27]") and the first subpoint ("1. Reckless accusation [vv. 22–24]") on the focal wall. **IN ADVANCE,** enlist a member to read the Scripture. Ask for Matthew 12:22–24 to be read at this time. Lecture briefly:

- Jesus healed a man possessed with a devil, and the people were amazed.
- The Pharisees accused Jesus of casting the demon out by using Beelzebub's power.
- Place the second subpoint on the wall ("2. Miracles wrought by the Spirit's power [vv. 25–29]"). Ask for this Scripture to be read aloud. Lecture briefly on these points:
- When a nation engages in a civil war, the result is a desolation of the country.
- Likewise, Satan's domain could not survive if Satan fought against himself.
- If Jesus cast out demons by Satan's power, all the exorcists must also rely on that power; the Pharisees were unwilling to admit that.
- Jesus used God's Spirit to cast out demons; this proves God's kingdom has come.
- Comment briefly on the three important Bible doctrines in this passage: (1) the Holy Spirit, (2) Christ's victory over Satan, and (3) the kingdom of God.

Place the third subpoint on the wall ("3. No neutrals in the cosmic struggle [v. 30]") and lecture briefly:

- No one can be neutral in this struggle between good and evil.
- Write on a chalkboard: *Not to choose is to choose* and ask members to respond.
- How can we know whose side we are on? If we are not helping gather in the scattered flock or the vast harvest (Matt. 9:36–38), we are not really with Christ.

Place the fourth subpoint on the wall ("4. The unpardonable sin [vv. 31–32]") and ask the reader to read verses 31–32. Lecture briefly:

- Emphasize that these verses contain the promise to forgive all sin but one.
- The heart of God yearns to forgive sinners; only when people make that impossible is God unable to forgive.
- Present the narrow and broad interpretations of the unpardonable sin.

Place the second main point ("II. Demanding That Jesus Give Them a Sign [Matt. 12:38–45]") and the first subpoint ("1. Request for a sign [v. 38]") on the wall. Ask the reader to read verse 38; explain how a sign differs from a miracle.

Place the second subpoint ("2. Sign of Jonah [vv. 39–42]") on the wall and ask the reader to read verses 39–40. Lecture briefly:

- Demanding a sign indicates arrogant unbelief.
- Share number 4, "Wrong Signs," in "Applying the Bible."
- What the sign of Jonah would reveal to all people.

Place the third subpoint on the wall ("3. Danger of spiritual emptiness [vv. 43–45]") and ask the reader to read these verses. Summarize these verses by saying: "An empty heart will soon be invaded by old and new evils unless God is allowed into a cleansed heart and life."

Give the Truth a Personal Focus

Read each of the six "Summary of Bible Truths" and ask, What relationship does this truth have to our lives?

---

1. John Dryden, "The Hind and the Panther" [1687], pt. III, l. 73.
2. François, Duc de La Rochefoucauld.

January

30

2000

Laborers in the Vineyard

Background Passage: Matthew 19:16–20:16

Focal Passage: Matthew 20:1–16

The laborers in the vineyard is one of the most difficult parables to understand. Evidence of this is seen in the many and varied interpretations of Jesus' story. The problem in Matthew 20:1–16 is why the employer paid all his workers the same, no matter how long they worked, and what this has to do with the saying that the last will be first, and the first, last.

Study Aim: *To explain the parable of the laborers in the vineyard.*

STUDYING THE BIBLE

OUTLINE AND SUMMARY

I. Renouncing All to Follow Jesus (Matt. 19:16–30)
 1. The young man's refusal (19:16–22)
 2. Who then can be saved? (19:23–26)
 3. Rewards for renunciation (19:27–30)

II. Parable of the Laborers in the Vineyard (Matt. 20:1–16)
 1. A parable of the kingdom (20:1–7)
 2. Grumbling about pay (20:8–12)
 3. The owner's fairness and generosity (20:13–16)

The young man refused to give up his riches and depend on God (19:16–22). Jesus said that the rich cannot be saved by human means, but only by God's grace and power (19:23–26). When Peter asked about their reward, Jesus described divine blessings but added a word of caution (19:27–30). Jesus told of a vineyard keeper who hired workers at five different times during the day, promising the first group a denarius (20:1–7). When the last group was paid a denarius, the first group grumbled (20:8–12). The employer said that he had acted fairly, freely, and generously (20:13–16).

I. Renouncing All to Follow Jesus (Matt. 19:16–30)

1. The young man's refusal (19:16–22)

A young man asked Jesus what good thing he could do to inherit eternal life (19:16). When Jesus spoke to him about the Commandments, the man claimed to have kept them (19:17–20). Jesus challenged him to sell everything and give it to the poor (19:21). The young man had many possessions and was not willing to give them up in order to follow Jesus (19:22).

2. Who then can be saved? (19:23–26)

Jesus told the disciples that it is humanly impossible for a rich man to be saved (19:23, 24). The surprised disciples asked, "Who then can be saved?" (19:25). Jesus said that the rich person can be saved only by the grace and power of God (19:26).

3. Rewards for renunciation (19:27–30)

Noting the disciple's renunciation of all things to follow Jesus, Peter asked, "What shall we have therefore?" (19:27). Jesus gave a twofold answer to Peter's question: First, Jesus assured the disciples that their renunciation would result in divine blessings (19:28, 29). Second, Jesus warned, "Many that are first shall be last; and the last shall be first" (19:30).

II. Parable of the Laborers in the Vineyard (Matt. 20:1–16)

1. A parable of the kingdom (20:1–7)

1 For the kingdom of heaven is like unto a man that is an householder, which went out early in the morning to hire labourers into his vineyard.

The parable begins like so many of Jesus' parables in Matthew's Gospel (see 13:24, 44, 45, 47; 25:1). In other words, Jesus told this story to illustrate some reality in our relation to God as our King. As you seek to understand this parable, keep in mind these facts about Jesus' parables.

1. People in Jesus' parables often acted in ways that people normally would not act. The "householder" was a man who owned a house and vineyard. In some ways, he acted like any vineyard owner; but in other ways, Jesus portrayed the man as acting very differently.

2. Most parables were designed to make one point, not to be allegories in which every detail represents something in God's kingdom.

3. The context is the key to many parables. Jesus told this story as an explanation of Matthew 19:30, which was part of His answer to Peter's question about rewards. The repetition of Matthew 19:30 in 20:16 shows this connection between Matthew 19:16–30 and Matthew 20:1–16.

2 And when he had agreed with the labourers for a penny a day, he sent them into his vineyard.

3 And he went out about the third hour, and saw others standing idle in the marketplace,

4 And said unto them; Go ye also into the vineyard, and whatsoever is right I will give you. And they went their way.

5 Again he went out about the sixth and ninth hour, and did likewise.

6 And about the eleventh hour he went out, and found others standing idle, and saith unto them, Why stand ye here all the day idle?

7 They say unto him, Because no man hath hired us. He saith unto them, Go ye also into the vineyard; and whatsoever is right, that shall ye receive.

The Jews defined the first hour of the day as the first hour after sunrise. Thus, the third hour would be about 9:00 A.M. The sixth hour was noon. The ninth hour was about 3:00 P.M. The eleventh hour was about 5:00 P.M.

The vineyard owner began the day as did any man in his position. During harvest season, vineyard owners hired extra workers to pick grapes. Therefore, the man went early to the marketplace where such workers gathered in hope of being hired for the day. He hired workers and promised to pay them a denarius ("penny"), which was a coin equal to pay for a day's work of picking grapes. The workers agreed and went to the vineyard and began working.

For some reason, the vineyard owner returned for more workers four other times during the day. The story does not explain why he did not hire all he needed at the beginning of the day. Jesus built into his story this repeated return in order to make a point about service to God. Jesus' vineyard owner did not act as most owners acted. Most would have hired all they needed at the beginning.

The word translated "idle" means literally "without work" or "unemployed." At times this word is used in the New Testament to mean "lazy" (Titus 1:12), but in Matthew 20:3, 6, "idle" means "unemployed." When the last group was asked why they stood idle all day, they replied, "Because no man hath hired us."

The vineyard owner did not promise to pay the later groups a denarius, as he had the first group. Instead, he told the group at 9:00 A.M. that he would pay them what was right. Apparently he made the same statement to each group hired.

2. Grumbling about pay (20:8–12)

8 So when even was come, the lord of the vineyard saith unto his steward, Call the labourers, and give them their hire, beginning from the last unto the first.

9 And when they came that were hired about the eleventh hour, they received every man a penny.

10 But when the first came, they supposed that they should have received more; and they likewise received every man a penny.

11 And when they had received it, they murmured against the goodman of the house,

12 Saying, These last have wrought but one hour, and thou hast made them equal unto us, which have borne the burden and heat of the day.

Paying this kind of workers at the end of each work day was normal, and the owner instructed his steward to distribute the pay. However, he gave the steward instructions that were not typical of vineyard owners. He told the steward to begin paying the last group first. Normally, the ones longest in the fields would be paid first. The owner also told the steward to pay everyone a denarius. Normally, an owner would pay people based on how long they worked.

Jesus was not giving instructions about how to pay workers. Employees expect to be paid for the work they have done; and if they are hourly employees, they expect to be paid according to the hours worked. Extra work deserves extra pay. Jesus deliberately had this employer pay the last first and pay everyone the same.

Jesus told the story to make a point about God and those who serve Him. In a human situation, the early workers' grievance was predictable and probably justified. However, in our relationship with God, people act sinfully when they insist on getting what they deserve and complaining about what they receive from God. As anyone saved by grace knows, we would be in real trouble if God truly gave us what we deserved. We can be glad that He relates to us with mercy and grace.

3. The owner's fairness and generosity (20:13–16)

13 But he answered one of them, and said, Friend, I do thee no wrong: didst not thou agree with me for a penny?

14 Take that thine is, and go thy way: I will give unto this last, even as unto thee.

15 Is it not lawful for me to do what I will with mine own? Is thine eye evil, because I am good?

16 So the last shall be first, and the first last: for many be called, but few chosen.

The owner's response was directed to one, who apparently was the spokesman for the group. If we assume the owner represents God, his response highlights several facts about God, His relationship to us, and our responses to Him.

God is like Jesus' vineyard owner in at least three ways:

1. Because He is God, He has the right to do whatever He chooses to do. Thus, the vineyard owner insisted that he was free to do as he pleased with what was his.
2. God chooses to be fair or just. This is seen in verse 13. The employer hired the first workers for a denarius, and he paid them what He had promised.
3. God is more than fair; He is generous. He chooses to give more than we deserve. The late workers had trusted the owner's word to do what was right. What he chose to do was to be generous with them.

The early workers were angry at the man who had hired them and begrudged what the man gave so generously to the late workers. An "evil eye" was used at times to refer to looking on someone with malice and evil intent. This may be its meaning in Mark 7:22. At other times, as in Deuteronomy 15:9 and probably in Matthew 6:23, it was used to describe greedy people who begrudged sharing anything of theirs with others. Both ideas may be implied in verse 15 because the early workers were angry with the employer and begrudged his generosity to the late workers.

Some people see their relation with God as a bargain in which God gives them what they deserve. Such people seldom experience His goodness, grace, and generosity. They are too busy complaining if they are not properly rewarded for their service. Peter had not complained, but his question implied that the faithful service of the disciples deserved something special. He had either forgotten or never learned that Christians' relationship with God is based on grace. This applies not only to salvation but also to service.

The only human response to God that enables one to enter the kingdom is a sense of dependence on God. Only the "poor in spirit" enter the kingdom (Matt. 5:3), and only the humble are great in the kingdom (Matt. 20:17–28). The problem with the rich young ruler was that he was unwilling to come to God as a sinner, poor and needy. He wanted to be rewarded for his obedience to the Commandments. When Jesus placed him in a situation in which he would have to trust God completely, he was unwilling to do that.

Peter left all to follow Christ, but he continued to harbor worldly ideas about prominence in the kingdom. Jesus was reminding him that although faithfulness results in blessings, these are not rewards for what Peter had done; they are gifts of God's grace. Thus, "blessings" is a better word than "rewards," which implies that we deserve the rewards because of what we have done.

Peter and the disciples thought of themselves as "first." Matthew 20:17–28 shows that they often argued among themselves about which of them was first or greatest. People who assume that rewards are based on human merit grumble against God and struggle with others in a competitive way for prominence in the kingdom. Jesus told this story to show that anyone who considers himself "first" for these mistaken reasons will be disappointed. Those who are willing to place themselves "last" in prominence by humble, self-giving service are "first" in God's eyes.

PRONUNCIATION GUIDE

denarius [dee NAHR ih uhs]

SUMMARY OF BIBLE TRUTHS

1. God shows His sovereignty by being not only fair but also generous.
2. God's grace, not human merit, is the basis for our relationship with Him and service in His name.
3. Faithfulness brings divine blessings, based on His grace, not rewards based on what we deserve.
4. People who insist on getting what they deserve will inevitably be disappointed.
5. Seeking to be first is characteristic of worldly standards, not kingdom standards.
6. Proper human responses to God include dependence, trust, gratitude, contentment, faithfulness, and humility.

APPLYING THE BIBLE

1. Fair pay. In a recent article titled "Musicians Finally Get What They Deserve," the Kingsmen were awarded a court decision that says they are entitled to thirty years' worth of royalties for the song "Louie Louie." Since a contract was signed in 1968, the group was supposed to receive 9 percent of the profits or licensing fees from the record. After thirty years, they finally got what they deserved.

Life does not always seem fair. However, one thing is certain: God has a way of balancing the scales! He is fair. The vineyard owner treated his workers fairly. A day's wage was promised to all who worked in the vineyard. We may feel that we deserve more at times than other people, but that is not the case. Salvation is a gift. No one deserves it, but God is equally gracious to all whom He calls.

2. He went away sad. The rich young man was possessed by his possessions. "There is enough for the needy but not for the greedy" (Mohandas K. Gandhi).

3. Greed. Clovis Chappell wrote in his book of sermons *Feminine Faces:* "When Pompeii was being excavated, there was found a body that had been embalmed by the ashes of Vesuvius. It was that of a woman. Her feet were turned toward the city gate, but her face was turned backward toward something that lay just beyond her outstretched hands. The prize for which those frozen fingers were reaching was a bag of pearls. Maybe she herself had dropped them as she was fleeing for her life. Maybe she had found them where they had been dropped by another. But, be that as it may, though death was hard at her heels, and life was beckoning to her beyond the city gates, she could not shake off their spell. She had turned to pick them up, with death as her reward. But it was not the eruption of Vesuvius that made her love pearls more than life. It only froze her in this attitude of greed."

4. God's nature. Third- and fourth-graders at Wheaton Christian Grammar School in Illinois were asked to complete the following sentence: "By faith, I know that God is . . ."

"**forgiving**, because he forgave in the Bible, and he forgave me when I went in the road on my bike without one of my parents" (Amanda).

"**providingful**, because he dropped manna for Moses and the people, and he gave my dad a job" (Brandon).

"**caring**, because he made the blind man see, and he made me catch a very fast line drive that could have hurt me. He probably sent an angel down" (Paul).

"**merciful**, because my brother has been nice to me for a year" (Jeremy).

"**faithful**, because the school bill came, and my mom didn't know how we were going to pay it. Two minutes later, my dad called, and he just got a bonus check. My mom was in tears" (anonymous).

"**sweet**, because he gave me a dog. God tells me not to do things that are bad. I need someone like that" (Hannah).

5. A prayer for generosity:

> Teach us, good Lord, to serve Thee as Thou deservest:
> To give and not to count the cost;
> To fight and not to heed the wounds;
> To toil and not to seek for rest;
> To labor and not ask for any reward
> Save that of knowing that we do Thy will.
>
> —Ignatius of Loyola

TEACHING THE BIBLE

- *Main Idea:* Jesus said we all get into heaven by God's grace.
- *Suggested Teaching Aim:* To lead these adults to accept and share God's grace.

A TEACHING OUTLINE

1. *Renouncing All to Follow Jesus (Matt. 19:16–30)*
2. *Parable of the Laborers in the Vineyard (Matt. 20:1–16)*

Introduce the Bible Study

Use number 1, "Fair Pay," in "Applying the Bible" to introduce the lesson.

Search for Biblical Truth

IN ADVANCE, enlist three people to read the comments in "Studying the Bible" on "I. Renouncing All to Follow Jesus." Copy the three paragraphs and distribute to three people to set the context out of which Jesus told the parable of the laborers. Ask members to listen for why Jesus told this parable after the experience with the man we sometimes call the rich young ruler.

IN ADVANCE, copy the six questions in "Give the Truth a Personal Focus" and give to six members of your class. Distribute these to six members or six groups at the beginning of the class and ask them to listen throughout the lesson and form an answer and share at the conclusion of the study.

Ask members to open their Bibles to Matthew 20:1–16 and scan these verses. Use the three statements in "Studying the Bible" to explain Jesus' use of parables.

If you have members with modern translations, ask them to determine what times the owner of the vineyard went out to hire laborers. (9:00, 3:00, and 5:00.) Also ask them if they can determine how much the workers were paid. (Most translations have something like the "normal or usual wage," possibly "minimum wage.") Ask: Why do you think the men went to work later in the day without knowing what wage they would receive? Why did the owner not tell them?

DISCUSS: How is God like the vineyard owner? (See "Studying the Bible.")

Give the Truth a Personal Focus

IN ADVANCE, copy the six questions in "Give the Truth a Personal Focus" and give to six members of your class. Distribute these to members at the beginning of the class and ask them to form an answer and share it.

Read each of the following questions (based on the "Summary of Bible Truths") and let members respond:

- How does God show that He is not only fair but also generous?

- What evidence can you give that God's grace, not human merit, is the basis for our relationship with God and service in His name?
- Why does God base His blessings on His grace and not on rewards based on what we deserve?
- Why do you think people who insist on getting what they deserve will inevitably be disappointed?
- If seeking to be first is characteristic of worldly standards, not kingdom standards, why do so many who call themselves believers seek to be first?
- Which of the proper human responses to God (dependence, trust, gratitude, contentment, faithfulness, and humility) do you need to develop in your life?

Close in prayer that members may be able to accept *and* share God's grace.

February

6

2000

Coming to Jerusalem

Background Passage: Matthew 21:1–17

Focal Passage: Matthew 21:1–13

The Old Testament prophets sometimes did unusual things to clarify or reinforce their spoken words. This is called prophetic symbolism. In connection with Jesus' final coming to Jerusalem, He did two acts of prophetic symbolism: His unusual entry into the city and His bold actions in the temple.

Study Aim: *To recognize what Jesus' royal entry and cleansing the temple reveal about His identity and mission.*

STUDYING THE BIBLE

OUTLINE AND SUMMARY

- **I. Royal Entry into Jerusalem (Matt. 21:1–11)**
  - **1. Came as the meek King (21:1–7)**
  - **2. Acclaimed as the Son of David (21:8, 9)**
  - **3. Created a great stir (21:10, 11)**
- **II. Cleansing the Temple (Matt. 21:12–17)**
  - **1. Attacked the money-makers (21:12)**
  - **2. Condemned making the temple into a den of thieves (21:13)**
  - **3. Aroused the anger of the chief priests (21:14–17)**

Jesus entered Jerusalem in a way to reveal Him as a humble Messiah (vv. 1–7). The people acclaimed Jesus as the Son of David (vv. 8, 9). His entry created a great stir throughout the city (vv. 10, 11). Jesus went into the temple and drove out the money changers and sellers of animals (v. 12). He accused them of making God's house of prayer into a den of thieves (v. 13). His actions in the temple made the chief priests very angry at Jesus (vv. 14–17).

I. Royal Entry into Jerusalem (Matt. 21:1–11)

1. Came as the meek King (vv. 1–7)

1 And when they drew nigh unto Jerusalem, and were come to Bethphage, unto the mount of Olives, then sent Jesus two disciples,

2 Saying unto them, Go into the village over against you, and straightway ye shall find an ass tied, and a colt with her: loose them, and bring them unto me.

3 And if any man say ought unto you, ye shall say, The Lord hath need of them; and straightway he will send them.

4 All this was done, that it might be fulfilled which was spoken by the prophet, saying,

5 Tell ye the daughter of Sion, Behold, thy King cometh unto thee, meek, and sitting upon an ass, and a colt the foal of an ass.

6 And the disciples went, and did as Jesus commanded them,

7 And brought the ass, and the colt, and put on them their clothes, and they set him thereon.

As Jesus prepared to enter Jerusalem for the final time, He gave instructions to two of His disciples. They were to enter a village (probably Bethphage), find a female donkey and her colt, and bring them to Jesus. The Lord told the disciples what to say if anyone questioned what they were doing. The two disciples followed Jesus' instructions, brought the animals to Jesus, spread their robes on the animals as a saddle, and set Jesus on the colt.

Verses 4, 5 emphasize that this action fulfilled Zechariah 9:9. The first line of the quotation probably reflects Isaiah 62:11. Zechariah 9:9 was considered by many Jews to relate to the coming of the Messiah-King. Jesus deliberately chose to fulfill that particular Old Testament promise because it describes the King as "meek," a word Jesus used of Himself in Matthew 11:29, and a word He used in one of the Beatitudes to describe kingdom citizens (Matt. 5:5). Jesus did not enter Jerusalem as a military and political King, riding a white horse and dressed as a king and warrior. He entered as a humble Servant-King.

Throughout His ministry, Jesus had faced a dilemma about how to reveal Himself as Messiah-King. From the beginning of Matthew, He is called the Christ (Messiah), the Son of David (1:1). Yet He had come to save His people from sin, not from the power of Roman domination (Matt. 1:21). To fulfill this mission involved crucifixion and resurrection. Jesus committed Himself to such a mission, and the Father's words at Jesus' baptism indicate His approval (Matt. 3:17).

The problem was that many of the Jewish people were expecting an earthly king. Even Jesus' disciples were expecting an earthly king. When Jesus began clearly to predict His rejection, suffering, death, and resurrection, Peter rebuked Jesus for saying such a thing (Matt. 16:13–25). Although Jesus continued to predict what was to happen in Jerusalem, the disciples did not understand. Even as they approached Jerusalem, the Twelve were arguing about which of them would be the greatest (Matt. 20:17–28).

2. Acclaimed as the Son of David (vv. 8, 9)

8 And a very great multitude spread their garments in the way; others cut down branches from the trees, and strawed them in the way.

9 And the multitudes that went before, and that followed, cried, saying, Hosanna to the son of David: Blessed is he that cometh in the name of the Lord; Hosanna in the highest.

Jesus was taking a calculated risk by entering Jerusalem as the Messiah. He came as King, but as a humble Servant-King, not as a mighty political king. However, the people failed to note this subtle difference.

Verses 8, 9 show that they disregarded the humility depicted by riding on a donkey colt and the word *meek* in Zechariah 9:9. All they saw was a King, their kind of king, one worthy of being called Son of David, the great warrior king of their glorious past.

Jesus entered Jerusalem during Passover season (Matt. 26:2). At this most famous of Jewish feasts, the city was always crowded with Jews from many places. Expectations of the Messiah ran high at Passover. As Jesus passed through Jericho, crowds were already with Him (Matt. 20:29). As Jesus approached the city, others joined the throngs about Him. By the time He rode into Jerusalem, Jesus had crowds in front of Him and behind Him. They were placing their cloaks in front of Him and paving the road with branches from trees. These acts signified great honor to Jesus by the multitudes.

Their words acclaimed Jesus as the Son of David. They were quoting from Psalm 118:25, 26, a hymn used by people going to worship in the temple. "Hosanna" meant "God, save us." However, by the first century, "Hosanna" had become a word used in praising God. Two of the titles in Psalm 118:25, 26 were titles for the Messiah. Of course, Son of David meant the descendant of David sent by God to fulfill divine promises of an everlasting kingdom ruled by one of David's descendants (2 Sam. 7:12–17). "He that cometh" was also at times used as a title for the One who was to come (see Matt. 11:3). Unfortunately, the actions of the people that day and later in the week showed that they welcomed Jesus as the kind of Messiah they wanted, not the kind of King He had come to be.

3. Created a great stir (vv. 10, 11)

10 And when he was come into Jerusalem, all the city was moved, saying, Who is this?

11 And the multitude said, This is Jesus the prophet of Nazareth of Galilee.

The word *moved* is too mild to describe the great stir of excitement in Jerusalem. The word was used in Matthew 27:51 to describe an earthquake. The whole city was asking, "Who is this?" The crowds answered this question by referring to Jesus as "the prophet of Nazareth of Galilee." Why didn't they acclaim Him as Son of David?

Perhaps they were thinking of Moses' promise of a prophet and thus intended "prophet" to mean Messiah. If not, perhaps they were merely being cautious. After all, even Jesus had cautioned people about publicly declaring Him as Messiah. Many of the people of Judea knew that Micah 5:2 predicted that the Messiah would come from David's native city Bethlehem in his home area of Judah, not from an obscure village in distant Galilee (John 7:40, 41).

II. Cleansing the Temple (Matt. 21:12–17)

1. Attacked the money-makers (v. 12)

12 And Jesus went into the temple of God, and cast out all them that sold and bought in the temple, and overthrew the

tables of the moneychangers, and the seats of them that sold doves.

Jews who came to worship in the temple needed animals to offer as sacrifices. The poorer people were allowed to bring doves. Many worshipers traveled great distances to come to Jerusalem, and the animals had to be declared unblemished by the priests. These two factors suggested a marketing opportunity for people always looking for new ways to make money. The temple authorities, who were always looking for ways to enrich themselves, also saw this opportunity. Thus, booths were set up in the court of the Gentiles where travelers could buy sacrificial animals guaranteed to pass inspection by the priests. No doubt, the chief priests, who ran the temple, received a percentage of this lucrative enterprise.

Jews also needed Jewish coins with which to pay the temple tax. Foreign coins, which were in wide circulation, often had heads of Roman emperors on them or some insignia that suggested paganism. Therefore, tables were set up where a Jew could exchange foreign money for Jewish money.

The sellers of animals and the exchangers of money thus justified their work as a service to worshipers. They justified their presence in the temple's outer court as a convenience for these same worshipers. Yet Jesus apparently didn't accept these as legitimate enterprises in the temple, even in the large outer court. When Jesus entered the temple, He acted anything but meekly, at least in the usual sense of our word *meek.* He boldly turned over the tables and the seats of those who made money in the temple. Matthew also says that He drove them out.

2. Condemned making the temple into a den of thieves (v. 13)

13 And said unto them, It is written, My house shall be called the house of prayer; but ye have made it a den of thieves.

Jesus explained His actions by quoting Isaiah 56:7 and Jeremiah 7:11. Mark 11:17 quotes all of Isaiah 56:7, including the words "for all nations." God's purpose all along has been to provide a way for all people—Gentiles as well as Jews—to worship Him. Under the old covenant, one sign of this was the provision in the Jewish temple for a place where Gentiles could worship. Although Gentiles could not enter the courts where Jews brought their animals to the priests, Gentiles were supposed to be able to pray in the court of the Gentiles. Those who made money had perverted the divine purpose of the court of the Gentiles from a place of prayer to a place of business.

Jeremiah 7:11 was part of the outspoken prophet's famous temple sermon. He condemned the hypocrites of his day for living in sin and coming to the temple to worship. Jeremiah compared them to thieves, who ventured forth to commit crimes and then retreated to a secret den. Jesus' use of Jeremiah 7:11 condemned the hypocrisy of those who used the temple for their own profit, and His use of "thieves" shows that the money-makers were robbing the people. The animal sellers sold animals for more than they were worth and the money changers charged an unfair fee for their services.

By cleansing the temple, Jesus showed not only the boldness of a prophet but also the authority of One who looked on the temple as His Father's house. Jesus in essence was claiming to have authority over the temple, an ultimate authority that dared to condemn the priestly authorities who ran the temple.

This bold action in the temple was a key factor that led to His death. The ruling Jewish religious court, the Sanhedrin, was presided over by the high priest, who also happened to administer the temple. On the Sanhedrin were both Pharisees and Sadducees. For a long time, the Pharisees had hated Jesus, because He defied their legalistic traditions. By invading the domain of the Sadducees, the temple, Jesus aroused their fury. Thus, these two groups, who seldom agreed on anything, decided to get rid of Jesus (Mark 11:18).

3. Aroused the anger of the chief priests (vv. 14–17)

Jesus showed His authority over the temple also by healing people there (v. 14). The scribes (Pharisees) and chief priests (Sadducees) had watched all these things, apparently including the royal entry. They were angry because even children were caught up in praising Jesus (v. 15). Jesus responded to their anger by quoting Psalm 8:2 (v. 16). Then Jesus left Jerusalem and went to the nearby village of Bethany, where he was staying (v. 17).

PRONUNCIATION GUIDE

Bethphage	[BETH fayge]
Sanhedrin	[san HE drihn]

SUMMARY OF BIBLE TRUTHS

1. Jesus was a Servant-King, who saves by humble self-giving.
2. Jesus' purpose in the royal entry was to emphasize this truth.
3. The people wanted a powerful earthly king.
4. Jesus condemned those who perverted God's purpose for the temple.
5. By cleansing the temple, Jesus claimed authority over the temple.
6. Jesus was meek in the sense of being humble, not in the sense of not showing righteous indignation and holy boldness.

APPLYING THE BIBLE

1. Lasting peace. Had Jesus come as the conquering Messiah-King, our ultimate response to him would be one of resentment. In a speech delivered to the U.S. Senate, President Woodrow Wilson stated that peace must be "without victory. . . . Victory would mean peace forced upon the loser, a victor's terms imposed upon the vanquished. It would be accepted in humiliation, under duress, at an intolerable sacrifice, and would leave a sting, a resentment, a bitter memory upon which terms of peace would rest, not permanently, but only as upon quicksand. Only a peace between equals can last."[1]

The wisdom of God made it happen. Jesus emptied Himself and took on the form of a servant (our equal) and made available a peace with no resentment. It seems like a strange way to save a world, but in riding to Jerusalem on a donkey, He did just that.

2. The meekness of Jesus. General George S. Patton said, "Wars may be fought with weapons, but they are won by men. It is the spirit of the men who follow and of the man who leads that gains the victory." Entering Jerusalem on the back of a donkey demonstrated the spirit and character of Jesus. The battle for redemption was won because of who He is.

3. Creating a great stir. When Jesus entered Jerusalem, it created a great stir. At Passover, people were hoping that God would send the Messiah. People were looking for a hero. People are still looking for heroes today, and in many ways we look for them in the same arenas as the people in Jesus' day.

Sixty percent of children ages 9-13 say they have a hero. The top five categories for their heroes are:

- relatives/friends (52.9%),
- athletes (31.5%),
- religious figures (11.3%),
- fictional characters (11.3%), and
- political/historical figures (8.7%)[2]

Religious leaders and fictional characters tie for influence, and their numbers combined still fall short of the influence held by sports heroes. Convincing people that spiritual things matter is the continuing challenge facing the church.

4. Cleansing the temple. Among several business principles held by Japanese businessman Konosuke Matsushita,[3] the following illustrate a strong commitment to business ethics.

- Treat the people you do business with as if they were part of your family.
- After-sales service is more important than assistance before sales.
- Don't sell customers goods they are attracted to; sell them goods that will benefit them.

The righteous indignation demonstrated by Jesus in cleansing the temple of the money changers may be due in part to the fact that each of these principles was violated. There were no ethics involved at all. The trade benefited the money changers and the religious leaders who received a kickback. There was no concern for the individual, no familial consideration, no service, and certainly nothing with their best interest in mind. It broke the heart of Jesus to see such abuse in a place that was intended for prayer.

5. Never an acceptable way to do a bad thing. An airline worker was convicted of stealing 100,000 cards from the mail he was loading on airplanes. He looked for envelopes that might contain cash or checks and over a three-year period may have helped himself to as much as $500,000. After pleading guilty, his attorney told news reporters that he took the money to play the lottery, hoping to pay expenses for two disabled children. His case reminds us that there is never an acceptable way to do a bad thing. The money changers in the temple were doing a bad thing. They were taking advantage of the poorest of the poor and making a profit in the process.

6. We need a house of prayer. The names of the towns in this study are significant. They further illustrate the reasons Jesus reacted with such anger in the temple at the sight of the money changers. Bethphage (Matt. 21:1), where today's lesson begins, means "house of the unripened fruit" while Bethany (Matt. 21:17), where today's lesson ends, means "house of misery." Jesus knew that between the bitterness of life (unripened fruit) and the pressures of life (misery) people needed a house of prayer. Life continues to be bitter and difficult for people today. Our churches need to be houses of prayer—not contention. How do you think people view your church today?

TEACHING THE BIBLE

- *Main Idea:* Jesus' royal entry into Jerusalem declared that He was a humble Servant-King.
- *Suggested Teaching Aim:* To lead adults to accept Jesus as a humble Servant-King and not try to force Him into the role of political king.

A TEACHING OUTLINE

1. *Royal Entry into Jerusalem (Matt. 21:1–11)*
2. *Cleansing the Temple (Matt. 21:12–17)*

Introduce the Bible Study

Use number 2, "The Meekness of Jesus," in "Applying the Bible" to introduce the lesson.

Search for Biblical Truth

Be sure every member has a Bible. You might have some extra ones available so all can participate in the Scripture search. Ask members to open their Bibles to Matthew 21:1–17. Locate Jerusalem and the possible location of Bethphage on a map of Jesus' ministry. Ask members who have reference Bibles to locate the Old Testament Scriptures referred to in verses 4, 5 (Zech. 9:9 and Isa. 62:11). Ask another member to look up Matthew 11:29 and find one word Jesus used to describe Himself that is similar to a word used in Zechariah. (Meek, lowly.) Using the material in "Studying the Bible," point out how Jesus' entrance emphasized His humbleness and not His political ambitions.

DISCUSS: If Jesus had asked you how He could have entered Jerusalem to communicate that He was a humble Servant-King, what would you have responded? What dangers did Jesus face if the people misunderstood?

Ask members to find two titles in Matthew 21:9 that the people applied to Jesus that indicated they believed Jesus to be the Messiah. ("Son of David" and "He that cometh in the name of the Lord.")

Use "Studying the Bible" to explain how the Jews expected the Messiah to come at Passover. Ask members to turn to Psalm 118:25–26 to find the psalm from which the people quoted their praise. Point out that the people sang this psalm as they went to worship in the temple. Ask, What kind of Messiah do you think the people expected?

DISCUSS: How have we forced Jesus to be the kind of Savior we want Him to be instead of the kind of Savior He really is? What can we do to keep this from happening again?

Ask half the members to look at Matthew 21:10 and the other half to turn to Matthew 27:51. Ask each group to find a word in their verse that describes how the city of Jerusalem was affected ("moved" and "quaked"). Point out that the Greek word is the same in both places. Ask, If you had been a reporter writing about Jesus' entry into Jerusalem, what headline would you have used?

Ask members to look at Matthew 21:12. Ask, What was the first thing Jesus did when He entered Jerusalem? What do you think the people expected Him to do? How do you think this made the people feel when He cleansed the temple instead of setting Himself up as king?

Explain why the Jews had set up shop to provide animals and coinage in the court of the Gentiles. Ask, Why do you think Jesus drove the shopkeepers out?

1. The traders were taking advantage of the people who traveled great distances to worship God.
2. The business interfered with the Gentiles' place of worship.
3. The traders were cheating the people by charging great prices to exchange coins and to buy "approved" sacrificial animals.

Give the Truth a Personal Focus

Read the six "Summary of Bible Truths" statements. Distribute paper and pencils. Ask members to think about ways they have tried to force Jesus to be the kind of Lord they want instead of allowing Him to be who He is. Close in prayer that all will accept Jesus as a humble Servant-King and not try to force Him into any other role.

---

1. Woodrow Wilson, Address to the Senate, Jan. 22, 1917.
2. "Sports Illustrated for Kids," cited in *USA Today,* March 4, 1995.
3. Cindy Kano, *Fortune,* March 31, 1997, 107.

February

13

2000

Watching for Christ's Return

Background Passage: Matthew 24:1–25:13
Focal Passage: Matthew 24:45–25:13

Matthew 24–25 focuses on Jesus' teachings about the future. These chapters provide the foundation for some basic Christian beliefs. The basic teachings are: (1) Christ's coming is certain, but the time is uncertain, and (2) people demonstrate their belief in this teaching by being ready for His coming. These chapters also contain some points on which Christians do not agree.

Study Aim: To explain what Jesus taught about watching for His return.

STUDYING THE BIBLE

OUTLINE AND SUMMARY

I. Questions About the Future (Matt. 24:1–3)

II. Events Prior to the End (Matt. 24:4–28)
- **1. The end is not yet (24:4–14)**
- **2. The abomination of desolation (24:15–28)**

III. Christ's Future Coming (Matt. 24:29–41)
- **1. Certainty of His coming (24:29–35)**
- **2. Uncertainty of the time (24:36–41)**

IV. Call to Watch (Matt. 24:42–25:13)
- **1. A faithful and wise servant (24:42–47)**
- **2. An evil servant (24:48–51)**
- **3. Wise and foolish virgins (25:1–5)**
- **4. Judgment on the unprepared (25:6–13)**

The disciples asked Jesus about the time of the destruction of the temple and of His return (24:1–3). Jesus warned against assuming that every time of trouble meant that the end had come (24:4–14). He spoke of the abomination of desolation and a time of troubles (24:15–28). He spoke of the certainty of His return (24:29–35) but the uncertainty of the time (24:36–41). He illustrated His call for watchfulness by telling of a faithful and wise servant (24:42–47). He illustrated what not to do by telling of an evil servant (24:48–51). Jesus told the parable of the wise and foolish virgins (25:1–5). The wise ones got ready, but the foolish ones were excluded because they did not prepare (25:6–13).

I. Questions About the Future (Matt. 24:1–3)

After the disciples spoke of the impressive buildings of the temple, Jesus predicted the destruction of the temple (24:1, 2). The disciples asked Jesus about the time when the temple would be destroyed and about His future coming (24:3).

II. Events Prior to the End (Matt. 24:4–28)

1. The end is not yet (24:4–14)

Jesus warned them not to assume that every disaster meant that the end had arrived. False messiahs (24:4, 5); wars and natural disasters (24:6, 7); persecution and betrayal (24:9, 10); false prophets, great evil, and apostasy (24:11, 12) are only the beginning of troubles to be expected by believers (24:8). During those times Christians are to remain faithful and take the good news to all nations (24:13, 14).

2. The abomination of desolation (24:15–28)

Many Bible students think these verses are Jesus' answer to the question about the fall of Jerusalem and the destruction of the temple, although these events foreshadow events related to Christ's coming (24:15). The instructions given in verses 16–20 were obeyed by Christians when they saw the Roman armies surround Jerusalem (see Luke 21:20–24). Some Bible students interpret verses 21 through 26 as a final great tribulation, and others see these verses describing troubles over a longer period of time. Verses 27 and 28 make clear that Christ's coming will be as visible as lightning.

III. Christ's Future Coming (Matt. 24:29–41)

1. Certainty of His coming (24:29–35)

The real but cataclysmic events of Christ's coming are summarized in verses 29 through 31. Verses 32 through 35 stress the nearness of Christ's coming.

2. Uncertainty of the time (24:36–41)

No one but God knows the time of Christ's coming (24:36). As in the time of Noah, people will be going about their usual tasks and will be caught unprepared for Christ's coming (24:37–39). A separation of people will take place, depending on their readiness for Christ's coming (24:40, 41).

IV. Call to Watch (Matt. 24:42–25:13)

1. A faithful and wise servant (24:42–47)

45 Who then is a faithful and wise servant, whom his lord hath made ruler over his household, to give them meat in due season?

46 Blessed is that servant, whom his lord when he cometh shall find so doing.

47 Verily I say unto you, That he shall make him ruler over all his goods.

Because no one knows when Christ will return, each should watch (24:42). Christ's coming will be like a thief in the night in that many will not be expecting Him at that time (24:43). Therefore, each person should be ready at all times (24:44). Two words describe one who is ready: *faithful* and *wise.* The word *servant* translates the Greek word for "slave." This particular slave was a steward or manager whom an owner left in charge of his household. Among his duties was to feed the other slaves.

A wise manager listens to the owner's instructions, and a faithful manager obeys what the owner said to do. Because the owner might return at any time, the only way to be ready is to follow his instructions. Therefore, when the owner returns unexpectedly, he will find the manager carrying out his orders. The owner will promote the manager as a reward.

2. An evil servant (24:48–51)

48 But and if that evil servant shall say in his heart, My lord delayeth his coming;

49 And shall begin to smite his fellow-servants, and to eat and drink with the drunken;

50 The lord of that servant shall come in a day when he looketh not for him, and in an hour that he is not aware of,

51 And shall cut him asunder, and appoint him his portion with the hypocrites: there shall be weeping and gnashing of teeth.

This servant had the same job as the one in verses 45 through 47; however, he was not just neglectful; he was evil. He not only did not care for the other slaves, but also he misused his authority to beat them. And he misused his position to get drunk.

These evil actions stemmed from the evil slave's attitude about the master and his warning that he might return at any time. When the master did not return right away, the evil slave noted that he was delaying his coming. He must have decided that he would continue to delay his return; perhaps he thought that the master would not return at all. At any rate, he used the master's delay as an opportunity to do as he pleased. His true nature came to the surface. He disobeyed the master's orders; he mistreated his fellow slaves; and he abused his own body with excessive drink.

One day—when the slave-manager least expected him to return—the master showed up. The master's unexpected arrival gave the manager no time to try to hide his sins. He was caught in the act. As punishment, the master cut him to pieces. The last part of verse 51 reflects the Lord's punishment of those who use the Lord's absence to do evil.

3. Wise and foolish virgins (25:1–5)

1 Then shall the kingdom of heaven be likened unto ten virgins, which took their lamps, and went forth to meet the bridegroom.

2 And five of them were wise, and five were foolish.

3 They that were foolish took their lamps, and took no oil with them:

4 But the wise took oil in their vessels with their lamps.

5 While the bridegroom tarried, they all slumbered and slept.

Like the parable in Matthew 20:1–16, the parable in Matthew 25:1–13 used a typical situation from life to illustrate realities about human relations with God. The former parable was about a landowner hiring workers for his harvest; the latter was about a wedding. Although the situations were familiar to Jesus' hearers, Jesus depicted some of the characters acting in ways different from the way people normally acted in such situations.

This parable focuses on ten virgins. The word *virgin* is used here to describe what we would call "bridesmaids." These were young women, who were probably friends of the bride (who is never mentioned in the story). According to the wedding customs of that time, the groom and a procession went to the bride's house, where she and her bridesmaids joined the procession to go to the groom's house for the wedding and banquet.

The bridesmaids' part in the procession was to have lamps and oil to provide illumination as the wedding party made its way through the unlighted streets. The word *lamps* referred to oil lamps, which were lighted, hoisted on poles, and used for light.

All the bridesmaids had their lamps, but only five had brought the oil necessary to make the lamps burn. This was the one fact that initially distinguished the wise from the foolish virgins. We are not told why five did not bring oil. Jesus' hearers could not imagine any bridesmaid being so foolish. That was exactly Jesus' point. This part of the parable reflects how people react toward the certainty of the Lord's coming and the uncertainty of the time of His coming. No bridesmaid would be so foolish as to risk not being ready to join the wedding party, but many people are foolish enough not to prepare for the much more important procession of the Lord to the marriage feast of the Lamb.

For some unexplained reason, the groom was late. This had been known to happen, but it was not normal. Jesus was illustrating the fact that many people consider His delayed coming an excuse for not being ready when He does come.

4. Judgment on the unprepared (25:6–13)

6 And at midnight there was a cry made, Behold, the bridegroom cometh; go ye out to meet him.

7 Then all those virgins arose, and trimmed their lamps.

8 And the foolish said unto the wise, Give us of your oil; for our lamps are gone out.

9 But the wise answered, saying, Not so; lest there be not enough for us and you: but go ye rather to them that sell, and buy for yourselves.

10 And while they went to buy, the bridegroom came; and they that were ready went in with him to the marriage: and the door was shut.

11 Afterward came also the other virgins, saying, Lord, Lord, open to us.

12 But he answered and said, Verily I say unto you, I know you not.

13 Watch therefore, for ye know neither the day nor the hour wherein the Son of man cometh.

The folly of the five unprepared bridesmaids became apparent when they were awakened by the cry that the groom was near. All ten were asleep. The wise could sleep because they were ready. The ones without oil should have been taking advantage of this last opportunity to purchase oil. Only after the groom arrived did they recognize their plight. The wise bridesmaids were not being selfish but practical in refusing to share their oil. They did not have enough for all ten to perform their functions.

The refusal of the groom to let the foolish girls in was probably not something true to life, but it illustrates the seriousness of not being ready when the Lord returns. It will be too late then to get ready. The foolish people who postponed getting ready for His coming will be left outside the door to the kingdom. Their fate will be sealed by their own foolish failure to get ready.

The word *watch* can mean "stay awake" (Matt. 26:38, 40, 41); but, in this passage, it has the more general meaning of "be ready" (24:44). The wise virgins were ready for the groom whenever he came; the foolish ones were not ready no matter when he came.

SUMMARY OF BIBLE TRUTHS

1. Because the time of Christ's return is unknown, people should be ready at any time.
2. "Watch" means "be ready" for the Lord's return.
3. Wise people prepare; foolish people don't.
4. Faithful servants of Christ will share in His glory.
5. Evil people and people who failed to get ready will be excluded.

APPLYING THE BIBLE

1. The importance of staying awake. Did you hear about the thief who fell asleep in a home he was burglarizing? A woman came home in the early morning hours and found her front door ajar, a window broken, and jewelry boxes emptied. She also found the intruder snoring at the foot of her bed.

The woman quietly made her way downstairs to call police, who arrived moments later to awaken and arrest the sleeping man. Jesus told the story of the ten virgins to emphasize the importance of being prepared and being alert to His coming. A church that fails to be alert is like a thief falling asleep. Neither is very effective in fulfilling their mission.

2. Seduction. G. Campbell Morgan said the great danger in our careless waiting would be "the seduction of a false Christ."[1] Growing cult activity in our day gives credibility to Morgan's warning. So does the growing attraction to secular idols that have found their way into the heart of mankind.

3. Looking for signs. The thirteen-year cicada bug made its appearance in the spring of 1998, the same year that the "blame it all on El Nino" weather pattern made its way into every arena of our lives. Some saw these events as cataclysmic parts of a prophetic event. Others saw them as natural events that just happened to occur in the same year. The Christian is encouraged to exercise discernment when looking at events that make their way into our lives.

4. No man knows the hour. In 1988 Edgar C. Wisenant published a book entitled *88 Reasons Why the Rapture Will Be in 1988*. Obviously, it didn't happen. I doubt anyone really expected it to, except maybe the author. Jesus said no one knows the day or the hour.

5. Common responses to difficult times. Warren Wiersbe[2] offers an encouraging application to the text for this lesson. Difficult days are inevitable. All believers will face trying times sooner or later as we await the second coming of Christ. The following five statements apply today's lesson to the heart of every believer:

- **Don't be deceived** (Matt. 24:4, 11). False prophets and teachers will arise, but we know the truth.
- **Don't be discouraged** (Matt. 24:6). Bad things happen, but God is still on the throne.
- **Don't be defeated** (Matt. 24:13). At times it may seem pointless, but our witness still matters.
- **Don't be doubtful** (Matt. 24:34, 35). Things change and disappointments happen, but God's word abides forever.
- **Don't be distracted** (Matt. 24:42). Everything vies for your attention, but we are watching and working until He comes.

6. What if it were today? Hymn texts can challenge us at a deeper level than mere words. "What If It Were Today" asks a haunting question:

> Faithful and true would He find us here
> If He should come today?
> Watching in gladness and not in fear,
> If He should come today?
> Signs of His coming multiply,
> Morning light breaks in eastern sky,
> Watch, for the time is drawing nigh,
> What if it were today?
>
> —Leila Naylor Morris

TEACHING THE BIBLE

- *Main Idea:* Jesus warns us to be ready at any moment for His return.
- *Suggested Teaching Aim:* To lead adults to identify what they can do to prepare for Jesus' return.

A TEACHING OUTLINE

1. *Questions About the Future (Matt. 24:1–3)*
2. *Events Prior to the End (Matt. 24:4–28)*
3. *Christ's Future Coming (Matt. 24:29–41)*
4. *Call to Watch (Matt. 24:42—25:13)*

Introduce the Bible Study

Use number 1, "The Importance of Staying Awake," in "Applying the Bible" to introduce the lesson. Point out that Jesus urged His followers to watch for His return.

Search for Biblical Truth

IN ADVANCE, enlist someone to present as a monologue by Jesus the information in the summary statements in "Outline and Summary." Begin by saying: "One day My disciples asked Me about the destruction of the temple and My return. This is what I told them. 'Don't assume that every time of trouble means that the end has come.'" Put each of the statements into a word of warning from Jesus and read this to the class to overview the Scripture.

Using the material in "Studying the Bible," lecture briefly covering points I and II in the outline on the previous page. (These verses set the context for the lesson.)

Organize the class into two groups and give each group one of the assignments. Allow six to seven minutes for study and then call for reports.

1. Based on Matthew 24:42–51:

- What two words describe one who is ready?
- Compare and contrast the faithful and wise servant with the evil servant.
- How are we like these two servants? How are we different?

2. Based on Matthew 25:1–13:

- Who are the main characters in this parable?
- Describe the wedding situation Jesus portrayed.
- Why were the five wise bridesmaids justified in not sharing their oil?
- How are we like the five wise bridesmaids? the five foolish bridesmaids?

Give the Truth a Personal Focus

IN ADVANCE, on a chalkboard or a large sheet of paper, write these statements. (Italicized words are the words that need to be changed and are for your convenience; do not italicize them when you write them out.) Ask members to change a word or words in each sentence to make it a true statement.

- Because the time of Christ's return is *known,* people should be ready at any time.
- "Watch" means "be ready" for the *devil's* return.
- *Foolish* people prepare; *wise* people don't.
- *Indifferent* servants of Christ will share in His glory.
- Evil people and people who failed to get ready will be *included.*

Ask, What do you need to do to be ready for Christ's return? (If you have unsaved members present, encourage any who need to accept Christ to talk with you after the class.) Challenge believers to live in such a way that they would not be embarrassed if Christ caught them at any point in their lives.

---

1. G. Campbell Morgan, *Life Applications from Every Chapter in the Bible* (Grand Rapids: Revell, 1994), 307.
2. Warren Wiersbe, *With the Word* (Nashville: Thomas Nelson Publishers, 1982), 650.

Death of Jesus

Background Passage: Matthew 27:32–61
Focal Passage: Matthew 27:38–54

The death and resurrection of Jesus are the heart of the good news (1 Cor. 15:3, 4). All four Gospels make these the climactic events of Jesus' life and ministry. The account of the death of Jesus in Matthew's Gospel is a series of brief looks at the people around the cross, with Jesus Himself as the focal point.

Study Aim: *To describe what the people at the cross said and did.*

STUDYING THE BIBLE

OUTLINE AND SUMMARY

- **I. Crucifixion of Jesus (Matt. 27:32–50)**
  1. **Those who crucified Him (27:32–37)**
  2. **Those who mocked Him (27:38–44)**
  3. **Jesus' cry from the cross (27:45–50)**
- **II. Events Following Jesus' Death (Matt. 27:51–61)**
  1. **Miracles (27:51–53)**
  2. **Centurion's confession (27: 54)**
  3. **Women's watch (27:55, 56)**
  4. **Burial of Jesus (27:57–61)**

The soldiers who crucified Jesus cast lots for His clothes (vv. 32–37). The passersby, the religious leaders, and the two thieves mocked Jesus (vv. 38–44). During Jesus' suffering, He cried out in the words of Psalm 22:1 (vv. 45–50). When Jesus died, the temple veil was torn, an earthquake occurred, and dead believers were raised up (vv. 51–53). The Roman centurion confessed Jesus as Son of God (v. 54). Three women followers were watching (vv. 55, 56). Joseph of Arimathea placed Jesus' body in his own tomb (vv. 57–61).

I. Crucifixion of Jesus (Matt. 27:32–50)

1. Those who crucified Him (vv. 32–37)

Because Jesus was unable to carry the cross, the soldiers conscripted Simon of Cyrene (v. 32). When they arrived at Golgotha, Jesus refused the drugged wine which was offered to Him by the soldiers (vv. 33, 34). The soldiers cast lots for Jesus' clothes (vv. 35, 36). Over the cross of Jesus was the accusation against Jesus, "THIS IS JESUS THE KING OF THE JEWS" (v. 37).

2. Those who mocked Him (vv. 38–44)

38 Then were there two thieves crucified with him, one on the right hand, and another on the left.

The word *thieves* can mean what our word means, or it can refer to rebels against Rome, who stole as part of their terrorism. Whatever their crime, these two men were sinners and criminals. The fact that Jesus died with sinners points to the purpose of the cross—Jesus died for sinners.

39 And they that passed by reviled him, wagging their heads,

40 And saying, Thou that destroyest the temple, and buildest it in three days, save thyself. If thou be the Son of God, come down from the cross.

The crowds who passed by insulted (blasphemed) Jesus. They taunted Him to save Himself. They knew about the false accusations made at His trial. Jesus was accused of saying that He would tear down the temple building and rebuild it in three days (Matt. 26:61; see John 2:19–22).

The passersby used the same clause that Satan had used in the wilderness temptations (Matt. 4:3). They taunted Jesus, "Since you are the Son of God, save yourself." This had been a recurring temptation for Jesus. Satan tempted Him again on the cross to use His power to save Himself. Jesus could have saved Himself. When Jesus was arrested, He said that He could have summoned twelve legions of angels to rescue Him (Matt. 26:53, 54). Instead, He voluntarily gave Himself into the hands of those who intended to crucify Him.

41 Likewise also the chief priests mocking him, with the scribes and elders, said,

42 He saved others; himself he cannot save. If he be the King of the Israel, let him now come down from the cross, and we will believe him.

43 He trusted in God; let him deliver him now, if he will have him: for he said, I am the Son of God.

44 The thieves also, which were crucified with him, cast the same in his teeth.

The chief priests also mocked (made fun of) Jesus, being joined by the scribes and elders—the groups that conspired to condemn Jesus (Matt. 26:3, 57; 27:1). They taunted Him by saying that Jesus claimed to have saved others, but He was unable to save Himself. Their intended mockery contained more truth than they realized. Jesus could have saved Himself from the cross; but He knew that if He saved Himself, He would be unable to save sinners.

They also taunted Jesus about His professed trust in God, whom He claimed was His Father. The religious leaders made fun of this man who claimed to be the Son of God. He trusted God, but where was God, that He allowed His Son to die in this terrible way? Even the two dying criminals echoed the words of the other mocking voices.

3. Jesus' cry from the cross (vv. 45–50)

45 Now from the sixth hour there was darkness over all the land unto the ninth hour.

46 And about the ninth hour Jesus cried with a loud voice, saying, Eli, Eli, lama sabachthani? that is to say, My God, my God, why hast thou forsaken me?

47 Some of them that stood there, when they heard that, said, This man calleth for Elias.

48 And straightway one of them ran, and took a spunge, and filled it with vinegar, and put it on a reed, and gave him to drink.

49 The rest said, Let be, let us see whether Elias will come to save him.

50 Jesus, when he had cried again with a loud voice, yielded up the ghost.

Jesus was crucified at the third hour of the Jewish day, or about 9:00 A.M. (Mark 15:25). At the sixth hour (noon) darkness spread over the land until the ninth hour (3:00 P.M.). Toward the end of the three hours of darkness, Jesus cried out in words that some misunderstood. Others knew Aramaic and were near enough to recognize His cry as the words of Psalm 22:1. The psalmist's sense of being forsaken by God was echoed in the cry of Jesus from the cross. His cry was a cry and a prayer. When the crucifixion accounts of all four Gospels are compared, we find seven sayings of Jesus from the cross (Luke 23:34, 43, 46; John 19:27, 28, 30).

Preachers, scholars, and every sincere believer stand in awe before Jesus' cry, "My God, my God, why hast thou forsaken me?" We do our best to understand and explain the cry, but all our efforts fall short of unlocking the full mystery of Christ's atoning death or of beginning to fathom the depths of what He suffered for us.

Being crucified was a painful, humiliating way to die; but the New Testament does not dwell on the horrors of being crucified. Instead it presents us with the Son of God enduring the worst of all sufferings—a sense of being forsaken by God. Sin separates from God; and somehow as Jesus died, God "made him to be sin for us, who knew no sin; that we might be made the righteousness of God in him" (2 Cor. 5:21). Yet we also must remember "that God was in Christ, reconciling the world unto himself" (2 Cor. 5:19); and that the cross reveals not only the love of Jesus but the love of God (Rom. 5:6–8).

II. Events Following Jesus' Death (Matt. 27:51–61)

1. Miracles (vv. 51–53)

51 And, behold, the veil of the temple was rent in twain from the top to the bottom; and the earth did quake, and the rocks rent;

52 And the graves were opened; and many bodies of the saints which slept arose,

53 And came out of the graves after his resurrection, and went into the holy city, and appeared unto many.

Just as the birth of Jesus was announced by miraculous signs, so was His death. In addition to the miraculous darkness of His final three hours of suffering, Matthew mentions three other miracles: the temple veil, the earthquake, and resurrections.

The veil refers to the veil that closed off the holy of holies, which represented the presence of God, from the rest of the temple. Only the high priest could enter and he only once a year with the proper sacrifices for himself and for the people's sins. When Jesus died, that veil was torn from top to bottom—as if by the hand of God. This signified that God had opened access to Himself for all sinners through the sacrifice of Jesus Christ, who is also our great High Priest. The Book of Hebrews emphasizes Christ as our priest and sacrifice. As a result, the inspired writer says, "Let us therefore come boldly unto the throne of grace, that we may obtain mercy, and find grace to help in time of need" (Heb. 4:16).

Later Jewish sources mention an earthquake about forty years prior to the fall of Jerusalem in A.D. 70. This may have been the earthquake mentioned in Matthew 27:51.

At the same time, many graves were opened—perhaps by the earthquake. Later after Jesus had been raised from the dead, the resurrected bodies of dead believers appeared to many people. Apparently these were the dead people of faith of Old Testament times. This miracle shows that the Old Testament believers would share in the new covenant salvation.

2. Centurion's confession (v. 54)

> **54 Now when the centurion, and they that were with him, watching Jesus, saw the earthquake, and those things that were done, they feared greatly, saying, Truly this was the Son of God.**

A centurion was an officer in the Roman army who commanded one hundred men. This particular centurion was apparently in command of the soldiers who crucified Jesus. He and his soldiers had been near enough to the cross to see and hear what took place.

His response when Jesus died is remarkable. Some translators and interpreters think that the centurion's words indicate a good man who was right to trust God as Father (see Luke 23:47). However, others are convinced that the centurion confessed Jesus as the Son of God. When others at the cross were mocking the dying Jesus, the pagan Roman army officer confessed Jesus as the Son of God.

With the exception of a few faithful women and one of the Twelve, even the close friends of Jesus chose not to come to the crucifixion. They considered it the end of their hopes and dreams for Jesus as Messiah, and they feared that the enemies of Jesus would soon be looking for them. Yet at that time, two people believed at the cross—the penitent thief and the Roman centurion. In a way, they were comparable to the first groups to seek the newborn Jesus—outcast shepherds and pagan wise men. The centurion's confession foreshadowed the millions of Gentiles who eventually would acclaim Jesus as the Son of God.

3. Women's watch (vv. 55, 56)

Matthew did not mention any of the male disciples being there, including himself. John's Gospel mentions the beloved disciple. However, some loyal women watched with sorrow as Jesus was crucified:

Mary Magdalene, Mary the mother of James and Joses, and the mother of Zebedee's children (James and John).

4. Burial of Jesus (vv. 57–61)

Joseph of Arimathea asked Pilate for permission to take the body of Jesus, and Pilate issued the order (vv. 57, 58). After wrapping the body in a clean linen cloth, Joseph laid the body in his own new tomb, which had been hewn out of rock. Then he rolled a great stone across the tomb's door (vv. 59, 60). Mary Magdalene and the other Mary were sitting near the tomb (v. 61).

PRONUNCIATION GUIDE

Arimathea	[ahr ih muh THEE uh]
Cyrene	[sigh REE nee]
Lama	[LAH muh]
Sabachthani	[sah BAHK thu nigh]
Zebedee	[ZEB uh dee]

SUMMARY OF BIBLE TRUTHS

1. Jesus died with sinners and for sinners.
2. He voluntarily chose to give Himself in order to save others.
3. Jesus endured the suffering of one separated from God.
4. Some people reject Jesus and His death for them.
5. Other people confess Jesus as Son of God and Savior.

APPLYING THE BIBLE

1. True confession. "Psychoanalysis is the probing of mind by mind; confession is the communion of conscience and God" (Fulton J. Sheen).

2. Two kinds of people. "There are only two sorts of men: the one the just, who believe themselves sinners; the other sinners, who believe themselves just" (Blaise Pascal).

3. Substitute. When you write the word *substitute,* you are spelling a one-word sermon on the theology of salvation. There are three "t's" in the word just as there were three crosses on Golgotha the day Jesus was crucified. The middle "t" is the cross of Christ because there is a place for both "u" and "I" beside it. When Christ died, He took the place that belonged to you and me. He became the sin substitute for us.

4. People like us. "God was executed by people painfully like us, in a society very similar to our own . . . by a corrupt church, a timid politician, and a fickle proletariat led by professional agitators."[1]

5. It is finished. In a sermon titled *It is Finished* by Wayne Brouwer, we are invited to see how different people understood the words of Jesus as He hung dying on the cross.

- For Judas, the words indicated betrayal complete, blood money gone, business taken care of.
- For Peter, his denial meant he would never be able to go home again, not even to Galilee. He would never be able to show his face in public. He was ruined. It is finished.

- Pilate endured a political pressure point, faced another sleepless night with a wife who heard voices, washed his hands again, and watched from the portico of his palace and with a sigh of relief whispered, "It is finished."
- An unrepentant thief said, "You're done for, and so am I. Here we go."
- A broken-hearted thief heard the words "It is finished" and discovered that his past had disappeared. He felt like a newborn baby. With Simeon he could say, "Now, Lord, let me die in peace. My eyes have seen your salvation. It is finished."
- The centurion looked up at Jesus and shook his head. It's finished now, but something good died today—something that I once believed in—justice. We're the worse for it. But it is finished.
- Shocked and discouraged disciples heard the words and to them it simply meant back to the fishing boats and fishing nets. It is finished.
- Joseph of Arimathea collected the body, wrapped it in some strips of cloth, and put it in a damp tomb. It is finished.

6. Tearing down the cross. During Holy Week at First Presbyterian Church, Orlando Florida, an individual stopped to look at the three crosses that were on display on the front lawn of the church. Enraged at the sight, he tore the center cross down. Repair work began as soon as the church was notified. Damon Willow, one of the associate ministers of the church, looked up at the cross in the midst of repairs and said, "You can tear down the cross, but you can't stop the Christ." The cross is foolishness to some, offensive to others. But to those who have placed faith and trust in the resurrected Lord, it is the power to save.[2]

TEACHING THE BIBLE

- *Main Idea:* Jesus' crucifixion affected people in different ways.
- *Suggested Teaching Aim:* To lead adults to identify different responses to Jesus' death on the cross.

A TEACHING OUTLINE

1. *Crucifixion of Jesus (Matt. 27:32–50)*
2. *Events Following Jesus' Death (Matt. 27:51–61)*

Introduce the Bible Study

Use number 4, "People Like Us," in "Applying the Bible" to introduce the lesson.

Search for Biblical Truth

IN ADVANCE, write the following names on strips of paper and tape them at random around the room: Soldiers (Matt. 27:32–37), Simon of Cyrene (Matt. 27:32–37), Thieves (Matt. 27:38, 44), Passersby (Matt. 27:39, 40), Religious Leaders (Matt. 27:41–43), Resurrected People (Matt. 27:51–53), Centurion (Matt. 27:54), Women (Matt. 27:55, 56), Joseph of Arimathea (Matt. 27:57–61).

Explain that to understand the cross, we need to see it from the different perspectives of the people involved. Ask members to open their Bibles to Matthew 27:32–37 and skim the verses. Point to *Soldiers* and ask: What was the attitude of the soldiers toward the crucifixion? How did the crucifixion affect them? What lessons can we learn from them? Follow the above procedure with the rest of the names.

Give the Truth a Personal Focus

IN ADVANCE, enlist three readers to read this biblical skit.

Father, Forgive Them

FIRST READER: I hate crucifixions. They are always so messy.

SECOND READER: Yes, and they take so much time. Besides, it's hot out here.

FIRST READER: You shouldn't complain. You were the lucky man with the dice today. You won His robe.

SECOND READER: Look at that! That's the man who was going around saving people! If He is really the Messiah, let Him save Himself now.

FIRST READER: Ha! Save Yourself, O king of the Jews! *(laughs)*

JESUS: "Father, forgive them; for they know not what they do."

SECOND READER: Hey, He's still alive. I wish He were already dead. I'd like to get this over with.

FIRST READER: Look at all those women over there. I wonder what they saw in this guy?

JESUS: "Woman, behold thy son!"

SECOND READER: He was supposed to have a whole group of followers. I don't see but one man in the bunch. I guess what we're doing to their leader put the fear of the gods in them.

JESUS: "Behold thy mother."

FIRST READER: Yeah, but this is such a messy business. I never have liked it.

SECOND READER: Oh, come now, he's just a Jew. He's not even a Roman citizen.

FIRST READER: I know, but He just doesn't look like a criminal. Have you looked into His eyes?

SECOND READER: *That's* your problem. Never look into a condemned man's eyes. The eyes will get you every time.

FIRST READER: But He's not even cursing like the other two. One filthy dog spat right in my face when I was trying to nail his arm. He made it easy for me.

JESUS: "Today shalt thou be with me in paradise."

SECOND READER: Well, don't ever look at their eyes. By the way, we're supposed to get this over with before sundown.

FIRST READER: Yeah, it's some kind of religious holiday. These Jews have some kind of dumb law about not having criminals on the cross over a holiday.

SECOND READER: As far as I'm concerned, they have a lot of strange laws. I'll be glad when I'm through with this tour. I'll be glad to get back to Rome.

FIRST READER: I wish my tour had ended before this. I tell you, I don't like it. Something is different about this one.

SECOND READER: Well, I'll admit that when everything went dark and stayed that way for three hours, I felt a little uncomfortable too.

FIRST READER: He just seems so different. I wish I weren't involved in this one.

JESUS: "I thirst."

FIRST READER: Hey, He's thirsty. You might as well give Him a drink of that cheap wine over there. That's the least we can do for the poor fellow.

SECOND READER: Well, it will soon be over. Get that mallet that we drove the spikes with. We need to break their legs.

FIRST READER: I hate to do that. I'd rather let that dirty dog who spat in my face suffer a while.

SECOND READER: I'd like to let them all suffer. Maybe that would teach these Jews that they can't mess with Caesar.

FIRST READER: But He didn't do anything against Caesar. You heard Pilate himself say that He was innocent.

JESUS: "It is finished!"

SECOND READER: Listen! Did you hear Him cry out? It sounded like a cry of victory!

JESUS: "Father, into thy hands I commend my Spirit."

FIRST READER: He looks like He's dead.

SECOND READER: Good. We won't have to break His legs.

FIRST READER: You know, I really believe He was the Son of God.[3]

---

1. Dorothy L. Sayers, "The Man Born to Be King," *Christianity Today.*
2. Howard Edington, *Downtown Church, the Heart of the City* (Nashville: Abingdon Press, 1996), 39.
3. James E. Taulman, *Help! I Need an Idea* (Nashville: Broadman Press, 1987), 42–44.

Resurrection and Commission

Background Passage: Matthew 27:62–28:20
Focal Passages: Matthew 28:1–10, 16–20

All the New Testament accounts of Jesus' resurrection are distinctive in some ways, but all emphasize the same basic facts: (1) The disciples were not expecting Jesus to be raised from the dead, in spite of all His predictions, (2) the tomb was empty, (3) Jesus appeared alive to many individuals and groups, and (4) the risen Lord commissioned His followers to tell the whole world about the risen Lord. Matthew 28 mentions two of the appearances, and it emphasizes the Great Commission.

Study Aim: *To explain how obedience to the Great Commission testifies to a person's faith in the risen Lord.*

STUDYING THE BIBLE

OUTLINE AND SUMMARY

I. Empty Tomb and Risen Lord (Matt. 27:62–28:15)
- **1. The sealed tomb (27:62–66)**
- **2. The empty tomb (28:1–8)**
- **3. The risen Lord (28:9, 10)**
- **4. A conspiracy of lies (28:11–15)**

II. The Commission of the Risen Lord (Matt. 28:16–20)
- **1. Responses to the risen Lord (28:16, 17)**
- **2. The Great Commission (28:18–20)**

The enemies of Jesus sealed His tomb and stationed guards (27:62–66). When women came to the tomb, an angel told them to go tell the disciples that Jesus had been raised from the dead (28:1–8). On their way, they encountered the risen Lord (28:9, 10). When the guards reported what had happened, they accepted a bribe to say that the disciples stole Jesus' body (28:11–15). When Jesus appeared to the disciples in Galilee, they worshiped; but some doubted (28:16, 17). The risen Lord commissioned His followers to make disciples of all nations (28:18–20).

I. Empty Tomb and Risen Lord (Matt. 27:62–28:15)

1. The sealed tomb (27:62–66)

The religious leaders asked Pilate to seal the tomb and station guards (27:62–64a). They wanted to be sure the disciples did not steal the body of Jesus and then claim that He had been raised from the dead (27:64b). After Pilate gave permission, the religious leaders posted guards (27:65, 66).

2. The empty tomb (28:1–8)

1 In the end of the sabbath, as it began to dawn toward the first day of the week, came Mary Magdalene and the other Mary to see the sepulchre.

As we study the sequence of events about the crucifixion and resurrection of Jesus, three days of the week are mentioned. "The day of the preparation" (27:62) was the Jewish way of describing Friday, the day of preparation for the sabbath, our Saturday. Jesus was crucified between 9:00 A.M. and 3:00 P.M. on Friday of Passover week. He was buried late that day, before sunset, which was the beginning of the Jewish sabbath. The wording of Matthew 28:1 is ambiguous enough to refer either to just after dark on what we would call Saturday or about dawn on Sunday. Luke 24:1 and John 20:1 clearly set the action early on Sunday morning.

According to Matthew 28:1, the two women who came were the same two mentioned in Matthew 27:61, watching the burial of Jesus' body. Mark 16:1 adds Salome to the list.

2 And, behold, there was a great earthquake: for the angel of the Lord descended from heaven, and came and rolled back the stone from the door, and sat upon it.

3 His countenance was like lightning, and his raiment white as snow:

4 And for fear of him the keepers did shake, and became as dead men.

The information in Matthew 28:2–4 is found only in Matthew's Gospel. None of the Gospels describe the actual resurrection, but verse 2 describes how the angel of the Lord came down and rolled away the stone. The angel's actions and appearance terrified the guards so much that they fell down like dead men. The women had been worried about how they would roll away the stone (Mark 16:3), but they found the stone rolled away and an angel sitting on it.

5 And the angel answered and said unto the women, Fear not ye: for I know that ye seek Jesus, which was crucified.

6 He is not here: for he is risen, as he said. Come, see the place where the Lord lay.

7 And go quickly, and tell his disciples that he is risen from the dead; and, behold, he goeth before you into Galilee; there shall ye see him: lo, I have told you.

8 And they departed quickly from the sepulchre with fear and great joy; and did run to bring his disciples word.

As was often the case when an angel appeared to humans, the angel tried to calm their fears. The angel told the women that he knew that they had come seeking Jesus, who had been crucified and whose body had been placed in this tomb. Quickly the angel told them that the tomb was empty because Jesus had been raised from the dead.

Notice the words "as he said." The angel reminded the women that Jesus had predicted not only His crucifixion but also His resurrection. Looking back from the safe distance of history, we wonder why none of His followers were expecting Jesus to be raised from the dead. The women had not gone to the tomb to see the risen Lord, but to anoint His body (Mark 16:1; Luke 24:1). The disciples did not believe the first reports of His resurrection; they had to see Him for themselves.

The most likely reason why they were not expecting His resurrection is that they had not really expected Him to suffer and die. When Jesus earlier had predicted His suffering, death, and resurrection, the minds of His followers never got past the first part of the prediction.

The angel invited the women to come and see the place where Jesus' body had been. Then the angel told them to go and tell the disciples that Jesus had been raised from the dead. Like a shepherd going ahead of his sheep, Jesus was going ahead of them to Galilee, where they would see Him. The wording did not rule out earlier appearances in Judea (see Luke 24:36–43; John 20:19–29), but it focused attention on the appearance described in Matthew 28:16–20.

The women quickly obeyed the angel. Their fears were not totally gone, but they were now overshadowed by their joy. They ran to tell the disciples the joyful news. Their instant obedience is a model for us who have received the Great Commission.

3. The risen Lord (28:9, 10)

9 And as they went to tell his disciples, behold, Jesus met them, saying, All hail. And they came and held him by the feet, and worshipped him.

10 Then said Jesus unto them, Be not afraid: go tell my brethren that they go into Galilee, and there shall they see me.

One of the many evidences that the New Testament is true is that no one in the first century would have made up a story in which women were the first to see the angel, meet the risen Lord, and tell others. Just as Matthew broke precedent at the beginning of the Gospel by naming women in the genealogy of Jesus (Matt. 1:3, 5, 6), so did he emphasize the crucial role of women as the first to see the Lord alive and to tell that good news to others.

Their initial response was to grasp Jesus about His feet and worship Him. Like the angel, Jesus told them not to be afraid. He also reinforced the command to go and tell the disciples that the Lord would appear to them in Galilee.

4. A conspiracy of lies (28:11–15)

Meanwhile, some of the terrified guards reported to the chief priests what had happened (28:11). The religious leaders bribed the guards to say that the disciples had stolen the body of Jesus while they slept (28:12–14). The guards accepted the bribe and thus began the first of many subsequent ways of trying to explain away the resurrection of Jesus (28:15).

II. The Commission of the Risen Lord (Matt. 28:16–20)

1. Responses to the risen Lord (28:16, 17)

16 Then the eleven disciples went away into Galilee, into a mountain where Jesus had appointed them.

17 And when they saw him, they worshipped him: but some doubted.

Matthew mentions only the eleven disciples, but some Bible students think that other believers also could have heard the Great Commission. Jesus certainly did not intend to confine this mission to the apostles.

One reason some people assume that others were present are the words "but some doubted." Some people wonder how the disciples could have doubted, especially if this appearance came near the end of the forty days between the resurrection and the ascension. We do know that the disciples did not believe the first report of the women (Luke 24:11). Thomas thus was not the only doubter. When Jesus appeared to them, their initial responses included fear and uncertainty (Luke 24:36–38). Even after Jesus reassured them, their joy was mixed with some unbelief (Luke 24:41). The Gospels emphasize their honest doubts to show that they became believers only after they saw Him and became totally convinced that it was Jesus raised from the dead.

2. The Great Commission (28:18–20)

> **18 And Jesus came and spake unto them, saying, All power is given unto me in heaven and in earth.**
>
> **19 Go ye therefore, and teach all nations, baptizing them in the name of the Father, and of the Son, and of the Holy Ghost:**
>
> **20 Teaching them to observe all things whatsoever I have commanded you: and, lo, I am with you alway, even unto the end of the world.**

The risen Lord has authority over all things as a result of the successful completion of His mission. This authority has not been openly asserted as it will be at His future coming, but believers already believe He is Lord of all, before whom some day every knee shall bow (Phil. 2:9–11). As Lord of all the earth, Jesus issued a command that encompasses all people. He commissioned His followers to make disciples of people of all nations.

During Jesus' ministry, He sometimes told people not to tell anyone (Matt. 9:30). Even after Peter confessed Jesus as the Christ, Jesus told the disciples not to tell (Matt. 16:20). He was afraid that the Jews of His day would see Him as only an earthly king. By contrast, after His death and resurrection, Jesus issued marching orders for His followers to make disciples of all nations.

Matthew 28:18–20 is called the Great Commission, because it is the fullest statement of the commission for world missions and evangelism. All the Gospels and the Book of Acts have some form of a commission spoken by the risen Lord (see Mark 16:15; Luke 24:47, 48; John 20:21; Acts 1:8).

The word translated "teach" in verse 19 is a different word than "teaching" in verse 20. The meaning in verse 19 is "make disciples." This is the main verb in the Great Commission. Three participles point to three aspects of making disciples. We are to make disciples by going, baptizing, and teaching.

"Go" is translated as a command, and this may be the force of the participle; or it may mean "as you go." Both are true. Sometimes we are called to go to certain places or people. Always we are to bear witness for Christ as we go about our tasks in daily life.

"Baptizing" assumes that those being baptized are people who have heard the good news and have trusted Jesus as Lord and Savior.

"Teaching" is the usual word for Jesus teaching the disciples and for instruction in the early church. This crucial aspect of the Great Commission reminds us that new believers need to be taught about Jesus and His teachings concerning how His followers are to live and serve.

To those who obey this Great Commission, Jesus promises His abiding presence until the end time arrives and His kingdom comes in all its glory. By His Spirit, the risen Lord is leading the way to make disciples of all nations. Our obedience in fulfilling the Great Commission bears testimony to our belief in His resurrection.

PRONUNCIATION GUIDE

Salome [suh LOH mih]

SUMMARY OF BIBLE TRUTHS

1. The resurrection was the climax of Jesus' earthly mission.
2. The apostles were not expecting His resurrection.
3. They had to be convinced by seeing Him alive.
4. The Great Commission is to make disciples of all nations.
5. Making disciples involves going, baptizing believers, and teaching them the things Jesus wants them to know.
6. The risen Lord promises to be with those who follow Him in fulfilling this commission.

Quotations of the Other Commissions
"Go ye into all the world, and preach the gospel to every creature" (Mark 16:15).
"Repentance and remission of sins should be preached in his name among all nations, beginning at Jerusalem. And ye are witnesses of these things" (Luke 24:47, 48).
"As my Father hath sent me, even so send I you" (John 20:21).
"Ye shall receive power, after that the Holy Ghost is come upon you: and ye shall be witnesses unto me both in Jerusalem, and in all Judaea, and in Samaria, and unto the uttermost part of the earth" (Acts 1:8).

APPLYING THE BIBLE

1. In Jesus' words. "It should ever be remembered that our Lord is never recorded as speaking of His coming cross without at the same time foretelling His resurrection" (G. Campbell Morgan).

2. Hope. Among the earliest manifestations of Christian art are the early third-century paintings of biblical figures on catacomb walls in Rome. Among the main themes portrayed are the hope of resurrection and immortality, symbolized by fish and peacock motifs.[1] From earliest days, it seems the Christian community has held on to the promise of the empty tomb.

3. Why we need hope. Peter Anderheggen became the first subscriber to a magazine called *Hope*. He told reporters, "We don't live without hope." He went on to predict, "The magazine will be successful because it demands us to look at things that do not naturally come to mind as hopeful."[2]

We don't live without hope. We certainly don't stand at the graveside of a loved one without hope. Things that do not naturally come to mind as hopeful have become transformed by the resurrection of Christ.

4. Easter's promise. No matter how bad things may seem, resurrection Sunday reminds us that things are going to get better.

5. Hope in our grief. "The most enduring emblems of tragedy often are poignantly impermanent," writes Mary Lord in an article in *U.S. News & World Report*. When employees of a Starbucks coffee shop were killed, chalk tributes to the three coworkers were lovingly etched on the sidewalk by a member of the community.[3]

6. Conspiracy. Sentinels of the Tomb of the Unknowns officially began guarding the tomb in 1948. But their story began shortly after World War I. The sentinels are held to some of the highest standards in the Army. Their training is rigorous, including about nine months of drilling exercises aimed at near-perfect expertise. They guard the tomb twenty-four hours a day, seven days a week.[4]

The soldiers who were sent to guard the tomb of Jesus were among Rome's best. Skilled and trained, they knew the significance of their task and the penalty that awaited them for failure. Yet it was impossible to stop the resurrection. These soldiers went from being among the elite to becoming part of a cover-up conspiracy.

7. The Great Commission. According to the 1995–96 Annual Church Profile of the Southern Baptist Convention, 10,713 churches reported no baptisms in the previous twelve months. The reason for this boils down to one simple fact: we have forgotten the urgency of the Great Commission. It is the only strategy Christ gave to the church. When we fail to participate in making disciples, we participate in the "Great Omission." Edmund Burke said it accurately: "The only thing necessary for the triumph of evil is for good men to do nothing."

TEACHING THE BIBLE

- *Main Idea:* Our obedience in fulfilling the Great Commission bears testimony to our belief in Jesus' resurrection.
- *Suggested Teaching Aim:* To lead adults to examine how their obedience to the Great Commission reflects their belief in Jesus' resurrection.

A TEACHING OUTLINE

1. *Empty Tomb and Risen Lord (Matt. 27:62—28:15)*
2. *The Commission of the Risen Lord (Matt. 28:16–20)*

Introduce the Bible Study

IN ADVANCE, make a poster of number 4, "Easter's Promise" in "Applying the Bible." Display this and read it to begin the lesson.

Search for Biblical Truth

Ask a member to read silently Matthew 27:62–28:10 and find the three days of the week that are mentioned.

Ask, What was the purpose of the earthquake? (To let people into the tomb, not to let Jesus out.) What was symbolic about the angel sitting on the stone? What was the angel's first word to the women? Can you think of another time this same word was used by an angel? (Luke 2:10.) Why were the women not expecting Him to be raised? (They hadn't expected Him to die.) Was it only coincidental that the women met Jesus as they obeyed the angel's message to go tell the disciples Jesus was alive?

DISCUSS: Do you see anything significant in women being the first messengers of the resurrection? How had Matthew emphasized women in the genealogy of Jesus? (Matt. 1:3, 5, 6.) Are these two purposes related?

Ask members to scan Matthew 28:16–20. Ask: Why would anyone doubt Jesus was alive? Where did Jesus get His power over all things?

On a chalkboard write *make disciples* ("teach" [v. 19] in KJV). Point out that making disciples is the primary objective of the Great Commission. Ask members to examine verses 19–20 to find three ways Christ's followers are to make disciples. (Go, baptize, teach.) Ask, What is the wonderful promise He gives us as we make disciples?

Give the Truth a Personal Focus

Read number 7, "The Great Commission," in "Applying the Bible." Ask: Does your obedience to the Great Commission reflect your belief in Christ's resurrection. If we do not make disciples, do we really believe Christ is alive? Close in prayer that members will make disciples as they go to their separate worlds of work this week.

---

1. *The Concise Columbia Encyclopedia* (Columbia University Press, 1989, 1991).
2. Cheryl Wetzstein, "Always Hope for the Best," *Insight on the News,* April 15, 1996, 38.
3. Mary Lord, "Finding a Way to Grieve," *U.S. News & World Report,* July 28, 1997, 16.
4. Tranette Ledford, "Tomb Sentinels Mark 50th Anniversary," *Army Times,* March 8, 1998.

Helping a Church Face Crisis

March

April

May

2000

INTRODUCTION

Paul's letters to the Corinthians are his longest correspondence with any one church. The letters reveal many problems in the church. Passages from the Corinthian letters provide the basis for this three-unit study of "Helping a Church Face Crisis."

Unit I, "Christ the Basis for Unity," is a four-lesson unit based on passages from 1 Corinthians. The unit, like the letter, begins with a focus on the need for unity. Other emphases include the role of the Holy Spirit as teacher, church leaders as servants and stewards of God, and church discipline.

Unit II, "Unity in Human Relationships," is a five-lesson study from 1 Corinthians. Sessions deal with marriage and celibacy, love and knowledge, spiritual gifts, future resurrection (Easter), and the way of self-giving love.

Unit III, "The Power of Christian Ministry," is a four-lesson unit based on 2 Corinthians. The first two sessions focus on victory through Christ, in spite of difficulties. The third session gives directions concerning giving. The fourth session is Paul's appeal to the Corinthians to live by the faith they professed.

Cycle of 1998–2004

1998–1999	1999–2000	2000–2001	2001–2002	2002–2003	2003–2004
Old Testament Survey	Exodus Leviticus Numbers Deuteronomy Joshua	Judges 1, 2 Samuel 1 Chronicles 1 Kings 1–11 2 Chronicles 1–9	Parables Miracles Sermon on the Mount	2 Kings 18–25 2 Chronicles 29–36 Jeremiah Lamentations Ezekiel Habakkuk Zephaniah	James 1, 2 Peter 1, 2, 3 John Jude
New Testament Survey	Matthew	Luke	Isaiah 9; 11; 40–66 Ruth Jonah Nahum	Personalities of the NT	Christmas Esther Job Ecclesiastes Song of Solomon
John	1, 2 Corinthians	Acts	Romans Galatians	Mark	The Cross 1, 2 Thessalonians Revelation
Genesis	Ephesians Philippians Colossians Philemon	1 Kings 12–2 Kings 17 2 Chronicles 10–28 Isaiah 1–39 Amos Hosea Micah	Psalms Proverbs	Ezra Nehemiah Daniel Joel Obadiah Haggai Zechariah Malachi	Hebrews 1, 2 Timothy Titus

OUTLINE OF 1 CORINTHIANS

Introduction: Greeting and Gratitude (1:1–9)

I. Disruptive Dissension over Church Leaders (1:10–4:21)
   1. Selfish Pride and Strife (1:10–17)
   2. God's Wisdom Versus Worldly Wisdom (1:18–31)
   3. The Spirit and Spiritual People (2:1–16)
   4. Leaders as Servants and Stewards (3:1–4:21)

II. Sexual Immorality and Church Lawsuits (5:1–6:20)

III. Marriage and Singleness (7:1–40)

IV. Meat Sacrificed to Idols (8:1–11:1)
   1. Knowledge and Love (8:1–13)
   2. Freedom and Self-Discipline (9:1–11:1)

V. Worship and the Lord's Supper (11:2–34)

VI. Spiritual Gifts (12:1–14:40)
   1. One Body, Many Members (12:1–31)
   2. The More Excellent Way (13:1–13)
   3. Prophecy and Tongues (14:1–40)

VII. Christ's Resurrection and Ours (15:1–58)

Conclusion: Final Exhortations and Greetings (16:1–24)

OUTLINE OF 2 CORINTHIANS

Introduction: Greetings and Doxology (1:1–11)

I. From Despair to Triumph (1:12–2:17)
   1. Painful Dealings with the Corinthians (1:12–2:11)
   2. Sharing in Christ's Triumph (2:12–17)

II. Characteristics of Paul's Ministry (3:1–6:2)
   1. Ministry of Christ's Spirit (3:1–4:6)
   2. Ministry of Renewal and Hope (4:7–5:10)
   3. Ministry of Reconciliation (5:11–6:2)

III. Paul and the Corinthians (6:3–7:16)
   1. A Personal Appeal (6:3–7:4)
   2. Rejoicing in Reconciliation (7:5–16)

IV. Offering for the Jerusalem Christians (8:1–9:15)
   1. Examples of Sacrificial Giving (8:1–15)
   2. Administration of the Offering (8:16–9:5)
   3. Principles of Giving (9:6–15)

V. Paul and His Critics (10:1–13:10)
   1. Responses to Critics (10:1–11:15)
   2. Paul's Accomplishments (11:16–12:10)
   3. Tough Love (12:11–13:10)

Conclusion: Exhortations, Greetings, and Doxology (13:11–14)

Appeal for Unity

March

5

2000

Background Passage: 1 Corinthians 1:1–17
Focal Passage: 1 Corinthians 1:2–17

First Corinthians reveals a church riddled with problems. First Corinthians 1:1–17 begins with Paul's usual greeting, moves through a typical expression of gratitude, and then focuses on the central problem at Corinth and hints at the solution.

➧**Study Aim:** *To describe the reasons for Paul's gratitude and for his concern about the church at Corinth.*

STUDYING THE BIBLE

OUTLINE AND SUMMARY

I. Greetings (1 Cor. 1:1–3)

II. Thanksgiving (1 Cor. 1:4–9)
  1. Grateful for the work of God's grace (1:4–7)
  2. Grateful for the faithfulness of God (1:8, 9)

III. Dissension in a Church (1 Cor. 1:10–17)
  1. Warning and appeal (1:10)
  2. Selfish strife (1:11, 12)
  3. Divine Lord or human leaders? (1:13–16)
  4. The cross versus human wisdom (1:17)

After greeting the saints in Corinth (vv. 1–3), Paul thanked God for His grace (vv. 4–7) and faithfulness (vv. 8, 9). He warned against dissension and urged oneness of spirit (v. 10). He was disturbed by reports of strife over preachers (vv. 11, 12). Paul emphasized that Jesus is Lord, not any human leader (vv. 13–16). Paul's mission was to preach the gospel of the cross (v. 17).

I. Greetings (1 Cor. 1:1–3)

2 Unto the church of God which is at Corinth, to them that are sanctified in Christ Jesus, called to be saints, with all that in every place call upon the name of Jesus Christ our Lord, both theirs and ours:

3 Grace be unto you, and peace, from God our Father, and from the Lord Jesus Christ.

Corinth was a major city of the first century. It had a population of over half a million. It was the capital of the Roman province of Achaia. Corinth was a thriving seaport. Like many seaports, Corinth had a poor reputation morally.

Paul visited Corinth on his second missionary journey. He spent eighteen months in Corinth; and when he left, a church had been established (Acts 18:1–18). During Paul's long missionary campaign in Ephesus, Paul wrote 1 Corinthians (1 Cor. 16:8). He wrote because they had misunderstood an earlier letter from Paul (1 Cor. 5:9). He wrote to answer some specific questions sent to him in a letter from the church (1 Cor.

7:1). Paul also had received reports from people who visited him in Ephesus and who had been in Corinth (1 Cor. 1:11; 16:17, 18).

In spite of the problems Paul had with the Corinthians, he greeted them as "sanctified in Christ Jesus, called to be saints." Many people think of "saints" as a title reserved only for especially holy people, but every Christian is a saint. The word *saints* comes from the same root as *sanctified.* Saints are people set apart by God and for God. Saints are not perfect, but they are set apart to become what God wants them to become.

Paul used "grace" and "peace" in his greeting in most of his letters. "Grace" is similar, yet different from the usual Greek greeting. "Peace" is the same word used by Jews in greeting, except that this peace is from God the Father and the Lord Jesus Christ.

II. Thanksgiving (1 Cor. 1:4–9)

1. Grateful for the work of God's grace (vv. 4–7)

4 I thank my God always on your behalf, for the grace of God which is given you by Jesus Christ;

5 That in every thing ye are enriched by him, in all utterance, and in all knowledge;

6 Even as the testimony of Christ was confirmed in you:

7 So that ye come behind in no gift; waiting for the coming of our Lord Jesus Christ.

Although the thanksgiving for the Corinthian church lacks the warmth of some of the other letters, Paul wrote it sincerely. In spite of their faults and problems, he considered them true believers; and although they lacked much, he was grateful for what God had done, was doing, and would do in and through them.

Paul expressed gratitude to God for His work of grace among them. This grace had enriched them in two areas they particularly prized: speaking and understanding. Paul felt that such evidence of the work of God's grace confirmed the testimony to Christ that he had borne when he was first in Corinth. This grace was also the source of the spiritual gifts in the church.

2. Grateful for the faithfulness of God (vv. 8, 9)

8 Who shall also confirm you unto the end, that ye may be blameless in the day of our Lord Jesus Christ.

9 God is faithful, by whom ye were called unto the fellowship of his Son Jesus Christ our Lord.

Paul was grateful not only for what God's grace had done and was doing, but he was grateful for what the faithful God was yet to do in the lives of the Corinthian believers. The rest of the letter reveals their faults and sins, but Paul was sure that the One who had begun a good work in them would complete it unto the day of Christ Jesus (Phil. 1:6).

Why was Paul so sure? His confident assurance was based not on any special qualities of the Corinthians, but on the faith that "God is faithful." The faithful God had called them into "the fellowship of his Son Jesus Christ, our Lord."

III. Dissension in a Church (1 Cor. 1:10–17)

1. Warning and appeal (v. 10)

10 Now I beseech you, brethren, by the name of our Lord Jesus Christ, that ye all speak the same thing, and that there be no divisions among you; but that ye be perfectly joined together in the same mind and in the same judgment.

Paul now got to his real reason for writing. Before he finished his lengthy letter, he named many problems in the Corinthian church; but he began with the basic problem of a divisive spirit. The church was not yet divided into groups that had formally separated themselves from one another. They were still meeting together, but they had already divided themselves into rival groups within the same church. Paul sternly warned against this; and at the same time, he fervently appealed for a spirit of unity.

"All speak the same thing" was not a call for uniformity, but for oneness of spirit. Paul based this fervent appeal on the fact that they were brothers and sisters in Christ. He appealed to them in the name of "our Lord Jesus Christ." None of us can relate to the Lord in isolation from others who know Him as Lord.

2. Selfish strife (vv. 11, 12)

11 For it hath been declared unto me of you, my brethren, by them which are of the house of Chloe, that there are contentions among you.

12 Now this I say, that every one of you saith, I am of Paul; and I of Apollos; and I of Cephas; and I of Christ.

Chloe apparently had a large household, with many servants. Some of them either were members of the church in Corinth or knew what was happening in the church. These members of Chloe's household visited Paul in Ephesus, and they told him what he reported in verse 12. Paul believed their report. He began verse 12 by speaking in his own name, not in the name of his informants.

The Corinthian church was arguing about leaders. Apollos was the eloquent preacher from Alexandria, whom Aquila and Priscilla helped instruct after they heard him preach in Ephesus (Acts 18:24–26). He went to Corinth from Ephesus (Acts 18:27–19:1). Cephas was the Aramaic name of Simon Peter. Other than this verse, we have no evidence that Peter himself was ever in Corinth. Even this verse may mean that some were loyal to Peter by reputation only.

Paul had started the church at Corinth. It is not surprising that some championed him, especially when others in the church began to criticize Paul and state their preferences for someone else. The issue was not doctrinal differences, but personal preferences. Some were probably impressed by the eloquence of Apollos, who was probably a better orator than Paul. Some were partial to Cephas because he represented the twelve apostles and Jewish Christianity. Yet Paul, Apollos, and Peter all preached the same good news of salvation by grace through faith for all who believe.

The fourth group is more difficult to identify. Some believe that those who said, "I of Christ" were all those who reacted against the idolatrous attachment to human leaders. However, if this were true, wouldn't Paul have identified with this position? In fact, that was his position; however, he spoke of the fourth group as another divisive faction. The most likely explanation is these people claimed a special loyalty to Christ that set them apart—at least in their own eyes—as the only true followers of Christ. This self-righteous attitude made them another divisive faction.

Look closely at verse 12. Notice how prominent is the little word *I.* It overshadows even the name of the leader being championed. It was as if one said: "Look at me! I am for Paul." This kind of selfish pride is the basic human sin, which makes it all the more out of place in a Christian church.

Put this fact with the word *contentions* in verse 11. This translates a word meaning "strife." This is one of the works of the flesh listed in Galatians 5:20 and one of the sins of the non-Christian world listed in Romans 1:29. It refers to the wrangling that is the mark of sinful people. It is the opposite of the self-giving love that should be a mark of those who know Christ.

3. Divine Lord or human leaders? (vv. 13–16)

13 Is Christ divided? was Paul crucified for you? or were ye baptized in the name of Paul?

14 I thank God that I baptized none of you, but Crispus and Gaius;

15 Lest any should say that I had baptized in mine own name.

16 And I baptized also the household of Stephanas: besides, I know not whether I baptized any other.

If Paul's supporters expected the apostle to praise them, they must have been surprised by the withering attack on them. Of course, what he said of his own supporters applied to all who substituted loyalty to a human leader for loyalty to the Lord Jesus. Paul's three questions in verse 13 were to help them see the folly of what they were doing.

The church is Christ's body. The body is one. A divisive spirit tears the one body into pieces. Christ, not Paul, died for them. They were baptized in the name of Christ, their Lord, not in the name of Paul. Paul was not minimizing the importance of baptism (see Matt. 28:18–20). However, he was reminding them that baptism signifies a commitment to Christ as Lord. The person who does the baptizing is only one of Christ's servants, not one's divine Lord.

4. The cross versus human wisdom (v. 17)

17 For Christ sent me not to baptize, but to preach the gospel: not with wisdom of words, lest the cross of Christ should be made of none effect.

Verse 17 introduces the basic solution to selfish pride and divisive strife. The solution is the cross of Jesus Christ. Paul contrasted the way of the cross with human wisdom. He elaborated on the differences between these two ways in 1 Corinthians 1:18–31 and in the rest of the letter. The cross is not only the door to the Christian life but also the way of the Christian life. After sinners have been saved at the cross, the crucified, risen Lord comes into their lives to enable them to deny themselves, take up their crosses, and follow Him daily (Luke 9:23).

PRONUNCIATION GUIDE

Achaia	[uh KAY yuh]
Apollos	[uh PAHL uhs]
Cephas	[SEE fuhs]
Chloe	[KLOH ee]
Corinth	[KAWR inth]
Crispus	[KRIS puhs]
Gaius	[GAY yuhs]
Sosthenes	[SAHS thih neez]
Stephanas	[STEF uh nuhs]

SUMMARY OF BIBLE TRUTHS

1. Christians are set apart by God and for God.
2. The work of God's grace produces good results in the lives of Christians.
3. God's faithfulness is the basis for Christian assurance.
4. Dissension and strife are the results of selfish pride.
5. Unity of spirit is an expression of the way of the cross.

APPLYING THE BIBLE

1. Grace. Spurgeon said, "The higher a man is in grace, the lower he will be in his own esteem."

2. Thanksgiving. Gratitude is the memory of the heart. Paul's opening prayer for the Corinthians is one of gratitude for the grace of God. Paul remembers what he was like before God's grace was demonstrated in his life, and he knows that living in Corinth was not easy. He prays a prayer of thanksgiving because he remembers (from the heart) what God has done for them.

3. Thoughts on pride:

- "If there is anything harder than breaking a bad habit, it is to refrain from telling people how you did it" (Tony Pettito).
- "When a man gets too big for his britches, his hat doesn't fit either."
- "Proud men end in shame, but the meek become wise" (Prov. 11:2).
- "The only effect of pride is fighting; but wisdom is with the quiet in spirit" (Prov. 13:10).

4. The mission. The mission of the early church is underscored by Paul in this opening chapter of his Corinthian correspondence. It is the cross of Christ. Failure to prioritize that would forever result in the church languishing in the surface-deep problems that characterized it upon Paul's writing.

Steven Spielberg's masterwork, *Saving Private Ryan,* raises the consciousness of younger generations who view the invasion of Normandy through the camera lens of Hollywood. The movie's plot involves a small platoon of American soldiers who are on a mission to find the surviving brother of three American GIs killed in combat within days of the initial invasion. Captain John Miller, played by actor Tom Hanks, tells his unsuspecting platoon, "This time, the mission is the man" when referring to their orders. When they temporarily lose focus on the mission, they turn against each other. When they get sidetracked, they not only lose momentum; they lose valuable members of the platoon. However, focus brings them back together and their mission is accomplished.

Focus is the only thing that can reshape a splintered congregation. The mission matters, and our mission is the cross of Christ: "For the message of the cross is foolishness to those who are perishing, but to us who are being saved it is the power of God" (1 Cor. 1:18).

5. Grace or mercy . . . or both. "I do not ask the grace which thou didst give Saint Paul; nor can I dare to ask the grace which thou didst grant to Saint Peter; but, the mercy which thou didst show to the Dying Robber, that mercy show to me" (confession of faith printed below the portrait of famed astronomer and scientist, Copernicus, hanging in Saint John's Church in Thorn).

6. Unity in the church body. "A Christian fellowship lives and exists by the intercession of its members for one another, or it collapses" (Dietrich Bonhoeffer).

7. God's faithfulness. The third stanza of the hymn "Great Is Thy Faithfulness" seems to underscore the truth found in 1 Corinthians 1:4–9:

Pardon for sin and a peace that endureth,
Thine own dear presence to cheer and to guide;
Strength for today and bright hope for tomorrow,
Blessings all mine with ten thousand beside!
Great is thy faithfulness! Great is thy faithfulness!
Morning by morning new mercies I see;
All I have needed thy hand hath provided;
Great is thy faithfulness, Lord, unto me!

TEACHING THE BIBLE

- *Main Idea:* Making the cross central to our lives keeps our vision on Christ and prevents our developing divisions.
- *Suggested Teaching Aim:* To lead adults to identify ways they can make the cross more central to their lives to eliminate divisiveness in their relationships.

A TEACHING OUTLINE

1. *Greetings (1 Cor. 1:1–3)*
2. *Thanksgiving (1 Cor. 1:4–9)*
3. *Dissension in a Church (1 Cor. 1:10–17)*

Introduce the Bible Study

Read the following to introduce the lesson:

Dear Paul,

Our church recently lost its pastor, and several people in the church wanted to call our assistant pastor, who is a great preacher. The pulpit search committee did not feel that the young man had enough maturity to handle the task of senior pastor. Members of our church have taken sides. Some are for the assistant pastor, some are against him; still others keep telling us to grow up and just trust the Lord and all will work out. This issue is about to divide our church. What can we do?

Terribly Troubled

Dear T.T.:

Read my first letter to the church at Corinth.

Paul

Search for Biblical Truth

Be sure every member has a Bible. Ask members to open their Bibles to 1 Corinthians 1:2. Locate Ephesus and Corinth on a map of Paul's missionary journeys. Ask, According to verse 2, who are the Corinthians to whom Paul is writing? (Church of God, sanctified, saints.) Explain the meaning of "saints."

Ask, According to verse 3, what did Paul wish for them? (Grace and peace.) Explain the meaning of grace and peace and their source for believers.

Ask, According to verses 4–6, in what two areas had God's work of grace enriched the Corinthians? (Speaking and understanding.)

DISCUSS: How can we express gratitude for people even when we are upset with them?

Ask, According to verses 8–9, how could Paul be certain that the Corinthians would be strong to the end? (He based his statement on God's faithfulness, not theirs; God calls, and God keeps.)

DISCUSS: What can you tell people who are worried that they cannot be strong in the faith to the end of their lives?

Ask, According to verse 10, what did Paul want the Corinthians to do? (He wanted them to agree with each other, not to take sides, and also to think alike—and they were doing just the opposite of all of this.)

DISCUSS: Would you agree or disagree with this statement: None of us can relate to the Lord in isolation from others who know Him as Lord? Why?

Ask, According to verses 11–12, what caused the contention at Corinth? (The church supported various leaders.) How were these leaders different? alike? Ask members to count the number of times the word *I* appears in verse 12 (five times in KJV). Ask, Based on the number of times the word *I* is used, what do you think might have been the cause of the conflict? ("I-trouble" or selfish pride.)

Ask: According to verses 13–16, how can the body of Christ—the church—be divided and still be a body? Point out that a divisive spirit tears the one body into pieces. Those who minister, whether by preaching, teaching, or baptizing, are all Christ's servants—not their lord!

Ask, According to verse 17, what is the answer? (Preach the cross of Christ.)

DISCUSS: How does proclaiming the cross keep us united?

Give the Truth a Personal Focus

Ask members to bow their heads. Read aloud the five "Summary of Bible Truths" statements. Pray that members will keep these truths before them this week. Distribute copies of the five statements you have made **IN ADVANCE.**

The Holy Spirit As Teacher

March

12

2000

Background Passage: 1 Corinthians 2:1–3:23

Focal Passages: 1 Corinthians 2:1, 2, 4–13, 15, 16

Several themes introduced in chapter 1 are interwoven with a new theme introduced in chapter 2. The themes introduced in chapter 1 are: arguments over human leaders (1:10–17), the cross as divine wisdom versus human wisdom (1:18–25), praise due only to God (1:26–31). The new theme in chapter 2 is the Spirit of God.

Study Aim: *To identify ways in which God's Spirit is leading Christians to give all praise to God.*

STUDYING THE BIBLE

OUTLINE AND SUMMARY

I. Empowering the Preaching of the Cross (1 Cor. 2:1–5)

1. Preaching the cross (2:1, 2)

2. Empowered by the Spirit (2:3–5)

II. Revealing God's Kind of Wisdom (1 Cor. 2:6–16)

1. The mystery of God's wisdom (2:6–9)

2. Revealed by the Spirit (2:10–13)

3. Natural man and spiritual man (2:14–16)

III. Praising God, Not Human Leaders (3:1–23)

1. Leaders as servants of God (3:1–9)

2. Building worthily on a firm foundation (3:10–17)

3. Belonging to God (3:18–23)

When Paul was in Corinth, he preached Christ crucified (2:1, 2). He relied not on eloquence, but on the power of the Spirit (2:3–5). He preached the revealed mystery of salvation by grace through faith for all people (2:6–9). This mystery was revealed by the Spirit (2:10–13). The natural man does not know the Spirit, but the spiritual man does (2:14–16). Human leaders like Apollos and Paul are only servants of God (3:1–9). People are responsible for the quality of the lives they build on the solid foundation of Jesus Christ (3:10–17). Children of God own all things because they are heirs of God (3:18–23).

I. Empowering the Preaching of the Cross (1 Cor. 2:1–5)

1. Preaching the cross (2:1, 2)

1 And I, brethren, when I came to you, came not with excellency of speech or of wisdom, declaring unto you the testimony of God.

2 For I determined not to know any thing among you, save Jesus Christ, and him crucified.

"And I" shows that Paul was about to explain how he had practiced the principles set forth in chapter 1. He did not practice the wisdom of the world; instead he preached the cross, which is God's wisdom. "Wisdom" is a key word. Paul used it in chapters 1 and 2 in two bad senses and two good senses. One of the bad senses is seen in chapter 2, verse 1 (see 1:17).

When Paul preached in Corinth, he did not rely on human intellect and eloquent oratory to persuade people. He had determined to preach Christ crucified, although he knew that this message was considered foolish by the Greeks and was a stumbling block to the Jews. Paul also knew that only in the cross is salvation possible. People persuaded by oratory might credit the speaker or even themselves. However, coming to the cross demands that people come just as they are—as needy sinners (see 2:5).

2. Empowered by the Spirit (2:3–5)

4 And my speech and my preaching was not with enticing words of man's wisdom, but in demonstration of the Spirit and of power:

5 That your faith should not stand in the wisdom of men, but in the power of God.

One indication that Paul was not trusting his own human skills was the fear and trembling he felt as he approached his mission in Corinth (v. 3). Repeating the idea in verse 1, Paul wrote that his "preaching was not with enticing words of man's wisdom." Instead Paul preached the cross in the power of the Spirit. This is Paul's first mention of the Spirit in the letter. He did not rely on his own persuasive powers, but on the power of the Spirit.

Verse 5 states Paul's reasons for preaching the cross in the power of the Spirit. People saved at the cross under the conviction of God's Spirit are not likely to give credit to the preacher or to take credit for themselves. Instead, they have faith that only God is to be praised for His work of salvation and His saving power.

II. Revealing God's Kind of Wisdom (1 Cor. 2:6–16)

1. The mystery of God's wisdom (2:6–9)

6 Howbeit we speak wisdom among them that are perfect: yet not the wisdom of this world, nor of the princes of this world, that come to nought:

7 But we speak the wisdom of God in a mystery, even the hidden wisdom, which God ordained before the world unto our glory:

8 Which none of the princes of this world knew: for had they known it, they would not have crucified the Lord of glory.

9 But as it is written, Eye hath not seen, nor ear heard, neither have entered into the heart of man, the things which God hath prepared for them that love him.

"Wisdom" is not a bad thing. It depends on whether the wisdom is God's or the world's. Paul wrote of the good wisdom of God that was known by mature believers. The word *perfect* here means "mature." This is the same group later referred to as "spiritual" (2:15).

This wisdom referred to God's wondrous salvation, which He planned before the world was created. This wisdom of God was a "mystery." Paul used this word not to describe a puzzle that human ingenuity could not solve. Paul meant something that the world did not grasp until it was revealed by God to people of faith.

The contrast to this wisdom of God is called "the wisdom of this world." This is the second bad use of the word. Paul was thinking here of the way of living and thinking of people who do not know God. All they know is the way of the world. The wisdom of God is foreign to anything in their experience.

Paul mentioned "the princes of this world" as being unaware of God's wisdom. Evidence of this ignorance was their crucifying the Son of God. Bible scholars debate whether these rulers are earthly rulers or spiritual powers arrayed against God. Acts 3:17 mentions the guilt of earthly rulers in crucifying Jesus. Colossians 2:15 speaks of Christ's death as a victory over spiritual rulers.

The irony of the world's rejection of God's wisdom is that it alone offers what the world's wisdom promises—glory. The world's glory is false, superficial, and temporary. Only in Christ does God bestow His glory on His people.

Even people of faith have no idea of the full glory that God is preparing for them. Verse 9, which seems to be a loose paraphrase of Isaiah 64:4, points to this future glory. Paul often contrasted the suffering of this present world and the future glory. He said the future glory is greater by far (Rom. 8:18; 2 Cor. 4:17).

2. Revealed by the Spirit (2:10–13)

10 But God hath revealed them unto us by his Spirit: for the Spirit searcheth all things, yea, the deep things of God.

11 For what man knoweth the things of a man, save the spirit of man which is in him? even so the things of God knoweth no man, but the Spirit of God.

12 Now we have received, not the spirit of the world, but the spirit which is of God; that we might know the things that are freely given to us of God.

13 Which things also we speak, not in the words which man's wisdom teacheth, but which the Holy Ghost teacheth; comparing spiritual things with spiritual.

The word *spirit* is used in three ways in these verses. The uppercase "Spirit" refers to the inner essence of God's being (John 4:24). When the first letter is not capitalized, the word can refer to the inner essence of a person ("the spirit of man") or to the attitude that characterizes a group.

For example, "the spirit of the world" is contrasted with "the spirit which is of God." (Some translations assume the latter means the Spirit of God, not the spirit of living that comes to believers from God.) When used of God, the word appears three ways in these verses: "the Spirit," "the Spirit of God," "the Holy Ghost" ("Ghost" is old English for "Spirit"). Thus, most translations have "Holy Spirit." The Spirit of God is the invisible presence of God as the Almighty deals directly with individuals.

Paul compared God's Spirit to a person's spirit. Who understands you? Your inner being or spirit hopefully has such understanding. In a far more infinite way, the Spirit of God understands the deep plans and purposes of God. The Spirit thus can choose to reveal these deep purposes of God to humans who are open to this revelation. This revelation is "freely given to us" by God.

The Holy Spirit is assigned many roles or tasks. One of these tasks is as Teacher of God's people. The Spirit gives us insight into the deep purposes of God and also gives us words to express this revelation. The last word in verse 13 can refer to things or people. In other words, the point may be that the Spirit helps us communicate spiritual words or things. Or the meaning may be that we can communicate spiritual realities only to spiritual people.

3. Natural man and spiritual man (2:14–16)

15 But he that is spiritual judgeth all things, yet he himself is judged of no man.

16 For who hath known the mind of the Lord, that he may instruct him? But we have the mind of Christ.

Paul contrasted two kinds of people, which he calls "the natural man" and the "spiritual." The former are those people who do not receive the Spirit of God. Thus, the purposes of God seem foolish to such people because such realities are discerned spiritually (2:14). By contrast, the spiritual person, in whom the Spirit of God dwells, has insight into all things. This discernment comes from the Spirit of God. This is the meaning of "judgeth all things," not that Christians pass judgment on others in ways forbidden by Christ (Matt. 7:1). Others may pass judgment on believers, but spiritual people realize that only God can truly judge them. Thus, they ignore the biased opinions of people who do not know the Lord (1 Cor. 4:3–5).

Paul quoted Isaiah 40:13 to show that God acts without human advice in ways beyond human comprehension, unless God chooses to reveal His ways to His people. Thus, believers' discernment of the mind of Christ is the result of the revelation by God's Spirit.

III. Praising God, Not Human Leaders (1 Cor. 3:1–23)

1. Leaders as servants of God (3:1–9)

Returning to the Corinthian problem of arguments over human leaders, Paul told his readers that they were not acting like mature believers, but spiritual infants. Using even stronger words, he told them they were not acting like spiritual people, but like carnal or non-Christian people (3:1–4). Paul reminded them that he and Apollos were only servants of God (3:5). Comparing them to farmers, Paul planted the seed; Apollos watered it; but only God made it grow (3:6–8). Paul and Apollos were fellow workers serving under the same Lord (3:9).

2. Building worthily on a firm foundation (3:10–17)

Paul changed the analogy to that of a builder. He laid a firm foundation by grounding faith in Jesus Christ (3:10, 11). Each preacher who followed Paul and each Christian who built a life on that foundation was accountable for what he built. He could build something valuable and lasting, or he could build something shoddy and temporary (3:12). The fires of divine judgment will consume all that is not lasting by God's standards, although a true believer will survive because of the fireproof foundation (3:13–15). Changing the analogy slightly, Paul reminded the Corinthians that their church was a temple in which God's Spirit dwelt. Paul warned of divine judgment against anyone who destroyed God's temple (3:16, 17; compare 1 Cor. 6:19, 20, which refers to each believer's body).

3. Belonging to God (3:18–23)

Worldly wise people ought to stop deceiving themselves. They will find true wisdom only when they admit their own folly (3:18). God considers worldly wise people to be fools (3:19, 20). Therefore, since one expression of worldly wisdom is idolatrous loyalties to human leaders, wise people will glory in God, not in themselves or other human beings (3:21a). Those who know God are children of the Owner of all things. As His heirs, they have all things (3:21b–23).

SUMMARY OF BIBLE TRUTHS

1. Preaching the cross demands that people come to God as needy sinners.
2. Preaching in the power of God's Spirit shows that the power comes from God alone.
3. God's kind of wisdom seems foolish to the worldly wise.
4. Worldly wise people seek worldly glory, but only God's people experience the true glory which God plans for His own.
5. God's Spirit reveals the mystery of God's purposes.
6. Only spiritual people perceive the mind of Christ.

Work of the Holy Spirit in People	
Convicts of sin	(John 16:8–11)
Glorifies Christ	(John 16:14)
Causes believers to be born anew	(John 3:1–8)
Abides in each believer	(Rom. 8:9; 1 Cor. 6:19, 20)
Abides in the church	(John 14:16, 17; 1 Cor. 3:17)
Fills those who surrender to Him	(Eph. 5:18)
Empowers witnesses for Christ	(Acts 1:8; 4:31)
Motivates and empowers doing right	(Rom. 8:1–13)
Enables believers to bear the fruit of the Spirit	(Gal. 5:22, 23)
Transforms into the image of Christ	(2 Cor. 3:17, 18)

Work of the Holy Spirit in People (Continued)	
Illumines the inspired Scriptures	(2 Pet. 1:21)
Helps in prayer	(Rom. 8:26, 27)
Gives spiritual gifts	(1 Cor. 12:4–13)
Guides	(Acts 16:6–10)
Teaches	(1 Cor. 2:13; John 14:26)
Assures of being God's children	(Rom. 8:14–17)
Assures of heaven	(2 Cor. 5:5)

APPLYING THE BIBLE

1. Functional ministry based on knowing Christ. Lynn Taylor, vice president and director of research at Accountemps, says, "Functional resumes are great for people changing careers, hiding flaws and showing off the qualities they can bring to a new job."[1]

Paul wrote the Corinthians to correct several problems in their church. He offered a functional resume of himself (not a chronological one) and emphasized his knowledge of the crucified Christ as the only personal resource that he brought to the table. He knew that the problems in the church were spiritual and that Christ alone could make the difference.

2. Falsified resumes. When the Port Authority of New York and New Jersey ran a help-wanted ad for electricians with expertise at using Sontag connectors, it got 170 responses—even though there is no such thing as a Sontag connector. The authority ran the ad to find out how many applicants falsify resumes.[2]

3. How not to write a resume. The second chapter of 1 Corinthians reads like a defense of Paul's experience with the Corinthian church. However, it seems as if he is trying hard not to impress the church by downplaying any of his human strengths.

Robert Half International, a worldwide executive-search firm based in Menlo Park, California, collects and publicizes bloopers like the ones listed below from real resumes.[3] If you want to impress a prospective employer, you should omit mistakes such as these.

- "I have lurnt Word Perfect 6.0."
- "Received a plague for Salesperson of the Year."
- "Reason for leaving last job: maturity leave."
- "Am a perfectionist and rarely if if ever forget details."
- "Note: Please don't misconstrue my 14 jobs as 'job-hopping.' I have never quit a job."
- "The company made me a scapegoat, just like my three previous employers."

Paul was not out to impress anyone. He told the Corinthians that he had a limited knowledge base (Christ alone, v. 2). He seemed only to emphasize the negative (Christ crucified, v. 2). He confessed weaknesses, fears, and trembling even though secular job hunters know they should *never* let a prospective employer see them sweat (v. 3). Finally,

Paul did not list good references. In fact, he said that those in charge weren't wise enough to be trusted anyway (vv. 6–8).

4. A work of the Spirit. Ken Hemphill, president of Southwestern Baptist Theological Seminary, says, "One of the dangerous trends of much current-day church growth material might be an over-emphasis and over-reliance on methods and marketing to the detriment of supernatural encounter and prayer. While we need to be open to new methodologies, we must constantly bear in mind that authentic church growth is supernaturally empowered."[4]

5. The Holy Spirit as teacher. The Christian gets OJT (on-the-job training) like no one else. The Holy Spirit is our teacher, and we begin our formal education the day we come to know Christ. As His students, we learn while:

- obeying,
- meditating,
- serving,
- waiting, and
- listening.

This is the wisdom Paul wanted the Corinthians to have. After nearly two thousand years, OJT is still the best (and only) education available to a believer.

6. Worldly experience and wrong decisions. During a question-and-answer session following a class lecture in a business college, an aspiring young collegian on the threshold of graduation asked the visiting "successful" businessman who had made a fortune on Wall Street, "Sir, what is the secret of your success?"

"Two words" he replied.

"What are they?" she asked.

"Right decisions."

Unimpressed, she prodded for more. "And how do you make right decisions?"

"One word," he replied

And with a bit of exasperation she followed, "And what is that?"

"Experience."

Before another student could change the subject, she asked, "And how do you get experience?"

"Two words."

"And what are they?"

"Wrong decisions."[5]

The wisdom of this age is made up of the experiences people have had making a series of right and wrong decisions. G. Campbell Morgan writes, "The child of God who has the Spirit of God has no right to be content not to understand the deep things of God. The Spirit is ours that we may know."[6]

TEACHING THE BIBLE

- *Main Idea:* The Holy Spirit enables believers to praise God.
- *Suggested Teaching Aim:* To lead adults to identify ways they can praise God.

A TEACHING OUTLINE

1. *Empowering the Preaching of the Cross (1 Cor. 2:1–5)*
2. *Revealing God's Kind of Wisdom (1 Cor. 2:6–16)*
3. *Praising God, Not Human Leaders (1 Cor. 3:1–23)*

Introduce the Bible Study

Use number 6, "Worldly Experience and Wrong Decisions," in "Applying the Bible" to introduce the lesson. Point out that the Holy Spirit provides believers wisdom and gives us insights about God that the wisest unbeliever cannot have.

Search for Biblical Truth

Plan a lecture for this lesson. **IN ADVANCE:**

- Make poster strips of the three major outline points above.
- Enlist someone to present "Work of the Holy Spirit in People" on pages 219–220 at the end of this lesson.
- Make copies of the following Study Guide for each member.

Use the questions as an outline for your lecture. Use "Studying the Bible" to provide information and explanations of the questions.

Study Guide	
1. How many times does "wisdom" occur in 2:1–13?	
2. In what two ways did Paul use "wisdom"?	
3. What two things did Paul not do to impress the Corinthians?	
4. What one thing did he do?	
5. Why did Paul not use human wisdom in his preaching?	
6. What is the mystery of God's wisdom?	
7. To whom did Paul speak God's wisdom?	
8. What does it mean to refer to God's wisdom as "a mystery"?	
9. Put the meaning of 2:9 in your own words:	
10. List two interpretations of "rulers of this world."	
11. How can we understand what God wants us to know?	
12. What is one role the Holy Spirit has in our lives?	
13. What three ways is "spirit" used in these verses?	
14. What two terms does Paul use in verses 14–15 to describe believers and unbelievers?	
15. Paraphrase verse 16b.	
16. In what way does the spiritual person "judgeth all things"?	

Distribute the Study Guides and ask members to open their Bibles to 1 Corinthians 2:1. Use the questions as an outline to guide your lecture.

DISCUSS: Use the following discussion questions:

After question 4, ask, Why does the cross draw people to Jesus in ways that human wisdom cannot?

After question 5, ask, How can we know when a preacher is using human wisdom in his preaching?

After question 9, ask, What would be the most wonderful thing you could think of in heaven?

After question 11, ask, What is the greatest thought you have ever had about God?

After question 12, ask the enlisted person to present "Work of the Holy Spirit in People."

After question 16, ask, What do you do with the insights that the Holy Spirit gives you into the workings of God?

Give the Truth a Personal Focus

To apply the lesson, say, This lesson reminds us of the following: (Read the six "Summary of Bible Truths" statements). Close in prayer.

---

1. Ann Chen, "Attention-Grabbing Resume Can Get Your Foot in the Door," *San Jose Mercury News,* Dec. 28, 1997.
2. Peter LeVine, "Boardroom Reports," *Leadership,* vol. 15, no. 1, July 15, 1993.
3. "How to Avoid Getting Hired: Stupid Resume Tricks," *Fortune,* July 21, 1997, 117.
4. Ken Hemphill, "Memorandum to State Baptist Paper Editors," March 16, 1993.
5. *Bits and Pieces,* vol. R, no. 29 (Fairfield, N.J.: The Economic Press, Inc.), 16.
6. G. Campbell Morgan, *Life Applications from Every Chapter of the Bible* (Grand Rapids: Fleming H. Revell, 1926), 338.

March
19
2000

The Church and Its Leaders

Background Passage: 1 Corinthians 4:1–13
Focal Passage: 1 Corinthians 4:1–13

Paul was still dealing with the issue of divisive dissension over leaders (1:10–12). As he neared the end of his words about this issue, Paul listed the qualities of the leaders about which the members were squabbling.

Study Aim: *To list qualities of good church leaders.*

STUDYING THE BIBLE

OUTLINE AND SUMMARY

I. Basic Qualities of Good Leaders (1 Cor. 4:1, 2)
II. How Leaders Handle Criticism (1 Cor. 4:3–5)
  1. Ignore criticism (4:3, 4)
  2. Don't play God (4:5)
III. Applications for Members (1 Cor. 4:6, 7)
  1. Don't be puffed up (4: 6)
  2. Replace pride with gratitude (4: 7)
IV. Sacrifices of Leaders (1 Cor. 4:8–13)
  1. Striking contrasts (4:8–10)
  2. Christlike responses (4:11–13)

Good church leaders are humble servants and faithful stewards (vv. 1, 2). They ignore criticism (vv. 3, 4). Christians should avoid passing judgment on brothers in Christ (v. 5). Christians should not be puffed up with pride (v. 6). They should remember that everything good that they have is from God (v. 7). Leaders who make sacrifices for the cause of Christ stand in marked contrast to members who have an inflated attitude toward themselves (vv. 8–10). Christlike leaders give back good for evil to those who persecute them (vv. 11–13).

I. Basic Qualities of Good Leaders (1 Cor. 4:1, 2)

1 Let a man so account of us, as of the ministers of Christ, and stewards of the mysteries of God.

2 Moreover it is required in stewards, that a man be found faithful.

"Let a man so account of us" was Paul's way of calling the attention of the Corinthians to the leaders whom they had been treating as rivals. "Us" may refer to Paul, Apollos, and Cephas, all of whom Paul had just mentioned (3:22). However, Paul mentioned only himself and Apollos by name in 4:1–13. He did mention "apostles" in verse 9. He could have been using the word in its usual technical sense, which would have included Peter, Paul, and the others whom Christ commissioned as apostles. On the other hand, "apostles" sometimes was used in the general sense of "missionary," which would have included Apollos.

Paul used two key words to describe good church leaders (and good church members too): *ministers* and *stewards.* This is not the usual word translated "ministers" or "servants." The word in verse 1 originally referred to the slaves who manned the oars on the lowest tier of oars on a ship. They were the lowest of the low.

A good leader is a servant-leader, who sets the example for humble service. Jesus exemplified and taught this. On the last night before His crucifixion, for example, Jesus washed the disciples' feet and told them that He was setting an example for them (John 13:1–17). Peter probably had that in mind when he wrote church leaders not to lord it over their flock but to be examples to them (1 Pet. 5:3).

"Stewards" were slaves or servants to whom their master or employer entrusted something belonging to the master. For example, Jesus told several parables of stewards entrusted with their masters' households or with their possessions. Christian leaders have been entrusted with the good news of God's revealed mystery of salvation by grace through faith. All Christians share this stewardship (1 Pet. 4:10).

Stewards are expected to be faithful in managing what is entrusted to them by doing what the master said to do with his possessions. When Jesus told the parable of the talents, the returned master commended his "good and faithful servant" (Matt. 25:21, 23).

II. How Leaders Handle Criticism (1 Cor. 4:3–5)

1. Ignore criticism (vv. 3, 4)

> **3 But with me it is a very small thing that I should be judged of you, or of man's judgment: yea, I judge not mine own self.**
>
> **4 For I know nothing by myself; yet am I not hereby justified: but he that judgeth me is the Lord.**

The existence of four factions—three of which supported a leader other than Paul—is evidence that Paul was not popular with many in the Corinthian church. Yet Paul considered their criticisms "a very small thing." In other words, he ignored their criticisms and the judgments passed on him by any one other than God, his only Judge.

Paul said that he did not even give much weight to his judgment of himself. Anyone's self-judgment is biased; thus, he did not relax just because he knew of nothing serious against himself. The only judgment that really matters is what the Lord thinks of us—not what others think of us or what we think of ourselves.

2. Don't play God (v. 5)

> **5 Therefore judge nothing before the time, until the Lord come, who both will bring to light the hidden things of darkness, and will make manifest the counsels of the hearts: and then shall every man have praise of God.**

Paul addressed the Corinthians, who were judging him, the other leaders, and one another. He warned them against doing what only God is qualified to do—passing judgment on other people. Only God has the character and the information to be Judge. Thus, the Bible often warns against playing God by condemning others or by justifying ourselves (Matt. 7:1–5; Rom. 2:1; 14:10).

In a sense, all human judgments are pre-judgments. Not even God renders final judgment until the end of time. Only then will a person's life and influence have borne its full fruit—either for good or for evil. At that time, God will bring into the light all the sins that people thought they had kept hidden and secret. And God will also judge people's thoughts and attitudes.

III. Applications for Members (1 Cor. 4:6, 7)

1. Don't be puffed up (v. 6)

6 And these things, brethren, I have in a figure transferred to myself and to Apollos for your sakes; that ye might learn in us not to think of men above that which is written, that no one of you be puffed up for one against another.

Paul called the Corinthian believers "brethren" to show how he regarded them and to set the stage for emphasizing that he and Apollos were also brothers in Christ. They viewed each other as brothers, friends, fellow-workers, not as rivals. Throughout his lengthy response to their attitude, Paul used himself and Apollos as examples of fellow-workers (3:5–9).

Paul told the Corinthians "not to think of men above that which is written." Bible scholars are not sure what he meant. One possibility is that he was telling them to follow the Scriptures in giving God His rightful place and human leaders their rightful places as servants of God. No one is justified in an idolatrous attachment to any human leader.

Paul warned them not to be puffed up by their selfish pride in their favorite leader in contrast to those who favored another leader. "Puffed up" was used by Paul more often in his Corinthian letters than in his correspondence to any other church. They were puffed up about leaders and about many other issues (1 Cor. 4:18, 19; 5:2; 8:1; 13:4; 2 Cor. 12:20). As noted in the first lesson, selfish pride was at the heart of the problems in the Corinthian church, just as it is at the heart of all human problems. It is the basic human sin.

2. Replace pride with gratitude (v. 7)

7 For who maketh thee to differ from another? and what hast thou that thou didst not receive? now if thou didst receive it, why dost thou glory, as if thou hadst not received it?

Several answers have been proposed to the first question, depending on what Paul meant by "differ from another." If he was thinking of their spiritual gifts, which is likely, he was saying that God is the giver of different spiritual gifts.

The answer to the second question is more obvious. The answer is "nothing." Everything good was from God, the giver of every good and perfect gift (James 1:17). None of their gifts or any other good thing was the result of their own efforts (Deut. 8:17). Thus, Jacob prayed with gratitude to God and acknowledged that he was not worthy of the least of God's many blessings (Gen. 32:10).

The third question is the logical one to follow the second. If all that we have is a gift from God, what basis do people have for acting as if they are responsible for what is good in their lives?

IV. Sacrifices of Leaders (1 Cor. 4:8–13)

1. Striking contrasts (vv. 8–10)

8 Now ye are full, now ye are rich, ye have reigned as kings without us: and I would to God ye did reign, that we also might reign with you.

9 For I think that God hath set forth us the apostles last, as it were appointed to death: for we are made a spectacle unto the world, and to angels, and to men.

10 We are fools for Christ's sake, but ye are wise in Christ; we are weak, but ye are strong; ye are honourable, but we are despised.

Paul used powerful ironic language to contrast how the proud Corinthians viewed themselves with the way in which the world and the apostles viewed themselves. The arrogant Corinthians acted as if the kingdom of God had already come in all its fullness and they were already reigning as they lived a rich, full life. Paul said sadly that he wished that the kingdom had fully come and that Christ had fully honored all His people by including them in His reign. But it was not so!

Instead of reigning, the apostles were treated like condemned criminals who were led last into the arena. There a spectacle was made of the deaths of the condemned. The apostles were made a spectacle not only for people but also angels.

The Corinthians reveled in those things the Greeks prized as marks of wise people; but Paul and the apostles preached the cross of Christ, which the Greeks considered foolish (1 Cor. 1:18–25). The Corinthians considered themselves so strong that they later had to be warned that anyone who thinks he stands needs to "take heed lest he fall" (1 Cor. 10:12). By contrast, the apostles had learned that only as they recognized their weakness did they become open to the strength of God working in and through them (2 Cor. 12:7–10). The Corinthians prized being considered people of honor by worldly standards. The apostles knew that in order to serve the One who was despised and rejected of man, they too must be despised.

2. Christlike responses (vv. 11–13)

11 Even unto this present hour we both hunger, and thirst, and are naked, and are buffeted, and have no certain dwellingplace;

12 And labour, working with our own hands: being reviled, we bless; being persecuted, we suffer it:

13 Being defamed, we intreat: we are made as the filth of the world, and are the offscouring of all things unto this day.

Right up to the time of Paul's writing, the apostles were not rich and full like the Corinthians; instead, they often were hungry, thirsty, poorly clothed, and homeless. Some of them—like Paul—worked to support themselves rather than exercise their right to receive pay from the churches. (See other lists of Paul's difficulties in 2 Cor. 4:8–10; 6:4–10; 11:23–33.)

At the same time the enemies of the cross of Christ reviled, persecuted, and defamed them, the apostles followed the example and teachings of Jesus in how they responded to evil acts. Rather than returning evil for evil, they returned good for evil. They blessed those who reviled them. They endured persecution. They witnessed to those who reviled them. All the while, they were being treated as if they were what we would call "scum of the earth."

SUMMARY OF BIBLE TRUTHS

1. Good leaders are humble servants of God and others.
2. Good leaders are faithful stewards of the gospel message.
3. Good leaders ignore criticism and seek to please only God.
4. Christians should treat one another as brothers, not as rivals.
5. Replace pride with humble gratitude and faithful stewardship.
6. Christlike people return good for evil.

APPLYING THE BIBLE

1. Leadership. What kind of leader was Paul? In today's lesson we see that he was a leader under attack. He defended himself against his critics but maintained a focus that enabled him to lead and minister. Experienced executives know that maintaining a focus on the future requires a conscious effort, since shorter term, operational issues (and criticisms) have a tendency to dominate their attention.[1] If you are a leader today, expect criticism but be "future focused."

2. What makes a leader? Andrea Cunningham, president and founder of Cunningham Communications, Inc., says that a leader must possess the following five characteristics:

- An undying and unquestionable belief in your abilities.
- The stick-to-it-iveness to do whatever it takes to make something happen.
- The electricity to light up the organization and keep it running.
- The desire to make heroes out of your subordinates.
- The personality to get people to join your parade.

3. Criticism. "Criticism comes easier than craftsmanship" (Pliny the Elder).

4. Ten commandments for church leaders:

- Practice grace. Everyone needs it once in a while.
- Be a bridge builder.
- Listen.
- Help others become free.
- Say "thank you" often.
- Say "please" every time you can.

- Laugh at yourself and with others.
- Enlarge the circle of the spotlight.
- Keep your shoulders free of all debris, including past hurts.
- Do one thing nice for at least one person every day.

5. The exercise of power. "A trusted deacon handed me a card one day upon which was written the following words: 'Because leadership is necessarily an exercise of authority, it easily shifts into an exercise of power. But the minute it does that, it begins to inflict damage on both the leader and the led.' I keep this card on my desk so that I can be reminded of it regularly. It speaks volumes to church leaders" (author unknown).

Paul understood the principle even though he did not have the quote. Leaders must be faithful stewards of the manifold grace of God. They cannot lead and abuse at the same time and be found faithful.

6. Church leadership and the formula for failure. International management consultant Van Oliphant offers a tongue-in-cheek approach for leadership failure:

- Develop a know-it-all attitude.
- Refuse to recognize the principle of delegation.
- Disregard the need to cultivate peer relationships.
- Procrastinate in making decisions.
- Place the blame for failure on others.[2]

7. Future church leaders. Van Oliphant says future leaders must

- be flexible,
- be adaptable,
- possess the ability to anticipate changes and the ability to respond to them,
- have a high frustration tolerance,
- develop credibility,
- earn respect,
- keep egos under control, and
- learn the difference between efficiency and effectiveness.[3]

TEACHING THE BIBLE

- *Main Idea:* Good church leaders handle criticism in a Christlike way.
- *Suggested Teaching Aim:* To lead adults to identify ways of handling criticism in a Christlike way.

A TEACHING OUTLINE

1. *Basic Qualities of Good Leaders (1 Cor. 4:1, 2)*
2. *How Leaders Handle Criticism (1 Cor. 4:3–5)*
3. *Applications for Members (1 Cor. 4:6, 7)*
4. *Sacrifices of Leaders (1 Cor. 4:8–13)*

Introduce the Bible Study

Use number 4, "Ten Commandments for Church Leaders," in "Applying the Bible" to introduce the lesson.

Search for Biblical Truth

Number and print the summary statements in "Outline and Summary" on large strips of paper and tape them around the room. Let members read them aloud to overview the lesson.

Ask members to open their Bibles to 1 Corinthians 4:1. On a chalkboard or a large sheet of paper, write: *Ministers* and *Stewards.* Ask half the class (Group 1) to list characteristics of good ministers. Ask the other half (Group 2) to list characteristics of good stewards. Use "Studying the Bible" and define both of these. Point out that these characteristics apply to all Christians.

Ask Group 1 to scan 1 Corinthians 4:3–5 and find one way a leader can handle criticism. (Ignore it.) Ask the other half (Group 2) to scan 1 Corinthians 4:5 and find another way. (Don't play God.) Ask Group 1, Whose criticism really mattered to Paul? (God's.) Ask Group 2, Why should we not judge others or even ourselves? (We don't have all the information.)

DISCUSS: How does the following statement make you feel? "Not even God renders final judgment until the end of time. Only then will a person's life and influence have borne its full fruit—either for good or for evil."

Ask, What term in verse 6 did Paul use to show how he felt about the Corinthians even though they were creating trouble? If members have different translations, ask them to share the translations of verse 6. Ask: How are we going "above that which is written" when we place leaders in a position in which God alone should be? What ways can this be done?

Ask members to look at verse 7. Ask Group 1 to paraphrase the first question in 7 and answer it. Ask Group 2 to paraphrase the second question in 7 and answer it. Ask both to paraphrase the third question in 7 and answer it.

DISCUSS: Do we have anything that has not come from God—whether talents, looks, physical bodies, intelligence, or motivation? Do we ever have anything to boast about?

Ask Group 1 to explain Paul's irony in verse 8 and why later in 1 Corinthians 10:12 they had to be warned that if they thought they were strong enough to withstand temptation, they likely would fall. Ask Group 2 to describe Paul's feelings in verses 9, 10.

Ask both Groups 1 and 2 to look at verses 11–13. Ask Group 1 to find ways Paul and other apostles worked in a Christlike manner. Ask Group 2 to find ways they responded to events and criticism in a Christlike manner.

Give the Truth a Personal Focus

IN ADVANCE, write the six "Summary of Bible Truths" statements on a large sheet of paper. Place this on the wall. Ask: Do these statements describe good leaders? Which of them does not apply to all believers? Pray that members will be able to respond to criticism in a Christlike way.

---

1. Michael E. McGrath, *Cahners Magazine,* April 1998, 9–10.
2. Van Oliphant, "Church Leadership Professor Offers Formula for Failure," Baptist Press, Nov. 18, 1996.
3. Ibid.

The Need for Discipline in the Church

Background Passage: 1 Corinthians 5:1–6:11
Focal Passage: 1 Corinthians 5:1–13

The content of 1 Corinthians is built around specific problems in the church. The problem of disruptive dissension (1:10–12) determined the content of 1 Corinthians 1:10–4:21. The problem of serious sin in a church member's life and the church's complacent attitude determined the content of the next section of the letter.

Study Aim: *To contrast the attitudes of Paul and the Corinthian church toward a member living in sexual immorality.*

STUDYING THE BIBLE

OUTLINE AND SUMMARY

I. When Discipline Is Needed (1 Cor. 5:1, 2)
- **1. Persistent and serious sin (5:1)**
- **2. Complacent and proud church (5:2)**

II. Goals of Discipline (1 Cor. 5:3–8)
- **1. Salvation of the member (5:3–5)**
- **2. Cleansing the church (5:6–8)**

III. Discipline and Fellowship (1 Cor. 5:9–13)
- **1. Contacts with unbelievers (5:9, 10)**
- **2. Close fellowship with sinful church members (5:11–13)**

IV. Discipline and Judgment (1 Cor. 6:1–11)
- **1. Avoiding lawsuits with Christians (6:1–8)**
- **2. Remembering Christians are saved sinners (6:9–11)**

Discipline was needed in the Corinthian church because the church was proud of a member who was living in flagrant sexual immorality (5:1, 2). The goals of discipline were to see the sinful member among the saved when the Lord comes (5:3–5) and to cleanse the church of shameful sin (5:6–8). Contacts with unbelievers are inevitable (5:9, 10), but close fellowship with sinful church members is inappropriate (5:11–13). Christians should avoid going to court against one another (6:1–8). Persistent sinners are not in God's kingdom, but believers were once such sinners before the Lord saved them (6:9–11).

I. When Discipline Is Needed (1 Cor. 5:1, 2)

1. Persistent and serious sin (5:1)

1 It is reported commonly that there is fornication among you, and such fornication as is not so much as named among the Gentiles, that one should have his father's wife.

Paul had heard of a shocking case of sexual immorality that was well-known in the Corinthian church. A man, who was apparently a member of the church, was living with his father's wife, who seems not to have been a Christian. The woman was not the man's mother, or Paul would have said so. She had been his stepmother, but she seems to have been either divorced or widowed from the man's father. Paul did not say whether the man was married to her or only living with her, but the word *have* indicates the continuing persistence of the sin.

Strictly speaking, this was not incest; but it bore the same kind of stigma. Even the pagan world, with its lax views of sex, considered this kind of relationship taboo. Roman law forbade a man from marrying his father's wife, even if the father had died.

2. Complacent and proud church (5:2)

> **2 And ye are puffed up, and have not rather mourned, that he that hath done this deed might be taken away from among you.**

Paul was shocked not only by the man's heinous sinning but also by the attitude of the Corinthian church. They had made no move to discipline the man; instead they were proud of what was happening. How could a church be proud of such blatant sinning? They could have seen it as a mark of their open-mindedness about such things. Distortion of Christian freedom is a theme in 1 Corinthians. They may have been like a group later called Gnostics. They believed that flesh is evil; some of them taught that what a person did in the fleshly part of his life had no bearing on his spiritual life.

II. Goals of Discipline (1 Cor. 5:3–8)

1. Salvation of the member (5:3–5)

> **3 For I verily, as absent in body, but present in spirit, have judged already, as though I were present, concerning him that hath so done this deed,**
>
> **4 In the name of our Lord Jesus Christ, when ye are gathered together, and my spirit, with the power of our Lord Jesus Christ,**
>
> **5 To deliver such an one unto Satan for the destruction of the flesh, that the spirit may be saved in the day of the Lord Jesus.**

Paul told the Christians that he had already cast his vote to exclude the sinner from the church. Although he was not actually there in Corinth, his position was already clear. Paul did not presume to dictate to the congregation. He wrote of their gathering together to decide what to do. Paul wanted them to know that if he were present, he would vote to discipline the man. Neither Paul nor the congregation were the head of the church; they would be acting in the name and by the power of the Lord Jesus Christ.

Delivering the man over to Satan meant removing him from the Lord's people and placing him in the world, the realm of Satan's influence and power. The "destruction of the flesh" might refer to sickness or death (see 1 Cor. 11:30), but Paul often used "flesh" to describe the old way of sinful living. Paul's hope was that this would force the man to face his spiritual plight. If he was a real believer, this could lead him to repent. At any rate, Paul's objective and hope was that by this stern action, the church would be used by God to see that the man was saved when the Lord returns.

2. Cleansing the church (5:6–8)

6 Your glorying is not good. Know ye not that a little leaven leaveneth the whole lump?

7 Purge out therefore the old leaven, that ye may be a new lump, as ye are unleavened. For even Christ our passover is sacrificed for us:

8 Therefore let us keep the feast, not with old leaven, neither with the leaven of malice and wickedness; but with the unleavened bread of sincerity and truth.

One of the goals of discipline is the redemption of the sinning member; the other goal is the cleansing of the church from evil. A church that tolerates such open and flagrant sinning among its members will have little influence for God and good.

Paul used the analogy of how even a little leaven permeates the entire lump of dough. He used leaven here as a symbol of evil. A familiar proverb states, "One rotten apple spoils the whole barrel." Thus, Paul said to remove the evil leaven. He named two specific sins—wickedness and malice—as examples. He named two acts of righteousness—sincerity and truth—as examples of the good that should characterize the church.

Since the feast following Passover was the Feast of Unleavened Bread, Paul compared Christians to the Israelites when they kept the Passover in commemoration of their deliverance from Egypt. Christ is to Christians what the Passover lamb was to the enslaved Israelites in Egypt. Just as the blood of the lamb sprinkled on the doorposts saved the Jews from the death angel, so does the blood of Jesus cleanse us from sin and save us from spiritual death.

When Paul wrote "keep the feast," he meant living the Christian life in light of our cleansing from sin (see 1 Cor. 6:9–11). After we have been cleansed from our sins, Christians are not to return to the old ways. Leaven symbolized the old sins; and the absence of leaven signified the new life in Christ.

III. Discipline and Fellowship (1 Cor. 5:9–13)

1. Contacts with unbelievers (5:9, 10)

9 I wrote unto you in an epistle not to company with fornicators:

10 Yet not altogether with the fornicators of this world, or with the covetous, or extortioners, or with idolaters; for then must ye needs go out of the world.

Paul referred to a letter, which he must have written to them before he wrote 1 Corinthians. In the letter, he told them not to have close fellowship with people who lived in sexual immorality. Apparently the Corinthians had limited Paul's words to non-Christians. And Paul did teach Christians to avoid potentially compromising relationships with unbelievers (2 Cor. 6:14). However, Paul was not addressing that problem in his earlier letter. He was warning against close fellowship with fellow Christians who were living sinful lives.

Paul said that some contacts with unbelievers are necessary. This was particularly true in pagan Corinth, where Christians were a small minority of the population. Jesus also taught and practiced the need to maintain contact with sinners in order to lead them to repentance (Matt. 9:11–13; Luke 15:1, 2).

2. Close fellowship with sinful church members (5:11–13)

11 But now I have written unto you not to keep company, if any man that is called a brother be a fornicator, or covetous, or an idolater, or a railer, or a drunkard, or an extortioner; with such an one no not to eat.

12 For what have I to do to judge them also that are without? do not ye judge them that are within?

13 But them that are without God judgeth. Therefore put away from among yourselves that wicked person.

Paul clarified the meaning of his earlier letter and extended the list beyond sexual immorality. The apostle emphasized that he had been writing about a Christian brother who was guilty of sexual immorality—of which the man in verse 1 was a case in point. "Keep company" refers to close relationship. Eating together was considered one of the closest kinds of relationships. The Christians ate meals together and took the Lord's Supper together. Christians, however, were not to do this with church members living in persistent sin. Paul spelled it out clearly at the end of verse 13: they were to exclude the man from church fellowship.

Notice that Paul expanded the list of sins to include sins like greed. He also listed people who worshiped idols and those who were drunkards, slanderers, and swindlers. Paul did not mean this to be an exhaustive list. His point is that any church member who persists in a life of sin—whatever the sin—should not be treated as if he were living for the Lord. Paul elsewhere (Gal. 6:1) taught that every attempt should be made to restore those who go astray. Jesus outlined a three-step process for dealing with sinful believers (Matt. 18:15–18). Exclusion from the church would be the final step if all attempts at restoration failed. However, both Jesus and Paul taught that such discipline was the Lord's will when all else had failed.

Paul said that he had no right to pass judgment on unbelievers. God would judge them. However, as a part of the Lord's body, Paul taught that he and his fellow believers were expected to exercise discipline in the name of the Lord.

This teaching seems to many people to involve judging others, which Jesus said His followers were not to do (Matt. 7:1–5). Jesus did warn against individuals passing judgment on other individuals. However, when a group of believers act together under the Spirit's leadership, they are acting in His name.

IV. Discipline and Judgment (1 Cor. 6:1–11)

1. Avoiding lawsuits with Christians (6:1–8)

Paul warned Christians not to take one another to court (6:1). Since Christians shall eventually be involved in judging the world and even angels, surely they can exercise judgment in the kinds of issues dealt with in human courts (6:2, 3). Even the least qualified person ought to be able to handle such issues; how much more ought a qualified brother be able to settle disputes between brothers (6:4, 5). Think what an impression it makes when brothers go to court before unbelievers (6:6). It would be better for a Christian to give up his rights than to do this (6:7, 8).

2. Remembering Christians are saved sinners (6:9–11)

People only deceive themselves if they believe that persistent sinners (and Paul listed a number of sins as examples) are in God's kingdom (6:9, 10). On the other hand, Christians cannot forget that they once were guilty of sins of various kinds; but they have now been saved and set apart to live Christ's way of life (6:11).

PRONUNCIATION GUIDE

Gnostics [NAHZ tiks]

SUMMARY OF BIBLE TRUTHS

1. Some church members persist in living sinful lives.
2. Churches often do not discipline such members.
3. The goal of Christian discipline is redemptive.
4. A church needs to be cleansed of sins that destroy the church's witness for Christ.
5. Some contacts with unbelievers are necessary.
6. Christians are not to have close fellowship with church members who are living in sin.

APPLYING THE BIBLE

1. Discipline. The *American Heritage Dictionary* defines discipline as "punishment intended to correct or train."

2. Appropriate disciplinary measures. A University of New Hampshire study says that children whose parents spank them at least once a week are more likely to lie, cheat, bully, break things, and show no remorse for their bad behavior. They also have trouble getting along with their teachers and other kids. Stacey Colino suggests the following disciplinary track:

- Scold without getting personal.
- Hand down brief, but limited, warnings.
- Let a child learn from natural consequences.
- Remove a privilege that relates to whatever the child did wrong.
- Require reparations.

Sometimes we would like to use similar methods in dealing with church disciplinary issues. Paul's letter to the Corinthians was intended to help them take disciplinary actions in a situation that had become a moral embarrassment to the church. They were not dealing with childish issues of misbehavior. They could not afford to treat this problem lightly.

3. We have forgotten how to blush. The attitude of the church toward this sin was surprising. Instead of being embarrassed or concerned, the church seemed to display a sense of pride. (One wonders if the man in question had lots of money.)

The words of Jeremiah seem appropriate for the Corinthians. "Were they ashamed when they had committed abomination? nay, they were not at all ashamed, neither could they blush: therefore they shall fall among them that fall; at the time that I visit them they shall be cast down, saith the LORD" (Jer. 6:15).

4. Instructions on morality. "When you know Christ and Him crucified, you do not need instruction on morality . . . one follows the other" (David Brainerd).

Paul's reason for "throwing the brother out" was a gracious one. If the action prompted the brother to recognize that he never knew Christ, Paul hoped he would repent and return to the fellowship of the church. As it was, there was no evidence that he knew Christ as Savior, and his was a dangerous association.

5. Jesus' three-step process:

Step one, personal confrontation. "And if your brother does wrong to you, go, make clear to him his error between you and him in private: if he gives ear to you, you have got your brother back again" (Matt. 18:15).

Step two, group confrontation. "But if he will not give ear to you, take with you one or two more, that by the lips of two or three witnesses every word may be made certain" (Matt. 18:16).

Step three, congregational decision. "And if he will not give ear to them, let it come to the hearing of the church: and if he will not give ear to the church, let him be to you as a Gentile and a tax-collector" (Matt. 18:17).

6. Reputation. The way to gain a good reputation is to endeavor to be what you desire to appear.

7. Does repentance really matter? Following President Clinton's national address to the American people regarding his "inappropriate relationship" with an intern young enough to be his daughter, the dean of Washington National (Episcopal) Cathedral, Rev. Nathan Baxter, said in a Sunday sermon: "Our desire to keep sin private . . . is a judgment upon all of us. Unless we acknowledge moral failing—without excuse—the soul of our nation will not heal. More importantly, our children will be even more confused as to whether the truest treasure of our common life is found in the state of the economy or the character of our moral integrity."

Paul's corrective words to the Corinthian church sounded the same message. Real repentance matters. It matters in terms of the authenticity of our ministry, and it matters for the true bearings of the spiritual compass we seek to pass down to future generations.

- *Main Idea:* Believers who live immoral lives damage the body of Christ.
- *Suggested Teaching Aim:* To lead adults to identify scriptural support for calling on believers to live moral lives.

A TEACHING OUTLINE

1. *When Discipline Is Needed (1 Cor. 5:1, 2)*
2. *Goals of Discipline (1 Cor. 5:3–8)*
3. *Discipline and Fellowship (1 Cor. 5:9–13)*
4. *Discipline and Judgment (1 Cor. 6:1–11)*

Introduce the Bible Study

Use number 1, "Discipline," in "Applying the Bible" to introduce the lesson.

Search for Biblical Truth

Organize members in two groups (or you can do this with the whole class). Write the following chart without the italicized answers on a chalkboard or large sheet of paper. Assign Group 1, Paul's attitudes, and Group 2, the Corinthians' attitude.

Contrasting Attitudes

Attitudes	Paul	Corinthians
Illicit relationship (5:1–2)	Shocked	Proud, approving
Response to the man (5:3–5)	Remove from church	Let remain in church
Leaven (5:6–8)	Remove	Let influence whole church
Contact with immoral Christians (5:9–10)	No	Yes
Contact with immoral unbelievers (5:9, 11–13)	Yes	(Not Applicable)

Ask the groups to search the Scriptures to find the answers for the chart. Members' answers may differ slightly from the ones given. Fill in the chart as they suggest their responses.

After the groups have finished, read aloud the following case study. Ask each group, based on their study, to write a solution to this case study. (Distribute paper and pencils if needed.)

Marie had been a member of the church for years. She had always been faithful and was a true spiritual "pillar" of the church. She was a gentle, caring person.

When her only child, Bill, was 13, her husband died. Bill rebelled against her, the church, God, and everyone else. Bill had made a profession of faith in a revival when he was 10 and had been baptized. After his father died, Bill attended only spasmodically. He had done drugs and had some light skirmishes with the police. This broke Marie's heart.

At 28, Bill had been married and divorced. He was now living with a woman, and they had recently had a child—a little girl who was the pride of Bill's life. Bill showed up one morning at church with his little girl and his live-in companion. When church members saw them, one group went to Marie and said, "It is so good to have Bill in church today." The other group went to Marie and said, "I don't see how Bill can come into this building after the kind of life he has led."

What should Marie do? What should the church do? What would you do if this were your church?

Call for responses and let the groups discuss each other's responses.

Give the Truth a Personal Focus

Assign the even numbered "Summary of Bible Truths" statements to Group 1 and the odd numbered statements to Group 2. Ask the groups to (1) read the statements aloud and (2) suggest one specific application for your church. Close in prayer that God will grant wisdom and courage, love and compassion, and the grace to know when to apply each.

Counsel Concerning Marriage

Background Passage: 1 Corinthians 6:12–7:16
Focal Passages: 1 Corinthians 7:1–5, 8–16

First-century Greek society was a sexual wilderness of immorality and perversion, and Corinth had the worst reputation in all of Greece. The Gentile converts often had been guilty of such sins and still lived in a city dominated by such sins. Paul tried to teach them about the biblical view of sex as God's good gift to be exercised only within the one-flesh union of marriage.

Study Aim: *To explain what Paul taught about marriage.*

STUDYING THE BIBLE

OUTLINE AND SUMMARY

- **I. Sexual Immorality (1 Cor. 6:12–20)**
  - **1. Why sexual immorality is wrong (6:12–17)**
  - **2. Flee sexual immorality (6:18–20)**
- **II. Marriage and Celibacy (1 Cor. 7:1–9)**
  - **1. Is it good not to have sex? (7:1)**
  - **2. Sex in marriage (7:2–6)**
  - **3. Celibacy for the unmarried (7:7–9)**
- **III. Permanence of Marriage (1 Cor. 7:10–16)**
  - **1. In a Christian marriage (7:10, 11)**
  - **2. In a stable mixed marriage (7:12–14)**
  - **3. When a non-Christian spouse leaves (7:15, 16)**

Sex is wrong when it is outside the one-flesh union of marriage (6:12–17). Christians should flee temptations to this sin (6:18–20). Some Corinthians wanted to know if sex was wrong, even in marriage (7:1). Paul taught that sex in marriage is essential in a Christian marriage (7:2–6). Paul personally preferred to remain single, but he realized that not everyone had the gift of remaining celibate (7:7–9). Christians should stay married (7:10, 11). If a Christian is already married to an unbeliever, the two should stay married (7:12–14). If a non-Christian spouse leaves, the Christian spouse is not bound (7:15, 16).

I. Sexual Immorality (1 Cor. 6:12–20)

1. Why sexual immorality is wrong (6:12–17)

Although Christians are not saved by keeping the Law, they are not free to do something that will enslave them (6:12). Although sex is a physical drive, it is a moral issue because it has to do with the body (6:13). Our bodies are who we are, and they will be raised (6:14). Members of Christ's body ought not to be made members of a prostitute (6:15). Sex outside the one-flesh union of husband and wife is a perversion of God's purpose for sex (6:16, 17).

2. Flee sexual immorality (6:18–20)

As Joseph fled from Potiphar's wife, Christians ought to flee any temptation to sexual immorality (6:18). The body of each Christian is a temple of the Holy Spirit of God (6:19). Because they have been redeemed, they ought to glorify God in their body (6:20).

II. Marriage and Celibacy (1 Cor. 7:1–9)

1. Is it good not to have sex? (7:1)

> **1 Now concerning the things whereof ye wrote unto me: It is good for a man not to touch a woman.**

This verse introduces the first of a series of issues in a letter from the Corinthians to Paul (see 8:1; 12:1; 16:1). We face two questions about the words: "It is good for a man not to touch a woman."

1. What did these words mean? One view says it means, "It is good not to get married." However, these words are used in Greek literature to describe having sexual relations. Thus, the meaning is that it is not good to have sex.

2. Who said this—Paul or the Corinthians? Paul's later comments show that he did not teach that having sex is wrong within marriage. More likely, therefore, this was a quotation from the Corinthians about a view that some of them had. Thus, some Corinthians insisted that all sex is all right (6:12, 13) and others insisted that all sex is wrong (7:1). Some married Christians in the early church accepted the latter view and thus tried to exclude sex from their marriage. This was probably true at Corinth.

2. Sex in marriage (7:2–6)

> **2 Nevertheless, to avoid fornication, let every man have his own wife, and let every woman have her own husband.**
>
> **3 Let the husband render unto the wife due benevolence: and likewise also the wife unto the husband.**
>
> **4 The wife hath not power of her own body, but the husband: and likewise also the husband hath not power of his own body, but the wife.**
>
> **5 Defraud ye not one the other, except it be with consent for a time, that ye may give yourselves to fasting and prayer; and come together again, that Satan tempt you not for your incontinency.**

Paul disagreed with the statement that all Christians should refrain from sex. Sex within marriage is normal and necessary. One reason is because marriage provides the way God gave for sexual expression. Paul has been accused of making marriage only a way to avoid sexual immorality. However, keep in mind that he was answering a specific question here, not giving an ideal description of Christian marriage.

His main point, of course, is that sexual relations is an essential part of marriage. A husband owes this to his wife, and she owes it to him. A married couple belong to each other. Verse 4 can be pressed too far as if to say that neither has any power over his or her body. That is not Paul's point. His point is that each also belongs to the other, and neither can arbitrarily act only on what he or she wants to do or not to do.

Paul made only one concession to those in Corinth who wanted marriage without sex. Paul admitted that at times a Christian couple may agree to refrain from sex for a higher purpose; but Paul set forth clear conditions: (1) Both must agree, (2) it must be temporary, and (3) the purpose must be for prayer and fasting. Verse 6 means that Paul did not command such a period of abstinence from sex; he only allowed it if a couple met these three conditions.

Two other things are noteworthy about Paul's teaching concerning sex in marriage: (1) Nothing is said here about having sex only to have a child. Procreation is one reason for the one-flesh union of marriage, but expressions of intimacy, commitment, and love are also reasons for sex. (2) Paul emphasized the mutuality of the marriage relationship. Notice that he included both husband and wife in each point he made.

3. Celibacy for the unmarried (7:7–9)

> **8 I say therefore to the unmarried and widows, It is good for them if they abide even as I.**
>
> **9 But if they cannot contain, let them marry: for it is better to marry than to burn.**

Some Bible students think that Paul may have been a widower, but all we know is that he was not married when he wrote 1 Corinthians 7. At various places in chapter 7, Paul stated his reasons for his personal preference for remaining single. For example, he felt that unmarried Christians could give more of their time and energy to the Lord (7:32–35). On the other hand, Paul's references to his married friends Aquila and Priscilla show that married Christians also have special opportunities of service (Rom. 16:3–5).

Paul not only stated his personal preference for the single life; he commended it to others. He advised unmarried Christians to remain single; however, Paul recognized that not every Christian had the gift and calling of God to the single life. Part of this gift was the ability to live a celibate life. Paul said that those who are unable to refrain from sex ought to get married, "for it is better to marry than to burn." He probably meant to burn with lust.

Paul was echoing Jesus' teachings in Matthew 19:1–12. Jesus said that being married requires lifelong marriage and total faithfulness to one's spouse. He also taught that the single life has its own demand—total abstinence from sex.

III. Permanence of Marriage (1 Cor. 7:10–16)

1. In a Christian marriage (7:10, 11)

> **10 And unto the married I command, yet not I, but the Lord, Let not the wife depart from her husband:**
>
> **11 But and if she depart, let her remain unmarried, or be reconciled to her husband: and let not the husband put away his wife.**

Since verses 12–16 deal with mixed marriages in which only one spouse is a Christian, Paul apparently was addressing Christian couples in verses 10, 11. These verses definitely show that Paul was thinking of Jesus' teachings about marriage. That is why he wrote, this is the Lord's command, not just Paul's.

Paul reinforced the Lord's command about marriage being a lifetime union. Jesus quoted Genesis 1:27 and 2:24 as scriptural evidence that this was God's intention for marriage. Thus, Paul told Christian wives not to leave their husbands, and he made the same demand on Christian husbands. If circumstances forced such a separation, Paul taught that the couple should remain unmarried or be reconciled to each other.

2. In a stable mixed marriage (7:12–14)

12 But to the rest speak I, not the Lord: If any brother hath a wife that believeth not, and she be pleased to dwell with him, let him not put her away.

13 And the woman which hath an husband that believeth not, and if he be pleased to dwell with her, let her not leave him.

14 For the unbelieving husband is sanctified by the wife, and the unbelieving wife is sanctified by the husband: else were your children unclean; but now are they holy.

Paul taught unmarried Christians to marry "only in the Lord" (1 Cor. 7:39; 2 Cor. 6:14). In other words, unmarried Christians who decide that it is God's will that they marry should marry only a Christian. But what about a Christian who is already married to an unbeliever? Perhaps both were unbelievers and then one was saved.

Paul could not quote a specific teaching of Jesus on this. That is what he meant by saying "I, not the Lord." Paul felt that the Spirit was leading him to share the mind of Christ; however, Paul did not know of a specific teaching of Jesus on this matter.

Paul wanted Christians who were already married to realize that theirs is a real marriage in the eyes of God. Thus, he told a Christian not to leave a non-Christian spouse, but to remain married. Paul used the word *sanctified* to describe the effect of a Christian spouse on an unbelieving mate, and he used the word *holy* to describe any children born of this union. He obviously was not saying that a Christian spouse automatically caused a non-Christian mate to be saved and sanctified in relation to God and sin. Nor did he mean that children of such a union come into the world saved and sanctified. What then did he mean?

For one thing, Paul used these strongly religious words to emphasize that the marriage is real and the children are legitimate. Paul also probably was implying that the presence of a Christian spouse added a spiritual dimension to the household, in spite of an unbelieving mate. And he meant that a child with one Christian parent is more likely to be influenced toward God than one raised by unbelievers.

3. When a non-Christian spouse leaves (7:15, 16)

15 But if the unbelieving depart, let him depart. A brother or a sister is not under bondage in such cases: but God hath called us to peace.

16 For what knowest thou, O wife, whether thou shalt save thy husband? or how knowest thou, O man, whether thou shalt save thy wife?

These verses have been interpreted in two different ways, depending on one's understanding of the meaning of "called us to peace." One interpretation emphasizes the words "called us to peace" and assumes that this refers to marital harmony: "God has called us to marital peace. So if the unbeliever is determined to go, let him or her go. This would be better than constant strife in the home. And besides, what real opportunity is there for winning the unbeliever under such circumstances?"

The other interpretation emphasizes verse 16 as a strong reason for trying to preserve the marriage: "There will be inevitable tensions in any mixed marriage. But do your best to stay together in the hope that your unbelieving spouse may be saved."

SUMMARY OF BIBLE TRUTHS

1. Sex is God's good gift, not a sin for married people.
2. Christian spouses owe normal sexual relations to each other.
3. God expects unmarried Christians to remain celibate.
4. Christians should marry for life.
5. If a Christian is already married to a non-Christian, the Christian should have a godly influence.
6. If a non-Christian spouse leaves, the Christian is not bound.

APPLYING THE BIBLE

1. Submission in marriage. A man entered the Boston library and asked for the location of the book, *Man, the Master of Women.* The librarian looked over the top of her glasses and said, "Try looking under fiction."

2. Successful marriage. Success in marriage requires more than finding the right mate; it involves being the right mate.

3. Questions for the person contemplating marriage:

- What is my gift from God?
- Am I marrying a believer?
- Are the circumstances such that marriage is right?
- How will marriage affect my service for Christ?
- Am I prepared to enter this union for life?

4. Marriage or people? "It is not marriage that fails; it is the people that fail" (H. E. Fosdick).

5. Ten ways to love your spouse:

- Assume responsibilty for your actions and be quick to say four important words: "I'm sorry" and "Forgive me."
- Follow through on commitments made to each other.

- Tell each other often what specific things you like about each other.
- Keep a good budget and manage it properly . . . don't overspend . . . don't rely on credit cards.
- Go over the weekly schedule and anticipate pressure spots in advance.
- Praise each other in public.
- Always remember the key holidays and other celebrations, such as birthdays and anniversaries!
- Provide each other time to be alone.
- Become your partner's "best friend."
- Go to a Christian marriage conference or retreat every three years.

TEACHING THE BIBLE

- *Main Idea:* Paul taught that sexual relationships for Christians should be confined to marriage.
- *Suggested Teaching Aim:* To lead adults to identify reasons why Paul taught that sexual relationships for Christians should be confined to marriage.

A TEACHING OUTLINE

1. *Sexual Immorality (1 Cor. 6:12–20)*
2. *Marriage and Celibacy (1 Cor. 7:1–9)*
3. *Permanence of Marriage (1 Cor. 7:10–16)*

Introduce the Bible Study

Use No. 1, "Submission in Marriage," in "Applying the Bible" to introduce the lesson.

Search for Biblical Truth

IN ADVANCE, do the following:

Copy the six "Summary of Bible Truths" statements on large strips of paper and place them around the room.

Write on a chalkboard or a large sheet of paper: *Sexual immorality is wrong . . .* Give members a piece of paper and a pencil as they enter and ask them to complete this sentence.

Copy the outline from "Outline and Summary" on a poster.

Place the first Roman numeral and the first two subpoints on the wall. Call for volunteers to read their responses to why sexuality is wrong. (Share these responses from "Studying the Bible": "Our bodies are who we are and will be raised . . . Sex outside the one-flesh union of husband and wife is a perversion of God's purpose for sex.")

Assign one-third of the class (Group 1) to look at both number 1 subpoints in the three sections of the outline; a second (Group 2) to look at both number 2 subpoints in the three sections of the outline, and a third (Group 3) to look at both number 3 subpoints in sections two and three of the outline. Ask each group to write a summary of the biblical truth in the section based on each of the points as they are being discussed. The summary should offer guidance in daily life. (See the summaries printed at the end of this lesson as suggestions but let members develop their own.)

Place the second Roman numeral and the first subpoint on the wall. Lecture briefly on 7:1, explaining (1) what the phrase means (good not to have sex in marriage), and (2) who said it (Corinthians asked Paul about this).

Place the second subpoint on the wall. Lecture briefly: (1) sex in marriage is normal and necessary; (2) each spouse belongs to the other, and neither can arbitrarily act only on what he or she wants to do or not to do; (3) the three reasons Christian couples may refrain from sex for a higher purpose; (4) sex is not just for having a child; (5) mutuality of both husband and wife is emphasized.

Place the third subpoint on the wall. Lecture briefly: (1) Paul may have been a widower; (2) Paul felt single Christians could give more time and energy to the Lord; (3) "to burn" probably means to "burn with passion" (NIV).

Place the third Roman numeral poster and the first subpoint on the wall. Lecture briefly, emphasizing the permanence of marriage. Place the second subpoint on the wall. Lecture briefly: (1) Christians should marry only believers; (2) a Christian should stay with unbelieving spouse; (3) a Christian spouse adds a spiritual dimension to the household; (4) children born to this union are more likely to be influenced for God than those raised by unbelievers.

Place the third subpoint on the wall. Lecture briefly, explaining the two meanings of "called us to peace." Ask, Which view do you support? Why?

Give the Truth a Personal Focus

Allow a couple of minutes for groups to write their Bible truths and then call for responses. Ask members if they can find a statement on the wall similar to theirs. Close in prayer.

April

9

2000

Concerning Love and Knowledge

Background Passage: 1 Corinthians 8:1–13
Focal Passage: 1 Corinthians 8:1–13

Meat sacrificed to idols was another divisive issue in Corinth. Although this is not an issue today, the principles apply to many modern issues that are potentially divisive.

Study Aim: *To identify abiding principles in Paul's teaching about meat sacrificed to idols.*

STUDYING THE BIBLE

OUTLINE AND SUMMARY

I. Knowledge, Love, and Morality (1 Cor. 8:1–8)

1. Proud knowledge and constructive love (8:1–3)

2. Knowledge about God and idols (8:4–6)

3. When a nonmoral issue becomes a moral issue (8:7, 8)

II. Freedom, Conscience, and Commitment (1 Cor. 8:9–13)

1. Danger of unrestrained freedom (8:9)

2. Sinning against conscience (8:10–12)

3. A commitment made in love (8:13)

Christian knowledge is personal knowledge of God, not knowledge that is proud and divisive (vv. 1–3). Mature Christians know that pagan gods are nothing; there is only one God (vv. 4–6). Eating meat is not a moral issue, but it becomes one when eating meat harms others (vv. 7, 8). Exercising our right to eat may cause weak brothers to stumble (v. 9). Causing someone to go against conscience is a serious sin (vv. 10–12). Paul made a commitment not to eat meat if it caused a brother to take offense (v. 13).

I. Knowledge, Love, and Morality (1 Cor. 8:1–8)

1. Proud knowledge and constructive love (vv. 1–3)

1 Now as touching things offered unto idols, we know that we all have knowledge. Knowledge puffeth up, but charity edifieth.

2 And if any man think that he knoweth any thing, he knoweth nothing yet as he ought to know.

3 But if any man love God, the same is known of him.

Corinth was a pagan city filled with temples to various gods. Much of the meat sold in the meat markets was from animals offered as sacrifices in those temples. A small portion was offered to the god and in some cases part was used either to feed the priests or to be eaten by the worshipers in a temple feast. The rest of the animal's meat was sold in markets and eaten in homes.

Many of the Corinthian Christians had worshiped idols before they heard the gospel and believed. Some of them felt that eating anything offered in a pagan temple was wrong. In their minds, such meat was tainted by having been presented to a pagan god. Other Corinthian Christians said that false gods were unreal; therefore, meat offered to a nonexistent god was no different from any other meat.

The latter group took pride in their enlightened knowledge that had freed them from any guilt about eating meat offered to idols. Paul basically shared this enlightened view. "We know that we all have knowledge" may have been a quotation from their letter. Paul basically agreed; however, he warned that such knowledge can lead to pride ("puffeth up") if it is insensitive to the opinions of believers who lack such knowledge.

Such pride is the opposite of Christian love, which is sensitive to the needs of others. Being puffed up about one's knowledge concerning meat and idols can become divisive, just as being puffed up about loyalties to human leaders was divisive. Love builds up ("edifieth"); whereas insensitive pride destroys individuals and the fellowship of the church.

Anyone who has a high opinion of his own knowledge does not know anything—at least not in the Christian sense. Christian knowledge is basically a knowledge of personal acquaintance with God, not a knowledge of facts about God. Paul wrote, "I know whom I have believed" (2 Tim. 1:12). Of course, he also knew what he believed; but his knowledge of God was personal.

Paul reminded the Corinthians in verse 3 that such knowledge of God is based on God's prior knowledge of us. We might expect Paul to write, "Those who love God, know God"; however, instead, he ended with "the same is known of him." Galatians 4:9 makes the same point, "Ye have known God, or rather are known of God." "We love him, because he first loved us" (1 John 4:19). In the same way, we know Him because He first knew us. Such knowledge of God is constructive, in contrast to proud knowledge, which is destructive.

2. Knowledge about God and idols (vv. 4–6)

4 As concerning therefore the eating of those things that are offered in sacrifice unto idols, we know that an idol is nothing in the world, and that there is none other God but one.

5 For though there be that are called gods, whether in heaven or in earth, (as there be gods many, and lords many,)

6 But to us there is but one God, the Father, of whom are all things, and we in him; and one Lord Jesus Christ, by whom are all things, and we by him.

Throughout this passage, Paul was addressing the group in Corinth that saw nothing wrong with eating meat sacrificed to idols. Paul shared the knowledge they had about God and idols. Paul's objection was not with the content of their knowledge, but with the proud way they boasted of their knowledge and the insensitive way they flaunted it to those who saw things differently.

Mature Christians know that God is the only true God; pagan gods are not real. Although pagans believed in many gods and built temples to worship the many names by which they called their gods, such gods were nonexistent. Later in his letter, Paul warned that evil spirits often used idols and false gods to deceive and tempt (10:20, 21). However, Paul did not believe that the gods themselves existed. The only God is the one Father and His Son Jesus Christ. Paul believed that the one God has revealed Himself; and we have experienced Him as Father, Son, and Spirit (2 Cor. 13:14).

3. When a nonmoral issue becomes a moral issue (vv. 7, 8)

7 Howbeit there is not in every man that knowledge: for some with conscience of the idol unto this hour eat it as a thing offered unto an idol; and their conscience being weak is defiled.

8 But meat commendeth us not to God: for neither, if we eat, are we the better; neither, if we eat not, are we the worse.

Paul considered some things always right or wrong. He dealt with some of those moral absolutes in 1 Corinthians 5–6. For example, sexual relations outside the one-flesh union of marriage are always sinful. He listed other moral absolutes in 6:9–10. Paul, however, also believed that some issues are nonmoral. That is, they are neither right nor wrong within themselves. However, such things can become either good or evil by how they are used.

In Paul's opinion, eating meat was such an issue. This was true whether the debate was about clean and unclean meat (Acts 10:14), about eating meat versus eating no meat (Rom. 14:2), or about eating meat sacrificed to idols (v. 8). Eating meat or not eating meat does not make a person better or worse morally or spiritually. "The kingdom of God is not meat and drink; but righteousness, and peace, and joy in the Holy Ghost" (Rom. 14:17).

However, eating meat sacrificed to idols became a moral issue when one group of Christians insisted on their right to eat it in the presence of those who felt that eating such meat was sinful. Verse 7 points out that not all Christians shared the view of Paul and other Corinthians that eating meat was not a moral issue. Some of them did not have the same knowledge Paul outlined in verses 4–6, 8. They felt that eating meat sacrificed to idols was to share in the worship of a pagan god.

II. Freedom, Conscience, and Commitment (1 Cor. 8:9–13)

1. Danger of unrestrained freedom (v. 9)

9 But take heed lest by any means this liberty of yours become a stumblingblock to them that are weak.

The word *liberty* means "authority," "right," or "freedom." They were free to eat meat sacrificed to idols, but Paul urged them not to insist on exercising this right if it caused others to stumble. Paul preached freedom in Christ from sin, death, and the law (Rom. 8:25). He warned against falling into the snare of legalism, which was a return to slavery (Gal. 5:1). Yet some believers claimed that freedom in Christ meant that they were free to do as they pleased. Paul, by contrast, taught that freedom must be consistent with the demands of self-giving love (Gal. 5:13).

As in verse 7, Paul used the word *weak* to refer to those who might stumble. Several times in this passage, Paul used the word *weak* to describe such believers or their conscience (vv. 7, 9–12). Perhaps Paul meant that they were weak in the sense of being immature in their grasp of the basic knowledge set forth in verses 4–6, 8. Perhaps he meant that they were easily influenced to go against their consciences when they saw a fellow Christian do something they considered wrong.

2. Sinning against conscience (vv. 10–12)

10 For if any man see thee which hast knowledge sit at meat in the idol's temple, shall not the conscience of him which is weak be emboldened to eat those things which are offered to idols;

11 And through thy knowledge shall the weak brother perish, for whom Christ died?

12 But when ye sin so against the brethren, and wound their weak conscience, ye sin against Christ.

Paul did not teach that conscience can always be our guide, but he did teach that it is wrong to go against one's conscience—even an overscrupulous conscience. He used a variety of words to describe the potential harm to the "weak" if they were influenced to go against conscience: defiled (v. 7), caused to stumble (v. 9), perish (v. 11), sinned against (v. 12), wounded (v. 12).

If Paul believed that eating meat sacrificed to idols is not sinful, then why did he think it would be sinful for people to do it if they went against their conscience? Conscience is like a flashing red light at a railroad crossing. Sometimes the light is flashing when the train is too far away to harm someone who runs the red light. However, suppose someone became callous to the flashing red light. That person might fail to stop in the face of real danger. If a person goes against conscience in a nonmoral issue, that person may begin to go against conscience in a real moral issue.

Tempting someone to go against conscience is wrong. Paul said it showed no concern for those for whom Christ died. It was not only a sin against fellow Christians; it was a sin against Christ.

3. A commitment made in love (v. 13)

13 Wherefore, if meat make my brother to offend, I will eat no flesh while the world standeth, lest I make my brother to offend.

Paul stated his own commitment not to eat meat sacrificed to idols in situations in which this could cause a brother to sin by going against conscience. He vowed to "eat no flesh while the world standeth," a very strongly stated commitment.

The specific example Paul used in verse 10 was eating in an idol temple. Later he used examples from social settings. For example, Paul said that he would freely buy any meat sold in the market and eat any meat served by a host without asking questions; however, if a weak brother objected, Paul would not eat it—for the sake of the brother's conscience (10:25–29).

Paul was not as liberal in his practice and counsel about eating meat in a pagan temple. He warned that Christians who did this not only set a bad example but also exposed themselves to the demonic forces that use idolatry to tempt even strong Christians (10:1–22).

In applying Paul's principle of not doing anything to offend a weak brother, Paul did not intend that Christians should allow legalistic people to tyrannize them. For example, Jesus did not keep the rigid rules of the Pharisees. There is a difference between sincerely weak believers whose scruples need to be respected and legalistic people who want to lay on us a burden of guilt for not going along with all their rigid human rules. Unfortunately, distinguishing these two groups is not always easy.

SUMMARY OF BIBLE TRUTHS

1. Worldly knowledge is proud and divisive.
2. Moral absolutes are always right or wrong.
3. Christians do not always agree on what are nonmoral issues.
4. Nonmoral issues become moral issues if doing these things hurts others.
5. Going against conscience is always dangerous.
6. Mature Christians should not cause weaker people to stumble.

APPLYING THE BIBLE

1. Don't let ego get in the way. Paul reminds the Corinthians to be careful so that they do not use their Christian liberty in such a way as to cause a new believer or a weaker Christian to stumble. This admonition requires us to look to the needs of others, not those of ourselves. It requires that our egos be surrendered.

It has been said, "When a man is wrapped up in himself, he makes a pretty small package." Christian freedom enables us to have a lasting influence on others and to grow far bigger than ego.

2. Influence:

My life shall touch a dozen lives before this day is done,
Leave countless marks for good or ill ere sets the evening sun,
This is the wish I always wish, the prayer I always pray;
Lord, may my life help other lives it touches by the way.

—Anonymous

3. Everything you do matters. C. S. Lewis said, "Every square inch in the universe is claimed by Christ and counterclaimed by the enemy." There are no neutral areas. No neutral decisions. No neutral activities. Perhaps this idea prompted Cal Stargel to write these words:

The things I do,
The things I say,
Will lead some person

Aright or astray.
So the things we do
Should be the best,
And the things we say
Should be to bless.

4. Costly stumbles. Some stumbles are more costly than others. Several years ago a technician tripped on the tail of his lab coat and stumbled into the exhaust nozzle of a space rocket being prepared for one of the Discovery shuttle missions. The accident caused a crack in the heat-resistant carbon nozzle that could not be repaired. NASA had to replace the entire first stage of the expensive rocket at a cost of about six million dollars.[1]

It's difficult to estimate the cost of some stumbles. But when a believer or a church leader causes a new Christian to stumble, the results can be devastating. Right or wrong, church leaders are held in high esteem by others. Their influence carries added weight. You need to be careful that your Christian liberty is not used carelessly. It has a lasting impact on the lives of others.

5. Knowledge. Someone has defined knowledge as "the process of passing from the unconscious state of ignorance to the conscious state of ignorance." Ignorance does not know that it does not know. True knowledge does not know, and it knows it.[2]

6. Caring for a weaker brother or sister. In deciding if an activity could cause one to stumble, John MacArthur's checklist may prove helpful. Ask yourself:

- Is it necessary?
- Is it helpful?
- Is it what Christ would do?
- Does it set a good example?
- Will it help or hinder my testimony?
- Will it make me stronger?
- Will it honor God?

7. Needed prayer. A prayer for "unity and caution" might be the way to describe the hymn titled "Dear Lord and Father of Mankind." It reads like a prayer and may be used as a written prayer or a sung prayer. The first stanza speaks clearly to the text of today's lesson.

Dear Lord and Father of mankind,
Forgive our foolish ways;
Reclothe us in our rightful mind;
In purer lives Thy service find,
In deeper reverence praise.

The issue of eating meat sacrificed to idols, the abuse of one's freedom, and the temptation to exercise less than care for the weaker individual in the Corinthian fellowship seem to be covered in the phrase "forgive our foolish ways." How rich we would be if this were our prayer.

TEACHING THE BIBLE

- *Main Idea:* Christians should be motivated by love to respect those who are weak in their Christian life and would be offended by certain actions.
- *Suggested Teaching Aim:* To lead adults to identify principles for engaging in activities some find offensive.

A TEACHING OUTLINE

1. *Knowledge, Love, and Morality (1 Cor. 8:1–8)*
2. *Freedom, Conscience, and Commitment (1 Cor. 8:9–13)*

Introduce the Bible Study

Read the following two true case studies: A man became a Christian. He had a large statue of the Hindu god Buddha in his home. After his conversion, he offered the statue to the evangelist who had led him to Christ. The evangelist refused the statue because he said it was a pagan god. The man placed it in his driveway, took a hammer and smashed the expensive jade statue to pieces.

A woman from the United States was in Mexico on a church-sponsored mission trip. One afternoon she visited a pyramid and purchased a pendant with a sun symbol on it because she thought it looked nice. That evening she wore the pendant to the church service. A church member told her that the symbol was offensive to the Christians in that area.

Ask, What would you have done in either of these cases? Why?

Search for Biblical Truth

Organize members into two groups. Give the groups the following assignments:

Group 1—Paul responded to questions from the Corinthians about eating meat offered to idols. That letter no longer exists. At the conclusion of this lesson, you will be asked to write a letter to Paul. This letter will be based on Paul's reply to the Corinthians, who asked Paul about eating meat offered to idols. Listen carefully to the lesson. Include in your letter comments that made Paul reply by saying, "We all have knowledge."

Group 2—How do you think the Corinthians responded to Paul's comments on eating meat sacrificed to idols? At the conclusion of this lesson, you will be asked to write a letter to Paul from the Corinthians, explaining how you understood his letter and what your response will be. Explain why you agree with him and what you will do in the future.

Using the material in "Studying the Bible," prepare a lecture covering the points that members will need to write their two letters. Use the following discussion questions in each subpoint:

DISCUSS: Since the false gods were unreal, what difference did it make to eat meat that had been offered to a nonexistent god? (vv. 1–3) What ways do spiritually mature persons today demonstrate pride that could damage immature believers? (vv. 4–6) What are some nonmoral issues that became moral issues when one group insisted on doing the action? (vv. 7–8) If freedom in Christ does not mean we are free to do as we please, what does it mean? (v. 9) Why is letting our conscience be our guide a good idea? a bad idea? (vv. 10–12) How can we distinguish between sincerely weak believers whose scruples need to be respected and legalistic people who want to lay on us a burden of guilt for not going along with all their rigid human rules? (v. 13).

Give the Truth a Personal Focus

Close by using number 7, "Needed Prayer," in "Applying the Bible." Read or sing "Dear Lord and Father of Mankind" as a closing prayer.

---

1. "The $6 Million Stumble," *Time,* Dec. 19, 1988, 30.
2. John MacArthur, *1 Corinthians*, The MacArthur New Testament Commentary (Chicago: Moody Press, 1984), 192.

April

16

2000

Spiritual Gifts

Background Passage: 1 Corinthians 12:1–30
Focal Passages: 1 Corinthians 12:4–20, 26

Spiritual gifts was another divisive issue in Corinth. Paul emphasized the unity and diversity of the church as a foundation for dealing with the problem. Unity kept diversity from degenerating into divisiveness, and diversity kept unity from becoming uniformity.

Study Aim: *To explain how spiritual gifts can express unity without uniformity and diversity without divisiveness.*

STUDYING THE BIBLE

OUTLINE AND SUMMARY

I. One Spirit—Different Gifts (1 Cor. 12:1–11)
- **1. Gifts of one Spirit (12:1–6)**
- **2. Different gifts (12:7–11)**

II. One Body—Many Members (1 Cor. 12:12–30)
- **1. Unity and diversity of Christ's body (12:12, 13)**
- **2. Many members, not just one (12:14–19)**
- **3. Many members in one body (12:20–26)**
- **4. Personal application (12:27–30)**

Different spiritual gifts are given by the same Spirit (vv. 1–6). God gives diverse gifts for the good of the church as a whole (vv. 7–11). The Spirit of God is the basis for the unity of the body of Christ (vv. 12, 13). No one member or kind of member constitutes the body (vv. 14–19). Because the many members of the body are interdependent, they share their joys and sorrows (vv. 20–26). As Paul reemphasized the church's diverse gifts, he challenged his readers to apply the teachings to themselves (vv. 27–30).

I. One Spirit—Different Gifts (1 Cor. 12:1–11)

1. Gifts of one Spirit (vv. 1–6)

4 Now there are diversities of gifts, but the same Spirit.

5 And there are differences of administrations, but the same Lord.

6 And there are diversities of operations, but it is the same God which worketh all in all.

Paul used two different Greek words for spiritual gifts. The word in verse 1 (see also 14:1) is built on the word for "Spirit." The word in verse 4 (see also vv. 9, 28, 30) is built on the word for "grace." The word in verse 1 emphasizes that these are gifts from God's Spirit. The word in verse 4 emphasizes that these are gifts of God's grace.

The English words *charisma* and *charismatic* are from the word in verse 4. We use these words in more restricted ways than the spiritual gifts of grace described in 1 Corinthians 12–14. According to Paul, all Christians have charisma and are charismatic. The problem in Corinth was that a small group wanted to claim that only they were truly spiritual and charismatic.

Paul mentioned diversity in verses 1–6, but he emphasized unity. The unity is based on the fact that all the spiritual gifts come from the same Spirit. As in the rest of the New Testament, the work of the Spirit is one with the work of the one God, who has revealed Himself as Father, Son, and Spirit (see also 2 Cor. 13:14). The key words are "the same Spirit" (v. 4), "the same Lord" (v. 5), and "the same God" (v. 6).

2. Different gifts (vv. 7–11)

> **7 But the manifestation of the Spirit is given to every man to profit withal.**

The words "to profit withal" could be taken to mean that the purpose of each gift is for the profit or advantage of the person who received the gift. Such an interpretation, however, would contradict everything else in 1 Corinthians 12–14. Therefore, most Bible students understand "to profit withal" to refer to the profit or good of the entire church. "To each one is given the manifestation of the Spirit for the common good" (NASB).

> **8 For to one is given by the Spirit the word of wisdom; to another the word of knowledge by the same Spirit;**
>
> **9 To another faith by the same Spirit; to another the gifts of healing by the same Spirit;**
>
> **10 To another the working of miracles; to another prophecy; to another discerning of spirits; to another divers kinds of tongues; to another the interpretation of tongues.**

Paul listed nine different gifts. He continued to remind his readers that these are all gifts of the same Spirit. This is spelled out for the first four gifts in verses 8, 9. Although Paul did not use "Spirit" in listing the next five gifts in verse 10, verse 11 makes clear that Paul intended his readers to know that each different gift comes from the one and same Spirit of God.

Paul began with two gifts of instruction: "the word of wisdom" and "the word of knowledge." Since wisdom and knowledge were occasions for pride in Corinth, Paul reminded them that true wisdom and knowledge are gifts of divine grace, not human achievements.

"Faith" is the kind that "could remove mountains" (13:2). This is hard to distinguish from the next two gifts of miracle-working power.

Prophecy is discussed at great length in chapter 14. In contrast to the gift of tongues, prophecy is inspired speech that others can understand. Thus in chapter 14, Paul gave clear guidelines for tongues, one of which was the necessity of someone interpreting.

"Discerning of spirits" apparently was the gift of being able to recognize which words and actions were prompted by God's Spirit and which were prompted by some other spirit. Jesus (John 16:14), Paul (1 Cor. 12:2, 3), and John (1 John 4:1–3) all gave a key guideline in such discernment: Anyone who speaks or acts in God's Spirit glorifies Jesus Christ.

Actually, there are two other lists of spiritual gifts in 1 Corinthians 12: one in verse 28 and another in verses 29, 30. Paul dealt in such detail with spiritual gifts because they were a special concern in Corinth. Paul also included a brief discussion and list of spiritual gifts in Romans 12:6–8. Ephesians 4:11 mentions some gifted leaders whom the Lord gave to the church.

When all five of these lists are placed side by side, we see some similarities and some differences. Sometimes a gift is mentioned, and sometimes the person who has the gift (prophecy and prophet). Only one gift—prophecy—is found in all five lists. Teaching or teacher is in four; and if we assume that the two gifts in 1 Corinthians 12:8 have to do with teaching, all five refer to this gift. Although different words are used to describe similar gifts, some of these may refer to the same gift ("governments" in 1 Cor. 12:28 and "he that ruleth" in Rom. 12:8). Because Paul did not give a definitive list of the only spiritual gifts, most people conclude that a rich variety of spiritual gifts is God's purpose.

> **11 But all these worketh that one and the selfsame Spirit, dividing to every man severally as he will.**

Paul reminded the Corinthians that God is the One who distributes the gifts. He does this according to His will. Thus, to boast about any gift or look down on any gift is to forget that these are gifts of God, which He has distributed as He chooses.

II. One Body—Many Members (1 Cor. 12:12–30)

1. Unity and diversity of Christ's body (vv. 12, 13)

> **12 For as the body is one, and hath many members, and all the members of that one body, being many, are one body: so also is Christ.**
>
> **13 For by one Spirit are we all baptized into one body, whether we be Jews or Gentiles, whether we be bond or free; and have been all made to drink into one Spirit.**

The diversity of the church is not only because we have different gifts but also because we have different backgrounds. In churches of the first century, some members were Jews, and others were Gentiles. These two groups came from totally different cultural, moral, and religious backgrounds. Many people in the early church were slaves, and others were free people. Most of the members of the Corinthian church were slaves or from the lower classes; only a few were wealthy or high-born (1 Cor. 1:26). Sometimes richer members mistreated poorer members (1 Cor. 11:18–22).

Thus, the diversity in the church sometimes led to a divisive spirit. Over against this, Paul kept reminding them of their unity in Christ. They were members of one body, Christ's body. Notice how often he repeated "one body" in verses 12, 13. The basis for this one body was what these diverse groups had in common because of the work of God's Spirit in them. They had all been baptized by one Spirit into one body. (See also Eph. 4:1–6.)

2. Many members, not just one (vv. 14–19)

14 For the body is not one member, but many.

15 If the foot shall say, Because I am not the hand, I am not of the body; is it therefore not of the body?

16 And if the ear shall say, Because I am not the eye, I am not of the body; is it therefore not of the body?

17 If the whole body were an eye, where were the hearing? If the whole were hearing, where were the smelling?

18 But now hath God set the members every one of them in the body, as it hath pleased him.

19 And if they were all one member, where were the body?

Verses 14 and 19 bracket these verses that deal with the false idea that one member or one kind of member is the whole church. Using the parts of the human body to illustrate members of Christ's body, Paul first showed that each member is important. The foot and the ear in verses 15 and 16 represent members who don't feel as important or as much a part of the body of Christ as do other members, which are represented by the hand and the eye. A hand may seem more important than a foot; and an eye may seem more prominent than an ear; however, all four are important parts of the body.

Verse 17 shows Paul had a sense of humor. Imagine the ludicrous picture of a big eye bouncing or rolling around like a big ball. Such a monstrosity would not be a functioning body. Yet some churches have a person or a small group of people who think of themselves as the church, or at least that is how they are perceived by others.

Verse 18 repeats the crucial point already made in verse 11. God set the members of the body into place according to His will. It is His church, not ours. Verse 19 repeats the point made in verse 14: The body of Christ is many members, not just one.

3. Many members in one body (vv. 20–26)

20 But now are they many members, yet but one body.

Verse 20 is the flip side of verses 14 and 19. The church is many members, not just one; yet the many members constitute one body in which all the members are important, needed, and interdependent. Thus, the eye can't say to the hand, "I don't need you," nor can the head get along without the feet (v. 21). Even the weaker, less attractive members of the body deserve special honor because they, too, are important to the rest of the body (vv. 22–24).

26 And whether one member suffer, all the members suffer with it; or one member be honoured, all the members rejoice with it.

Paul summed up his main applications to the church in verses 25, 26. From the negative side, the recognition of interdependence helps prevent a divisive spirit. Positively, it causes members to care for one another (v. 25). Verse 26 elaborates on this spirit of caring for one another. In the human body, an injury or illness affecting one part of the body affects the entire body. In the body of Christ, the same ought to be true.

Another biblical analogy for the church is a family of faith and love bound together by the Father's love for each as brothers and sisters. In any family worthy of being called a family, when one member suffers, all share the burden of that grief and pain. Likewise, when one family member comes in with good news, all the family celebrates (Rom. 12:15).

4. Personal application (vv. 27–30)

The word *ye* in verse 27 made clear that Paul intended the Corinthians to apply all this to themselves. Then he once again emphasized the diversity of gifts in the church. He named as most crucial gifts: apostles, prophets, and teachers. Then he listed five other gifts (v. 28). Then he asked a series of questions with one obvious answer. As important as they are, "Are all teachers?" (vv. 29, 30). No. The one body of Christ functions when all its members exercise their different gifts.

SUMMARY OF BIBLE TRUTHS

1. Diverse spiritual gifts of grace are given by the same Spirit.
2. God decides who receives which gifts.
3. The unity of the body of Christ is based on having the same spiritual experiences.
4. No one member or kind of member is the church.
5. Members of Christ's body are important and interdependent.
6. Members of Christ's body share one another's joys and sorrows.

APPLYING THE BIBLE

1. Christian spirituality. "Christian spirituality is nothing other than life in Christ by the presence and power of the Spirit, being conformed to the person of Christ, and being united in communion with God and with others. Spirituality is not an aspect of Christian life; it is the Christian life" (Michael Downey).

2. The Holy Spirit. "Let the Spirit in, that you may be emptied" (D. L. Moody).

3. Everything in the body seems connected. Several years ago in a midwestern town, a lawsuit was filed by a woman against the county for injuries suffered in a fall in the icy parking lot of the local high school. She claimed injury to nearly everything in her body: all the bones, organs, muscles, tendons, tissues, nerves, veins, arteries, ligaments, disks, cartilages, and the joints of her body were fractured, broken, ruptured, punctured, compressed, dislocated, separated, bruised, narrowed, abraded, lacerated, burned, cut, torn, wrenched, swollen, strained, sprained, inflamed, and infected.

When part of the body hurts, all of the body hurts. Paul knew this truth not only had physical application, but also spiritual application to the church as well. Spiritual gifts were being wrongly emphasized in the congregation in Corinth, creating an *us* versus *them* mentality. Some "had it" and some "didn't" when it came to spiritual gifts. Those who did assumed a false air of spiritual superiority. The result was a broken fellowship. It's a good thing for us to remember that when one part of the body is hurt, all of the body hurts. In the church, we are all connected.

4. Class discussion. There are several new paradigms being thrown around today. Some that apply to the church are listed below.

- Unity does not mean uniformity.
- The larger we grow, the smaller we need to think.
- Unity depends on the affirmation of our diversity.
- You can be organized and fail to be an organism.

5. Learn the language of fellowship. For church fellowship to thrive, members must learn to communicate with several new words. These are the most important words for building fellowship in the church.

- The six most important words: I admit I made a mistake.
- The five most important words: You did a good job.
- The four most important words: What is your opinion?
- The three most important words: I love you.
- The two most important words: Thank you.
- The one most important word: We.
- The least important word: I.[1]

6. Building a championship team. Vince Lombardi was once asked "What does it take to build a championship team?"

The veteran coach and winner of Super Bowl championships answered, "There are three things. First, you must get players to pay attention to the fundamentals. Second, there must be discipline. Finally, everyone on the team must care for each other."

Paul had to address the misuse of spiritual gifts because the members of the congregation had forgotten to care for one another. Gifts had become marks of spiritual pride and exclusion. When members of a body care for one another, gifts will be used to edify and encourage and God will be honored.

TEACHING THE BIBLE

- *Main Idea:* Our spiritual gifts express unity without uniformity and diversity without divisiveness.
- *Suggested Teaching Aim:* To lead adults to recognize and affirm their gifts and the gifts of others.

A TEACHING OUTLINE

1. *One Spirit—Different Gifts (1 Cor. 12:1–11)*
2. *One Body—Many Members (1 Cor. 12:12–30)*

Introduce the Bible Study

Use number 6, "Building a Championship Team," in "Applying the Bible" to introduce the lesson.

April

16

2000

Search for Biblical Truth

IN ADVANCE, on large sheets of paper, copy the six Scripture references for the six outline subpoints. Tape these at random around the room where members can see them. Ask members to open their Bibles. One at a time, read the six summary statements from the "Outline and Summary" and ask members to find verses on the wall that support each statement.

Ask members to rank the positions in the church from most important to least important. List these on a chalkboard or a large sheet of paper. When the list is complete, ask: Can number 1 get by without the person lowest on the list? Can the pastor be as effective if there is no minister of music? Can either of them function well without adequate child care? Can child care function without adequate cleaning services?

DISCUSS: If God has given the gifts to all those who lead, is any gift more important than any other?

Ask two members you have enlisted **IN ADVANCE** to read the whole focal passages at this time. Ask the readers to alternate sections based on the outline points.

IN ADVANCE, make the following poster: "Unity keeps diversity from degenerating into divisiveness, and diversity keeps unity from becoming uniformity." Ask members to react to this statement.

Ask members to look at 1 Corinthians 12:4–11 and identify the spiritual gifts Paul listed. List these on a chalkboard or a large sheet of paper. If members have different translations, ask them to see if their translations help explain any of these terms.

Point out that since Paul later lists other gifts, these gifts are to be understood to be just a partial listing—not a complete list.

Ask members to look at verses 12–13. Ask half the class to count the number of times "one body" (or similar phrases) (four times in KJV) appear in these verses. Ask the other half to count the number of times "one Spirit" appears (two times in KJV).

DISCUSS: What is the danger of diversity? What is the benefit?

Ask members to find a verse in chapter 12 that describes the benefits and the disadvantages of being a part of the body of Christ (v. 26).

Give the Truth a Personal Focus

IN ADVANCE, prepare an envelope for each person you will have present. Also, provide each member with as many 3-by-5-inch cards (or slips of paper) as you have members present. If you have ten people present, each member will need ten cards or a total of one hundred cards. Ask members to write their names on the outside of the envelope. Then ask members to write a card for each person, telling the person what they see as the person's spiritual gift or gifts. Ask members to pass their envelopes and let each person put his or her card inside the envelope. Let members take the cards home to read them. Allow enough time for this activity.

---

1. Adapted from Michael Green, *Illustrations for Biblical Preaching* (Grand Rapids: Baker Book House, 1989), 351.

Christ's Resurrection and Ours

Background Passage: 1 Corinthians 15:1–58
Focal Passages: 1 Corinthians 15:20–27, 35–44

First Corinthians 15 is the most complete discussion of the resurrection in the New Testament. The theme of this amazing passage is that the resurrection of Christ guarantees the future resurrection of believers.

➧**Study Aim:** *To testify to personal faith in the resurrection of Christ and in the future resurrection.*

STUDYING THE BIBLE

OUTLINE AND SUMMARY

I. Because Christ Lives (1 Cor. 15:1–34)
1. Reality of Christ's resurrection (15:1–11)
2. If Christ had not been raised from the dead (15:12–19)
3. The death of death 15:20–28)
4. Defying death (15:29–34)

II. How Are the Dead Raised? (1 Cor. 15:35–58)
1. Doubts about the resurrection (15:35)
2. A spiritual body (15:36–44)
3. Biblical support 15:45–50)
4. Thanks be to God (15:51–58)

Christ was raised from the dead and appeared to many (vv. 1–11). If He had not been raised, there would be no Christian faith and hope (vv. 12–19). Christ's resurrection ensures the resurrection of believers and final victory over death (vv. 20–28). Christian hope enables Christians to defy death (vv. 29–34). Some asked about the nature of the resurrected body (v. 35). Paul taught that it will be a spiritual body (vv. 36–44). Christ makes it a spiritual body fit for heaven (vv. 45–50). Paul praised God for victory over sin and death (vv. 51–58).

I. Because Christ Lives (1 Cor. 15:1–34)

1. Reality of Christ's resurrection (vv. 1–11)

Paul reminded the Corinthians of the gospel of the cross and resurrection that he preached and they believed (vv. 1–4). Paul listed some of those to whom the risen Lord appeared: Cephas, the Twelve, over five hundred, James, all the apostles (vv. 5–7). Christ appeared last of all to Paul himself (vv. 8–11).

2. If Christ had not been raised from the dead (vv. 12–19)

Paul asked how some of the Corinthians could be denying the future resurrection (v. 12). To deny the resurrection of believers is to deny the resurrection of Christ (v. 13). If Christ has not been raised, the results would be false preaching, empty faith, unforgiven sins, no eternal life, deceptive hope (vv. 15–19).

3. The death of death (vv. 20–28)

20 But now is Christ risen from the dead, and become the firstfruits of them that slept.

But Christ has been raised from the dead. Nothing was more certain to Paul. He and the other apostles had seen the crucified, risen Lord. How do you and I know that Christ has been raised from the dead? We have the written testimonies of those who saw Him in the New Testament. Our personal experience with the risen Lord confirms the truth of the inspired Scriptures.

"Firstfruits" refers to the practice of waving the first sheaf of the harvest and presenting it with offerings to the Lord (Lev. 23:10–14). As the first sheaf was a promise of the harvest, Christ's resurrection guarantees the resurrection of believers.

"Them that slept" is one of many biblical references that compare the Christian dead to people who are asleep (Matt. 9:24; John 11:11–14; 1 Thess. 4:13–18). The meaning of the comparison is that just as people who are asleep awaken, so will the dead awaken to eternal life.

21 For since by man came death, by man came also the resurrection of the dead.

22 For as in Adam all die, even so in Christ shall all be made alive.

Adam by his sin brought death into the world; Jesus, the second Adam, made possible the resurrection from the dead. All die as a result of choosing the sin that Adam brought into the world. Christ's resurrection does not mean that all people automatically shall be made alive. Only those "in Christ" shall be made alive.

23 But every man in his own order: Christ the firstfruits; afterward they that are Christ's at his coming.

Verse 23 builds on the mention of "firstfruits" in verse 20. Christ's resurrection took place at the end of His earthly ministry and after His crucifixion. The resurrection of Christians is yet future. This final harvest of the redeemed will take place "at his coming."

The focus of New Testament hope is not what happens when an individual dies, but what will happen when the Lord comes again. Thus, the focus for Christian hope of eternal life is not an individual's survival of death, but the fulfillment of God's redeeming purpose for all His people.

24 Then cometh the end, when he shall have delivered up the kingdom to God, even the Father; when he shall have put down all rule and all authority and power.

25 For he must reign, till he hath put all enemies under his feet.

26 The last enemy that shall be destroyed is death.

27 For he hath put all things under his feet. But when he saith all things are put under him, it is manifest that he is excepted, which did put all things under him.

The Bible consistently declares that Christ is already enthroned at the right hand of God with divine authority over all things. Some day every knee shall bow and every tongue confess that Jesus is Lord to the glory of God the Father.

Christ is already in the process of putting all things under His feet, but the culmination will be at the end "when he shall have put down all rule and all authority and power." Christians disagree about the process and time period of verse 25. Some believe that Christ will reign on earth for one thousand years, before Christ puts down all authority. Others believe that He shall do this in connection with His coming. All agree that He shall do it, and that the final enemy to be destroyed will be death.

By His death for our sins and His resurrection from the dead, Christ defeated sin, death, and the devil. However, this evil trinity continues in spite of Christ's victory. However, their days are numbered; and meanwhile, believers can be saved from sin, promised eternal life, and empowered to resist the devil. At the end, sin, death, and the devil will face their final doom. The beautiful picture of the new Jerusalem in Revelation 21:4 promises, "God shall wipe away all tears from their eyes; and there shall be no more death, neither sorrow, nor crying, neither shall there be any more pain."

After Christ subjects all things unto Himself, "then shall the Son also himself be subject unto him that put all things under him, that God may be all in all." This will not be a subjection of inferiority, but a subjection of completion of mission.

4. Defying death (vv. 29–34)

Whatever verse 29 meant to Paul and the Corinthians, baptism itself is a testimony to faith in Christ's resurrection and to our future resurrection. Verses 30–32a testify to how the resurrection hope enabled Christians to defy death. Verses 32b–34 testify to the moral transformation of those who believe in a future resurrection.

II. How Are the Dead Raised? (1 Cor. 15:35–58)

1. Doubts about the resurrection (v. 35)

35 But some man will say, How are the dead raised up? and with what body do they come!

Verses 12 and 35 are the best clues of the problem or problems in Corinth that caused Paul to write chapter 15.

Some Bible scholars believe that some of the Corinthians had problems with any form of life after death. This could have been what some meant when they denied the resurrection. We know that most Greeks and Romans did not believe in any life after death (1 Thess. 4:13; Eph. 2:12; Acts 26:23, 24.)

Most Bible scholars think that the primary doubt in Corinth was about the resurrection of the body. Some Greeks believed in the immortality of the soul, but they had problems believing that a body could be raised from the dead (Acts 17:31, 32).

2. A spiritual body (vv. 36–44)

36 Thou fool, that which thou sowest is not quickened, except it die:

37 And that which thou sowest, thou sowest not that body that shall be, but bare grain, it may chance of wheat, or of some other grain:

38 But God giveth it a body as it hath pleased him, and to every seed his own body.

Paul compared the dead body and the resurrection body to a seed and the plant that grows from the seed.

1. *A living plant comes from a dead seed.* When a seed is placed in the ground, in a sense it dies; however, the seed makes possible a living plant that sprouts and grows from the seed (John 12:24).

2. *Just as seeds differ, so do the plants that grow from the seeds.* Paul insisted on a resurrection of the body, but he wanted his readers to avoid restricting "body" to one kind of body. "Body" can mean many things other than a resuscitated corpse.

3. *God decides what kind of body is appropriate for each situation.* The key words in verse 38 and in verses 35–44 are the words "God giveth it a body as it hath pleased him."

39 All flesh is not the same flesh: but there is one kind of flesh of men, another flesh of beasts, another of fishes, and another of birds.

40 There are also celestial bodies, and bodies terrestrial: but the glory of the celestial is one, and the glory of the terrestrial is another.

41 There is one glory of the sun, and another glory of the moon, and another glory of the stars: for one star differeth from another star in glory.

Paul continued to enlarge his readers' concepts of "body." He pointed to differences in the flesh of living creatures: Humans, animals, fish, and birds all have different kinds of flesh and bodies. He pointed to bodies on earth and to the so-called "celestial bodies." He even noted differences between the sun, moon, and stars. He ended by observing that stars differed from one another in glory.

42 So also is the resurrection of the dead. It is sown in corruption; it is raised in incorruption:

43 It is sown in dishonour; it is raised in glory: it is sown in weakness; it is raised in power:

44 It is sown a natural body; it is raised a spiritual body. There is a natural body, and there is a spiritual body.

Paul used four pairs of words to contrast the mortal body with the resurrection body:

1. The human body obviously is subject to corruption. It decays and returns to the dust from which it was made. The resurrection body will not decay.
2. "Dishonour" translates a word meaning "without citizenship." When people die, they lose all earthly possessions and status. However, as citizens of a heavenly realm, resurrected believers will experience glory.

3. Our mortal bodies are weak: subject to illness, aging, injuries, and death. Resurrected bodies will have power over all.
4. A natural body is a physical body that is suited for earthly life; a spiritual body will be a body suited for a new kind of reality. It will not be pure spirit; nor will it be a mortal body (v. 50). We can trust God to give us the bodies we will need.

3. Biblical support (vv. 45–50)

Using Genesis 2:7, Paul again contrasted Adam and Christ (v. 45). Adam was from the earth; Christ was from heaven. Therefore, the first body is of the earth; the new bodies from Christ's life-giving power will be from heaven (vv. 46–50).

4. Thanks be to God (vv. 51–58)

Paul revealed the mystery of what will happen when the trumpet sounds. The dead in Christ will receive resurrection bodies and living believers will be transformed into incorruptible bodies (vv. 51–54). Paul broke into a doxology of praise to God for victory over sin, death, and the law (vv. 55–57). Such a confident hope challenges Christians to be faithful to the Lord (v. 58).

SUMMARY OF BIBLE TRUTHS

1. Christ has been raised from the dead.
2. His resurrection guarantees our resurrection.
3. The final victory over death will take place at His coming.
4. Some don't believe in life after death; many don't believe in resurrection of the body.
5. The resurrection body will be neither pure spirit nor a flesh-and-blood body, but a spiritual body.

APPLYING THE BIBLE

1. Hope beyond the grave. The Hope System is a standard of care for dying patients developed by Cathleen Fanslow-Brunjes. The Hope System recognizes that dying people have three basic needs:

- to know they won't be abandoned,
- to have the opportunity to express themselves, and
- to maintain hope.

Fanslow-Brunjes says, "We define hope as an inner dynamic life force that helps each dying patient live his life until the moment of death. It can take many forms—hope for a cure, hope to see one more Christmas, hope to live through the night."[1]

Hope is what keeps many people going. As Christians face death and dying, we do so with the absolute promise in Scripture that our hope will not be disappointed. There is a hope beyond the grave, and we know it. Paul says that we grieve "not as those who have no hope" (1 Thess. 4:13).

2. Four stages of hope. Patients and their families typically experience hope in four stages:

- hope for cure,
- hope for treatment,
- hope for prolongation of life, and
- hope for peaceful death.[2]

3. Interest in death and dying. Dozens of new books on the subject of death and dying are coming to bookstores, with titles like *The Dying Time* and *A Newcomer's Guide to the Afterlife,* covering subjects from treating the terminally ill to life after death. Colleges now offer courses in thanatology, or the study of death. And death has quietly sidled into the marketplace. Hallmark is introducing cards for the terminally ill, their families and their caregivers.[3]

4. Our death-defying society. For many years death was discussed in hushed, solemn tones. Indeed, for much of the twentieth century, America has been a death-defying society. More than two million of us die each year, yet we try to deny the inevitable. Nutritionists tout strategies to reverse the aging process. Anti-wrinkling creams are big sellers. Plastic surgery keeps sagging bodies uplifted.[4]

5. Helping patients prepare for death. St. Patrick Hospital in Missoula, Montana, became the first health-care facility in the United States to retain twenty-four harpists-in-residence, as part of their music thanatology program. The program is designed to help the dying disengage from pain as they take leave of the world.[5]

6. Quotes on death and dying:

"Men fear death as children fear to go in the dark; and as that natural fear in children is increased with tales, so is the other."

—Francis Bacon

Death be not proud, though some have called thee
Mighty and dreadful, for thou art not so,
For those whom thou think'st thou dost overthrow,
Die not, poor death, nor yet canst thou kill me.

—John Donne

"It is not death, but dying, which is terrible."

—Henry Fielding

"They that love beyond the world cannot be separated by it. Death is but crossing the world, as friends do the seas; they live in one another still."

—William Penn

"Our Constitution is in actual operation; everything appears to promise that it will last; but in this world nothing is certain but death and taxes."

—Benjamin Franklin

"All men think all men mortal, but themselves."

—Edward Young

Teach me to live that I may dread
The grave as little as my bed.

—Tomas Ken

7. Resurrection life:

Call it not death, this is life begun.
The waters are past and Heaven is won.
This ransomed soul hath reached the shore
Where they suffer and sorrow and cry no more.
To depart from this world of sin and strife and be with the Lord Jesus, Tis not death but life.

—Charles B. Arendall

TEACHING THE BIBLE

- *Main Idea:* The resurrection of Christ guarantees the future resurrection of believers.
- *Suggested Teaching Aim:* To lead adults to identify ways Christ's resurrection guarantees the future resurrection of believers.

A TEACHING OUTLINE

1. *Because Christ Lives (1 Cor. 15:1–34)*
2. *How Are the Dead Raised? (1 Cor. 15:35–58)*

Introduce the Bible Study

Use number 1, "Hope Beyond the Grave," in "Applying the Bible" to introduce the lesson.

Search for Biblical Truth

On a chalkboard or a large sheet of paper, write: *Is resurrection real?* Ask members to open their Bibles to 1 Corinthians 15:20. Suggest that today's study will answer the question written on the board. Ask, how do we know Christ has been resurrected? (Eyewitnesses recorded their testimonies; our personal experience with the risen Lord confirms it.) Explain the concept of "firstfruits."

On a chalkboard write the following (omit italicized answers):

Adam	Christ
Brought death	Brought life
All die	All made alive

Ask members to look at 1 Corinthians 15:21–23. Ask members to compare and contrast Adam and Christ based on these verses. Fill in the chart. Point out that Adam introduced death into the world and Christ introduced life. However, we each have to choose for ourselves this death and life. We are sinners because we, like Adam, choose to sin; we gain life eternal, because we choose to follow Christ. Neither eternal death nor eternal life is thrust upon us. We choose.

Ask members to look at verses 24–27. Ask, Based on these verses, what will happen at the end of time? (Christ will deliver up the kingdom to God, He will destroy all powers and authorities, Christ will rule until all His enemies are defeated, the last enemy destroyed will be death.)

Ask members to look at verse 35. Say, The Bible is not afraid of questions. Apparently, some of the Corinthians had asked in their letter to Paul how the dead are raised and what kind of bodies they will have—questions most of us have raised ourselves. Let's see how Paul answers these in verses 36–44. Ask, What comparison does Paul use to explain how the body dies and is raised? (Seed sprouting.) Write the following on a chalkboard (omit italicized answers):

Seed	Body
Must be planted	Must die and be buried
Changes from a dried seed to plant	Changes from a dead body to a resurrected body
Sprout differs from the seed	Resurrected body differs from the dead body

Ask: What has to happen to a seed before it can sprout? to a body before it can be resurrected? What happens to a seed when it does sprout? to a body when it is resurrected? What is the difference between the seed and the sprout? between the dead body and the resurrected one?

Ask members to look at verses 38–41. Ask members to identify all the various types of "bodies" mentioned in these verses. Ask members to put in one sentence why they think Paul mentioned all these bodies and the point he is trying to make. (Consider: As God can make many different bodies, so He can make different resurrected bodies.)

Write on the chalkboard (omit italicized answers):

Mortal Body	Resurrected Body
Will die, is corrupt	Will live forever, incorrupt
Without honor, without citizenship	Will experience glory, heavenly citizenship
Weak, subject to illness	Will have power over all
Suited for earthly life	Suited for heavenly life

Give the Truth a Personal Focus

IN ADVANCE, enlist two readers to read alternately the five statements in "Summary of Bible Truths." Close in prayer of gratitude for Christ's resurrection and ours.

---

1. Cathleen Fanslow-Brunjes, Patricia E Schneider, and Lee H. Kimmel, "Hope: Offering Comfort and Support for Dying Patients," *Nursing,* March 1997, 54–57.
2. Ibid.
3. Cathy Hainer, *USA Today,* Aug. 11, 1997.
4. Ibid.
5. Therese Schroeder-Sheker, "Swan Songs," *Omni,* Sept. 1993, 76.

The Way of Love

Background Passage: 1 Corinthians 12:31–13:13
Focal Passage: 1 Corinthians 12:31–13:13

A list of favorite Bible chapters will surely include 1 Corinthians 13, the famous love chapter. Although the chapter has a beauty and power of its own, we gain new insight and appreciation of it as we see it within the context of 1 Corinthians in general and chapters 12–14 in particular.

Study Aim: *To list the characteristics of love as set forth in 1 Corinthians 13.*

STUDYING THE BIBLE

OUTLINE AND SUMMARY

I. More Excellent Way (1 Cor. 12:31)
II. Indispensable Way (1 Cor. 13:1–3)
III. Christlike Way (1 Cor. 13:4–7)
IV. Eternal Way (1 Cor. 13:8–13)

Although Christians should seek the best spiritual gifts in God's sight, they should do everything in the more excellent way of Christian love (12:31). Anything we do without love amounts to nothing (13:1–3). Love's characteristics are those seen perfectly only in Jesus Christ (13:4–7). Spiritual gifts will end with this age, but love will be part of God's eternal kingdom (13:8–13).

I. More Excellent Way (1 Cor. 12:31)

31 But covet earnestly the best gifts: and yet shew I unto you a more excellent way.

The first part of verse 31 sounds like a contradiction of verses 1–30. Had Paul not been making the points that each gift is important, that no gift is the entire church, and that all gifts are interdependent? Why suddenly urge the Corinthians to seek the best gifts? In order to find the answer, we have to study chapter 14. In that chapter, Paul ranked gifts in terms of how they built up the church and communicated. He, thus, ranked prophecy above tongues because the primary value of tongues is to an individual; whereas prophecy builds up the church. Thus, verse 31a set the stage for that discussion.

However, before moving on to clarify what he meant, Paul emphasized something more important than spiritual gifts. He showed them a more excellent way of Christian love. This is the spirit with which any gift or any Christian action must be done. Thus, chapter 13 is crucial to the specific problem of spiritual gifts at Corinth. Paul combated the divisiveness by pointing to the antidote for the selfish pride that spawns dissension. Christian love is also the solution to all the problems of divisiveness in Corinth.

II. Indispensable Way (1 Cor. 13:1–3)

1 Though I speak with the tongues of men and of angels, and have not charity, I am become as sounding brass, or a tinkling cymbal.

2 And though I have the gift of prophecy, and understand all mysteries, and all knowledge; and though I have all faith, so that I could remove mountains, and have not charity, I am nothing.

3 And though I bestow all my goods to feed the poor, and though I give my body to be burned, and have not charity, it profiteth me nothing.

The Greeks had several words for "love." They had one for erotic love and another for the love of friends and family. The New Testament, however, emphasizes the word *agape,* which was seldom used by the Greeks. Christians poured all the content of the self-giving love of God into this word. This is the kind of love that caused God to send His only Son, and this is the love revealed at the cross. It is the kind of love to which God calls His people. It is doing good for one another, for other people, and even for enemies.

"Charity" fails to communicate the meaning of *apape*. In fact, verse 3 says that an ultimate act of charity—giving everything to feed the poor—means nothing without Christian love. Paul's point in verses 1–3 is that nothing that Christians do amounts to anything if it is not done in love—that is, if it is not done for God's glory and to meet the needs of others. In other words, things done for our own benefit amount to nothing.

Verses 1, 2 obviously refer to spiritual gifts. Because speaking in tongues was so highly prized in Corinth, Paul began with it. Suppose that a person could speak not only with the gift of tongues but also with the very language of the angels. Such tongues would sound more like the noise of pagan worship than anything productive.

Paul listed prophecy next. He was soon to make a strong case for prophecy as the gift to seek instead of tongues; however, if someone (notice that Paul uses "I" throughout) has this valuable gift, he is nothing if the gift is not exercised in self-giving love. If I have perfect understanding and knowledge of all mysteries, I am nothing if my knowledge expresses selfish pride. If I were able to move mountains by my strong faith in God's miracle-working power and did not do it in love, I would be nothing in God's eyes.

Verse 3 does not deal with spiritual gifts, but with two acts that are usually considered ultimate expressions of Christian love. Suppose I gave everything I had to feed the poor. Suppose I was burned to death as a martyr for Christ. If I did these things for any reason other than to glorify God and help others, these sacrificial actions would bring me no gain in God's eyes.

III. Christlike Way (1 Cor. 13:4–7)

4 Charity suffereth long, and is kind; charity envieth not; charity vaunteth not itself, is not puffed up,

5 Doth not behave itself unseemly, seeketh not her own, is not easily provoked, thinketh no evil;

6 Rejoiceth not in iniquity, but rejoiceth in the truth;
7 Beareth all things, believeth all things, hopeth all things, endureth all things.

Rather than trying to define Christian love, Paul listed fifteen short descriptions of it—seven stated positively and eight stated negatively. Love is patient in both senses of the Greek word: It waits patiently for something God has promised, and it patiently endures with something or someone that causes suffering. Love is kind, the kindness that does good not just to friends but also to enemies.

Envy is worse than coveting. Covetousness is greed; envy is coveting something belonging to someone else. Love is not envious; neither is it boastful or arrogantly proud.

"Behave itself unseemly" includes any behavior that is inappropriate for Christians. Christian love is self-giving, the opposite of self-seeking. Christian love does not have a short fuse. "Thinketh no evil" does not refer to having a mind free from evil thoughts. The Bible teaches that elsewhere (Phil. 4:8, 9), but the Greek word in verse 5 means that we do not keep records of the bad things that others do or say about us. Christian love doesn't bear grudges.

Some people find satisfaction in the moral downfall of others. Some even condone and are glad when evil seems to be winning (Rom. 1:32). People with Christlike love do not find any joy in evil or evildoers. Christian love finds joy in people who do what is right and true, and thus bring glory to God.

"Beareth" in verse 7 literally means "cover." Some translate the word as "protects." Others retain "bears" in the sense of forbearing what others do that hurts or annoys them. Love trusts God and people. Love has confident hope based on the sure promises of God. Love endures or bears up under the worst that comes.

These fifteen characteristics were exemplified perfectly in only one person—Jesus Christ. He is the ultimate expression and example of Christian love. Although we fall short of His ideal love, His Spirit is with us to continue to narrow the gap between where we are and where He wants us to be.

IV. Eternal Way (1 Cor. 13:8–13)

8 Charity never faileth: but whether there be prophecies, they shall fail; whether there be tongues, they shall cease; whether there be knowledge, it shall vanish away.

9 For we know in part, and we prophesy in part.

10 But when that which is perfect is come, then that which is in part shall be done away.

11 When I was a child, I spake as a child, I understood as a child, I thought as a child: but when I became a man, I put away childish things.

12 For now we see through a glass, darkly; but then face to face: now I know in part; but then shall I know even as also I am known.

13 And now abideth faith, hope, charity, these three; but the greatest of these is charity.

Love never lets us down because it is always at work and because it will never come to an end. The point of verses 8–13 is that Christian love is part of God's eternal order, not just an instrument of His for the present age. In this, love stands in contrast to the spiritual gifts, which were so divisive in Corinth. Spiritual gifts like prophecy, knowledge, and tongues are all confined to the present age; they are not part of the eternal order. When God's kingdom comes in its fullness, spiritual gifts will have served their purpose—like other methods of God's work now. They will end, cease, and vanish away.

Paul illustrated this in two ways. First, he compared the knowledge of children with that of adults. Elsewhere, Jesus taught that we must have the simple trust of a child to enter God's kingdom. Paul was using children in verse 11 to make a different point. Children have a partial and childish knowledge of life as compared with the more mature knowledge of those who have learned God's lessons with the passing years. No illustration is perfect. All of us know that even adults have imperfect knowledge. However, Paul was making only one point. The future age will bring more complete knowledge just as adulthood does (however imperfectly).

Paul used a mirror as a second illustration. The "glass" in verse 12 is not a window but a mirror, probably made of polished metal. The mirrors of that day did not provide perfect images of what they reflected. Looking at your reflection in a mirror, therefore, did not show the real you in a sharp, clear image. Looking at God and His kingdom in our present age is like looking at one's reflection in a first-century mirror. It is imperfect. Looking at God and His kingdom in the future age will be like seeing ourselves and God face to face. "When he shall appear, we shall be like him; for we shall see him as he is" (1 John 3:2).

Most of the things that are part of earthly life will pass away in God's eternal kingdom. Hebrews 12:26–29 reminds us that God will shake all things and only the things of God's kingdom will remain. First Corinthians 13:13 lists three things that shall remain—faith, hope, and love. Paul often described the Christian life in terms of these three things (Gal. 5:5, 6; Col. 1:4, 5; 1 Thess. 1:3; 5:8). Faith describes the way we come to God through commitment and trust in Jesus Christ and the way in which we continue to relate to Him. Hope is not human wishful thinking, but confident hope in God and in His promises. Love is how we act toward God and other people.

These three will be part of who we are forever. The character of each may change in some ways. We will not need to walk by faith because we will be able in many ways to walk by sight. We will not be praying and hoping for the coming of God's kingdom. We will not have the need to give back good for evil when there is no evil. However, we will always be people of faith, hope, and love; and because we know so little about the new heavens and new earth, God may have new ways for us to express our faith, hope, and love.

Paul said that faith, hope, and love are eternal; but he said that the greatest of these is love. Perhaps he meant that since God is love (not faith or hope), this quality of God Himself is the greatest of the three. Perhaps he was thinking of what he had just written in verse 7. Love believes, and love hopes. At any rate, after reading chapter 13, no one really wants to argue with Paul about the preeminence of Christian love.

SUMMARY OF BIBLE TRUTHS

1. Everything Christians do should be done in love.
2. If not, all our efforts amount to nothing.
3. Christian love is the opposite of the world's sinful ways.
4. Christian love was perfectly seen only in Jesus Christ.
5. Spiritual gifts will pass away, but love is eternal.
6. Faith, hope, and love are eternal; and love is the greatest of the three.

APPLYING THE BIBLE

1. The right motive. A former head of the New York Stock Exchange once said, "The public may forgive us for mistakes in judgment, but it will not forgive us for mistakes in motive."[1] Love is not greedy; it does not seek its own. Love is the more excellent way because it comes from the right motive.

2. What love is. Love is swift, sincere, pious, pleasant, gentle, strong, patient, faithful, prudent, long-suffering, manly, and never seeking her own; for wheresoever a man seeketh his own, there he falleth from love.[2]

3. What love brings forth. Perhaps better known for the prayer that bears his name, St. Francis of Assisi writes of the benefits known to the life that has cultivated among other virtues, that of love (charity).

"Where there is charity and wisdom, there is neither fear nor ignorance. Where there is patience and humility, there is neither anger nor vexation. Where there is poverty and joy, there is neither greed nor avarice. Where there is peace and meditation, there is neither anxiety nor doubt."[3]

4. What love does. "I've never met a person whose greatest need was anything other than real, unconditional love. It is the common fiber of life, the flame that heats our soul, energizes our spirit and supplies passion to our lives. It is our connection to God and to each other."[4]

5. Love, according to the experts. Answering the question, "What does it take to keep love alive," a panel of six experts offered the following pointers:

- honesty,
- empathetic listening,
- creating an atmosphere without judgment,
- praise and encouragement; love cannot survive in an atmosphere of constant criticism,
- sharing responsibilities,
- knowing that hard times will come and being willing to work together when they do, and
- lots of giving and forgiving.[5]

6. The labor of love. "To love somebody is not just a strong feeling—a feeling may come and it may go. Rather, love is a decision, a judgment, a promise."[6] Those words could have been written to the

Christian community in Corinth. Divisions in the fellowship were driving the congregation apart. Paul's words to them in the thirteenth chapter are healing words, but they still require a decision.

7. Love in the midst of our differences. First Corinthians shows a church that was experiencing growing pains. The non-Christians in Corinth didn't know what the issues were, but as long as the church remained divided, the Christian witness was hindered. That witness is still hindered today when Christians ignore the rule of love. Francis Schaeffer put it this way: "Before a watching world an observable love in the midst of difference will show a difference between Christians' differences and others' differences. The world may not understand what the Christians are disagreeing about, but they will very quickly understand the difference of our differences from the world's differences if they see us having our differences in an open and observable love on a practical level."[7]

TEACHING THE BIBLE

- *Main Idea:* Paul lists the characteristics of love in this chapter.
- *Suggested Teaching Aim:* To lead adults to list the characteristics of love as set forth in 1 Corinthians 13.

A TEACHING OUTLINE

1. *More Excellent Way (1 Cor. 12:31)*
2. *Indispensable Way (1 Cor. 13:1–3)*
3. *Christlike Way (1 Cor. 13:4–7)*
4. *Eternal Way (1 Cor. 13:8–13)*

Introduce the Bible Study

Use number 4, "What Love Does," in "Applying the Bible" to introduce the lesson.

Search for Biblical Truth

IN ADVANCE, make four strip posters of "A Teaching Outline" above. Place the first strip on the wall. Read aloud or summarize the first paragraph in "Studying the Bible" under this verse. (Or **IN ADVANCE** enlist a member to do this.)

Place the second strip on the wall. Explain the Greek words for love and how the meaning of "charity" has changed. Point out that Paul begins these three verses with "What if . . ." phrases ("Though"). Write the following on a chalkboard (omit italicized answers). Let members suggest answers; add explanations from "Studying the Bible."

What if . . .	but I did not love . . .
I spoke all foreign languages and angel languages	I would be a noisy gong or cymbal
I could prophesy and knew everything	I would be nothing
I used everything I had to feed the poor and was burned alive	I would have nothing

Place the third strip on the wall. If members have different translations, ask them to read verses 4–7 in as many different translations as possible. On the chalkboard write, *Love is* . . . Ask members to compose a definition of love based on these four verses.

Place the fourth strip on the wall. Read aloud this statement: "The point of verses 8–13 is that Christian love is part of God's eternal order, not just an instrument of His for the present age." Ask members to look at verses 8–13 and find evidence that supports this statement.

Ask, What two illustrations did Paul use in verses 11, 12 to illustrate that spiritual gifts would have served their purpose when God's kingdom comes. Explain that first-century mirrors were made of polished metal, not glass with a silvered backing.

IN ADVANCE, write these definitions on large strips of paper and place on the wall at this time:

- **FAITH** describes the way we come to God through commitment and trust in Jesus Christ and the way in which we continue to relate to Him.
- **HOPE** is not human, wishful thinking, but confident hope in God and in His promises.
- **LOVE** is how we act toward God and other people.

Use the comments in "Studying the Bible" to explain how these three definitions will be a part of who we are forever and why Paul considered love the greatest of the three.

Give the Truth a Personal Focus

Distribute paper and pencils to members. **IN ADVANCE,** copy on a large sheet of paper the six statements in "Summary of Bible Truths." Display these six statements and read them aloud to the class. Ask members to choose one of these statements and write a paragraph to describe how this statement could help them this coming week to let love be the guiding force of their lives. (If you choose not to do this individually, you can use the six statements to lead a group discussion with the whole class; or you can organize members in six groups and assign each group one of the statements.)

---

1. Alfred Decrane, "Leadership for the Future," *Executive Excellence, Inc.,* Dec. 1997, 16-17.
2. Thomas à Kempis, *Imitation of Christ,* bk. III, ch. 5.
3. St. Francis of Assisi, *The Counsels of the Holy Father St. Francis,* admonition 27.
4. Elisabeth Kubler-Ross, *The Wheel of Life.*
5. Lynne Gold-Bikin, Frank Farley, et al., "What Does It Take to Maintain Love?" *Psychology Today,* March-April 1996, 88.
6. Erich Fromm, *The Art of Loving.*
7. Francis A. Schaeffer, "The Mark of the Christian," *Christianity Today,* March 6, 1995, 27.

May

7

2000

The Christian March of Triumph

Background Passage: 2 Corinthians 1–2
Focal Passage: 2 Corinthians 2:4–17

Paul dealt with a host of problems in 1 Corinthians. He dealt with another problem in 2 Corinthians. By reading what Paul wrote and sometimes reading between the lines, we can try to put together what had happened between 1 and 2 Corinthians in the relationships of Paul and the Corinthians.

Study Aim: *To summarize the relationship between Paul and the Corinthian church.*

STUDYING THE BIBLE

OUTLINE AND SUMMARY

I. Greetings and Doxology (2 Cor. 1:1–11)
II. Dealing with Issues (2 Cor. 1:12–2:17)
1. **Paul's defense against criticism (1:12–22)**
2. **Painful visit and letter (1:23–2:4)**
3. **Forgiving the chief offender (2:5–11)**
4. **Preoccupation with the church's internal problems (2:12, 13)**
5. **Gratitude for Christ's triumph (2:14–17)**

Paul praised God as the source of comfort (1:1–11). He defended himself against the charge of being untrustworthy (1:12–22). He had made a painful visit and written a harsh letter (1:23–2:4). Paul urged the Corinthians to forgive the one they had disciplined (2:5–11). When Paul was in Troas, he was too upset to preach (2:12, 13). He thanked God for being led in the triumph of Christ (2:14–17).

I. Greetings and Doxology (2 Cor. 1:1–11)

After greeting the Corinthians (1:1, 2), Paul praised God for His comfort, which enabled Paul to comfort others (1:3–7). Paul told how their prayers had helped when his life was in danger (1:8–11).

II. Dealing with Issues (2 Cor. 1:12–2:17)

1. Paul's defense against criticism (1:12–22)

Paul declared that he had always acted with sincerity (1:12–14). Paul defended himself against the criticism that he did not keep his word because he changed his travel plans (1:15–17). He spoke and lived by God's truth (1:18–22).

2. Painful visit and letter (1:23–2:4)

4 For out of much affliction and anguish of heart I wrote unto you with many tears; not that ye should be grieved, but

that ye might know the love which I have more abundantly unto you.

When Paul wrote 1 Corinthians 16:5, 6, he planned to come to Corinth through Macedonia. Some time after he wrote 1 Corinthians, he planned to go from Ephesus directly to Corinth, then go to Macedonia, and return to Corinth. However, an emergency in Corinth forced him to make an unscheduled visit to Corinth. That visit proved to be so painful that he wanted to spare them another such visit (1:23–2:2).

We are not told why Paul made such a painful visit, but passages in 2 Corinthians strongly suggest that the church majority had repudiated Paul's leadership. Paul tried to resolve the issue by a visit to Corinth. The visit proved painful, and it was apparently unsuccessful in resolving the issue because Paul followed up on the painful visit with a harsh letter (2:3, 4).

Paul mentioned the letter in 2 Corinthians 2:3, 4, 9 and in 7:8, 12. Some Bible students believe that this was the letter we call 1 Corinthians, but Paul's description of the letter doesn't seem to fit 1 Corinthians. (For example, in 2 Cor. 7:8, Paul admitted that he regretted writing the harsh letter at first. Nothing in 1 Corinthians implies that he ever regretted writing it.) Apparently the harsh letter is now lost. Many Bible scholars believe that Paul wrote four letters to Corinth, only two of which are in the Bible (the other is mentioned in 1 Cor. 5:9).

Paul wrote the letter mentioned in verses 3 and 4 "out of much affliction and anguish of heart." He wrote it "with many tears." When Paul sent this harsh letter, he intended to show them how much he loved them. Tough love is not an easy thing to do; only those with real love are willing to risk using tough love.

3. Forgiving the chief offender (2:5–11)

5 But if any have caused grief, he hath not grieved me, but in part: that I may not overcharge you all.

6 Sufficient to such a man is this punishment, which was inflicted of many.

7 So that contrariwise ye ought rather to forgive him, and comfort him, lest perhaps such a one should be swallowed up with overmuch sorrow.

8 Wherefore I beseech you that ye would confirm your love toward him.

9 For to this end also did I write, that I might know the proof of you, whether ye be obedient in all things.

10 To whom ye forgive any thing, I forgive also: for if I forgave any thing, to whom I forgave it, for your sakes forgave I it in the person of Christ;

11 Lest Satan should get an advantage of us: for we are not ignorant of his devices.

Bible scholars debate the identity of this offender. Those who believe that the painful letter of verses 3 and 4 was 1 Corinthians identify this person with the man in 1 Corinthians 5. Most Bible scholars think that the offender in 2 Corinthians 2:5–11 was the ringleader of Paul's critics in Corinth. He likely had taken the lead in guiding the majority of the church to repudiate Paul.

A lot happened between 1 and 2 Corinthians. Paul never gave a blow-by-blow account, but we can piece much together by looking at several passages. We have already noted that Paul for some reason made a painful visit and wrote a harsh letter to Corinth. The rest of this chapter and 2 Corinthians 7:5–16 provide other key pieces to the puzzle.

Verse 5 notes that the man had "caused grief," but Paul insisted that it was not so much his grief as grief for the whole church. When Paul wrote, "He hath not grieved me," he was not denying that the man's attacks had grieved him personally. Paul, however, was emphasizing that he had done even more harm to the church as a whole than to Paul personally. The last part of verse 5 is difficult to translate, but this seems to be what Paul was saying.

Paul used "sufficient" to indicate that the punishment already given to the man was enough. The punishment had been "inflicted of many" (v. 6). "Many" here probably means that the majority of the church voted to punish the man in a certain way.

Paul urged the Corinthian church to forgive and comfort the disciplined member. They needed to confirm their love for him. Otherwise, he might be overwhelmed with sorrow. Apparently the man was repentant, or Paul would not have advised forgiveness.

Verse 9 provides more insight into the letter mentioned in verses 3 and 4. Paul wrote the harsh letter to test their obedience. Very likely, in that letter he called for the church to discipline the one who was leading the opposition to him. Now they had proved their loyalty to Paul; therefore, he urged them to forgive the man. Paul said that he would support them in forgiving the man. Christians ought to forgive one another as God in Christ has forgiven us (Eph. 4:32).

Failing to discipline the man would have given an advantage to Satan, but so would failing to forgive the man after he repented. Paul knew that the evil one is constantly looking for ways to gain an advantage over Christ's work by exploiting the weaknesses of Christians. Since "we are not ignorant of his devices," we ought not to give Satan any advantage.

4. Preoccupation with the church's internal problems (2:12, 13)

12 Furthermore, when I came to Troas to preach Christ's gospel, and a door was opened unto me of the Lord,

13 I had no rest in my spirit, because I found not Titus my brother: but taking my leave of them, I went from thence into Macedonia.

These verses provide one of the tantalizing flashbacks in 2 Corinthians. Each of these flashbacks provides a piece of the puzzle of what happened between Paul and the Corinthians after he sent 1 Corinthians.

For the first time in the letter Paul mentions Titus, who had played such a key role in resolving the problem at Corinth. Based on these verses and 2 Corinthians 7:5–16, we learn that Paul had sent Titus to Corinth on just such a mission. Titus was a kind of troubleshooter for Paul. In his three main appearances in the New Testament, he had been given some tough situations to handle (see 2 Cor. 8:6, 16, 23; Titus 1:4, 5, 10–12).

Paul became restless as he waited at Ephesus. Having not heard from Titus, Paul decided to head along the route over which Titus would be traveling. He hoped to meet Titus along the way. Paul arrived at Troas, where he earlier had had the vision of the man of Macedonia (Acts 16:8–10). He hoped to use his time in Troas to preach the gospel. A door was opened for Paul to preach, but Paul was too upset about the situation in Corinth to take advantage of an opportunity to tell the good news. Nothing takes the heart out of Christians so much as dissension in a church.

5. Gratitude for Christ's triumph (2:14–17)

14 Now thanks be unto God, which always causeth us to triumph in Christ, and maketh manifest the savour of his knowledge by us in every place.

15 For we are unto God a sweet savour of Christ, in them that are saved, and in them that perish:

16 To the one we are the savour of death unto death; and to the other the savour of life unto life. And who is sufficient for these things?

17 For we are not as many, which corrupt the word of God: but as of sincerity, but as of God, in the sight of God speak we in Christ.

Between verses 13 and 14, Paul moved from despair to joyous gratitude without explaining why to later readers of 2 Corinthians. The first readers of the letter—the Corinthian church—knew what had happened. Later readers have to wait for 2 Corinthians 7:5–7 to learn the rest of the story. Paul left Troas for Macedonia, where he met Titus, who told him the good news from Corinth. Just thinking of it caused Paul to burst forth in praise to God. Paul knew that neither his letter nor Titus's work had been the real power that resolved the crisis at Corinth. God had used both Paul and Titus, but only God could work such a miracle.

Paul compared his ministry and that of other servants of Christ to a Roman triumph. When a Roman general had won an especially great victory, he was honored with a victory parade. His officers and troops marched behind him. Bringing up the rear were the chained captives. Paul used the same analogy in Colossians 2:15, where the victorious Christ leads as defeated captives the spiritual powers of evil.

"Causeth us to triumph" is usually translated as "leads us in His triumph." However we translate it, we need to emphasize that Christ is the victorious general. Any victory of God's people is because they follow the victorious Lord Jesus.

One of the features of a Roman triumph was the lavish use of incense. Paul said that Christ's leading His servants in victory is a sweet savor to God and a sweet savor to those who follow Christ. The incense at the triumph did not smell so sweet to condemned captives. For many of them, the victory march was a march to the grave. Likewise, the victory of

Christ means life abundant and eternal for believers; but it means the second death for Satan and all who choose to reject the Savior.

Paul asked, "Who is sufficient for these things?" His answer was that no one is sufficient in his own strength. However, Paul elsewhere testified that he could do all things through Christ who strengthened him (Phil. 4:13).

Paul then contrasted his ministry and the ministries of all true servants of Christ to many others who corrupt the word of God. True servants of Christ serve in sincerity because they constantly remember that they live and serve in the sight of God and in the name of Christ.

PRONUNCIATION GUIDE

Macedonia [mass uh DOH nih uh]
Troas [TROH az]

SUMMARY OF BIBLE TRUTHS

1. Tough love sometimes works.
2. When disciplined church members repent, forgive them.
3. Dissension in a church hinders evangelism.
4. Give thanks to God for solving church problems.
5. Christ the victor leads His servants in a march of triumph.
6. Christ's victory means life for some and death for others.

Events Between 1 and 2 Corinthians
Critics of Paul led by one man became active.
They influenced the majority of the church to repudiate Paul.
Paul made an unscheduled and painful visit to Corinth.
Paul wrote a harsh letter to the church.
Paul sent Titus to Corinth.
Paul went to Troas and was too upset to preach.
Paul went to Macedonia, where he met Titus.
Titus reported that the church majority had reaffirmed Paul.
He also reported that the church majority had disciplined Paul's chief critic.
Paul wrote 2 Corinthians.

APPLYING THE BIBLE

1. Handling criticism. A five-point plan for facing criticism might be similar to that for facing gossip.

- Stay calm; consider the source.
- Don't overreact, and don't react too quickly.
- Investigate; try to discover not only what was said, but how and why it was said.
- Decide whether to confront the critic.

- Move on; don't expend emotional and mental energy over something you've already dealt with.

2. Quotes about criticism:

"To escape criticism—do nothing, say nothing, be nothing."
—Elbert Hubbard

"It is much easier to be critical than to be correct."
—Benjamin Disraeli

"In judging others, folks will work overtime for no pay."
—Charles Edwin Carruthers

"Criticism comes easier than craftsmanship."
—Zeuxis

"Honest criticism is hard to take, particularly from a friend, an acquaintance, or a stranger."
—Franklin P. Jones

"The person who can't dance says the band can't play. One survives all wounds except those of critics."
—North African saying

3. Forgiveness. "He who forgives ends the quarrel." Paul urged the Corinthians to practice forgiveness in the case of the individual who had been disciplined. When we practice forgiveness, we write "The End" at the bottom of a page representing a difficult chapter in life. Only then are we able to move on, and in a case such as the church in Corinth, are we able to get on with our mission "unencumbered."

4. Forgive as Christ forgave. Horace Bushnell said, "Forgiveness is man's deepest need and highest achievement." Paul said, Christians ought to forgive one another as God in Christ has forgiven us (Eph. 4:32).

5. Americans are in a forgiving mood. In a recent Gallup Poll, Americans indicated six to one that if given a choice, they would prefer to forgive someone who wronged them than seek revenge. Forty-eight percent would "try to forgive" while eight percent would "try to get even."

6. Rebuilding a relationship with the one who hurt you. Louis McBurney, founder of the Marble Retreat, Marble, Colorado, guides those whose trust has been shattered in relationships through the following steps toward reconciliation.

- Acknowledge the problem.
- Choose to forgive.
- Verbally commit.
- Risk wisely.
- Work together.
- Celebrate the victory.[1]

These are similar to steps necessary for biblical reconciliation for the church. Paul's words to the Corinthians involve the same steps where repentance and grace are sincere.

7. A great way to get even. In writing about Eleanor Roosevelt, Ralph McGill said, "One of the shameful chapters of this country was how many of the comfortable—especially those who profited from the misery of others—abused her. . . . But she got even in a way that was almost cruel. She forgave them."

TEACHING THE BIBLE

- *Main Idea:* God works in the midst of our conflicts to bring healing.
- *Suggested Teaching Aim:* To lead adults to express gratitude for God's healing our past conflicts and to express hope for healing in present conflicts.

A TEACHING OUTLINE

1. *Painful Visit and Letter (2 Cor. 1:23–2:4)*
2. *Forgiving the Chief Offender (2 Cor. 2:5–11)*
3. *Preoccupation with Church's Internal Problems (2 Cor. 2:12–13)*
4. *Gratitude for Christ's Triumph (2 Cor. 2:14–17)*

Introduce the Bible Study

Use number 1, "Handling Criticism," in "Applying the Bible" to introduce the lesson.

Search for Biblical Truth

IN ADVANCE:

- Display a map of Paul's missionary journeys.
- Make strip posters of the four points of "A Teaching Outline" above.
- Enlist two members to read the Scripture passage alternately when called on.
- Make a large poster of "Events Between 1 and 2 Corinthians" on page 283 at the end of this lesson.
- Enlist a member to give a two- to three-minute report on Titus and his relationship with Paul.

Place the first strip poster on the wall and ask one of the readers to read 1 Corinthians 1:23–2:4. Locate Corinth on the map. Lecture briefly:

1. Using the material in "Studying the Bible," describe the "painful visit" Paul made to Corinth.
2. Other passages in 2 Corinthians suggest that the church majority had rejected Paul's leadership in Corinth.
3. The visit was unsuccessful in resolving the conflict and Paul wrote a "harsh letter."

DISCUSS: What steps can we take to help assure that tough love will work when we deal with conflicts?

Place the second strip poster on the wall. Ask the second reader to read verses 5–11. Lecture briefly:

1. Describe the offender and the possible circumstances at Corinth.

2. Display the "Events Between 1 and 2 Corinthians" poster and use it to help describe the situation in Corinth.
3. Point out that the man had been disciplined by the church, and they should now forgive him so Satan would not have an opportunity to work in their midst.

DISCUSS: Why is it so hard to forgive someone after we have disciplined the person?

Place the third strip poster on the wall. Ask the first reader to read verses 12–13. Lecture briefly:

1. Locate Troas and Macedonia on the map.
2. Call for the report on Titus and his relationship with Paul.
3. Paul was so upset over the Corinth matter that he could not preach even though God had provided an opportunity.

DISCUSS: What are some ways dissension in a church hinders evangelism?

Place the fourth strip poster on the wall. Call for the second reader to read verses 14–17. Lecture briefly:

1. Between verses 13 and 14, Paul had left Troas for Macedonia where he had met Titus who told him the good news from Corinth.
2. Paul compared his ministry to a Roman triumph in which Christ the victorious general will lead his servants in a triumphal march.
3. Romans used incense at the triumph to celebrate, but to the condemned it was the smell of death.
4. Christ's victory means life for some and death for others.

DISCUSS: Can you think of a church problem that you can thank God for solving?

Give the Truth a Personal Focus

Read the six "Summary of Bible Truths" statements aloud. Close by letting members express sentence prayers of gratitude for God's healing past conflicts and for healing in present conflicts.

---

1. Louis McBurney, *Leadership Journal,* Spring 1996, 86.

May

14

2000

Trials and Triumphs of Christian Ministry

Background Passage: 2 Corinthians 4:1–18
Focal Passage: 2 Corinthians 4:5–18

In many ways, 2 Corinthians is one of Paul's most personal letters. Because he had been under attack at Corinth, he spent the heart of the letter describing his ministry. Chapter 4 describes what kept Paul going in a ministry that was often filled with trials of various kinds.

Study Aim: *To summarize the trials Paul encountered and the ways he overcame them.*

STUDYING THE BIBLE

OUTLINE AND SUMMARY

I. Preaching Christ, Not Ourselves (2 Cor. 4:1–6)
II. Relying on God, Not Ourselves (2 Cor. 4:7–18)
1. Weak, yet strong (4:7)
2. Down, but not out (4:8, 9)
3. Dying, yet living (4:10–15)
4. Aging, yet being renewed (4:16)
5. Suffering, yet hopeful (4:17, 18)

Paul preached Christ, not himself (vv. 1–6). He relied on God's power, not his own (v. 7). He encountered many trials, but Christ enabled him to overcome them (vv. 8, 9). Although he lived under danger of death, he trusted the resurrection power of Christ in life and death (vv. 10–15). Outwardly he was wasting away, but inwardly he was renewed each day (v. 16). Earthly suffering is light compared to the glory of eternal glory (vv. 17, 18).

I. Preaching Christ, Not Ourselves (2 Cor. 4:1–6)

Two sources of Paul's trials were critics within the church and the blindness of unbelievers. He dealt with these in verses 1–6. Because he had been entrusted with the ministry, he did not lose heart (4:1). He had renounced all dubious methods of ministry and concentrated on dealing with God's Word in truth (4:2). He realized that Satan was constantly at work seeking to blind the hearts of unbelievers "lest the light of the glorious gospel of Christ, who is the image of God, should shine upon them" (4:3, 4).

5 For we preach not ourselves, but Christ Jesus the Lord; and ourselves your servants for Jesus' sake.

6 For God, who commanded the light to shine out of darkness, hath shined in our hearts, to give the light of the knowledge of the glory of God in the face of Jesus Christ.

Paul's critics had accused him of promoting Paul himself. Paul answered that lie in verses 5 and 6. Paul's basic approach to preaching was to preach Jesus Christ, keeping himself in the role of preacher only. Jesus Christ is the only Lord and Savior. Closely related to this first priority was Paul's commitment to serve others for Jesus' sake. These two priorities match Jesus' two great commandments of loving God and loving neighbors.

Genesis 1:3 is in the background of verse 6. Paul, no doubt influenced by his own experience on the Damascus Road, often spoke of light in connection with salvation and living the Christian life. He had just done that in verse 3 (see also Col. 1:13; Eph. 5:8). Jesus is the Light of the world, who came to bring the light of salvation and new life (John 8:12; Matt. 4:16).

Paul was also still thinking of the powerful word picture in 2 Corinthians 4:6 when he wrote of "the light of the knowledge of the glory of God in the face of Jesus Christ." Light brings salvation and revelation. They go together. We see God's glory revealed in Jesus Christ and experienced through a personal knowledge of God when we exercise saving faith.

II. Relying on God, Not Ourselves (2 Cor. 4:7–18)

1. Weak, yet strong (v. 7)

7 But we have this treasure in earthen vessels, that the excellency of the power may be of God, and not of us.

This verse provides the key to the rest of the chapter. Paul's critics in Corinth said he was weak, not strong. Paul insisted that suffering is part of a Christian's lot, and that the power is divine, not human power. The power of God was able to work in Paul only when he recognized his weakness (2 Cor. 12:7–10).

"This treasure" is the saving light of the knowledge of God described in verse 6. The "earthen vessels" were the frail mortals in whose hearts the Lord's Spirit dwelt and through whose lives He does His work. In the first century, people sometimes hid their treasures in clay pots. Paul used this familiar ancient practice to describe the greatness of the treasure and the earthly nature of those with the treasure.

Paul's point is clear. The wonder, glory, and power come from the treasure, not from the frail vessels to whom the treasure is entrusted. The power for Christian living and service do not come from us, but from God. We are privileged to be entrusted with the treasure, but we are not able to convict or convert sinners. We grow old and die, but the treasure—although in a series of mortal lives—continues to exert its power down through the ages.

Later in this letter, Paul described his experience with what he called "a thorn in the flesh." He prayed for God to remove this painful messenger of Satan, because it seemed to interfere with his ministry. However, the Lord told Paul, "My grace is sufficient for thee." From this Paul said that God was teaching him that when he was weak, he was strong. That is, when he realized his human frailty and limitations, he relied more on the strength of the Lord (2 Cor. 12:7–10).

May

14

2000

2. Down, but not out (4:8, 9)

8 We are troubled on every side, yet not distressed; we are perplexed, but not in despair;

9 Persecuted, but not forsaken; cast down, but not destroyed.

Paul gave four examples of ways the power of God sustains believers in the kinds of trials faced by His people. Each is stated as a kind of paradox.

1. *Outward pressure.* "Troubled on every side" translates words that describe being under pressure from all directions. "Not distressed" communicates not being crushed by the pressure.

2. *Inward perplexity.* "Perplexed" is a word meaning being subjected to what causes people to become despondent. In other words, at times God's people grow despondent; but they are kept from despair by God's power.

3. *Persecution.* Paul and the early Christians knew what it was to be persecuted, but they also knew that they would never be forsaken by the Lord.

4. *Life's hard blows.* "Cast down" can be translated "knocked down." "Destroyed" can mean "knocked out." Like a boxer, the Christian may be knocked down by troubles; but the Lord promises that He will not allow us to be knocked out.

3. Dying, yet living (vv. 10–15)

10 Always bearing about in the body the dying of the Lord Jesus, that the life also of Jesus might be made manifest in our body.

11 For we which live are alway delivered unto death for Jesus' sake, that the life also of Jesus might be made manifest in our mortal flesh.

12 So then death worketh in us, but life in you.

13 We having the same spirit of faith, according as it is written, I believed, and therefore have I spoken; we also believe, and therefore speak;

14 Knowing that he which raised up the Lord Jesus shall raise up us also by Jesus, and shall present us with you.

15 For all things are for your sakes, that the abundant grace might through the thanksgiving of many redound to the glory of God.

The central paradox of the Christian life is dying, yet living. "Whosoever will save his life shall lose it: and whosoever will lose his life for my sake shall find it" (Matt. 16:25). Paul later testified, "I am crucified with Christ: nevertheless I live; yet not I, but Christ liveth in me" (Gal. 2:20). The way of the cross is not something we can live in our own strength. Jesus was not just calling His disciples to do their best to follow His example. He was promising to come into their lives as the crucified, risen Lord to enable them to live by the way of the cross and the power of the resurrection.

This principle of living by dying applies in three main ways: (1) dying to self and sin and becoming more like Jesus; (2) suffering for Jesus' sake but overcoming by God's power; (3) facing death with confident hope of eternal life. The second of these is dominant in verses 10–15, but the first and third are here also.

Paul was like a man on death row. More than once his life had been in danger (Acts 14:5, 19; 19:29; 21:31; 23:12; 2 Cor. 1:8, 9). He was "bearing about in the body the dying of the Lord Jesus," and "alway delivered unto death for Jesus' sake." He described the deliverances made possible by God's resurrection power as "the life also of Jesus . . . made manifest in our mortal flesh."

Verse 12 reinforces a point made throughout this passage—that Christians live for others. They are willing to die so others may live.

Verse 13 quotes Psalm 116:10, a psalm of gratitude, faith, and testimony in the face of affliction and possible death. Just as the psalmist maintained his faith and bore his testimony, so did Paul under similar circumstances.

Paul knew that eventually he would die. He probably expected to die a martyr's death for Jesus' sake—as indeed he did (2 Tim. 4:6–8). God had often delivered him from death, but Paul did not expect God always to save him from dying. He was not worried because death held no fears for one who knew the crucified, risen Lord.

Verse 15 shows that Paul endured dangers and death for the sake of others. He did it when he came to Corinth so they could hear the gospel. Their conversion in turn led them to glorify God.

4. Aging, yet being renewed (v. 16)

16 For which cause we faint not; but though our outward man perish, yet the inward man is renewed day by day.

The word translated "faint not" is also in 4:1. The word can mean "grow weary" (Luke 18:1; Gal. 6:9), but it can also mean "lose heart." "Perish" can refer to all the outward dangers of death that Paul faced, but it probably here emphasizes the gradual loss of health and strength as a person grows older. When applied to the human body, the Greek word translated "perish" means "waste away."

Paul's thorn in the flesh was probably some physical ailment that comes as one grows older. Paul was aware that his mortal body was wearing out; yet he did not lose heart because he was being renewed inwardly each day. The presence of the Lord brought daily strength and renewal of spirit (see Isa. 40:31).

5. Suffering, yet hopeful (vv. 17, 18)

17 For our light affliction, which is but for a moment, worketh for us a far more exceeding and eternal weight of glory;

18 While we look not at the things which are seen, but at the things which are not seen: for the things which are seen are temporal; but the things which are not seen are eternal.

Verses 17 and 18 contain four striking contrasts: "light" and "weight," "affliction" and "glory," "temporal" and "eternal," "seen" and "not seen." "Affliction" is a general word for troubles. In a similar passage in Romans 8:18, Paul used the word for "sufferings." He likely had sufferings in mind here also.

"Light affliction" does not imply that sufferings are not real and painful; however, Paul was viewing earthly sufferings from the perspective of eternity. Sufferings are real and painful, but they are temporary. Sufferings are "temporal," which means "immediate" or "for the present" only. And when our present sufferings are compared with the glory of eternity with God, they are "light" compared to the weightiness of eternal glory. "I reckon that the sufferings of this present time are not worthy to be compared with the glory which shall be revealed in us" (Rom. 8:18).

"Look at" means "fix one's attention on." Unbelievers say that "seeing is believing." People of faith say that "believing is seeing" (Heb. 11:1). Only those who fix their attention on God and His kingdom will see the realities of this life and the life beyond. Paul elaborated on the life beyond in 2 Corinthians 5:1–10.

SUMMARY OF BIBLE TRUTHS

1. Bear witness to Jesus Christ, not ourselves.
2. Rely on God's power, not our own.
3. Allow God to enable us to overcome troubles.
4. Let Christ empower us to live for God and others.
5. Let God renew you inwardly day by day.
6. Live in the light of eternity.

APPLYING THE BIBLE

1. Trouble and prayer. Trouble may drive you to prayer, but prayer will drive away trouble.

It has been my experience that prayer is never an imposition during times of trouble, but unfortunately, when things are going great, we slow down in this area of spiritual discipline. Since prayer is an exercise in experiencing the presence of God, perhaps trouble should be viewed as a blessing.

2. Good words for difficult times. An old preacher admonished his congregation by saying: "Fret not, for He loves you; faint not, for He holds you; fear not, for He keeps you." Paul demonstrated the truth of this statement and shared from his heart as he ministered to the Corinthians. In difficult times, Paul knew that the Lord was with him.

3. Faith as a source of difficulty. Faith and its ethical demands are often the source for suffering, especially for those who take their faith seriously. Deitrich Bonhoeffer was executed for participating in a plan to assassinate Hitler. He did this because of his convictions in the area of faith and ethics. While he could have enjoyed a career in theological education or some other ministry in the United States, he returned to Germany to fight to keep the German church from selling out to national socialism. He was arrested, imprisioned, and shortly before allied troops liberated his POW camp, executed. Paul faced difficulties for his faith, too. Eventually, his faith demanded his life. He would not retreat, even when things got tough. Faith doesn't do that.

4. Enduring difficulties. "God prepares us for what God is preparing for us" (Warren Wiersbe).

5. Quotes for difficult times:

"To extraordinary circumstances we must apply extraordinary remedies." —Napoleon Bonaparte

"There cannot be a crisis next week. My schedule is already full." —Henry Kissinger

"People who don't have nightmares don't have dreams." —Robert Paul Smith

"Life doesn't do anything to you, it only reveals your spirit." —anonymous

"A diamond is a chunk of coal that made good under pressure." —anonymous

"A brook would lose its song if God removed the rocks." —anonymous

TEACHING THE BIBLE

- *Main Idea:* The sufferings we endure for Jesus are minor compared to the reward we receive.
- *Suggested Teaching Aim:* To lead adults to commit themselves to suffer for Christ so they may experience His glory.

A TEACHING OUTLINE

1. *Preaching Christ, Not Ourselves (2 Cor. 4:1–6)*
2. *Relying on God, Not Ourselves (2 Cor. 4:7–18)*

Introduce the Bible Study

Use number 1, "Trouble and Prayer," in "Applying the Bible" to introduce the lesson.

Search for Biblical Truth

Point out that Paul had two sources of trials: critics within the church and unbelievers outside the church. Ask, Which do you think was more difficult for Paul to deal with?

Ask members to open their Bibles to 2 Corinthians 4:5–6 and identify Paul's two priorities in his preaching. (Jesus and serving others.) Ask members how this compares to Jesus' two great commandments in Matthew 22:37–39.

Ask members to look at 2 Corinthians 4:6. Ask, What experience in Paul's life may have influenced his using the concept of light shining out of darkness?

DISCUSS: How do witnessing activities that we engage in point to ourselves rather than to Christ?

Write on a chalkboard: *1. Weak, yet strong (2 Cor. 4:7)*. Ask members to look at this verse and answer these questions: What is "this treasure"? (The saving light of the knowledge of God described in v. 6.) What are the "earthen vessels"? (Frail mortals in whose hearts the Spirit dwelt.) What point is Paul making? (We may grow old and die, but the treasure continues to exert his power through the ages.)

Write on a chalkboard: *2. Down, but not out (2 Cor. 4:8, 9)*. Use "Studying the Bible" to explain the four examples of ways God's power sustains believers in the kinds of trials faced by His people.

Write on a chalkboard: *3. Dying, yet living (2 Cor. 4:10–12)*. Ask a volunteer to read Matthew 16:25. Point out that this is the theme of Paul's words to the Corinthians. Use "Studying the Bible" to explain the three main ways the principle of living by dying applies.

Write on a chalkboard: *4. Aging, yet being renewed (2 Cor. 4:16)*. Ask, What phrase could indicate that Paul was experiencing some of the problems of aging? ("Outward man perish.")

Write on a chalkboard: *5. Suffering, yet hopeful (2 Cor. 4:17–18)*. On a chalkboard write (omit italicized answers):

Now	Then
Light	*Weight*
Affliction	*Glory*
Temporal	*Eternal*
Seen	*Unseen*

Ask members to identify the four striking contrasts between *Now* and *Then*. Use "Studying the Bible" to explain each of the terms.

Give the Truth a Personal Focus

IN ADVANCE, copy the six statements on a small sheet of paper and give a copy to each member. Ask six members each to read one of the statements as a summary of the lesson. Ask members to keep the list in their Bibles as a reminder that the sufferings we endure for Jesus are minor compared to the reward we receive.

The Collection for Jerusalem Christians

Background Passage: 2 Corinthians 9:1–15
Focal Passage: 2 Corinthians 9:1–13

The Bible says a lot about money. The longest passage on this subject is 2 Corinthians 8–9. Chapter 9 contains most of the biblical principles about giving.

Study Aim: *To identify the principles of giving.*

STUDYING THE BIBLE

OUTLINE AND SUMMARY

I. Finishing What You Start (2 Cor. 9:1–5)
  1. Making preparations (9:1, 2)
  2. Implementing the preparations (9:3–5)
II. Principles of Giving (2 Cor. 9:6–15)
  1. Manner of giving (9:6, 7)
  2. Means for giving (9:8–10)
  3. Motives for giving (9:11–15)

Paul reminded the Corinthians of their earlier preparations for the offering (vv. 1, 2). He urged them to have the offering ready when he came (vv. 3–5). He taught giving that is generous, intentional, voluntary, and joyful (vv. 6, 7). He promised that God would give generous givers enough to continue to be generous (vv. 8–10). Motives for giving are gratitude to God, deep human needs, and the blessings of giving (vv. 11–15).

I. Finishing What You Start (2 Cor. 9:1–5)

1. Making preparations (vv. 1, 2)

1 For as touching the ministering to the saints, it is superfluous for me to write to you:

2 For I know the forwardness of your mind, for which I boast of you to them of Macedonia, that Achaia was ready a year ago; and your zeal hath provoked very many.

Romans 15:25–33 reveals that Paul was intent on taking to the poor believers of Jerusalem a love offering from the Gentile churches. Paul had explained this offering to the Corinthians, and he wrote to them about it in 1 Corinthians 16:1–4. The Corinthians had already made preparations for participating in the offering a year earlier. "The forwardness of your mind" translates a Greek word meaning "readiness" or "willingness." The word is found also in 2 Corinthians 8:11, 12, 19. They had not actually made the offering, but they had shown a "readiness to will" (8:11).

When promoting the offering in the churches of Macedonia, Paul had boasted to them of the preparations of Corinth (chief city in the province of Achaia). Paul's description of the zeal of the Corinthian church had aroused a similar zeal among those who heard what Paul said. The word translated "provoked" usually had a negative meaning: as it does, for example, in Colossians 3:21. Here, however, it has a positive meaning.

2. Implementing the preparations (vv. 3–5)

3 Yet have I sent the brethren, lest our boasting of you should be in vain in this behalf; that, as I said, ye may be ready:

4 Lest haply if they of Macedonia come with me, and find you unprepared, we (that we say not, ye) should be ashamed in this same confident boasting.

5 Therefore I thought it necessary to exhort the brethren, that they would go before unto you, and make up beforehand your bounty, whereof ye had notice before, that the same might be ready, as a matter of bounty, and not as of covetousness.

The "brethren" mentioned in verses 3 and 5 were Titus and two others, whose task Paul had just described in 8:16–24. Paul was sending them on before he personally went to Corinth. Meanwhile, Paul stayed in Macedonia putting the finishing touches on their offering and also probably allowing the Corinthians time to finish what they had begun a year earlier. They apparently had delayed the offering during the time they were wrangling among themselves and with Paul. Now that a reconciliation had taken place, Paul sent the committee of three to assist in organizing the Corinthians to finish what they had started.

"May be ready" in verse 3 is the same word as "ready" in verse 2. In verse 2, however, they were only getting ready or making preparations to give; in verse 3, Paul urged them to actually implement the preparations by making the offering.

Paul probably had with him some of the representatives of the Macedonian churches when he returned to Corinth. Because he had boasted of the Corinthians to the Macedonians, Paul did not want the Corinthians to embarrass themselves in front of the Macedonians by not having a worthy offering ready to go to Jerusalem.

Paul wrote in 2 Corinthians 8:1–5 of the sacrificial giving of the Macedonian churches. This may have been due in part to what Paul had told the Macedonians about the Corinthians. Paul in turn wrote the Corinthians about the sacrificial giving of the Macedonian churches, hoping that their example of actual giving would provoke the Corinthians to carry through with their earlier preparations.

Paul used "bounty" to describe the generous gifts that he hoped the Corinthians would give. "Not as of covetousness" is the opposite kind of giving. The person who gives "of covetousness" asks, "How little do I have to give?"

II. Principles of Giving (2 Cor. 9:6–15)

1. Manner of giving (vv. 6, 7)

6 But this I say, He which soweth sparingly shall reap also sparingly; and he which soweth bountifully shall reap also bountifully.

7 Every man according as he purposeth in his heart, so let him give; not grudgingly, or of necessity: for God loveth a cheerful giver.

1. *Generously.* The general law of the harvest, which is stated so well in Galatians 6:7, is here applied to giving. Farmers of that day scattered seed abundantly (Matt. 13:3–9). Not all of it grew into healthy, fruitful plants; but the more seed sowed, the more plants that sprouted, grew, and bore fruit. If a farmer was stingy sowing the seed, he would reap less of a harvest. Paul applied this to giving. The more generous giver will see a greater harvest of good from the gifts. Thus, one principle of the manner of giving is to give generously.

2. *Intentionally.* "As he purposeth in his heart" means giving based on a deliberate decision. When Jesus spoke of not letting one hand know what the other is doing, He was not attacking knowing what you give. He was warning against using the amount as a basis for personal pride and boasting (Matt. 6:3). The Bible teaches intentional giving as the only way for regular, systematic giving.

3. *Voluntarily.* Closely related to intentional giving is voluntary giving. Each person decides what to give. Giving is not "of necessity." Paul felt that the offering was necessary in order to meet the needs of the poor in Jerusalem. However, he did not assess each person a certain amount. He left this decision for each person to make as he was led by God's Spirit.

4. *Joyfully.* "Grudgingly" is the opposite of being a "cheerful giver." The word translated "grudgingly" means "sorrow," "grief," "pain." For some people, any giving is painful for them; and they give as little as possible. The opposite kind of giver acts out of gratitude to God and love to others; such givers find joy in giving. They have discovered the secret of life. God has shown us that life is for giving (Acts 20:35).

2. Means for giving (vv. 8–10)

8 And God is able to make all grace abound toward you; that ye, always having all sufficiency in all things, may abound to every good work:

9 (As it is written, He hath dispersed abroad; he hath given to the poor: his righteousness remaineth for ever.

10 Now he that ministereth seed to the sower both minister bread for your food, and multiply your seed sown, and increase the fruits of your righteousness).

Generous giving is an act of faith. The person who gives has no way of knowing that he and his family may not face future difficulties in which they will need what they have given to others. In order to give generously, a person must believe what Paul wrote in verses 8–10. Notice the key words, "God is able." People who give believe that God is the source of all their blessings past, present, and future. Therefore, they trust that God will provide all they need to do His will. And since God's will is that we give in His name to meet the needs of others, we trust that He will give us enough to be able to do that.

Notice the words *all* and *every* in verse 8: "all grace," "always," "all sufficiency," "all things," "every good work." (Each of these translates the Greek word for "all.") The word *abound* means to have more than enough.

Another key word is *sufficiency.* The Greek word was used by the Stoic philosophers of Paul's day to describe their goal of learning to be self-sufficient, which included learning how to get by with the bare minimum. Paul used an adjective form of this word in Philippians 4:11, when he described how God had taught him to be content with little or with much. Paul, however, was no advocate of achieving contentment through self-sufficiency. In the same passage in Philippians, he wrote, "I can do all things through Christ which strengtheneth me" (Phil. 4:13).

We might translate "sufficiency" as "enough." Verses 8–10 promise generous givers that God will always give enough for their personal needs and enough to give to others. He gives the gift of learning to be content with enough; He does not promise to give us all we want, but all we need.

The sower analogy from verse 6 is enlarged on in verses 9, 10. People who give generously to the poor are promised that God will provide bread for them and their families and plenty of seed to sow for another harvest from which they will share generously with others. The words translated "ministereth" and "minister" in verse 10 mean to supply bountifully.

First Kings 17:11–16 illustrates this principle of faith in giving. The poor widow gave the last of her oil and meal to feed the hungry Elijah. God in turn made her barrel of meal always have meal and her cruse of oil never to run dry.

3. Motives for giving (vv. 11–15)

11 Being enriched in every thing to all bountifulness, which causeth through us thanksgiving to God.

12 For the administration of this service not only supplieth the want of the saints, but is abundant also by many thanksgivings unto God;

13 Whiles by the experiment of this ministration they glorify God for your professed subjection unto the gospel of Christ, and for your liberal distribution unto them, and unto all men.

The final verses focus on three reasons or motives for giving: thanksgiving to God, needs of others, and personal blessings.

1. *Personal blessings.* Verses 9, 10 show that generous people grow in "righteousness." This is one way of saying that the lives of generous people are enriched spiritually. This theme continues in verse 11.

2. *Needs of others.* "Want" in verse 12 refers to deep needs, not to "wants" as "desires." Money can't buy everything, but some things only money can buy: food, clothing, housing. Poverty and wealth are often

relative terms. The Macedonian and many of the Corinthian believers were poor; so were the Jerusalem believers. The Gentile believers took Paul's word for the depth of the needs of the poor Jewish Christians.

3. *Thanksgiving to God.* Paul's prayer was that the Jewish believers would give thanks to God for these generous gifts from Gentile believers. The Jews would glorify God because the gifts from Gentile Christians would prove that the Gentile believers had truly responded to the gospel.

Of course, generous givers are motivated primarily by their own gratitude to God for what He has done for them. Paul thus ended his appeal with these words: "Thanks be unto God for his unspeakable gift" (9:15). Bible scholars debate which of God's "unspeakable" gifts Paul had in mind. Whatever it was, Paul's shout of praise shows that gratitude to God motivates our giving.

PRONUNCIATION GUIDE

Achaia	[uh KAY yuh]
Macedonia	[mass un DOH nih uh]

SUMMARY OF BIBLE TRUTHS

1. Carry through with good intentions about giving.
2. Give generously, intentionally, voluntarily, and joyfully.
3. God will provide what generous givers need to keep being generous.
4. Give because of gratitude to God and to cause others to thank God.
5. Give because only money meets some needs of others.

APPLYING THE BIBLE

1. Money matters. The Bible contains 500 verses of Scripture on prayer, less than 500 verses on faith, and more than 2,000 verses on finances and possessions.

2. Quotes on giving:

"Every gift, though it be small, is in reality great if given with affection."

"A gift is never lost; only what is selfishly kept impoverishes."

"Generosity does not come naturally; it must be taught."

3. Motive for giving. You may give without loving, but you cannot love without giving. Paul's appeal to the Corinthians was out of love for the brethren. He was teaching not only the principal of stewardship, but also the principal of fellowship.

4. Prayer for generosity. St. Ignatius of Loyola penned the following prayer in 1548. It continues to be a good model for the church today.

Teach us, good Lord, to serve Thee as Thou deservest:
To give and not to count the cost;
To fight and not to heed the wounds;
To toil and not to seek for rest;
To labor and not ask for any reward
Save that of knowing that we do Thy will.

5. Stewardship story. The following story comes from the Internet. It is entitled "The Rich Family in Our Church," and is attributed to Eddie Ogan.

"I'll never forget Easter 1946. I was fourteen, my little sister Ocy, twelve, and my older sister Darlene, sixteen. We lived at home with our mother, and the four of us knew what it was to do without many things. My dad had died five years before, leaving Mom with seven school kids to raise and no money. By 1946, my older sisters were married, and my brothers had left home.

"A month before Easter, the pastor of our church announced that a special Easter offering would be taken to help a poor family. He asked everyone to save and give sacrificially. When we got home, we talked about what we could do. We decided to buy fifty pounds of potatoes and live on them for a month. This would allow us to save $20 of our grocery money for the offering. Then we thought that if we kept our electric lights turned out as much as possible and didn't listen to the radio, we'd save money on that month's electric bill. Darlene got as many house and yard cleaning jobs as possible, and both of us baby sat for everyone we could. For fifteen cents, we could buy enough cotton loops to make three potholders to sell for $1. We made $20 on potholders.

"That month was one of the best of our lives. Every day we counted the money to see how much we had saved. At night we'd sit in the dark and talk about how the poor family was going to enjoy having the money the church would give them. We had about eighty people in church, so we figured that whatever amount of money we had to give, the offering would surely be twenty times that much. After all, every Sunday the pastor had reminded everyone to save for the sacrificial offering.

"The day before Easter, Ocy and I walked to the grocery store and got the manager to give us three crisp $20 bills and one $10 bill for all our change. We ran all the way home to show Mom and Darlene. We had never had so much money before. That night we were so excited we could hardly sleep. We didn't care that we wouldn't have new clothes for Easter; we had $70 for the sacrificial offering. We could hardly wait to get to church!

"On Sunday morning, rain was pouring. We didn't own an umbrella, and the church was over a mile from our home, but it didn't seem to matter how wet we got. Darlene had cardboard in her shoes to fill the holes. The cardboard came apart, and her feet got wet. But we sat in church proudly. I heard some teenagers talking about the Smith girls having on their old dresses. I looked at them in their new clothes, and I felt so rich.

"When the sacrificial offering was taken, we were sitting on the second row from the front. Mom put in the $10.00 bill, and each of us girls put in a $20 bill. As we walked home after church, we sang all the way. At lunch Mom had a surprise for us. She had bought a dozen eggs, and we had boiled Easter eggs with our fried potatoes! Late that afternoon the minister drove up in his car. Mom went to the door, talked with him for a moment, and then came back with an envelope in her hand. We asked what it was, but she didn't say a word. She opened the envelope and out fell a bunch of money. There were three crisp $20 bills, one $10 bill and seventeen $1 bills. Mom put the money back in the envelope. We didn't talk, just sat and stared at the floor.

"We had gone from feeling like millionaires to feeling like poor white trash. We kids had had such a happy life that we felt sorry for anyone who didn't have our mom and dad for parents and a house full of brothers and sisters and other kids visiting constantly. We thought it was fun to share silverware and see whether we got the fork or the spoon that night. We had two knives which we passed around to whoever needed them. I knew we didn't have a lot of things that other people had, but I'd never thought we were poor. That Easter day I found out we were. The minister had brought us the money for the poor family, so we must be poor.

"I didn't like being poor. I looked at my dress and worn-out shoes and felt so ashamed that I didn't want to go back to church. Everyone there probably already knew we were poor! I thought about school. I was in the ninth grade and at the top of my class of over one hundred students. I wondered if the kids at school knew we were poor. I decided I could quit school since I had finished the eighth grade. That was all the law required at that time.

"We sat in silence for a long time. Then it got dark, and we went to bed. All that week, we girls went to school and came home, and no one talked much. Finally on Saturday, Mom asked us what we wanted to do with the money. What did poor people do with money? We didn't know. We'd never known we were poor. We didn't want to go to church on Sunday, but

Mom said we had to. Although it was a sunny day, we didn't talk on the way.

"Mom started to sing, but no one joined in and she only sang one verse. At church we had a missionary speaker. He talked about how churches in Africa made buildings out of sun-dried bricks, but they needed money to buy roofs. He said $100 would put a roof on a church. The minister said, "Can't we all sacrifice to help these poor people?" We looked at each other and smiled for the first time in a week.

"Mom reached into her purse and pulled out the envelope. She passed it to Darlene. Darlene gave it to me, and I handed it to Ocy. Ocy put it in the offering. When the offering was counted, the minister announced that it was a little over $100. The missionary was excited. He hadn't expected such a large offering from our small church. He said, "You must have some rich people in this church." Suddenly it struck us! We had given $87 of that "little over $100." We were the rich family in the church! Hadn't the missionary said so?

"From that day on I've never been poor again. I've always remembered how rich I am because I have Jesus."

TEACHING THE BIBLE

- *Main Idea:* Paul laid out certain principles of giving.
- *Suggested Teaching Aim:* To lead adults to identify at least one way they will improve their stewardship.

A TEACHING OUTLINE

1. *Finishing What You Start (2 Cor. 9:1–5)*
2. *Principles of Giving (2 Cor. 9:6–15)*

Introduce the Bible Study

Use number 3, "Motive for Giving," in "Applying the Bible" to introduce the lesson.

Search for Biblical Truth

IN ADVANCE:

- Copy the five summary statements under "Outline and Summary" on small pieces of paper. Make enough copies so that every person in the class can have one statement. (If you have more than five members, some will have the same statement.)
- Enlist a scribe to record the translation you will write. Provide paper and pen.

- Enlist two members to read about the offering Paul was taking in Romans 15:25–33 and 1 Corinthians 16:1–4.
- Secure a map of Paul's missionary journeys.
- Be sure every person has a Bible. Different translations may be of help if you have access to them.

Distribute copies of the summary statements to each member. Ask them to read the statement and find verses that support that statement as the lesson progresses. Call on the two persons you enlisted **IN ADVANCE** to read about the offering Paul was taking in Romans 15:25–33 and 1 Corinthians 16:1–4. Locate Macedonia and Achaia on the map and explain Paul's plan to take an offering among the Corinthians. Explain difficult phrases in this passage, and ask members with different translations to read 2 Corinthians 9:1–2. Let the class suggest their own paraphrase of these verses. Ask the scribe to record it.

Ask members to look at verses 3–5. Explain the difficult phrases in this passage, using "Studying the Bible." Ask members to read any different translations they have and suggest their own paraphrase for these verses. Ask the scribe to record it.

Follow the above procedure for each of the other Scripture sections.

When you have finished each of the sections, ask the scribe to read the paraphrase members have written.

Give the Truth a Personal Focus

Ask volunteers from the five different groups to read their summary statement and identify the Scripture verses they have chosen to support their statement. Other members may want to suggest other Scriptures.

Ask all those who have the same summary statement to form a group and take their summary statement and make a principle of the biblical truth in that passage. (These should be similar to the five "Summary of Bible Truths" statements at the end of "Studying the Bible.") Let members read these statements aloud.

Close by sharing number 5, "Stewardship Story," in "Applying the Bible."

May

28

2000

Living in the Faith

Background Passage: 2 Corinthians 13:1–13
Focal Passage: 2 Corinthians 13:1–13

The most difficult part of 2 Corinthians is chapters 10–13. After the joy of reconciliation expressed in earlier chapters, these final chapters contain an emotional defense by Paul and stern warnings to his critics.

Study Aim: *To explain the reason for and the meaning of Paul's stern words.*

STUDYING THE BIBLE

OUTLINE AND SUMMARY

I. Needed Preparations for Paul's Visit (2 Cor. 13:1–10)
  1. Warning from an apostle of Christ (13:1–4)
  2. Challenge to examine themselves (13:5–7)
  3. Desire to build them up (13:8–10)
II. Final Exhortations (2 Cor. 13:11–13)

Paul warned critics that he would come with the power of a judge if necessary (vv. 1–4). He challenged them to examine themselves (vv. 5–7). He prayed that he could go to Corinth to help build them up (vv. 8–10). His final exhortations focused on restoring harmony in the church (vv. 11–13).

I. Needed Preparations for Paul's Visit (2 Cor. 13:1–10)

1. Warning from an apostle of Christ (vv. 1–4)

1 This is the third time I am coming to you. In the mouth of two or three witnesses shall every word be established.

2 I told you before, and foretell you, as if I were present, the second time; and being absent now I write to them which heretofore have sinned, and to all other, that, if I come again, I will not spare.

Paul's first visit to Corinth was when he went there for eighteen months to preach the gospel and to start the church (Acts 18:1–18). His second visit was the painful visit between 1 and 2 Corinthians (2 Cor. 2:1, 2). He was headed to Corinth for a third visit.

The last part of verse 1 refers to requirements for witnesses in a trial. The Law demanded that there be two or three witnesses before an accusation could be verified (Deut. 19:15). Jesus had established the same rule for dealing with situations in the church, when one person has a grievance against another (Matt. 18:16). This implies that Paul was warning that he might have to come as a judge to deal with some of the Corinthians.

When Paul made the painful visit of 2 Corinthians 1:23–2:2, he warned them that he would exercise his authority as an apostle of Christ if he was forced to do so by their refusal to repent. What he had told them in person when he was there "the second time," he now wrote to them when he was "absent." His warning was directed to those "which heretofore have sinned" (sinned prior to his second visit) and "to all other" (those who had joined them in sin since Paul's second visit).

His warning was, "If I come again, I will not spare." Paul was on his way to Corinth. Their actions would determine in what spirit he came. If his critics continued in their sins, Paul would come clothed with the authority of Christ as Judge. If this happened, he would not spare the guilty from being punished for their sin.

All serious students of 2 Corinthians become aware of a change in tone when they compare chapters 10–13 with earlier passages that express the relief and joy Paul felt over being reconciled with the Corinthians (see especially 2:5–17; 7:5–18). When we read a passage like 2 Corinthians 13:1, 2, which is typical of most of chapters 10–13, we wonder, "Who were these sinners and critics about whom Paul wrote?"

Bible scholars divide into two groups in answering this question: One group says that the critics of 2 Corinthians 10–13 were the entire group of highly vocal critics of Paul that caused him to make the painful visit. In fact, this group of scholars has the theory that 2 Corinthians 10–13 is all or part of Paul's harsh letter of 2:3, 4, which somehow became attached to the letter of reconciliation of 2 Corinthians 1–9.

The other group of Bible scholars insists that these final chapters were written as part of one letter. They point to the fact that all ancient copies of 2 Corinthians contain all thirteen chapters. They believe that the final chapters were directed to an unrepentant minority in Corinth.

3 Since ye seek a proof of Christ speaking in me, which to you-ward is not weak, but is mighty in you.

4 For though he was crucified through weakness, yet he liveth by the power of God. For we also are weak in him, but we shall live with him by the power of God toward you.

The critics of Paul in Corinth questioned whether Christ was speaking through Paul. They said that Paul was weak, not strong. Paul quoted them as saying of him, "His letters . . . are weighty and powerful; but his bodily presence is weak, and his speech contemptible" (2 Cor. 10:10).

His critics placed great value on displays of what the world considers power. At the same time, they looked down on anyone who was considered weak by worldly standards. Paul had admitted in 1 Corinthians 2:3 that he first came to them "in weakness." But it was the so-called weakness of a person who came as a servant of others and preached Christ crucified. Paul told them that the cross, which the world considers weak, is "the power of God" (1 Cor. 1:24).

Paul thus linked his experience as a weak, yet powerful person to Christ, the ultimate weak-powerful One. During His earthly ministry and especially in His death, Jesus was weak by worldly standards. Allowing Himself to be crucified was the ultimate weakness; yet God raised Him from the dead and showed the power of God in both the cross and the resurrection (Phil. 2:5–11). Those who know the crucified-risen Lord know from personal experience what it is to be considered a weak servant by worldly standards, but through faith they also know the power of the Lord.

If they forced him to do so, Paul whom they considered so weak would show them what they had demanded to see. They should have seen the proof of the crucified, risen Lord's weakness and power through Paul's Christlike ministry among them. Indeed, they also should have experienced the weakness and power of Christ in their own lives as they allowed Christ into their lives. But if they demanded further proof that Christ was speaking through Paul, the apostle would live with Christ "by the power of God toward you."

2. Challenge to examine themselves (vv. 5–7)

> **5 Examine yourselves, whether ye be in the faith; prove your own selves. Know ye not your own selves, how that Jesus Christ is in you, except ye be reprobates?**
>
> **6 But I trust that ye shall know that we are not reprobates.**
>
> **7 Now I pray to God that ye do no evil; not that we should appear approved, but that ye should do that which is honest, though we be as reprobates.**

Paul's critics had challenged him to show them proof that Christ was speaking through him (v. 3). Paul then challenged them to examine themselves in order to prove that their profession of faith was genuine. The word translated "prove" means to prove that something is genuine by putting it to the test. Thus, if they passed the test, this would show that Jesus Christ truly was in them. If they failed the test, they would be shown to be "reprobates."

Verse 6 shows that Paul was confident that both the Corinthians and the apostle would pass the test. If they proved to be genuine Christians—as Paul expected, what could be better proof that Paul's ministry among them had been genuine?

Paul, however, was not so concerned about his own approval as he was about their not doing evil. His prayer was that they might do good, not evil. Then Paul would not need to prove his power as judge because their repentance would make that unnecessary. This is the meaning of the difficult closing line of verse 7.

Verse 7 is a difficult verse, especially the words "though we be as reprobates." One key is to recognize that the words translated "approved" and "reprobates" come from the same root as "proof" (v. 3) and "prove" (v. 5). "Approved" is an adjective that means "with proof." "Reprobate" is the negative form of the same adjective. Its basic meaning is "without proof"; but the word at times came to mean "unqualified," "worthless," or "base."

The same word is translated "reprobates" in verses 5, 6, and 7. Our English word has a negative meaning, which the word does not have in verse 7. The word means "without proof" in verse 7, but it means "worthless" or "reprobates" in verses 5 and 6. In verse 7, Paul used the word to mean that they would not have proof of his power to come to them as a stern judge because their repentance would make such judgment unnecessary.

3. Desire to build them up (vv. 8–10)

> **8 For we can do nothing against the truth, but for the truth**

9 For we are glad, when we are weak, and ye are strong: and this also we wish, even your perfection.

10 Therefore I write these things being absent, lest being present I should use sharpness, according to the power which the Lord hath given me to edification, and not to destruction.

Paul would do nothing against the truth and everything possible for it. He rejoiced at the prospect of their change of heart, for this would enable him to go to Corinth as a humble servant ("weak") so that the power of the gospel would work in the Corinthians. The word translated "wish" is the same word translated "pray" in verse 7.

The word *perfection* denotes repairing something that was broken or restoring harmony and efficient functioning. The verb form of this noun is found in verse 11. Paul prayed that harmony might be restored to the Corinthian church.

This was the reason for Paul's harsh tone to the unrepentant critics in Corinth. He wanted to avoid having to confront them personally. If he was present, he would have to deal sharply with them. Therefore, he wrote in the hope that they would heed the letter. This would enable him to spend his time among them helping to build them up, rather than having to bring judgment. He was called to build up people in the Lord. If unrepentant sinners forced him to deal with judgment, Paul had the power of Christ to do so; however, he prayed that this kind of negative action might not be necessary.

II. Final Exhortations (2 Cor. 13:11–13)

11 Finally, brethren, farewell. Be perfect, be of good comfort, be of one mind, live in peace; and the God of love and peace shall be with you.

12 Greet one another with an holy kiss.

13 All the saints salute you.

In spite of Paul's problems with the Corinthians, he still called them "brethren." His final words are a series of short exhortations. "Farewell" is the word *rejoice.* "Be perfect" is the verb meaning to repair or restore. If harmony could be restored to the church, they would have come a long way (1 Cor. 1:10–12).

The other three exhortations reinforce this call for them to mend their broken fellowship. "Be of good comfort" means to respond to the help given, whether comfort, encouragement, warning, or challenge. "Be of one mind" and "live in peace" clearly have to do with restoring and practicing harmony in the church.

If they obeyed these exhortations from the God of love and peace, His presence would abide with them (see v. 14 for a beautiful doxology to this God.)

Paul asked them to express their harmony with warm affection. The holy kiss is comparable to our handshakes. You can be sure that Paul would not have advocated anything with sexual overtones to the church to which he had written 1 Corinthians 5–7.

As a reminder that they were part of a larger fellowship of believers, Paul sent greetings from all the saints.

SUMMARY OF BIBLE TRUTHS

1. Tough situations sometimes call for tough love.
2. The way of Christ includes both weakness and power.
3. Christians should examine themselves to ensure that their faith is genuine.
4. Genuine faith passes the test.
5. Christians find joy in humble service rather than in stern rebukes.
6. Christians should live in peace and oneness of spirit.

Evidences of an Unrepentant Minority in Corinth

1. In the account of the action of the church against the ringleader of Paul's critics (2:5–11), Paul used the word *many.* This implies that the majority acted to discipline the man; but this leaves open the possibility that a minority opposed such discipline, possibly because they were still critical of Paul.
2. Scattered throughout the earlier chapters of 2 Corinthians are indications that Paul was still defending himself. Near the beginning of the letter, for example, he defended himself against the charge that he was fickle because he changed his travel plans (1:12–22).
3. The heart of the letter is a description of Paul's ministry through which are scattered hints that he was still having to defend the integrity of his ministry as an apostle (see 3:1, 2; 4:2, 5; 5:9–15; 6:1–10).
4. Paul made a strongly worded appeal for the Corinthians to open their hearts to him (6:11–7:2).

Therefore, this seems to be what happened. Titus reported that Paul had been vindicated by the majority ("many"), but Titus also reported that a number of unrepentant critics of Paul were continuing their verbal attacks. Paul wrote words of joy and reconciliation in light of the action of the majority (2:5–17; 7:5–18); however, he continued to defend himself against the critics and ended by directly addressing himself to these critics (10–13).

APPLYING THE BIBLE

1. A strategy for victims of criticism. "If men speak ill of you, live so that no one will believe them." This was Paul's strategy, and it should be ours.

2. **Examination.** Watch your thoughts; they become words. Watch your words; they become actions. Watch your actions; they become habits. Watch your habits, they become character. Watch your character; it becomes your destiny.[1]

3. Courageous words. Manuel de Dios Unanue, an emigre from Cuba, was a journalist in New York City. He knew the risks when he published the names and photographs of drug dealers terrorizing Hispanic communities. Executed by a drug-dealing member of the gang he exposed, he will be remembered as a man of courage. After his death, colleague Rossana Rosado wrote, "Fear of death never stopped him from writing the truth."[2]

Paul's second letter to the Corinthian church bears a striking similarity. Paul could have found a way to live with the critical-spirited antagonists in the congregation, but he exposed them for who and what they were. His letter may appear stern, his comments even harsh, but in reality, his words are courageous. The ministry of the church to a lost and dying world is too valuable to be deeded over to trouble-making individuals. They are to be exposed, called into accountability, disciplined, and allowed to participate in the fellowship only when biblical repentance is demonstrated and reconciliation has begun.

4. Courage. "Every time we lose courage, we lose several days of our life" (Maurice Maeterlinck).

5. Courage and majority. Andrew Jackson said, "One man with courage makes a majority." Paul faced his critics with the same conviction. What he was fighting for was a kingdom issue. With courage, he wrote to correct and admonish. We do no less when we take our stand on kingdom issues. We are a majority when we speak the truth courageously, for Christ is on our side.

6. Experience or surrender? In a collection of "letters to God" twelve-year-old Jamie wrote:

> Dear God,
>
> Why are grandparents so much nicer than parents? Is it their experience? Or is it that they just give up being mean?

Experience is a great teacher. Paul's antagonists cause us to wonder if they had ever had the experience of God's grace, for they certainly did not demonstrate grace in their lives. There is the possibility that they had once known grace, but due to making wrong choices now saw themselves in a position of psuedo-spiritual elitism. Paul's words challenged them to either get real or get over it. At any rate, they were useless to the kingdom in their present condition. All church antagonists fit this category and should examine their experience with grace to see if it is genuine or not.

7. Proof. "No sadder proof can be given by a man of his own littleness than disbelief in great men" (Thomas Carlyle).

TEACHING THE BIBLE

- *Main Idea:* Living in the faith means at times that we must confront people who are opposing Christ.
- *Suggested Teaching Aim:* To lead adults to list ways they can confront people with a Christlike spirit.

A TEACHING OUTLINE

1. *Needed Preparations for Paul's Visit (2 Cor. 13:1–10)*
2. *Final Exhortations (2 Cor. 13:11–13)*

Introduce the Bible Study

Use number 5, " Courage and Majority," in "Applying the Bible" to introduce the lesson.

Search for Biblical Truth

IN ADVANCE:

- Enlist a member to read the Scripture passages.
- Enlist a member to read the four summary statements in "Outline and Summary."
- Enlist a member to present the material in "Evidences of an Unrepentant Minority in Corinth" on page 304 at the end of this lesson.

Ask the enlisted member to read aloud the first summary statement, followed by the member reading 2 Corinthians 13:1–4. Point out that Paul was planning a third visit to Corinth. Explain the last part of verse 1 as a reference to the judicial requirement. Paul was saying that he might have to come as a judge to deal with some of the problems, and those who had made accusations had better have enough witnesses to support their charges.

Ask, Who were these people that Paul "will not spare" when he comes? One possibility is that they were an unrepentant minority in Corinth. Call on the member enlisted to present the material on "Evidences of an Unrepentant Minority in Corinth." Ask, According to verses 3–4, what "proof" did the Corinthians seek about Paul's ministry? (Did Christ speak through him?) Why did they question this? (Paul came to them in weakness—the weakness of a servant modeled after Jesus.)

On a chalkboard write the following:

Now	Then
Ultimate weakness	Ultimate power
Ultimate power	Ultimate weakness

DISCUSS: How can we keep from falling into the trap of trying to use ultimate power to prove our ultimate weakness?

Ask the enlisted member to read aloud the first summary statement, followed by the member reading 2 Corinthians 13:5–7. Use the material in "Studying the Bible" to define the two ways "reprobate" is used in these verses. Ask: What did Paul expect the Corinthians to find when they examined their profession of faith? (Their faith was genuine.) If the Corinthians' faith was genuine, what did that prove about Paul's ministry that had led them to that faith?

DISCUSS: What do we need to look at to examine our faith?

Ask the enlisted member to read aloud the first summary statement followed by the member reading 2 Corinthians 13:8–9. Explain the meaning of "perfection" (v. 9) and ask, Why did Paul want them to repent? (He could spend his time building them up, not correcting them.)

DISCUSS: Is there a relationship you need to repair?

Ask the enlisted member to read aloud the first summary statement, followed by the member reading 2 Corinthians 13:11–13. Ask, What clue do we get about how Paul felt about the Corinthians? (Brethren.) Ask: What four things did Paul want the Corinthians to do? What did he say God would do?

DISCUSS: How can we be of one mind when we have honest differences with other Christians?

Give the Truth a Personal Focus

Ask members to bow their heads as you summarize the lesson by reading the six "Summary of Bible Truths" statements. Close in prayer.

---

1. Frank Outlaw, *Bits and Pieces*, vol. R., no. 29 (Fairfield, N.J.: The Economic Press, Inc.), 7.
2. "Our Times," *Life,* May 1992, 23.

New Life in Christ

June

July

August

2000

INTRODUCTION

This quarter's study is based on Paul's Prison Letters: Philippians, Ephesians, Colossians, and Philemon.

Unit I, "Living in Christ," is a four-lesson study of Philippians. The titles are "Living Is Christ," "Having the Mind of Christ," "Pressing On in Christ," and "Rejoicing in Christ."

Unit II, "Called to Be a New Humanity," is a five-lesson study of Ephesians. The five lessons focus on the following things to which Christians are called: spiritual blessings, oneness in Christ, use of spiritual gifts, responsible living, and standing firm.

Unit III, "Christ Above All," has three lessons based on Colossians and one lesson drawn from Philemon. The lessons from Colossians focus on Christ's supremacy, the completeness of life in Christ, and the new, righteous life in Him. Philemon focuses on welcoming fellow Christians.

Cycle of 1998–2004

1998–1999	1999–2000	2000–2001	2001–2002	2002–2003	2003–2004
Old Testament Survey	Exodus Leviticus Numbers Deuteronomy Joshua	Judges 1, 2 Samuel 1 Chronicles 1 Kings 1–11 2 Chronicles 1–9	Parables Miracles Sermon on the Mount	2 Kings 18–25 2 Chronicles 29–36 Jeremiah Lamentations Ezekiel Habakkuk Zephaniah	James 1, 2 Peter 1, 2, 3 John Jude
New Testament Survey	Matthew	Luke	Isaiah 9; 11; 40–66 Ruth Jonah Nahum	Personalities of the NT	Christmas Esther Job Ecclesiastes Song of Solomon
John	1, 2 Corinthians	Acts	Romans Galatians	Mark	The Cross 1, 2 Thessalonians Revelation
Genesis	Ephesians Philippians Colossians Philemon	1 Kings 12–2 Kings 17 2 Chronicles 10–28 Isaiah 1–39 Amos Hosea Micah	Psalms Proverbs	Ezra Nehemiah Daniel Joel Obadiah Haggai Zechariah Malachi	Hebrews 1, 2 Timothy Titus

OUTLINE OF PHILIPPIANS

I. Introduction (Phil. 1:1–11)
 1. Greetings (1:1, 2)
 2. Thanksgiving and intercession (1:3–11)
II. Outcomes of Paul's Imprisonment (Phil. 1:12–26)
 1. Good results from his confinement (1:12–18)
 2. Paul's readiness for living or dying (1:19–26)
III. Christian Togetherness (Phil. 1:27–2:30)
 1. Call to stand together against foes (1:27–30)
 2. Call to oneness based on self-giving love (2:1–11)
 3. Call to obedience (2:12–16)
 4. Examples of self-sacrifice (2:17–30)
IV. Salvation: Past, Present, and Future (Phil. 3:1–21)
 1. Self-righteousness versus righteousness in Christ (3:1–11)
 2. Pressing on toward perfection (3:12–21)
V. Christian Joy and Peace (Phil. 4:1–9)
VI. Gratitude and Contentment (Phil. 4:10–20)
VII. Final Greetings (Phil. 4:21–23)

Living Is Christ

Background Passage: Philippians 1:12–30

Focal Passage: Philippians 1:12–26

Many people have no center for their lives. Their lives are disjointed, and their energies are scattered. Others have a focal point for their living. For some, this is not an adequate objective for a constructive life. Paul had a focal point, and it was the right one.

Study Aim: *To testify what it means to make Christ central in one's life.*

STUDYING THE BIBLE

OUTLINE AND SUMMARY

I. Magnifying Christ at All Times (Phil. 1:12–20)

1. Good results out of a bad situation (1:12–14)

2. Mixed motives for preaching (1:15–18)

3. Paul's driving ambition (1:19, 20)

II. Ready to Die and Ready to Live (Phil. 1:21–26)

1. Ready to die (1:21–24)

2. Ready to live (1:25, 26)

III. Standing Together for Christ (Phil. 1:27–30)

Paul's imprisonment had resulted in many unbelievers hearing the gospel and in many believers becoming bolder witnesses (vv. 12–14). Paul was glad for all who were preaching the gospel, even if the motives of some were unworthy (vv. 15–18). Paul was confident that the prayers of Christians and the help of the Spirit would enable him to magnify Christ, whether in life or death (vv. 19, 20). Paul would welcome death, when he would depart to be with Christ (vv. 21–24). He expected to continue to live for a while longer and to bear fruit for the Lord (vv. 25, 26). Paul appealed for the Philippians to stand together for Christ (vv. 27–30).

I. Magnifying Christ at All Times (Phil. 1:12–20)

1. Good results out of a bad situation (vv. 12–14)

12 But I would ye should understand, brethren, that the things which happened unto me have fallen out rather unto the furtherance of the gospel;

After a warm opening greeting from Paul to one of his favorite churches (1:1–11), Paul quickly assured them that God had brought some good results out of his confinement. The word *rather* means that God had used his confinement for "the furtherance of the gospel" rather than allowing it to become a hindrance.

13 So that my bonds in Christ are manifest in all the palace, and in all other places;

14 And many of the brethren in the Lord, waxing confident by my bonds, are much more bold to speak the word without fear.

Paul listed two good results of his confinement. Paul had sought God's will for what to do in this difficult situation. He found that he had unique opportunities of Christian witnessing to a group of Roman soldiers. The word translated "palace" can refer to a place like the palace of the emperor or a governor or to the barracks of the praetorian guard, or the word can refer to the guards themselves. Many Bible students think the word referred to the soldiers; however, even if it referred to a place, Paul's testimony was to those who lived or worked in that place.

The praetorian guard were ten thousand elite soldiers hired to protect the emperor and to serve his purposes. One of their duties apparently was to guard prisoners who were to appear before the emperor. During Paul's two years of confinement, he had contact with many of these rough soldiers. During that time, they became aware of Paul's "bonds in Christ." This probably means that they learned that Paul was facing trial because of his loyalty to Jesus Christ. Paul was not claiming to have won all or even many of the guards to Christ, but he was saying that many of them heard his testimony for Christ. Since Philippians 4:22 mentions "saints in Caesar's household," we know that some of Caesar's staff, which included more than his guards, had become Christians.

The second good result of Paul's confinement was that his boldness as a witness emboldened many other Roman believers to tell of Jesus Christ without fear.

2. Mixed motives for preaching (vv. 15–18)

15 Some indeed preach Christ even of envy and strife; and some also of good will:

16 The one preach Christ of contention, not sincerely, supposing to add affliction to my bonds:

17 But the other of love, knowing that I am set for the defence of the gospel.

18 What then? notwithstanding, every way, whether in pretence, or in truth, Christ is preached; and I therein do rejoice, yea, and will rejoice.

Among those who had been emboldened to preach were two groups. One group is described by such words as "envy," "strife," "not sincerely," "contention," and "pretence." The other group is described by the words "good will" and "love."

Two questions confront us about the former group:

1. *Who were they?* Some Bible students have thought these were false teachers, probably Judaizers, who gave Paul such problems in the Galatian churches. However, Paul had nothing good to say about those who preached a false message. See, for example, Philippians 3:1, 2 and Galatians 1:6–9. Yet Paul did not condemn the message preached by those in Philippians 1:15, 16, 18. He assumed that they were preaching the true gospel. He was glad for the message they preached, but he criticized their motives for preaching. They preached out of envy for Paul. The words

“not sincerely” means “not pure.” Their motives were not pure. Paul was grateful for anyone who preached the gospel—whatever his motives.

2. *How did these preachers hope that their success would add to Paul’s afflictions?* Perhaps they hoped that the increase in converts to Christianity would get the emperor upset with Christians, and he would take it out on Paul. More likely, they hoped that Paul would be jealous of their success in preaching. In other words, they expected Paul to have the same selfish, petty attitudes toward them that they had toward Paul. They were wrong. Paul rejoiced whenever the gospel was preached, even if the preachers had selfish motives.

3. Paul’s driving ambition (vv. 19, 20)

19 For I know that this shall turn to my salvation through your prayer, and the supply of the Spirit of Jesus Christ,

20 According to my earnest expectation and my hope, that in nothing I shall be ashamed, but that with all boldness, as always, so now also Christ shall be magnified in my body, whether it be by life, or by death.

“Salvation” may be used here in the sense of the final stage of God’s saving process from sin and death, in the sense of “salvation” or deliverance from prison, or in the sense of “salvation” or deliverance from failing to bear bold witness for Jesus Christ. Each of these three interpretations has Bible students who support it. I think the context best supports the third view.

Would Paul have spoken of their prayers as contributing to his final salvation? This seems unlikely. Paul elsewhere spoke with confidence of his final salvation. Was being set free from prison his main concern? He did not say that it was. Instead, he wrote of his deep yearning and hope that he might not be ashamed, but instead that he might with boldness magnify Christ—no matter what the outcome of his trial. If he was sentenced to die, Paul wanted to be a bold witness for Christ: one whose attitudes, actions, and words would magnify Christ.

This was something to which he was committed and for which he prayed (Rom. 1:16). This is something that he often asked Christians to pray for in the letters he wrote during his imprisonment (Eph. 6:18, 19; Col. 4:3). Paul was not superhuman; he was just a man. As a man, he was tempted as all of us are to keep quiet when speaking out might bring ridicule or worse. Paul, therefore, knew that only in the power of God’s Spirit could he remain a bold witness. And he believed that the prayers of God’s people could be used to strengthen him as a Spirit-filled witness—even in the worst situations.

Paul’s one fear seems to have been that life might get so overwhelming that he in some way would fail to magnify Christ. His prayer was that God would empower him as a bold and faithful representative for Jesus Christ—no matter what happened to him.

II. Ready to Die and Ready to Live (Phil. 1:21–26)

1. Ready to die (vv. 21–24)

21 For to me to live is Christ, and to die is gain.

June

4

2000

22 But if I live in the flesh, this is the fruit of my labour: yet what I shall choose I wot not.

23 For I am in a strait betwixt two, having a desire to depart, and to be with Christ; which is far better:

24 Nevertheless to abide in the flesh is more needful for you.

Because Paul's life was centered in Jesus Christ, Christ gave meaning to his life; and Christ gave him assurance in the face of death. Life and death were both under Christ's lordship. Thus, life was joyful and meaningful; and death meant going to be with Christ. If the choice between life or death was left up to Paul (which it was not), he would not know which to choose. Both were desirable to him. Life and death are win-win situations for Christians.

Paul was thinking about his coming trial before Nero. If he was condemned of some capital crime, he would be put to death. Yet death held no terrors for Paul. When he died, Paul expected to depart and be with Christ. "Depart" translates a word used to describe a ship weighing anchor and sailing away. Paul would depart from his mooring in this life. People would say, "Paul is dead and gone." Yet in paradise, Paul would be very much alive because he would be with the Lord who has the keys to death and the grave.

Many people do not know Christ. Their lives lack meaning and are filled with fear and guilt. They are unhappy with living and afraid of dying. By contrast, Christians are ready to die; and the One who makes us ready to die also makes us ready to live. We can leave the issue of when we die in the Lord's capable hands. Either way, Christ is with us.

2. Ready to live (vv. 25, 26)

25 And having this confidence, I know that I shall abide and continue with you all for your furtherance and joy of faith;

26 That your rejoicing may be more abundant in Jesus Christ for me by my coming to you again.

Although the outcome of Paul's trial was still in doubt, Paul sounded fairly confident of his release in verses 25, 26. Contrast the tone of these verses with the tone of Paul's final letter (2 Tim. 4:6–8). At the end of Paul's second imprisonment, Nero's persecution was killing Christians in Rome. Paul knew that he soon would be executed as he wrote 2 Timothy. However, although Nero was emperor during Paul's first imprisonment, the persecution had not yet started. Paul knew that if he got a fair hearing, Nero would see that Paul was not guilty of any crime against Rome.

Paul hoped soon to be released, and he hoped to visit Philippi after his release. Paul was ready, even eager to go and be with the Lord; however, he felt the Lord was going to give him more time for fruitful service before he died. Paul was ready for either.

Would this not be an appropriate prayer based on what Paul wrote: "Lord, we are grateful that your Spirit enables us to bear fruit for you, that you will be with us when we pass through life's dark valleys, and that you will carry us to be with you when we die. Help us to use whatever life and health you give us to magnify Christ."

III. Standing Together for Christ (Phil. 1:27–30)

Paul challenged the Philippians to live in a way worthy of citizens of God's kingdom. Regardless of what happened to Paul, he appealed for them to stand together with courage for the truth of the gospel (vv. 27, 28). He wanted them to believe in Christ and be willing to suffer for Him if necessary (vv. 29, 30).

PRONUNCIATION GUIDE

Judaizers	[JOO duh igh zurs]
Praetorian	[prih TAWR ih uhn]

SUMMARY OF BIBLE TRUTHS

1. Christians can witness for Christ in difficult situations.
2. The example of one courageous witness emboldens others.
3. Some people have unworthy motives for preaching Christ.
4. Christians should pray that God's Spirit will enable us to magnify Christ at all times.
5. Christians are ready to die because at death we will go to be with the Lord.
6. While we are alive, Christ makes our lives fruitful.

APPLYING THE BIBLE

1. When Jesus is the center. Fanny Crosby wrote many of the hymns still sung in churches today. Blinded at the age of only six weeks, she might well be the poster child for today's lesson, especially when considering the centrality of Christ. Observe the words found in one of her hymns:

All the way my Savior leads me, What have I to ask beside?
Can I doubt his tender mercy who through life has been my guide?
Heavenly peace, divinest comfort, here by faith with him to dwell,
For I know whatever befall me, Jesus doeth all things well.

When facing life-or-death situations, remember what Miss Crosby discovered in Scripture: "Jesus doeth all things well."

2. It's always too soon to quit. Hubert Humphrey said, "Some people look upon any setback as the end. They're always looking for the benediction rather than the invocation. . . . But you can't quit. That isn't the way our country was built."

That's not the way our faith was built, either. Christians endure difficult times today as they have from the beginning. It's always too soon to quit.

3. Setbacks. Ask members of the class to offer possible "setbacks" that might have threatened their effectiveness as a witness. Ask them to tell how God turned what might have been a setback into a time of victory.

4. No fear. Paul's greatest fear seemed to be that life would overwhelm him to the point of his not being able to magnify Christ. Ask class members to formulate a list of their top ten fears. Disease, fear for the future of children, fear of death, financial fears, and other similar concerns will probably be noted. We rarely consider the spiritual consequences of dishonoring the Lord.

5. When good comes out of bad. At 39 years of age, Franklin Delano Roosevelt contracted the polio virus while vacationing with his family. Twelve years later and struggling with paralysis, Franklin D. Roosevelt became president of this country. Following his first year in office, an impassioned plea went out to gather resources that would be used for the study of this disease in the hopes of finding a cure.

Roosevelt's former law partner, Basil O'Connor, founded the National Foundation for Infantile Paralysis and became its first director. He started the "March of Dimes" fundraising campaign and led it so successfully that, ten years later, after polio came under control in the United States, there were still millions of dollars left in reserve.

A greater work, however, took place during this time in the life of President Roosevelt. Mrs. Roosevelt herself was perhaps the first to notice it. She wrote: "He had to think out the fundamentals of living and learn the greatest of all lessons—infinite patience and never-ending persistence." During painful years of trial, the handsome, debonair, somewhat frivolous and spoilt young man developed "a new seriousness about himself, and a deeper empathy for other people."

In the midst of Paul's many setbacks, God was also teaching him something. Lessons like this continue for each of us. What has God allowed you to learn in the midst of the difficult times you've faced?

6. When God says "no." There are times when God answers our prayers with a negative response. Paul probably asked God to deliver him from prison so he could continue preaching. But after discerning God's plan, he accepted the negative answer, knowing that God's plan included the spread of the gospel from within the confines of the prison. Paul was in the place God wanted him.

Sometimes God says "no" to our prayers. During times like that we need to try to see things from His perspective. The following monologue by an unknown author illustrates this well.

And God Said, "No"

I asked God to take away my pride and God said, "No." He said it was not for Him to take away but for me to give up.

I asked God to make my handicapped child whole, and God said, "No." He said, "His spirit is whole, his body is only temporary."

I asked God to grant me patience, and God said, "No." He said that patience is a by-product of tribulation. It isn't granted; it's earned.

I asked God to give me happiness, and God said, "No." He said that He gives blessings; happiness is up to me.

I asked God to spare me pain, and God said, "No." He said, "Suffering draws you apart from worldly cares and brings you closer to Me."

I asked God to make my spirit grow, and God said, "No." He said that I must grow on my own, but He will prune me to make me fruitful.

I asked God if He loved me, and God said, "Yes." He gave His only Son who died for me, and I will be in heaven some day because I believe.

I asked God to help me love others as much as He loves me, and God said, "Ah, finally you have the idea."

TEACHING THE BIBLE

- *Main Idea:* When we trust Christ, we are not afraid of the future.
- *Suggested Teaching Aim:* To lead adults to make Christ central in their lives so they will not be afraid of the future.

A TEACHING OUTLINE

1. *Magnifying Christ at All Times (Phil. 1:12–20)*
2. *Ready to Die and Ready to Live (Phil. 1:21–26)*
3. *Standing Together for Christ (Phil. 1:27–30)*

Introduce the Bible Study

Use number 1, "When Jesus Is the Center," in "Applying the Bible" to introduce the lesson.

Search for Biblical Truth

IN ADVANCE:

- Enlist a member to prepare a two- to three-minute report on the "Praetorian Guard."
- Secure a map of Paul's missionary journeys.
- Make a poster of the suggested teaching aim and display it on the focal wall.
- Copy the "Summary of Bible Truths" statements 1–3 on a small sheet of paper and 4–6 on another sheet.

Read the suggested teaching aim from the poster on the wall. Ask members to open their Bibles to Philippians 1. On the map of Paul's missionary journeys, locate Rome (Paul's place of writing) and Philippi (the recipients of the letter). Ask, What happened in Philippi the first time Paul visited there? (See Acts 16.) Ask members to look at verse 12 and put it in their words. (Possible paraphrase: What has happened to me has been good because the gospel has been preached.) Call on the person enlisted to present the report on the Praetorian Guard. Ask half the class (Group 1) to look at verse 13 and the other half (Group 2) to look at verse 14 and list ways that Paul's imprisonment had been good for the cause of Christ. (The teaching plan will call for you to use these two groups throughout the lesson.) Allow two to three minutes for study and then call for reports.

Ask members to look at verses 15–18. On a chalkboard or a large sheet of paper, write the following (omit italicized answers):

Preaching Christ for . . .

Negative Reasons	Positive Reasons
Envy	Good will
Strife	Love
Not sincerely	
Contention	
Pretense	

Ask Group 1 to list the negative reasons Paul said the gospel was being preached; ask Group 2 to list the positive reasons. Using the material in "Studying the Bible," suggest the two possible explanations of who these people were who were preaching the gospel. Ask both Group 1 and Group 2 to spend three minutes answering this question: How did these preachers hope that their success would add to Paul's afflictions? Call for reports.

Ask members to look at verses 19 and 20. Write on the chalkboard the three explanations in "Studying the Bible" of what Paul meant by the phrase, "shall turn to my salvation" (v. 19). Ask Group 1 and Group 2 to spend three minutes discussing why each reason could not be what Paul meant and why it could. Read: "Paul's one fear seems to have been that life might get so overwhelming that he in some way would fail to magnify Christ." Ask, Why do you think this was a legitimate fear for Paul?

Explain that Paul was thinking about his coming trial before Nero as he wrote these next verses. Ask Group 1 to look at verses 21–26 and list indications and reasons Paul said that he was willing to die. Ask Group 2 to look at verses 21–26 and list indications and reasons Paul said that he was willing to live.

Give the Truth a Personal Focus

Assign Group 1 the first three statements (1–3) in "Summary of Bible Truths" and Group 2 the second three (4–6). Ask the groups to read their statements and cite one example of how each truth can be acted on today. Allow six minutes for study and call for reports. Close by singing or reading the first stanza of "All the Way My Savior Leads Me."

Having the Mind of Christ

June

11

2000

Background Passage: Philippians 2:1–18
Focal Passage: Philippians 2:1–13

Paul was concerned about early signs of dissension in the Philippian church. He, therefore, appealed for oneness of spirit, which is made possible by humble self-giving. He called this an appeal to have the mind of Christ.

Study Aim: *To describe the need for and the way to have the mind of Christ.*

STUDYING THE BIBLE

OUTLINE AND SUMMARY

- I. **Appeal for Unity and Humility (Phil. 2:1–4)**
  1. **Oneness of spirit (2:1, 2)**
  2. **Humble self-giving (2:3, 4)**
- II. **Sharing the Mind of Christ (Phil. 2:5–11)**
  1. **The mind of Christ (2:5)**
  2. **Christ's humble self-giving (2:6–8)**
  3. **God's exaltation of Christ (2:9–11)**
- III. **Related Experiences (Phil. 2:12–18)**
  1. **A salvation that works (2:12, 13)**
  2. **A shining life (2:14–16)**
  3. **A living sacrifice (2:17, 18)**

Paul appealed for the Philippians to fill up his joy by having oneness of spirit (vv. 1, 2). He called for humble self-giving as an antidote for selfish pride (vv. 3, 4). He challenged them to have the mind of Christ (v. 5); then described how Christ's humble self-giving (vv. 6–8) was followed by God's exaltation of Christ (vv. 9–11). He exhorted them to work out their own salvation as God worked within them (vv. 12, 13). He challenged them to be lights in the darkness (vv. 14–16). Paul testified of his willingness to pour out his life for Christ's sake (vv. 17, 18).

I. Appeal for Unity and Humility (Phil. 2:1–4)

1. Oneness of spirit (vv. 1, 2)

1 If there be therefore any consolation in Christ, if any comfort of love, if any fellowship of the Spirit, if any bowels and mercies,

2 Fulfil ye my joy, that ye be likeminded, having the same love, being of one accord, of one mind.

"Therefore" shows that this continues Paul's appeal for unity from 1:27. The verb in verses 1, 2 is "fulfill," which means "fill up." Paul appealed to the Philippians to make his joy full by being one in mind and spirit. Because of Paul's frequent use of "joy" and "rejoice" in Philippians, it is often called "the joy letter."

Paul had seen in Corinth what disruptive dissension could do to a church. He was concerned when he heard about some early signs of dissension in Philippi (2:3, 14; 4:2, 3). Paul, therefore, wanted to forestall these things. He already had joy in the Philippians. Now he asked them to make his joy full by being one in spirit.

Paul based his appeal on a fourfold description of the Christian life. Paul appealed to these four aspects of Christian experience, each introduced by "if" in verse 1:

1. *The encouragement or challenge of being in Christ.* "Comfort" can mean "encouragement" or "exhortation." "In Christ" means not only that Christ is in each believer but also that all believers are joined together in Christ.

2. *The persuasive power of love.* "Comfort" translates a word meaning "persuasion."

3. *Shared life in the Spirit.* "Fellowship" translates the important New Testament word *koinonia.* That includes not only fellowship but far more.

4. *Hearts of mercy.* "Bowels" were once considered the place of feelings. We would say "hearts."

The unity for which Paul appealed is also described in four ways in the last part of verse 2. The use of words such as "like," "same," and "one" must not be understood as a call for sameness and uniformity in everything. Paul elsewhere (Rom. 12:6–8; 1 Cor. 12) emphasized that unity and diversity both enrich the church.

2. Humble self-giving (vv. 3, 4)

> **3 Let nothing be done through strife or vainglory; but in lowliness of mind let each esteem other better than themselves.**
>
> **4 Look not every man on his own things, but every man also on the things of others.**

Paul had seen in Corinth what "strife or vainglory" could do. "Strife" can mean either the selfish ambition that leads to strife or to the strife itself. "Vainglory" is a compound word meaning the empty glory of egotistical pride.

The antidote to these worldly sins is Christian humility. The Greeks considered humility a sign of weakness and inferiority. Jesus Christ made it the way of life for Himself and His followers. Paul described "lowliness of mind" in two ways, each of which runs in the opposite direction from the secular way of looking at life.

Paul overstated each of these in order to make a point. In verse 3b, 4, Paul was not denying the need for each person to recognize his or her value in God's eyes; however, he knew that most people tend to place too much emphasis on themselves and not enough on others. Paul, therefore, called for Christians to focus on the value and things of others.

II. Sharing the Mind of Christ (Phil. 2:5–11)

1. The mind of Christ (v. 5)

5 Let this mind be in you, which was also in Christ Jesus.

The word *was* is not in the Greek text. Therefore, the verse can be translated two ways. The King James Version emphasizes Jesus Christ as the ultimate example of humble self-giving, whom Christians are called to imitate. However, it can be translated, "Let this mind be in you, which you have in Christ Jesus." The two translations are not contradictory, but complementary. Christians are to follow Christ's example, but this is possible only as we abide in Him. The fact that we live in Christ and He lives in us motivates and empowers us to be like Christ.

2. Christ's humble self-giving (vv. 6–8)

6 Who, being in the form of God, thought it not robbery to be equal with God:

7 But made himself of no reputation, and took upon him the form of a servant, and was made in the likeness of men:

8 And being found in fashion as a man, he humbled himself, and became obedient unto death, even the death of the cross.

Paul described three stages in Christ's humble self-giving:

1. *Laying aside His preexistent glory.* He was "in the form of God" and "equal with God" (see John 1:1, 2). Yet he did not consider this something to hold on to. The word translated "robbery" can refer either to grasping something one doesn't have or holding on to something one does have. In Christ's case, He already had His preexistent glory; however, He voluntarily gave that up. "Made himself of no reputation" means "emptied himself."

2. *Choosing the servant role in His incarnate life.* "The form of a servant" refers here to His descent from glory to life as a human being. "Likeness of men" and "fashion as a man" might seem to call into question the reality of the incarnation; however, Paul's intent was to emphasize both the full deity and full humanity of Jesus.

3. *Dying the humiliating death of crucifixion.* "Humbled" in verse 8 is the verb form of the first part of "lowliness of mind" in verse 3. The ultimate lowliness to which any one could sink was to die the humiliating death of crucifixion. It was designed to torture and humiliate criminals condemned of capital crimes. For the Lord of glory to give Himself to such a death on our behalf and in obedience to the Father was the ultimate in humble self-giving.

3. God's exaltation of Christ (vv. 9–11)

9 Wherefore God also hath highly exalted him, and given him a name which is above every name:

10 That at the name of Jesus every knee should bow, of things in heaven, and things in earth, and things under the earth;

11 And that every tongue should confess that Jesus Christ is Lord, to the glory of God the Father.

Many Bible scholars believe that verses 6–11 were part of an early Christian hymn. We cannot know if these verses were part of a hymn, but they surely have a poetic, lyrical quality.

Christ is the subject in verses 6–8; God the Father is the subject of verses 9–11. God is the one who "highly exalted" His Son following the humiliating death on the cross. Although Paul did not mention the resurrection and ascension, he apparently had these events in mind. The world had condemned and crucified Jesus. God reversed the world's judgment of His Son and exalted Him.

These verses look back to the resurrection and ascension, remind us that Christ is at God's right hand even now, and point to the future when His sovereignty will be revealed to all. Believers already worship Him as Lord and Savior. We do so by faith. The world ignores or rejects Him. But the time will come when everyone will see His lordship. Every knee will bow and every tongue will confess that Jesus is Lord. This doesn't mean that some day everyone will be saved; it does mean that someday all will bow and confess. However, only those who have confessed Him as Lord by faith will enter the eternal kingdom.

III. Related Experiences (Phil. 2:12–18)

1. A salvation that works (vv. 12, 13)

12 Wherefore, my beloved, as ye have always obeyed, not as in my presence only, but now much more in my absence, work out your own salvation with fear and trembling.

13 For it is God which worketh in you both to will and to do of his good pleasure.

At first, verse 12 seems to introduce a new topic. Paul did move into a new area, but it is related to verse 11. Notice that "obedient" in verse 8 corresponds to "obeyed" in verse 12. As Christ obeyed, so are Christians to obey. Paul was not there to see personally that they did, but he was confident that they would act no differently in either case.

What did Paul mean by "work out your own salvation"?

1. *He obviously did not mean that people can save themselves by their own good works.* Paul consistently preached that no one can be saved by keeping the law or by doing its works; instead, we are sinners who can be saved only by God's grace through faith in Christ. He emphasized that doctrine in Philippians 3:2–11 as he did in most of his letters.

2. *He did mean that real salvation leads to a life of good works.* Paul was emphasizing here that if someone is truly saved, that person's life will be changed. We are saved by God's grace, but we are responsible for allowing God to work His will in us. Good works are not the *root* of salvation, but they are the *fruit* of salvation.

3. *Paul was referring here to the broader meaning of salvation.* He used "saved" of our past salvation from the penalty of sin, our present salvation from the power of sin, and our future salvation from the presence of sin. He was referring here to the present salvation from sin's power.

4. *God is at work in us to accomplish His will.* Verse 12 should never be read without verse 13; just as Ephesians 2:8, 9 should not be detached

from verse 10. We have a responsibility to work out our own salvation, but we do not do this in our own strength. God is at work in us "to will and to do of his good pleasure." He is working out His will by motivating us to want to do His will and to have the power to do so.

2. A shining life (vv. 14–16)

The warning against murmurings and disputings is related to Paul's appeal for oneness of spirit (v. 14). Although the world is crooked and broken, believers should live lives that are above reproach; and thus shine as lights in a dark world (v. 15). Paul challenged the Philippians to hold fast and hold forth (the word can mean either) the word of life in a dying world (v. 16).

3. A living sacrifice (vv. 17, 18)

Using the language of sacrifice, Paul was ready to be poured out (v. 17). Such humble and total self-giving brought joy to Paul and to others who followed his example as he sought to have the mind of Christ (v. 18).

SUMMARY OF BIBLE TRUTHS

1. Oneness of spirit among believers enhances joy.
2. Humble self-giving is the antidote for selfish strife.
3. Christians are in Christ and are to be like Christ.
4. Christ is the ultimate example of humble self-giving.
5. Christ is Lord.
6. God works in saved people to enable them to do good works.

APPLYING THE LESSON

1. Sacrifice: investing yourself for what matters most. Armistice Day, the eleventh day of the eleventh month at eleven o'clock in the morning, the armistice to end the "war to end all wars" was sounded. The carnage of a foreign conflict fought "to make the world safe for democracy" was stopped. The issues that drove the most civilized nations of the world to the barbarities of bayonet, gas, and trench may not have been understood or even known to most, but everyone knew somebody who knew somebody who went and fought "over there."

The Memorial Church was built in the shadow of Harvard University to honor the dead of that war. Hardly a decade passed after the dedication of the Memorial Church to this noble purpose before World War II burst upon us. The names of those dead adorn the walls, now joined by the dead of Korea and Vietnam.

The "mind that was in Christ" was the mind of sacrifice. He gave himself willingly. The conflict was great and we were in the balance scales between heaven and hell. Christ died so we might live. Now, with life, we learn the blessing of dying to self, so that others might live.

If your name was going to be etched upon the wall of your church as a memorial, what would people remember about you?

2. Your best efforts. The best athletes in sports, such as Michael Jordan and Larry Bird, are usually defined by their ability to play their best when it counts most. They possess the ability and the determination that always rises to the occasion. This is true in athletic arenas, and it should be true of the church today.

When does it matter most? Ask members of the class to brainstorm the times when the church has to be at its very best. Included in the answers could be phrases like "in times of crisis" or "in times of community changes." Other responses might include "during times of transition" (between pastorates). Finally, provided no one brings up the question, ask if there is a time when the church can afford to be less than its best.

3. Hidden treasures. The Academy of Natural Sciences located in Philadelphia, Pennsylvania, has many of America's scientific treasures. You can find plants gathered by Lewis and Clark, a 180-year-old collection of butterflies, and paintings of birds (some now extinct) by John J. Audubon. However, you can't see any of them. They are hidden treasures. The museum is short on money and space, so these and other nineteenth-century treasures are stored on shelves, warehoused away from the public eye.

Paul wrote the Philippians to encourage them not to be "hidden treasure." Instead, he appealed to them on the fourfold basis of what it means to be "in Christ and to let nothing hinder their witness. Warehoused Christianity is of no value.

4. A shining life reflects His light. "Heart of the Ocean," a 170-carat sapphire and diamond necklace modeled after a piece of jewelry in the movie "Titanic," sold for $2.2 million at a fundraiser held in honor of Princess Diana. In the movie, "Heart of the Ocean" was just a piece of costume jewelry used to support the story line of the movie. Still it inspired the Asprey London company to create the real thing—a marine-blue gem set in platinum and encased by a collection of 36 carats of diamonds.

It is fascinating that a piece of costume jewelry used in a fictionalized movie plot inspired something as costly as the piece of jewelry auctioned for $2.2 million. It shines today even though it is born out of a fictionalized past. How much more then should we shine. Rescued and redeemed by the Son of God, we are called to be in fellowship with Him, our sins forgiven and our lives completely changed.

5. Character. "Character is the result of two things—mental attitude and the way we spend our time" (Elbert Hubbard).

6. Attitude. "A bad attitude is the worst thing that can happen to a group of people. It's infectious" (Roger Allan Raby).

7. Example. "Setting an example is not the main means of influencing another, it is the only means" (Albert Einstein).

TEACHING THE BIBLE

- *Main Idea:* Christians are to have the mind of Christ.
- *Suggested Teaching Aim:* To lead adults to identify how they can have Christ's mind in their lives.

A TEACHING OUTLINE

1. *Appeal for Unity and Humility (Phil. 2:1–4)*
2. *Sharing the Mind of Christ (Phil. 2:5–11)*
3. *Related Experiences (Phil. 2:12–18)*

Introduce the Bible Study

Use number 1, "Sacrifice: Investing Yourself for What Matters Most," in "Applying the Bible" to introduce the lesson.

Search for Biblical Truth

IN ADVANCE, copy all the summary statements on one sheet of colored paper and all the Scripture references on another sheet. Place the sheets at random around the room.

To overview the passage, ask members to match the summary statements on the wall with the appropriate Scripture. After all statements are matched, read all eight statements.

Point out that "If" in verse 1 might more accurately be translated "since": "*Since* your life in Christ gives you strength, *since* His love comforts you, *since* we share together in the Spirit, *since* you have mercy and kindness, won't you make me very happy by thinking alike, sharing the same love, and having one purpose? Use "Studying the Bible" to explain these "Four Aspects of Christian Experience."

DISCUSS: What do you think is the biggest barrier to unity in our church?

On a chalkboard write:

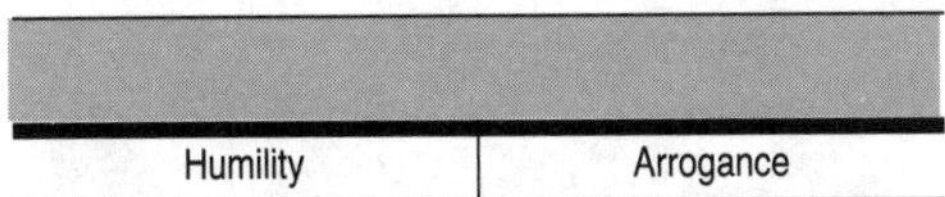

Humility	Arrogance

Ask half the class to look at verses 3 and 4 and find what Paul said would represent humble self-giving; ask the other half to identify what the opposite of this would be.

DISCUSS: How have you seen examples of humility furthering the cause of Christ?

Ask members to read verse 5 silently. Ask, What does it mean for a Christian to have the mind of Christ?

Ask a volunteer to read verses 6–8. Lecture briefly, describing the three stages in Christ's humble self-giving: (1) Laying aside His preexistent glory; (2) Choosing the servant role in His incarnate life; (3) Dying the humiliating death of crucifixion.

On a chalkboard write, *Who? What? When? Where?* and *Why?* Ask members to look at verses 9–11 and answer these questions: *Who* has highly exalted Jesus? (God.) *What* did God do for Jesus? (Gave Him the greatest name.) *When* will this name be recognized? (At some point in the future.) *Where* will this happen? (In heaven.) *Why* did God do this? (For God's glory.)

Ask members to read silently verses 12 and 13. Lecture briefly, using the four points in "Studying the Bible" to explain what Paul did not mean and did mean by the phrase, "Work out your own salvation."

DISCUSS: What steps can you take to "work out your own salvation"?

Give the Truth a Personal Focus

Ask these questions based on the "Summary of Bible Truths" statements: (1) How does oneness of spirit among believers enhance joy? (2) How does humble self-giving serve as an antidote for selfish strife? (3) How does God work in saved people to enable them to do good works? (4) What do we need to do to have Christ's mind in us?

Close in prayer that all members of the class will have Christ's mind in them.

Pressing On in Christ

Background Passage: Philippians 3:1–21
Focal Passage: Philippians 3:7–21

Paul warned the Philippians against false teachers; and, in the process, he shared much about his own experience before and after coming to know Christ. He testified to a salvation that is past, present, and future. The surest sign that he had been saved and would be saved was that he was pressing on in Christ.

Study Aim: *To testify why pressing on in Christ grows out of knowing Christ and leads to future resurrection.*

STUDYING THE BIBLE

OUTLINE AND SUMMARY

I. Salvation: Past, Present, and Future (Phil. 3:1–11)
  1. Deception of self-righteousness (3:1–6)
  2. Righteousness in Christ (3:7–9)
  3. Motivating power of past and future (3:10, 11)

II. Pressing on Toward Perfection (Phil. 3:12–21)
  1. Not perfect, but pressing on (3:12–14)
  2. Living an exemplary life (3:15–19)
  3. Living as citizens of heaven (3:20, 21)

Paul confessed that he once was self-righteous (vv. 1–6). He now considered his greatest treasure to be righteousness in Christ (vv. 7–9). He wanted to grow in his knowledge of Christ and in his experience of Christ's death and resurrection (vv. 10, 11). He was not yet perfect, but he was pressing on (vv. 12–14). Paul contrasted an exemplary life with the sinful lives of false teachers (vv. 15–19). He reminded the Philippians of the hope of resurrection for citizens of heaven (vv. 20, 21).

I. Salvation: Past, Present, and Future (Phil. 3:1–11)

1. Deception of self-righteousness (vv. 1–6)

After calling for the Philippians to rejoice in the Lord (v. 1), Paul warned against those who teach that circumcision is essential for salvation (v. 2). Paul insisted that those who rejoice in Christ are the true circumcision because their confidence is in the Spirit, not in the flesh (v. 3). Paul listed the reasons he had convinced himself that he had perfectly kept the law (vv. 4–6).

2. Righteousness in Christ (vv. 7–9)

7 But what things were gain to me, those I counted loss for Christ.

8 Yea doubtless, and I count all things but loss for the excellency of the knowledge of Christ Jesus my Lord: for whom I have suffered the loss of all things, and do count them but dung, that I may win Christ.

9 And be found in him, not having mine own righteousness, which is of the law, but that which is through the faith of Christ, the righteousness which is of God by faith.

Paul exchanged his old self-righteousness for Christ's righteousness. Using accounting terms, Paul testified that he placed all he had considered as assets in the category of liabilities. "Counted" in verse 7 referred back to his conversion; "count" in verse 8 referred to his present experience. He still felt that he had lost nothing but sins in laying aside his old life and that he had gained everything worthwhile in "the excellency of the knowledge of Christ Jesus."

Verse 9 has a future aspect to it. Paul believed that he had already been accepted as righteous by God. Therefore, when the final judgment came, Paul would be accepted as righteous because he was trusting Christ's righteousness, not his own.

The three aspects of salvation stated in terms of righteousness are justification (a sinner being declared right with God through faith in Christ), sanctification (a believer growing in Christlikeness by the power of Christ's Spirit, and glorification (being Christlike at Christ's coming). None of these is the result of human efforts; all are by the grace and power of Christ.

3. Motivating power of past and future (vv. 10, 11)

10 That I may know him, and the power of his resurrection, and the fellowship of his sufferings, being made conformable unto his death;

11 If by any means I might attain unto the resurrection of the dead.

Paul already knew Christ ("excellency of the knowledge of Christ Jesus," v. 8), but he wanted to know Him better. And he looked forward to the face-to-face knowledge of Christ when he would see Christ (1 John 3:2).

Likewise, Paul had already been saved through faith in Christ, who died for our sins and was raised from the dead (1 Cor. 15:3–5). Yet the cross and the resurrection also have a present and a future dimension. These saving acts of God in Christ not only provide the door to the Christian life for sinners, but they also provide the pattern and the power of the Christian life for believers. This is what Jesus meant about crossbearing (Luke 9:23) and what Paul meant by being crucified with and risen with Christ (Rom. 6:3, 4; Gal. 2:20).

Resurrection definitely has past, present, and future dimensions. We have passed from death to life (John 5:24; Eph. 2:1–7). We have been raised to walk in newness of life by the power of the resurrected Lord (Rom. 6:3, 4; Eph. 1:19, 20). We shall experience the resurrection or else the transformation of our bodies if we are alive when Christ comes (1 Thess. 4:13–18; Phil. 3:21).

The "if" clause in verse 11 was not intended by Paul to communicate any doubt on his part about the transformation of his body. What he may have doubted was whether he would be alive or dead when Christ came.

Or, Paul may have been dealing with a group who believed that the resurrection was already past, as he mentioned in 2 Timothy 2:17, 18.

II. Pressing on Toward Perfection (Phil. 3:12–21)

1. Not perfect, but pressing on (vv. 12–14)

12 Not as though I had already attained, either were already perfect: but I follow after, if that I may apprehend that for which also I am apprehended of Christ Jesus.

13 Brethren, I count not myself to have apprehended: but this one thing I do, forgetting those things which are behind, and reaching forth unto those things which are before,

14 I press toward the mark for the prize of the high calling of God in Christ Jesus.

Paul clearly denied that he was already perfect, but he was equally insistent that he was pressing on toward perfection. He "had [not] already attained" the future dimensions of salvation of which he had just written in verses 9–11. "Follow after" is a translation of the same word that is translated "press" (v. 14). The word means "pursue" and was translated "persecuting" in verse 6. As Paul had once zealously pursued Christians, now he pursued perfection in Christ.

"Apprehend" means "lay hold on." It appears twice in verse 12 and once in verse 13. His objective was to lay hold on that for which Christ had laid hold on him. He had not yet laid hold of this, but he was exerting every effort to do so. Paul used the picture of a runner straining forward toward the finish line in order that he might win the prize.

A runner could not look back; therefore, Paul was "forgetting" those things which were behind and concentrating on his objective. He described this as the high or upward calling of God in Christ Jesus. This was no less than perfection (Matt. 5:48).

2. Living an exemplary life (vv. 15–19)

15 Let us therefore, as many as be perfect, be thus minded: and if in any thing ye be otherwise minded, God shall reveal even this unto you.

16 Nevertheless, whereto we have already attained, let us walk by the same rule, let us mind the same thing.

The word *perfect* in verse 15 is the same word from verse 12. In verse 12, Paul clearly said that he was not perfect; in verse 15, he called on those who were perfect to be of the same mind as he was. The word translated "perfect" may be translated "mature." Paul may have been using it in this way, or he may have been using it ironically of a group who claimed that they were already perfect.

Verses 15b, 16 are not easy to translate or explain. The most likely meaning of verse 15b is that God will reveal what people need to know. The main idea in verse 16 is that they should hold on to the level of maturity that they had already attained—as well as pressing on toward perfection.

In Philippians 3, Paul set forth some principles of a doctrine of Christian perfection: (1) No living Christian has yet attained perfection,

(2) perfection is Christ's ultimate goal for all His people, (3) true believers are pressing on toward perfection, and (4) when Christ comes, He will transform us into His image.

17 Brethren, be followers together of me, and mark them which walk so as ye have us for an ensample.

Why would Paul tell them to imitate him? Before we condemn Paul as an egotist, let us remember these facts: (1) Paul had already clearly denied that he was perfect. (2) Paul was a missionary writing to people with few real examples of how Christians live. Paul had told them with words; but like all missionaries, he had to show them with his life. (3) Paul also pointed the Philippians to other mature Christians. In Philippians 2:16–30, Paul mentioned not only his own example but also the examples of Timothy and Epaphroditus. (4) Paul made plain that he was only an imperfect follower of the only perfect one, Jesus Christ (Phil. 2:5–11).

18 (For many walk, of whom I have told you often, and now tell you even weeping, that they are the enemies of the cross of Christ:

19 Whose end is destruction, whose God is their belly, and whose glory is in their shame, who mind earthly things.)

In contrast to the exemplary lives of real Christians, Paul warned of the evil example of some who were "enemies of the cross." Bible scholars debate what group Paul had in mind. Some think that he was still describing the Judaizers of verse 2. Other scholars believe that Paul had in mind a group that claimed to be perfect, but lived evil lives. This group is often identified as an early form of those later called Gnostics. Some Gnostics taught that flesh has nothing to do with one's spiritual state. Therefore, they lived sinful lives while claiming perfection.

The fact that Paul wept about them implies that they professed to be true Christians. Paul denied that they were. Instead, he said they were enemies of the cross who were headed for destruction. The last part of the verse accuses them of worshiping earthly things and even boasting of shameful things.

3. Living as citizens of heaven (vv. 20, 21)

20 For our conversation is in heaven; from whence also we look for the Saviour, the Lord Jesus Christ:

21 Who shall change our vile body, that it may be fashioned like unto his glorious body, according to the working whereby he is able even to subdue all things unto himself.

"Conversation" translates a word meaning "citizenship." Christians are citizens of heaven (see Heb. 11:13–16; 13:14). Philippi was a colony of Rome, and many of its people were citizens of Rome. Not everyone in the Roman Empire was a citizen. Those who were citizens tried to be faithful representatives of Rome. Paul reminded Philippian believers that their true citizenship was in heaven. Thus, their ultimate loyalty was to God.

The hope of citizens of heaven is fixed on the coming again of the Lord Jesus. When He comes, Christians will be given glorified bodies fit for the new heavens and new earth. John wrote that at His coming, we shall see Christ and be made like Him (1 John 3:1–3). This change will be wrought by the power of Christ, who at that time will subdue all things, including putting an end to death.

Verses 20 and 21 describe the perfection toward which Paul said he and other believers are constantly pressing. We are already being transformed as we walk with Him, but the final transformation will be in the future (2 Cor. 3:18).

PRONUNCIATION GUIDE

Epaphroditus [ih PAF roh DIGH tuhs]

SUMMARY OF BIBLE TRUTHS

1. Sinners gain far more than they lose by following Christ.
2. Salvation involves exchanging self-righteousness for Christ's righteousness.
3. Christ's cross and resurrection provide the door to and the way of the Christian life.
4. Christians are not perfect, but they are pressing on toward perfection.
5. Christians should live exemplary lives.
6. Christians are citizens of heaven.

APPLYING THE BIBLE

1. Imitation. Benjamin Franklin said, "There is much difference between imitating a good man and counterfeiting him." Paul encouraged the Philippians to imitate him as he sought to imitate Christ. This poses a good question for us today: "Are we imitators, or counterfeiters?"

2. Don't give up:

Christ's cause is hindered everywhere,
And folks are dying in despair,
The reason why? Just think a bit.
The church is full of folks who quit.

—Author unknown

3. Take on the day. Laura Schleshinger signs off her nationally syndicated radio program every day with these words: "Now, go take on the day." Paul does the same thing. Having given us a theological framework for handling the difficulties of life, making the application and calling us to servanthood, he then said, "Finally . . . go take on the day."

Our ability to do this is directly related to our knowledge of Christ. As we remember the sacrifice He paid for our sin, His sufferings, and the promise of resurrection made possible through Him, we can endure difficulties and press on to perfection.

4. Forgetting the best. An ancient Scottish legend tells of a shepherd boy tending a few straggling sheep on the side of a mountain. One day he saw at his feet a beautiful flower—one that was more beautiful than any he had ever seen before. The boy knelt down, scooped the flower in his hands, and held it close to his eyes, drinking in its beauty. The boy then heard a noise and looked up. There he saw a great stone mountain opening up right before his eyes. The sun began to shine on the inside of the mountain, and his eyes widened as he saw the sparkling of the beautiful gems and precious metals that it contained.

With the flower in his hands, the shepherd boy rushed inside. Laying the flower down, he began to gather gold, silver, and precious gems in his arms. Finally, with all that his arms could carry, the boy turned and started to leave the great cavern. Suddenly a voice said to him, "Don't forget the best."

Thinking that perhaps he had overlooked some choice piece of treasure, the boy turned around and quickly picked up additional pieces of priceless treasure. As his arms literally overflowed with wealth, he began to run out of the great mountainous vault. Again the voice said, "Don't forget the best."

But the boy's arms were filled, and he hurried outside. Suddenly, the precious metals and stones turned to dust. The boy looked around and saw the great stone mountain closing its doors.

A third time the shepherd boy heard the voice, and this time it said, "You forgot the best. The beautiful flower is the key to the vault of the mountain."

The boy forgot the best, and lost a treasure. We too can lose a treasure. We get so busy that in our haste we miss things in life that are just waiting to be enjoyed. As William Feather said, "Plenty of people miss their share of happiness, not because they never found it, but because they didn't stop to enjoy it."

There's another lesson we can learn from the legend about the shepherd boy. Just as the flower was the key to the treasure of the mountain, Jesus is the key to the treasure of life. But like the boy, you can get so involved in activities and so focused on material things that you forget the best and lose that treasure.[1]

5. Tear it down. A businessman owned a warehouse which had sat empty for months and needed repairs. Vandals had damaged the doors and smashed the windows, and trash was everywhere inside the building.

The businessman showed a prospective buyer the property and took great pains to say that he would replace the broken windows, bring in a crew to correct any structural damage, and clean out all the garbage.

"Forget about the repairs," the buyer said. "When I buy this place, I'm going to build something completely different, something entirely new. I don't want the building. I just want the site!"

You can't keep your "old building" when you come to Jesus. He doesn't want the building—but he does want the site. The site is the real you—the you that was created in the image of God. And the old building—with its dark rooms and bad habits—is demolished. You become a new creation in Christ Jesus.[2]

TEACHING THE BIBLE

- *Main Idea:* Pressing on in Christ grows out of knowing Christ and leads to future resurrection.
- *Suggested Teaching Aim:* To lead adults to identify ways they can continue to grow in their knowledge of Christ.

A TEACHING OUTLINE

1. *Salvation: Past, Present, and Future (Phil. 3:1–11)*
2. *Pressing on Toward Perfection (Phil. 3:12–21)*

Introduce the Bible Study

Use number 4, "Forgetting the Best," in "Applying the Bible" to introduce the lesson.

Search for Biblical Truth

IN ADVANCE:

- Make strip posters of the above two points in "A Teaching Outline."
- Write the six Scripture references of the background Scripture on a chalkboard or a large sheet of paper.
- Secure paper and pencils to distribute.
- Copy on small slips of paper the definitions of *justification*, *sanctification*, and *glorification* from "Studying the Bible" and give the definition to three people.
- Make a poster with the four principles of a doctrine of Christian perfection based on the material in "Studying the Bible" under verses 15 and 16.
- Make a poster of the six "Summary of Bible Truths" statements.

As members enter, ask those with birthdays in the months of January–April to form one group, those with birthdays in May–August to form a second group, and those with birthdays in September–December to form a third group. Ask members: (1) to look up the six Scripture references written on the chalkboard; (2) to read the passages in their Bibles; and (3) to write a one-sentence summary for each reference. Call for reports.

Place the first outline strip poster on the wall. Ask a volunteer to read verses 6 and 7. Ask, What word in verse 7 points to the past? ("Counted.") What word in verse 8 points to the present? ("Count.") What words in verse 9 point to the future? (Will "be found in him.") On a chalkboard write, *Justification, Sanctification,* and *Glorification.* Ask: Which of these words points to what happened in the past? (Justification.) In the present? (Sanctification.) In the future? (Glorification.) Ask members with definitions to read them aloud.

Ask a volunteer to read aloud verses 10 and 11. Ask, How does what happened to Christ in the past motivate us to live in the present so we might attain the resurrection of the dead in the future?

DISCUSS: What have you done to be crucified with Christ? What do you need to do to be crucified with Christ?

Ask members to open their Bibles to Philippians 3:12–14. On a chalkboard, write: *Rules for Running the Christian Race.* Ask members to look at these verses and identify rules or guidelines for pressing on toward the high calling.

DISCUSS: What is the biggest barrier in your desire to reach the high calling to which Christ has called you?

Ask a member to read aloud verses 15–17. Display the poster you made showing the four principles of a doctrine of perfection. Ask, Which of these statements keep us from getting discouraged? (3 and 4.) Read aloud the four statements in "Studying the Bible," explaining verse 17. Ask, How would you feel about telling people to imitate you?

Ask members to look at verses 18 and 19. Explain the two suggested explanations of who Paul described as "enemies of the cross": Judaizers and Gnostics. Ask, Why did Paul weep over this group?

Ask a member to read aloud verses 20 and 21. Explain that "conversation" translates a word meaning "citizenship."

DISCUSS: Where is your true citizenship? Where will you have your final homecoming? What will Christ subdue that thrills you the most?

Give the Truth a Personal Focus

To summarize the lesson, place the poster of the "Summary of Bible Truths" on the wall. Uncover the first statement and read it aloud. Do this with the other five statements. Close in prayer that members will seek the high calling in Christ.

---

1. Rich McLawhorn, *Forgetting the Best,* Daily Wisdom.
2. Wayne Rice, *More Hot Illustrations for Youth Talks* (Youth Specialties, Inc., 1995).

Rejoicing in Christ

June

25

2000

Background Passage: Philippians 4:4–20

Focal Passage: Philippians 4:4–18

Philippians has been called "the joy letter" because of its many references to joy and its calls to rejoice. Joy is closely related to peace. These twin themes are prominent in Paul's closing words to the Philippians.

➧ **Study Aim:** *To identify the distinctive characteristics of joy and peace in Christ.*

STUDYING THE BIBLE

OUTLINE AND SUMMARY

- **I. Joy and Peace (Phil. 4:4–9)**
  - **1. Distinctives of Christian joy (4:4, 5)**
  - **2. Prescription for peace (4:6, 7)**
  - **3. Thinking and doing the best (4:8, 9)**
- **II. Contentment and Generosity (Phil. 4:10–20)**
  - **1. Secret of contentment (4:10–13)**
  - **2. Gratitude for generous givers (4:14–18)**
  - **3. Blessings of generous giving (4:19, 20)**

Christian joy is a fruit of being in Christ (vv. 4, 5). Prayer with thanksgiving produces peace that exceeds understanding (vv. 6, 7). The God of peace will be with those who think and do the best (vv. 8, 9). Believers find their sufficiency in Christ (vv. 10–13). Paul was more grateful for generous givers than for their gifts (vv. 14–18). God will supply the needs of generous givers (vv. 19, 20).

I. Joy and Peace (Philippians 4:4–9)

1. Distinctives of Christian joy (vv. 4, 5)

4 Rejoice in the Lord alway: and again I say, Rejoice.

5 Let your moderation be known unto all men. The Lord is at hand.

Three distinctives of Christian joy are found in verses 4 and 5:

1. *Christian joy is in the Lord.* The happiness the world seeks is dependent on creating or finding a set of circumstances or achieving a state of mind in which one is happy. Christian joy is not something that people can find, create, or achieve. It is a fruit of a right relation with Jesus Christ.

2. *Christians who are right with God can always rejoice.* "Alway" has the same meaning as "rejoice evermore" (1 Thess. 5:16). Worldly happiness is dependent on outward, happy circumstances, but Christians can rejoice even in trouble (Rom. 5:2–5).

3. *Christian joy is forbearing toward others.* "Moderation" means "forbearance." Worldly happiness depends on being with people whom you like and who help to make you happy. Christian joy is enhanced by

practicing Christlike love, forgiveness, and forbearance to others—including those with whom you have differences.

"The Lord is at hand" refers not just to the continuing presence of Christ's Spirit but to the coming of Christ. We find joy as we live in the light of the Lord's abiding presence and future coming.

2. Prescription for peace (vv. 6, 7)

6 Be careful for nothing; but in every thing by prayer and supplication with thanksgiving let your requests be made known unto God.

7 And the peace of God, which passeth all understanding, shall keep your hearts and minds through Christ Jesus.

"Careful" means "anxious" (see Matt. 6:25–34). The antidote for this common human malady of worry is prayer that includes trust in God with thanksgiving to God. Someone has summed up verse 6:

1. Be anxious about nothing.
2. Be prayerful about everything.
3. Be thankful for anything.

This antidote for anxiety is a prescription for peace—not the kind of peace that eludes those who seek it by manipulating circumstances and people, but the peace of God. This "peace of God" is God's gift. It includes peace with God (Rom. 5:1), peace with others (Eph. 2:14; Rom. 12:18), and inner peace of mind. It keeps or guards our hearts and minds. The world can neither create nor understand this amazing peace of God.

3. Thinking and doing the best (vv. 8, 9)

8 Finally, brethren, whatsoever things are true, whatsoever things are honest, whatsoever things are just, whatsoever things are pure, whatsoever things are lovely, whatsoever things are of good report; if there be any virtue, and if there be any praise, think on these things.

9 Those things, which ye have both learned, and received, and heard, and seen in me, do: and the God of peace shall be with you.

"Think" means more than thinking about; it means to reflect on these things to the degree that they shape your attitudes and actions. In verse 8, Paul listed eight qualities. These were widely recognized by first-century moralists as basic virtues. Paul used them to remind Christians that they should be at least as good as the best non-Christians. The Bible says, "As [a person] thinketh in his heart, so is he" (Prov. 23:7).

Verse 8 goes beyond pagan virtues to distinctive Christian qualities. Paul wrote of what he had taught them and shown them by his example: humble self-giving of chapter 2 and persistent pressing on of chapter 3. Verse 8 also goes beyond "think" to "do." Good intentions are not enough. Christians must act.

Notice the similarity of the promises at the end of verses 7 and 9. Peace "which passeth all understanding" or the "peace of God" comes from "the God of peace." Paul promised those who do His will that the God of peace would be with them.

II. Contentment and Generosity (Phil. 4:10–20)

1. Secret of contentment (vv. 10–13)

10 But I rejoiced in the Lord greatly, that now at the last your care of me hath flourished again; wherein ye were also careful, but ye lacked opportunity.

11 Not that I speak in respect of want: for I have learned, in whatsoever state I am, therewith to be content.

12 I know both how to be abased, and I know how to abound: every where and in all things I am instructed both to be full and to be hungry, both to abound and to suffer need.

13 I can do all things through Christ which strengtheneth me.

Verses 10–13 reveal that Paul was speaking in these verses about money that the Philippians had sent him. The gift came from the Philippians, and Paul called them "my joy and crown" (4:1). But their action caused him to rejoice "in the Lord" because Paul knew that the Lord had inspired their generous gift.

The middle part of verse 10 sounds as if Paul was giving them a mild rebuke for being so slow to send him help. However, the last part of the verse clarifies his meaning. "Now at the last your care of me hath flourished again" was not a complaint that they had taken so long to send help. "But ye lacked opportunity" shows that they were concerned all along, but for some reason they had not had an opportunity to act earlier.

Verse 11 offers a further clarification of Paul's attitude. He did not want to leave the impression that he was suffering great hardship until their offering arrived. He did not "speak in respect of want." To the contrary, Paul testified, "I have learned, in whatsoever state I am, therewith to be content."

Did Paul ever write anything more challenging for our "want-it-all," "never-get-enough" generation? Paul had found what eludes most people today—contentment with whatever he had. In fact, not many people are looking for this; most are too busy trying to get more than they have.

What was Paul's secret? The word *content* translates a Greek word that was often used by the Stoic school of philosophers to describe their goal of "self-sufficiency." The Stoics tried to get along with the bare minimum. The difference is that they thought that they could achieve this contentment by effort of mind and will. By contrast, Paul trusted Christ for the gift of contentment.

Verse 13 is probably the most precious verse in the letter to the Philippians. Our sufficiency is not something we have achieved; it is something we have received from the abiding presence of the Lord with us. Paul did not end the sentence after "all things." A Stoic might boast, "I can do all things"; however, Paul always added "through Christ."

2. Gratitude for generous givers (vv. 14–18)

14 Notwithstanding ye have well done, that ye did communicate with my affliction.

15 Now ye Philippians know also, that in the beginning of the gospel, when I departed from Macedonia, no church communicated with me as concerning giving and receiving, but ye only.

16 For even in Thessalonica ye sent once and again unto my necessity.

"Communicate" in verse 14 translates a Greek verb meaning "sharing as brothers and sisters in Christ together with" Paul. A shorter form of the same basic root is translated "communicated" in verse 15. This root is the same as the word *koinonia,* which is used throughout the New Testament to describe the common life shared by those in Christ. One expression of this common life is generous sharing of material things with one another.

"The beginning of the gospel" refers to the time when the good news first made its impact in Philippi (see Acts 16:10–40). From the beginning, the Philippian church had shared what they had with Paul. The apostle did not accept gifts from all the churches he helped to start, but he always had an especially close partnership with the believers in Philippi.

When Paul left Philippi the first time, he went to Thessalonica to preach the good news (Acts 17:1–9). Then he went to Berea, another city in the Roman province of Macedonia (Acts 17:10–14). Verse 16 reveals that the Philippians helped to support Paul more than once when he was in neighboring Thessalonica. Verse 15 reveals that when Paul left the province for missionary work in the next province, only the Philippian believers sent him money.

17 Not because I desire a gift: but I desire fruit that may abound to your account.

18 But I have all, and abound: I am full, having received of Epaphroditus the things which were sent from you, an odour of a sweet smell, a sacrifice acceptable, well pleasing to God.

Paul was more concerned about raising generous givers than he was interested in raising generous gifts. He was grateful for the generous gifts, and he said so; however, he found his highest joy in the Philippians' growth in Christlikeness. They had learned what Jesus taught: that life is for giving (Acts 20:35). This is what Paul meant when he wrote, "Not because I desire a gift: but I desire fruit that may abound to your account."

He had been content before their generous gift arrived. Now he wrote, "I have all, and abound: I am full." He described their gift as being like a sweet sacrifice that brought joy to Paul because he knew that it was well-pleasing to God.

Verse 18 ties in with Philippians 2:25–30 in helping us reconstruct how the gift of the Philippians reached Paul, why Paul wrote Philippians, and how the letter got to them. One of their members, Epaphroditus, had carried the gift and had come prepared to provide personal help for Paul. While in Rome, Epaphroditus became gravely ill. Therefore, when he was well, Paul sent him back to Philippi with this letter—one purpose of which was to thank them for their generous gift.

3. Blessings of generous giving (vv. 19, 20)

Paul promised that God would supply every need for generous givers to continue being generous (v. 19; see 2 Cor. 9:6–11). He closed the body of his letter with a doxology (v. 20).

PRONUNCIATION GUIDE

Berea	[bih REE uh]
Epaphroditus	[ef PAF roh DIGH tuhs]
Macedonia	[mass uh DOH nih uh]
Thessalonica	[THESS uh loh NIGH kuh]

SUMMARY OF BIBLE TRUTHS

1. Christian joy is a fruit of a right relationship with God.
2. Christians can always rejoice in the Lord.
3. Prayer with thanksgiving leads to a peace that exceeds human understanding.
4. Thinking and doing the best is a sign that the God of peace is with us.
5. The secret of contentment is sufficiency in Christ.
6. Generous givers bring joy and find joy.

APPLYING THE BIBLE

1. Joy. "To be happy all the time is one of the most nonconformist things you can do. . . . To be always joyful is not just rebellion, it's *radical*"(John-Roger and Peter McWilliams).

2. Quotes on peace:

"Ambition is the grand enemy of all peace."
—John Cowper Powys

"The mere absence of war is not peace."
—John F. Kennedy

"Give peace in our time, O Lord."
—*The Book of Common Prayer*

"Peace is a journey of a thousand miles and it must be taken one step at a time." —Lyndon B. Johnson

"Peace hath her victories, no less renown'd than war."
—John Milton

"Only a peace between equals can last."
—Woodrow Wilson

"Peace hath higher tests of manhood than battle ever knew."
—John Greenleaf Whittier

"A soft answer turneth away wrath."
—Proverbs 15:1

3. Quotes on contentment:

"To be content with what we possess is the greatest of all riches."

"Contentment makes poor men rich; discontent makes rich men poor."

"There's none so poor as he who knows not the joy of what he has."

"Poverty without debt is real wealth."

4. A shortage of chocolate? A recent news story warned that a chocolate shortage is coming and by all counts, "it isn't going to be pretty" for consumers. According to recent reports, the cacao tree, which produces the cocoa beans essential for chocolate making, is in trouble. Diminishing tropical forest conditions are taking their toll on the trees that produce cocoa beans. Experts predict that there will be a shortage of chocolate candy products as chocoholics begin to hoard the remaining products in stores.

The early church faced a far more severe threat in its day. Paul encouraged the Philippian church to give generously in the face of an economic shortage. Times were difficult, especially in the context of religious persecution. Still the church gave, and apparently, gave from the heart.

Such giving increases joy—not only to the one who will receive the gift, but to the one who learns the joy of being free from possessions.

5. What money brings. "Money may be the husk of many things, but not the kernel. It brings you food, but not appetite; medicine, but not health; acquaintances, but not friends; servants, but not loyalty; days of joy, but not peace or happiness" (Henrik Ibsen).

TEACHING THE BIBLE

- *Main Idea:* Christians can have joy and peace in Christ.
- *Suggested Teaching Aim:* To identify the distinctive characteristics of joy and peace in Christ.

A TEACHING OUTLINE

1. *Joy and Peace (Phil. 4:4–9)*
2. *Contentment and Generosity (Phil. 4:10–20)*

Introduce the Bible Study

As members enter, give them a sheet of paper. Ask them to complete one of these statements: *Joy is* . . . or *Peace is* . . . .

Search for Biblical Truth

IN ADVANCE:

- On large sheets of paper, copy the six Scripture references for the six outline subpoints. Tape these at random around the room.
- Have pencils and a sheet of paper for each member.

Ask volunteers to read their statements on joy and peace.

Read the six summary statements from the "Outline and Summary" and ask members to find a reference on the wall that would support each statement.

Distribute a sheet of paper to each member. Ask half the class to listen for the number of times "joy" is mentioned in the lesson groups and to list distinctive characteristics of joy in Christ that they hear during the lesson. Ask the other half to listen for the number of times "peace" is mentioned in the lesson groups and to list distinctive characteristics of peace in Christ that they hear during the lesson.

Ask members to open their Bibles and read silently Philippians 4:4, 5. Lecture briefly on these points:

1. Christian joy is in the Lord.
2. Christians who are right with God can always rejoice.
3. Christian joy is forbearing toward others.

Ask members to look at verses 6 and 7. On a chalkboard, write:

Antidote for Anxiety

- Be anxious about nothing.
- Be prayerful about everything.
- Be thankful for anything.

Ask members to look at verses 8 and 9. Ask: Which of these are basically Christian virtues? Which virtue do you find the hardest to practice? What is the promise for those who practice these virtues? (Peace.)

Ask members to read silently verses 10–13. Ask, According to Paul, what is the secret of contentment?

DISCUSS: What is the biggest barrier to your gaining genuine contentment?

Ask members to read silently verses 14–16. Ask, How did the Philippians help Paul? What other church supported Paul in his missionary work?

Ask members to read silently verses 17 and 18. Ask, What made Paul's statement believable that it wasn't a gift from them that he wanted, but he wanted them to receive a blessing from God?

DISCUSS: Is it more blessed to give than to receive? Would you rather be on the receiving end of a Thanksgiving basket or the giving end?

Give the Truth a Personal Focus

Ask groups to share the number of times *joy* and *peace* were mentioned in the lesson. Now ask them to identify the distinctive characteristics of joy and peace in Christ that they have identified in the lesson.

Ask the group who had "joy" to write a hymn about *joy* to be sung to a familiar tune. Ask the group who had "peace" to write a hymn about peace. Call on the two groups to sing their hymns. Pray that all will experience joy and peace this week.

July

2

2000

Called to Spiritual Blessings in Christ

Background Passage: Ephesians 1:1–23
Focal Passage: Ephesians 1:1–14

Paul began this great document with a doxology of praise to God. Paul dealt with some theological ideas that go beyond our ability to understand fully. We do need to understand God and His ways in order to know Him, trust Him, follow Him, and praise Him.

Study Aim: *To praise God for the spiritual blessings in the doxology in Ephesians 1:3–14.*

STUDYING THE BIBLE

OUTLINE AND SUMMARY

I. Greeting (Eph. 1:1, 2)
II. Doxology of Praise to God (Eph. 1:3–14)
1. Keynote: blessed be God (1:3)
2. His loving and eternal purpose (1:4–6)
3. Fulfilling His purpose in Christ (1:7–12)
4. Sealing all believers by His Spirit (1:13, 14)
III. Prayer for the Church (Eph. 1:15–23)
1. For insight into their calling (1:15–18)
2. For power to fulfill their calling (1:19, 20)
3. For allegiance to the head of the body (1:21–23)

After a greeting (vv. 1, 2), Paul praised God as the source of all spiritual blessings (v. 3). He praised God for His loving, eternal purpose (vv. 4–6), which centers in the work of His beloved Son (vv. 7–12), and which is sealed by His Holy Spirit in the lives of all believers (vv. 13, 14). He prayed that the church might grasp its calling (vv. 15–18), use the power available (vv. 19, 20), and see the vision of the head of the church (vv. 21–23).

I. Greeting (Eph. 1:1, 2)

1 Paul, an apostle of Jesus Christ by the will of God, to the saints which are at Ephesus, and to the faithful in Christ Jesus:

2 Grace be to you, and peace, from God our Father, and from the Lord Jesus Christ.

Ephesians is one of Paul's greatest writings. Most of Paul's letters focused on issues and problems of a local congregation, but Ephesians looks at the church in terms of God's purpose for all His people. This is one reason why many Bible scholars believe the letter was not just for the Ephesian church but was intended to be circulated also to other churches.

Paul described readers as "saints" (those set apart by God and for God), "faithful," and "in Christ Jesus." The last of these is a theme in Paul's writings and is especially prominent in the doxology of verses 3–14. It emphasizes not only that Christ is in each believer but also that all believers are in Christ.

II. Doxology of Praise to God (Eph. 1:3–14)

1. Keynote: blessed be God (v. 3)

3 Blessed be the God and Father of our Lord Jesus Christ, who hath blessed us with all spiritual blessings in heavenly places in Christ.

The words *blessed, blessed,* and *blessings* are translations for three Greek words from the same root. The first "blessed" was a familiar Jewish way of praising God. The second word refers to how the blessed God has blessed His people, and the third word is a noun identifying the "blessings."

Paul praised "the God and Father of our Lord Jesus Christ." Christians believe in the one true God who has revealed Himself and acted to save us in Jesus Christ. This God is our Father, and He is very different in character from the false gods that many people worship.

God is the source of every good thing, including all our blessings. Paul focused on "all spiritual blessings in heavenly places in Christ." This means that God brings to us now the blessings that we shall know in full in heaven. And they are ours because we are "in Christ."

2. His loving and eternal purpose (vv. 4–6)

4 According as he hath chosen us in him before the foundation of the world, that we should be holy and without blame before him in love:

5 Having predestinated us unto the adoption of children by Jesus Christ to himself, according to the good pleasure of his will,

6 To the praise of the glory of his grace, wherein he hath made us accepted in the beloved.

Believers were "chosen . . . in him before the foundation of the world." God took the initiative in calling believers to be in Christ. This was part of God's eternal purpose.

Being "chosen" is a privilege but also a responsibility. He chose us in Christ "that we should be holy and without blame before him." These words could refer to justification (declared right with God), sanctification (becoming righteous by His Spirit), and/or glorification (being made like Christ at His coming).

"In love" could go with what precedes or with what follows. In either case, this shows that God's purpose is not only eternal but also loving.

"Predestinated" is the most debated word in the passage. The Greek word means to draw a circle of love around something or someone. This word, like "chosen," emphasizes God's sovereign grace in salvation. Neither word is used in the Bible to teach that God fixed the eternal destiny of some people, but both words emphasize that believers can

OUTLINE OF EPHESIANS

I. Introduction (Eph. 1:1–23)
  1. Greeting (1:1, 2)
  2. Doxology of praise to the triune God (1:3–14)
  3. Prayer for the church (1:15–23)
II. God's Plan for Making People One in Christ (Eph. 2:1–22)
  1. Saved from death unto life (2:1–10)
  2. Reconciled from alienation into oneness (2:11–22)
  3. Paul's ministry (3:1–13)
  4. Prayer for God's fullness (3:14–21)
III. What God Expects of His People (Eph. 4:1–6:24)
  1. Oneness and maturity in Christ (4:1–16)
  2. A new Christlike way of living (4:17–5:20)
  3. A Christian household (5:21–6:9)
  4. Overcoming Satan's temptations (6:10–20)
  5. Final words (6:21–24)

trace the source of their salvation back to the loving heart of the eternal God.

"Adoption" is one way to describe the goal of this eternal and loving purpose. In a Roman adoption, an adopted son had all the privileges of a son born to the parents. Christians are adopted to God "by Jesus Christ." The "good pleasure of his will" is another way of saying that God's purpose was loving and gracious.

"To the praise of the glory of his grace" is a refrain found three times in this doxology (vv. 12, 14). In general, the refrain distinguishes God's eternal purpose (vv. 4–6), His fulfilling that purpose in Christ (vv. 7–12), and His sealing believers for future redemption (vv. 13, 14). "Glory" describes the majestic fullness of God. "Grace" is God's unmerited favor for sinners.

The last part of verse 6 provides a transition to verses 7–12. "The beloved" is the beloved Son of God. It was in Him that believers were "accepted" by God's grace.

3. Fulfilling His purpose in Christ (vv. 7–12)

7 In whom we have redemption through his blood, the forgiveness of sins, according to the riches of his grace;

8 Wherein he hath abounded toward us in all wisdom and prudence;

9 Having made known unto us the mystery of his will, according to his good pleasure which he hath purposed in himself:

10 That in the dispensation of the fulness of times he might gather together in one all things in Christ, both which are in heaven, and which are on earth; even in him:

11 In whom also we have obtained an inheritance, being predestinated according to the purpose of him who worketh all things after the counsel of his own will:

12 That we should be to the praise of his glory, who first trusted in Christ.

"Redemption" means "deliverance" from sin's captivity at the cost of the "blood" of Christ. "Forgiveness of sins" means to remove sin as a barrier to fellowship, again by paying the price of bearing the pain of that sin at the cross. These are expressions of "the riches of his grace."

Not only does God in Christ forgive our guilt and break the power of sin, but He also is moving history toward the fulfillment of His loving and eternal purpose. "The mystery of his will" has now been revealed by God. At the end of the ages ("the fulness of times"), God's purpose is to "gather together in one all things in Christ." Ephesians 2:11–22 shows that the focus of this oneness will be the oneness of God's people, but Ephesians 1:10 reminds us that Christ will gather together all things in God's creation.

"We have obtained an inheritance" can also be translated as "we have been made a heritage." The Old Testament speaks of the chosen people as God's heritage, and it also speaks of the inheritance they received from God. Paul referred to God's "inheritance in the saints" in 1:18. All of this is God's loving and eternal plan, and it will be done in God's own time and way.

This glorious vision of present redemption and future inheritance led Paul to the second refrain: "That we should be to the praise of his glory." We are His people, His heritage. Not only should our voices praise Him and exalt His glory, but our lives should reflect His glory. The way we live should result in praise to God.

The last part of verse 12 sets the stage for verse 13. Strictly speaking, the "we" in verse 12 referred to Jewish believers; although the principle applies to all believers. At any rate, the Jewish Christians were those "who first trusted in Christ."

4. Sealing all believers by His Spirit (vv. 13, 14)

13 In whom ye also trusted, after that ye heard the word of truth, the gospel of your salvation: in whom also after that ye believed, ye were sealed with that holy Spirit of promise,

14 Which is the earnest of our inheritance until the redemption of the purchased possession, unto the praise of his glory.

"Ye" in verse 13 refers to Gentile believers. This goes with the last part of verse 12. The people of Israel were the first to hear the gospel of Christ, and thus the first believers were Jews. But due to the efforts of Jewish Christians like Paul, the gospel of salvation had been preached also to Gentiles; and some of them believed. "Our," like most of the "we's" in the doxology (except for v. 12), refers to both Jewish and Gentile believers.

Verse 13 speaks of Gentiles having "heard" and "believed." This reminds us not to press the meaning of "predestinated" to the point where people have no freedom to chose or reject the good news. The

Bible teaches both God's sovereignty and human freedom. Human freedom is a result of God's sovereign decision to create us that way. In dealing with sticky questions that seem to pit divine sovereignty and free will against each other, we need to maintain a balance that preserves both truths.

What then does it mean for believers to realize that they have been predestinated or chosen by God? Trace back your salvation to its source. It leads back to the person who told you of Christ, back through all the Spirit-led witnesses since Pentecost, back to the cross and resurrection, and back beyond the coming of Christ to the loving heart of the eternal God.

The work of the Holy Spirit is mentioned in verses 13 and 14. Two words are used: "sealed" and "earnest." In ancient times, documents were sealed in warm wax with an official ring or seal. This seal meant that the document belonged to the owner of the seal and that the document was under his protection. Thus, being "sealed with that holy Spirit of promise" is a sign that we belong to God and are under His protection.

"Earnest" was and still is a financial term. It refers to earnest money that a purchaser pays a buyer as a guarantee of full payment at the appointed time. Paul referred to God's people as "the purchased possession." Our future redemption is assured because the presence of God's Spirit is a guarantee.

The doxology ends with the refrain, "unto the praise of his glory."

III. Prayer for the Church (Eph. 1:15–23)

1. For insight into their calling (vv. 15–18)

Paul thanked God for their faith and love (vv. 15, 16). He asked God to open the eyes of their hearts to the hope of their calling (vv. 17, 18).

2. For power to fulfill their calling (vv. 19, 20)

Paul prayed that they would realize that the power that raised Jesus was available to God's people.

3. For allegiance to the head of the body (vv. 21–23)

Paul described Christ as head of all things, especially of His body the church.

PRONUNCIATION GUIDE

Ephesus [EF uh suhs]

SUMMARY OF BIBLE TRUTHS

1. Christ is in believers, and believers are in Christ.
2. God be praised for all His spiritual blessings.
3. Salvation has its source in the loving heart of the eternal God.
4. Christ died to redeem us from our sins.
5. God has given humans the freedom to hear and believe the gospel.
6. Believers are securely sealed by God's Spirit.

APPLYING THE BIBLE

1. Adoption. Conna Craig will never forget the day she met her two-year-old foster sister, Halie. The little girl's face was severely burned—the work of a mother and her boyfriend who had used a heater to discipline the child for refusing to eat supper. Conna said, "Imagine holding this child in your lap and gently putting cream on a burn while she's crying—all the time knowing someone deliberately did this to her."[1]

When we come to faith in Christ, we are adopted into God's family, and the church becomes our family too. The abuses and hurts of the past, some self-inflicted, others the evidence of the hold of the enemy on our life, are comforted in the arms of this new family.

Little Halie was eventually "reintroduced" to the environment where her abuse began, and no doubt continued. The state felt it was in the best interest of the family. Can you imagine it? Spiritual adoption means that we never have to go back to the old way of life. Those relationships are forever severed.

2. Adopting the children nobody wanted. Former college teacher Norma Claypool has adopted fifteen severely handicapped children over the years. Many of them could not speak, and she obtained plastic surgery for several who were facially deformed.[2]

Adopting the children that nobody wants, Norma Claypool becomes a living parable demonstrating the love of God. The story goes on to say that Norma has lost her sight. Certainly we know that God is not blind, but isn't it good to know that He chooses not to look at us and treat us as our sins deserve? He bids us to come home, and by His grace He changes us into the image of His Son.

3. What happens in adoption?

- Old relationships are severed.
- Old debts and obligations are canceled.
- We are placed under the authority of a new father.
- The new father is considered owner of all the adoptee's possessions and is in control of his behavior.
- Adoption means that we owe no allegiance to our old masters (Gal.3:26–4:7).
- We owe total allegiance to God, and all that we have is His.
- God commits Himself to guide us and to discipline us that we might bring credit to His household.[3]

4. Adoption defined. Adoption is the giving to anyone the name and place and privileges of a son who is not a son by birth.[4]

5. The parable of the child nobody wanted. Two young ladies, one a social worker and the other a community health nurse, were summoned to the weather-beaten residence of an elderly woman in Gaithersburg, Pennsylvania. She had not been seen for several days. Phone calls had been unanswered. Mail was left in the mailbox. To the few who paid any attention to the ninety-year-old, childless widow, concern for her safety was rising.

Finding her frail, limp body in an overstuffed chair in the den at the back of the house, the nurse began checking vital signs. The house smelled musty and old. Violets lay black and lifeless in dry pots lined up in the window sills, their flowers long ago fallen and never picked up. An untouched glass of skim milk stood guard over the half-eaten bowl of oatmeal on the nearby T.V. tray. Bottles of prescription drugs lined the counter, but it had been days since they had been opened. Both women tried to make sense of it all as they waited for an ambulance to come to take the old woman to the hospital.

That's when fright replaced compassion. A noise from the attic let them know that they were not alone. At first, the social worker thought it might be a cat. She called, but no one answered. Curious, she made her way to the stairs that led to the makeshift second story, in reality an attic. The light switch produced no light at all. The hall was dark except for the faint daylight coming through an attic dormer. A door at the end of the hall was locked with a keyless deadbolt. The social worker turned the bolt and slowly opened the door. And there was a sixty-five-year-old man, gaunt, toothless, unbathed, soiled, with shoulder-length hair and a long, matted beard. When asked his name, he answered in a raspy whisper, "Me, Paul."

As far as anyone could determine, he had not been out of the house in more than thirty years. The attic in which he had lived for decades was hot and malodorous. A pot in one corner of the filthy room served as his toilet, and the unmade bed sagged in the middle where Paul had sat patiently waiting, wondering when his next meal would arrive. On the exposed mattress lay a carefully arranged collection of rocks.

Authorities could find no record of Paul's birth. A next-door neighbor's account, corroborated by files at a local public school, indicated that Lena (the ninety-year-old who died two days after Paul was discovered) and her husband, Gleason, a carpenter who died some thirty years earlier, were not his natural parents, but that Paul apparently had lived with them most of his life. The doctors determined that he had the mental capacity of a seven-year-old. He could not tie his shoes, bathe, or correctly use a knife and fork. He was partially deaf in both ears, and his speech was limited to "Me, Paul" and a few guttural sounds.

All that changed rather quickly. As Marian Smith Holmes, a reporter for *People Weekly,* put it when she met him, "Paul bends over his white leather sneakers, gathers the laces in his hands and deftly knots a neat bow. Standing up, he smooths his sweater vest and flashes a proud grin that stretches across his clean-shaven face. Such childlike joy at mastering a simple task might seem odd, but for Paul, thought to be unteachable, such small triumphs are profoundly delicious."[5]

What made the difference? Adoption. Someone cared. Someone opened their home to Paul and simply loved him.

Like it or not, there's a little bit of Paul in every one of us. Locked away and lonely. Dirty. Comfortable in the unmade, sagging condition of our lives. Wanting so much to hear an invitation to come, but not really sure what it means to sit at the table. Some searching for themselves, others knowing little more than "Me, Paul." Helpless. Abandoned. Dying without even knowing it. Surrounded by the filth and stench of our own lives.

And then Jesus comes along and changes it all. He unlocks the door and removes the barriers that kept us from knowing Him. He rescues us from certain death. He takes us into His care and washes away the stain of sin. We are chosen. Adopting the child nobody wanted, He gives us a home.

TEACHING THE BIBLE

- *Main Idea:* God is worthy of our praise.
- *Suggested Teaching Aim:* To lead adults to praise God.

A TEACHING OUTLINE

1. *Greeting (Eph. 1:1, 2)*
2. *Doxology of Praise to God (Eph. 1:3–14)*

Introduce the Bible Study

Use No. 2, "Adopting the Children Nobody Wanted," and number 3, "What Happens in Adoption" in "Applying the Bible" to introduce the lesson.

Search for Biblical Truth

IN ADVANCE:

- Plan an illustrated lecture for this lesson.
- Make the two outline strip posters of "A Teaching Outline" above.
- Copy the six statements in "Summary of Bible Truths" on a large sheet of paper.
- Make a theological word list of significant words in the lesson. Write the words on posters and write the definitions on separate posters. Place all posters at random on the wall.

Grace	God's unmerited favor for sinners
Peace	Guards our hearts and minds
Saints	People set apart by God and for God
Predestined	Emphasizes God's sovereign grace in salvation
Glory	The majestic fullness of God
Redemption	Deliverance from sin's captivity at the cost of the blood of Christ
Forgiveness	Removing of sin as a barrier to fellowship with God
Sealed	Indicates document is under protection of owner
Earnest	Guarantee of a full payment at a later date

Place the first strip poster on the wall. Ask a volunteer to read Ephesians 1:1, 2. Using the material in "Studying the Bible": (1) explain to whom Ephesians is written, (2) explain two terms Paul used to describe believers (v. 1), (3) define "grace," "peace," and "saints." (See the lesson on June 25 for a definition of "peace.") Ask members to match the appropriate theological word with the correct definition.

DISCUSS: What implication can you draw for our lives from the three terms Paul used to describe believers?

Place the second strip poster on the wall. Ask a volunteer to read Ephesians 1:3–14. Using the material in "Studying the Bible," (1) explain how God is the source of every good thing; (2) define "predestined," "glory," "redemption," "forgiveness," "sealed," "earnest"; (3) explain the process of spiritual adoption; (4) explain that our human freedom is a result of God's sovereign decision to create us that way. Ask members to match the appropriate theological word with the correct definition.

DISCUSS: If we are to be "the praise of his glory," how can we praise God?

Give the Truth a Personal Focus

Distribute paper and pencils to members. Display the six summary statements and read them aloud to the class. Ask members to choose one of these statements and write a paragraph to describe how this statement could help them learn to be effective followers of Christ this coming week. As an alternate idea, if you choose not to do this individually, you can use the six statements to lead a group discussion with the entire class or organize members in six groups and assign each group one of the statements.

Use number 5, "The Parable of the Child Nobody Wanted," in "Applying the Bible" to conclude the lesson.

---

1. Gregg Zoroya, "Fighting for a Child's Right to Be Loved," *Good Housekeeping,* March 1997, 24.
2. Marilyn Johnson, "What Happens to Children Nobody Wants?" *Life,* May 1997, 56.
3. Lawrence O. Richards, *Expository Dictionary of Bible Words* (Regency/Zondervan, 1985), 20–21.
4. *Eaton's Bible Dictionary.*
5. Marian Smith Holmes, *People Weekly,* May 29, 1989, 42.

Called to Oneness in Christ

July

9

2000

Background Passage: Ephesians 2:1–22

Focal Passage: Ephesians 2:8–22

Ephesians 2 is the heart of the letter. In this chapter Paul set forth in some detail God's eternal plan to reconcile Jews and Gentiles into one new kind of humanity in Christ.

Study Aim: *To describe God's plan for making Jews and Gentiles one in Christ.*

STUDYING THE BIBLE

OUTLINE AND SUMMARY

- **I. Saved from Death unto Life (Eph. 2:1–10)**
  1. **Dead in sins (2:1–3)**
  2. **Made alive in Christ (2:4–7)**
  3. **By grace through faith unto good works (2:8–10)**
- **II. Reconciled from Alienation to Oneness (Eph. 2:11–22)**
  1. **Alienated from God and others (2:11, 12)**
  2. **Christ the peacemaker (2:13–15)**
  3. **Reconciled to God and one another (2:16–18)**
  4. **The church as one family (2:19–22)**

Sinners are dead in sins (vv. 1–3) until they are made alive in Christ (vv. 4–7). They are saved by God's grace through faith unto a life of good works (vv. 8–10). Unsaved Gentiles were once alienated from God and from God's people (vv. 11, 12). Through His death, Christ became the peacemaker for those who are in Him (vv. 13–15). Christ reconciled Jewish and Gentile believers to God in one body (vv. 16–18). The church is like a united nation, a family of faith and love, and a holy temple for God's Spirit (vv. 19–22).

I. Saved from Death unto Life (Eph. 2:1–10)

1. Dead in sins (vv. 1–3)

Paul reminded believers that they once lived under the devil's control. Although they were alive physically, they were spiritually dead in sins.

2. Made alive in Christ (vv. 4–7)

God in Christ made them come alive by saving them from their sins. Paul used several similar words to describe what this revealed about God: love, kindness, grace, mercy.

3. By grace through faith unto good works (vv. 8–10)

8 For by grace are ye saved through faith; and that not of yourselves: it is the gift of God:

9 Not of works, lest any man should boast.

10 For we are his workmanship, created in Christ Jesus unto good works, which God hath before ordained that we should walk in them.

Verses 8 and 9 are the most familiar verses in Ephesians, and they should be. They sum up the way to be saved. Many people do not quote or memorize verse 10 also. These three verses belong together; for they state the source of salvation ("by grace"), the necessary human response ("through faith"), and the result of being saved ("unto good works").

Paul fought a two-front war against opposite distortions of salvation. On one hand were those who insisted that keeping the Law was the means of deserving God's acceptance. This is still the most common misunderstanding of Christianity. People confuse living a Christian life with becoming a Christian. On the other hand, Paul had to deal with people who said that if good works are not necessary for salvation, they are unimportant in how Christians live. The sinful living of many professing Christians is evidence that this is still a big problem.

Paul's message to the first group is that none of us is good enough to deserve God's acceptance. We are sinners who need to be saved. This is possible only by God's grace. It is not of ourselves; "it is the gift of God: Not of works." Thus, none can boast; all can only praise God. The message to sinful church members is that although we were not saved by good works, we are saved "unto good works." However, even these fruits of a saved life are possible only by the grace and power of God. "We are his workmanship, created in Christ Jesus unto good works."

II. Reconciled from Alienation to Oneness (Eph. 2:11–22)

1. Alienated from God and others (vv. 11, 12)

11 Wherefore remember, that ye being in time past Gentiles in the flesh, who are called Uncircumcision by that which is called the Circumcision in the flesh made by hands;

12 That at that time ye were without Christ, being aliens from the commonwealth of Israel, and strangers from the covenants of promise, having no hope, and without God in the world.

Paul reminded Gentile Christians of their alienated state before they met Christ. Verse 11 reflects the disdain Jews felt toward Gentiles. The Jews called Gentiles, "uncircumcision." They took pride in being "the circumcision," because the ritual signified that they were God's chosen people.

"Without Christ" may refer to the fact that they had no hope of the Messiah (Christ). This parallels the next two descriptions: They were foreigners (aliens) from the chosen nation of Israel and thus "strangers from the covenants of promise." The most devastating description of the pagan Gentiles was that they had "no hope" and were "without God." They had lots of hopes in the same way that people hope for many things, but they had no real hope of life—either here or hereafter. The crux of their plight was that they did not know God. They had many gods, but not the one true God.

Sin alienates from God and from others. When Adam and Eve sinned, they were separated from God and from each other. This aspect of alienation became obvious when Cain murdered Abel.

2. Christ the Peacemaker (vv. 13–15)

13 But now in Christ Jesus ye who sometimes were far off are made nigh by the blood of Christ.

14 For he is our peace, who hath made both one, and hath broken down the middle wall of partition between us;

15 Having abolished in his flesh the enmity, even the law of commandments contained in ordinances; for to make in himself of twain one new man, so making peace.

"But now" introduces a striking contrast because of two things: "the blood of Christ" and being "in Christ Jesus." "God was in Christ, reconciling the world unto himself" (2 Cor. 5:19). The death of Jesus is the means for reconciling sinners to God and to one another. However, this avails only if they are "in Christ Jesus." Christ is in each of them, and all of them are in the same Christ—thus brothers and sisters in Him. The Gentile sinners who were "far off" from God and the chosen people of Israel have now been "made nigh" to both God and Jewish believers.

Christ is "our peace." He is the peacemaker through whom God reconciles sinners to God and one another. Christ has made both Jewish and Gentile believers "one." He did this by breaking down the wall of sin and the walls that sin erects. Paul referred to the "middle wall of partition." This may refer to the barriers of hostility that sin had built between Jews and Gentiles, but Paul likely had in mind a specific wall that epitomized that barrier.

Gentiles were not allowed into the worship area of the Jewish temple. They were restricted to the outer court. A screen separated that court from the next court, into which Jews could enter. A sign on the screen warned Gentiles that they would be put to death if they went past that screen.

When Jesus died, the veil in the innermost part of the temple was torn from top to bottom. This signified that God had opened access to Himself. The screen that excluded Gentiles was not literally destroyed in the same way that the veil was torn; however, Paul said that it may as well have been as far as God is concerned. God opened access for sinners to come to Him, but He opened access not only for Jews but also for Gentiles.

Verse 15 makes the same point in a different way. Christ "abolished in his flesh the enmity" between Jewish and Gentile believers. Paul saw the Jewish law as part of the basis for the enmity. This was not the Law as God intended it to be, but the law as groups like the Pharisees had made it. They used the law and their traditions about the law to thwart God's concern for people. During His ministry, Jesus often clashed with the Pharisees over this issue. In His death, Jesus did away with the kind of legalism that excluded other people from God unless they met the standards of the Pharisees.

The end result of all this was that Christ made of the two alienated groups—Jews and Gentiles—"one new man, so making peace." Christ makes a new person of each Christian, and He makes a new kind of community of believers. The "one new man" in verse 15 is the new people of God. Christ the peacemaker has made peace between the former enemies.

3. Reconciled to God and one another (vv. 16–18)

16 And that he might reconcile both unto God in one body by the cross, having slain the enmity thereby:

17 And came and preached peace to you which were afar off, and to them that were nigh.

18 For through him we both have access by one Spirit unto the Father.

For the first time in the passage, the word *reconcile* appears. The idea runs through the entire passage. Christ made possible a twofold reconciliation that corresponds to the twofold alienation caused by sin. Sin separates from God and others; Christ reconciles to God and others. He reconciled both Jewish and Gentile believers "unto God in one body." The church is the body of Christ to which he referred (1:22, 23). The words "by the cross" are parallel to "by the blood of Christ" in verse 13. The cross was the means of destroying the old animosity.

Christ the peacemaker preached inclusiveness of all sinners during His earthly ministry. After His resurrection and ascension, His Spirit preached twofold reconciliation through people like Paul. Christ calls both Jews and Gentiles to peace with God and thus to peace with fellow believers.

Christ was God's way of opening access to Himself, and God's Spirit is the way this happens. Verse 18 is an excellent example of the one God at work as Father, Son, and Spirit. Through Christ believers have access by one Spirit to the heavenly Father. There are not two Holy Spirits, one for Jews and another for Gentiles. God's one Spirit binds together as one all who come to God through Christ by the one Spirit.

4. The church as one family (vv. 19–22)

19 Now therefore ye are no more strangers and foreigners, but fellowcitizens with the saints, and of the household of God;

20 And are built upon the foundation of the apostles and prophets, Jesus Christ himself being the chief corner stone;

21 In whom all the building fitly framed together groweth unto an holy temple in the Lord:

22 In whom ye also are builded together for an habitation of God through the Spirit.

These verses describe the "one body" resulting from the reconciliation of Jews and Gentiles in Christ. Gentiles, who had once been "strangers and foreigners" (v. 19), are now "fellowcitizens with the saints." That is, they are equally citizens of God's kingdom.

Paul also described them as "of the household of God." That is, they are members of God's one family of faith and love.

Whether the church is compared to a nation or a family, it is built on the solid foundation of the witness to Jesus Christ that was borne by the apostles and prophets. Christ is sometimes compared to the foundation (1 Cor. 3:10) and sometimes to the chief cornerstone, but He is head of the church in either case.

Verses 21 and 22 carry forward this building analogy by comparing the church to a holy temple. Under the old covenant, the temple signified the presence of God among His people. That foreshadowed the spiritual temple of the people of God in whom dwells the presence of God by His Spirit. Each Christian is a temple of the Holy Spirit (1 Cor. 6:19, 20), and the church is also a temple of the Holy Spirit of God (1 Cor. 3:17).

SUMMARY OF BIBLE TRUTHS

1. Sinners are saved by grace through faith unto good works.
2. Sin separates us from God and from other people.
3. Christ died to make reconciliation possible.
4. He reconciles believers to God and to other believers.
5. The one family of God is the result of reconciliation.
6. God's purpose is oneness of all believers in Christ.

APPLYING THE BIBLE

1. Saving grace. Vance Havner used the following acrostic to teach the valuable truths of grace.[1]

G stands for Gift, the principle of grace.

R stands for Redemption, the purpose of grace.

A stands for Access, the privilege of grace.

C stands for Character, the product of grace.

E stands for Eternal Life, the prospect of grace.

2. Fellowship. "A man finds his identity by identifying. A man's identity is not best thought of as the way in which he is separated from his fellows but the way in which he is united with them" (Robert Terwilliger).

3. Oneness/unity. The love that unites Christians is stronger than the differences that divide them.

4. Called to fellowship. "God calls us not to solitary sainthood, but to fellowship in a company of committed men" (David Schuller).

5. No hope. What would you do with ten million dollars in prize money? What would you do to claim your winnings if you were misled into thinking they were yours already? A single mother of two borrowed $1,500 from her sister so she could fly to Florida to claim a ten million dollar prize. But when she showed up at the offices representing a publishing conglomerate, the only thing she got was ridicule from a non-caring receptionist. The woman was misled by advertising that appeared to say she was one of two winning ticket holders competing for an eleven million dollar prize.

She had a hope; the only problem was, it was a false hope. It was based on something that had no substance in fact. The lesson text for today reminds us that once we were a people of no hope. Then we were brought close by the blood of Christ. The only hope for individual reconciliation, global reconciliation, and lasting reconciliation finds its substance in Jesus' atoning work on the cross. All other offers are false hopes.

6. Bridging the gap. Time and the elements have taken their toll on one of the nation's oldest covered bridges. In 1994, an ambulance attempting to pick up a six-year-old girl had to make a half-hour detour because the timbers of the old bridge couldn't bear the weight. Constructed in 1829, the Haverhill-Bath covered bridge tilts downstream and can barely support its own weight. With only a three-ton limit, the covering over the bridge offers low clearance and narrow width, making it unsafe for anything more than one car at a time.

Christ gave Himself as a bridge to all who would dare cross over from death to eternal life. The bridge is not weathered and worn, even though it predates the Haverhill-Bath bridge by some 1,800 years. It stands before every living person, offering a chance to cross over. There simply are no detours, and there will never be another way. You must cross the bridge.

TEACHING THE BIBLE

- *Main Idea:* God has made one body all people who accept Christ.
- *Suggested Teaching Aim:* To lead adults to recognize that all people who accept Christ are part of Christ's body.

A TEACHING OUTLINE

1. *Saved from Death unto Life (Eph. 2:1–10)*
2. *Reconciled from Alienation to Oneness (Eph. 2:11–22)*

Introduce the Bible Study

Use number 1, "Saving Grace," in "Applying the Bible" to introduce the lesson.

Search for Biblical Truth

IN ADVANCE:

- Write on a chalkboard or a large sheet of paper:

Then Now

- Enlist two readers; one will read aloud the seven summary statements under "Outline and Summary" and the other will read the corresponding Scripture.

Call on the two enlisted readers to read the seven summary statements and the Scripture to overview the lesson. Ask the first reader to read a summary statement and then the other reader to read the corresponding Scripture.

Explain that this chapter is the heart of Ephesians and today's lesson will help adults recognize that all people who accept Christ are part of

Christ's body. Point to the words *Then* and *Now* on the chalkboard. Explain that Paul describes the Ephesians by who they had been before and after they came to know Christ. Ask half the class (Group 1) to listen for characteristics of the Ephesians before they came to know Christ and the other half (Group 2) for characteristics after they came to know Christ.

Ask members to look at 2:1–7. Briefly summarize these statements by reading from "Studying the Bible" the two sentences under "1. Dead in sins" and the one sentence in "2. Made alive in Christ." Ask groups to suggest what words should go on the chart. (They should have something like "Dead in Sins" and "Alive in Christ.")

Ask members to look at verses 8–10. Write on a chalkboard (omit italicized words):

The Way to Be Saved	
The source of salvation	Grace
The necessary human response	Faith
The result of salvation	Good Works

Ask: What is the source of salvation? What is the necessary human response to God's grace? What is the result of salvation?

DISCUSS: Where are you in this response to salvation? Have you accepted God's grace? Have you responded in faith? Are you engaging in good works? Point out the necessary order in which these must come.

Ask members to look at verses 11 and 12. Ask the groups to suggest words for the chart. (*Then:* Uncircumcision, without Christ, aliens, strangers, no hope, without God; *Now:* Circumcision.)

Ask members to look at verses 13–15. Point out that the words "But now" introduce a striking contrast between the past and the present. Ask: According to verse 13, what made the difference? (Blood of Christ.) Ask Group 2 to suggest words for the chart. (Christ is their peace, made one in Jesus, partition broken down, abolished enmity, made peace.) Explain that as a result of these, the Ephesians were a part of the new people of God.

Ask members to look at verses 16–18. Ask both groups to search these verses to find before and after characteristics of the Ephesians. (*Then:* separated from God and others; *Now:* reconciled to God and others.)

Ask both groups to look at verses 19–22 to find before and after characteristics of the Ephesians. (*Then:* strangers, foreigners; *Now:* fellow citizens, household of God, built on foundation of apostles and prophets, Christ as cornerstone, God's dwelling.)

Give the Truth a Personal Focus

Use number 5, "No Hope," in "Applying the Bible" to close the session. Remind members that God has formed into one body all people who accept Christ. Close in a time of silence in which class members examine their own lives to be sure they have accepted Christ.

---

1. Vance Havner, *The Vance Havner Notebook*, compiled by Dennis J. Hester (Grand Rapids: Baker Book House, 1989), 118.

Called to Use Your Spiritual Gifts

Background Passage: Ephesians 4:1–16
Focal Passage: Ephesians 4:1–16

Like many of Paul's letters, Ephesians begins with doctrinal truths and concludes with exhortations based on those truths. Ephesians 1–3 presents the great truths of God's purpose in Christ; Ephesians 4–6 contains practical applications for Christians. Ephesians 4:1–16 focuses on the role of gifted people in the oneness and maturity of the church.

Study Aim: *To describe the importance of exercising personal spiritual gifts.*

STUDYING THE BIBLE

OUTLINE AND SUMMARY

I. Christian Calling (Eph. 4:1–6)
  1. Appeal for worthy living (4:1–3)
  2. Marks of oneness (4:4–6)
II. Christ's Gifts to the Church (Eph. 4:7–12)
  1. Gifts of grace (4:7–10)
  2. Gifts of gifted people (4:11, 12)
III. Church Growth (Eph. 4:13–16)
  1. Goal of growth (4:13)
  2. Means of growth (4:14–16)

Paul appealed for Christians to live worthy of their common calling (vv. 1–3). The hope of their calling involved unity of Spirit (vv. 4–6). Christ gives gifts to believers and then gives gifted people to the church (vv. 7–10). The pastor's role is to equip church members for the work of ministry of the body of Christ (vv. 11, 12). The goal of church growth is maturity in Christ (v. 13). The body of Christ grows toward its purpose as all church members act in mature faith and love to do their part (vv. 14–16).

I. Christian Calling (Eph. 4:1–6)

1. Appeal for worthy living (vv. 1–3)

1 I therefore, the prisoner of the Lord, beseech you that ye walk worthy of the vocation wherewith ye are called,

2 With all lowliness and meekness, with longsuffering, forbearing one another in love;

3 Endeavouring to keep the unity of the Spirit in the bond of peace.

"Beseech" marks the beginning of Paul's appeal. Verse 1 sets the tone for the rest of the letter. His basic appeal was that believers live in a way worthy of their calling.

"Vocation" means "calling," which is the noun form of the verb translated "called." Calling is an important idea in the Bible in general, and in Ephesians in particular (1:18; 4:4). All Christians have one calling in common, and each Christian has a personal calling. The general calling describes those things to which all of us have been called as children of God. A personal calling includes one's individual gifts and ways to do one's part in fulfilling the larger calling.

Verses 2 and 3 list some aspects of the calling we all have from God. Verse 2 shows that He expects all of us to strive to be humble, gentle, patient, forbearing, and loving. All of these qualities were considered signs of weakness and inferiority in first-century society. "Lowliness" is a humble spirit, which is the opposite of self-exaltation. "Meekness" means the kind of gentleness that is considerate of others, the opposite of self-assertion.

"Longsuffering" refers to patience in dealing with others, especially those who annoy you or hurt you. "Forbearing one another in love" means living at peace with people who sometimes annoy you or rub you the wrong way. Ephesians 4:32 mentions also the need for forgiving one another, which is needed when someone has hurt you.

Verse 3 grows directly out of God's purpose of oneness of believers in Christ. "Endeavouring" means to give diligence to something, in this case, "to keep the unity of the Spirit in the bond of peace." Ephesians 2:11–22 described the oneness or unity created by Christ through His Spirit. "Peace" is what binds believers together as one in the Spirit.

2. Marks of oneness (vv. 4–6)

4 There is one body, and one Spirit, even as ye are called in one hope of your calling;

5 One Lord, one faith, one baptism,

6 One God and Father of all, who is above all, and through all, and in you all.

Paul listed seven marks of oneness of believers. "One body, and one Spirit" comes from Ephesians 2:16 and 18. The last part of verse 4 goes back to 1:18 and sums up the theme of Ephesians 1–3. "One hope of your calling" was Paul's way of emphasizing that our hope is bound up with God's purpose, not with our individual hopes. Thus, the fulfillment of Christian hope is the consummation of God's redemptive purpose.

Our saving experience with Christ involved "one Lord, one faith, one baptism." "One God and Father of all" is "the God and Father of our Lord Jesus Christ" (1:3). The doxology in 1:3–14 and the marks of oneness in 4:4 and 5 show that His oneness is incapable of being isolated and defined in one way by human minds. The last part of verse 6 reinforces this broad concept of His oneness. He "is above all, and through all, and in you all."

II. Christ's Gifts to the Church (Eph. 4:7–12)

1. Gifts of grace (vv. 7–10)

7 But unto every one of us is given grace according to the measure of the gift of Christ.

8 Wherefore he saith, When he ascended up on high, he led captivity captive, and gave gifts unto men.

9 (Now that he ascended, what is it but that he also descended first into the lower parts of the earth?

10 He that descended is the same also that ascended up far above all heavens, that he might fill all things.)

These verses show that the "unity of the Spirit" does not mean "uniformity," but unity of many diverse parts. Each Christian "is given grace." We received grace when we were saved (2:8, 9), but we also received grace when Christ gave us gifts of grace. All believers have received from Christ gifts of grace. "According to the measure" implies the diversity of the gifts.

Verse 8 is Psalm 68:18, adapted to make Paul's point. In Psalm 68:18, God is the victor who is given gifts. In Ephesians 4:8, Christ is given gifts, which He in turn imparts to others. Verses 9 and 10 interpret Paul's intention in adapting Psalm 68:18 the way he did. He pictures Christ's descent to earth, where He won the victory. Then when He ascended, He distributed gifts to His people.

2. Gifts of gifted people (vv. 11, 12)

11 And he gave some, apostles; and some, prophets; and some, evangelists; and some, pastors and teachers;

12 For the perfecting of the saints, for the work of the ministry, for the edifying of the body of Christ.

Instead of listing spiritual gifts as he did in Romans 12:6–8 and 1 Corinthians 12, Paul listed gifted people as the gifts of Christ to the church. Each of these groups had received spiritual gifts that qualified them to be given as gifts to the church. In other words, "apostles," "prophets," "evangelists," and "pastors and teachers" are gifts that Christ gave to the church. Isn't this the most natural way to understand what he meant in verse 11?

"Apostles" was used primarily of those eyewitnesses of the risen Lord whom Christ appointed as His apostles. "Prophets" were those who exercised the Spirit-led gift of plain speaking of God's message. "Evangelists" went from place to place telling the good news. "Pastors and teachers" probably refers to one person who served as a shepherd and teacher of the flock. Thus, your pastor is one of God's gifts to your congregation.

The relationship between verses 11 and 12 is crucial. How we understand this relationship determines how we view the role of the pastor and the church in ministry. The King James Version sounds as if Paul was listing three equal tasks of a pastor-teacher: to perfect or equip the saints (Christians), to do the work of the ministry, and to build up the body of Christ. And that is how many pastors and many laypeople view the role of the pastor. Church members hire him to do the work of the ministry.

The Greek manuscripts did not have the kind of punctuation marks that appear in our English translations. The use of punctuation, therefore, is a choice of translators. Suppose we left out the commas in verse 12, especially the first comma. How does that change the meaning and application? Then Paul was saying that the role of the pastor-teacher is to equip Christians for the work of the ministry so that the body of Christ will be built up. Most people today believe that was Paul's meaning. It is consistent with the rest of the New Testament, which teaches that every Christian is a minister, a saint, and a priest.

In verse 7, Paul wrote that "every one of us is given grace according to the measure of the gift of Christ." Each Christian has at least one spiritual gift. These gifts differ from person to person. The body of Christ is able to minister to the world and to the needy in its midst only as all the members use their gifts for the advancement of the cause of Christ. The idea of a professional clergy to do the work of the ministry developed after biblical times. The recovery of the meaning of Ephesians 4:12 is revolutionizing the work of pastors and church members.

III. Church Growth (Eph. 4:13–16)

1. Goal of growth (v. 13)

13 Till we all come in the unity of the faith, and of the knowledge of the Son of God, unto a perfect man, unto the measure of the stature of the fulness of Christ.

This statement of the goal of church growth is only another way of saying what Paul had been saying earlier. Notice "we all." When all Christians mature fully in faith, hope, and love, they will reflect the likeness of Christ. This is the "fulness of Christ." This is when all things will be subject to Christ, the head of all things, including the church (1:21–23). This is when Jewish and Gentile believers are in one family of faith and love and become a temple for the presence of the Spirit of God (2:15, 20–22). This is when all believers will be filled with the fulness of God's presence, love, and power (3:14–19). This is when the body of Christ will be built up to its intended perfection.

2. Means of growth (vv. 14–16)

14 That we henceforth be no more children, tossed to and fro, and carried about with every wind of doctrine, by the sleight of men, and cunning craftiness, whereby they lie in wait to deceive;

15 But speaking the truth in love, may grow up into him in all things, which is the head, even Christ:

16 From whom the whole body fitly joined together and compacted by that which every joint supplieth, according to the effectual working in the measure of every part, maketh increase of the body unto the edifying of itself in love.

In order for the body of Christ to mature, each member must mature. Too many believers are not mature enough in the faith to tell truth from error. As long as they remain so immature, they are easy prey for all the clever deceivers who can speak lies as if they were the truth. Such immature believers are like a helpless ship blown about by every wind that comes along.

Truth is important, but so is love. They are inseparable. Thus, mature Christians learn to "speak the truth in love." Truth without love can be devastating. Love without truth can degenerate into sentimentalism. Together the truth spoken in love fulfills its true purpose of honoring Him, who is truth and love personified.

Verse 16 is hard to translate and interpret. The main point seems to be that the entire body of Christ will function properly and with maturity when all the parts (which consist of church members) work together to fulfill the work of the body of Christ.

SUMMARY OF BIBLE TRUTHS

1. Christians are to live lives worthy of their divine calling.
2. Christians share one calling, and each Christian has an individual calling.
3. Christians must work at maintaining harmony in the church.
4. Each believer is gifted by Christ and given to the church.
5. The work of the ministry belongs to every member of the body.
6. The church grows as Christians mature in faith and love.

All Christians Are Ministers

1. The pastor equips Christians for the work of the ministry of the body of Christ (Eph. 4:11, 12).
2. Each member of Christ's body is important (1 Cor. 12:14–29).
3. All members have spiritual gifts to be used for the good of the body (Rom. 12:6–8).

Saints

1. "Saints" are sinners who have been sanctified, or set apart by and for God (1 Cor. 6:9–11).
2. All Christians are saints (Eph. 1:1; 4:12).
3. Even Saint Paul was not perfect, but he was pressing on (Phil. 3:12–14).

Priests

1. Because Christ is our High Priest, each of us has access to God through Him (Heb. 4:14–16).
2. Old covenant promises of a kingdom of priests are fulfilled in Christians (1 Pet. 2:9; Rev. 1:6).
3. Christians offer sacrifices (Rom. 12:1; Heb. 13:15, 16).

APPLYING THE BIBLE

1. Gifted to get the job done. Perhaps you have heard the slogan, "The difficult we do immediately; the impossible takes a little longer." This slogan could be very appropriate for the church. We have the promise of God's presence as we faithfully do His will. He has also given spiritual gifts to us to enable us to minister effectively through the church. Nothing is impossible to those who believe.

2. Ways to a healthier walk. A healthy walk is intentional. That is why we use the word *discipline* to describe it. Walking with God requires discipline. But the benefits are well worth it. Walking in a manner worthy of our calling requires that we answer four basic diagnostic questions. The answers have a direct bearing on the next step we take in our walk. At times, correction is needed. At other times, the confirmation helps in the days that are marked by difficulty and the occasional doubt.

The worship question. Am I consistent in the discipline of private and corporate worship? Am I in right relationship to others so that my worship is not hindered? Do I offer God a clean vessel by confessing my sin?

The attention question. Have I allowed my affections and my attentions to be drawn off of God and on to something that He has already condemned or judged?

The learning question. What is God teaching me in my quiet times with Him? Am I abiding and learning anything that is helping the image of Christ to become more evident in my life to others?

The knowing question. Is my knowledge of God growing more intimate as a result of the disciplines of my walk with Him, or am I simply going through the routines of a tradition that has become an idol in itself?

3. One body. A child was moved to write a letter to God to express his thanks for the way his mother was designed. While the references in the letter show an obvious love for his mother, it also demonstrates the lesson that God puts the church together so it can function like a body.

> Dear God,
>
> I like the way you built my mommy. She's really special and I like all her different parts. She has the perfect lap. It's just the right size for me to sit in whenever I am lonely or afraid. Her arms are just long enough to give me a hug all over. Her hands are soft when I hold them, tender when they bathe me, and smart enough to make things that I didn't know mommies knew how to make. I like the way her hair smells. Her fingers are pretty. I like the way they scratch my back at night when it's past bedtime. And mommy's eyes always sparkle when they see me after a long day. I think she can see something about me that no one else can. Maybe that's why she stares at me sometimes. Mommy has to have strong feet because there are so many places that she has to take me. And I like the way her lips turn into a smile each time she says my name. God, the most important part about my mommy is something I cannot see. You gave her a special heart that is big enough to take care of everything and still find time to love me.
>
> Thank you, God,
>
> AMEN

4. Is your church like a train? Someone once said, "The church is fairly well supplied with conductors. It shows a shortage of engineers, but an over supply of brakemen."

5. When does the service begin? A visitor entered a gathering of Quakers as they met for worship. Unfamiliar with the way in which

Quakers worship, the visitor sat quietly with the others in the room. Not much was said (as is customary) and the visitor looked again at his watch to make sure he had arrived at the time indicated in the yellow pages. Finally, he leaned over to one of the brethren sitting beside him and whispered, "When does the service begin?" The worshiper whispered back, "The service begins when the worship is complete."

This is as it should be. We gather for worship and the body of Christ (the church) is equipped for ministry. At the benediction, a week of service begins. Spiritual gifts and the unique calling of God make it so.

6. What is a church? "A church is not a museum, an exhibition of saints, a show-ring of pious purebreds. A church is a school. A group of people in various stages of development, from beginners in the Christian life with the dirt of the world still on them to those clad in white robes of the saints."[1]

7. Gifts. What you are is God's gift to you; what you become is your gift to God.

TEACHING THE BIBLE

- *Main Idea:* God has given each believer certain spiritual gifts to exercise for the church's benefit.
- *Suggested Teaching Aim:* To lead adults to describe the importance of exercising their personal spiritual gifts.

A TEACHING OUTLINE

1. *Christian Calling (Eph. 4:1–6)*
2. *Christ's Gifts to the Church (Eph. 4:7–12)*
3. *Church Growth (Eph. 4:13–16)*

Introduce the Bible Study

Place a large sheet of paper on the wall. Draw an outline of a human on it. As members enter, ask them to go to the figure and write their name at the appropriate place to indicate their gift for the church. For example, if they see their gift as ministry, write their name on the body's hands. Let each person explain what gifts he or she has.

Search for Biblical Truth

IN ADVANCE, number and write the six summary statements from "Outline and Summary" on large strips of paper and tape them to the backs of six chairs.

Ask the first member to read aloud the first statement. Ask, How are Christians to live? (Worthy of their calling.) Continue this with the rest of the statements and these questions:

(2) What is the hope of our calling? (Unity of spirit.)
(3) Why does Christ give gifts to believers? (To serve the church.)
(4) What is the pastor's/staff's role? (Equip.)
(5) What is the goal of church growth? (Maturity in Christ.)

(6) How does the body of Christ grow? (All members acting in mature faith and desiring to do their part.)

Explain that Paul's letters normally contained two parts: doctrine and application. The first part normally contains doctrine and the latter part contains application. Point out that Ephesians 4 begins the application part of Paul's letter.

On a chalkboard write, *What?* Ask members to glance back over the first three chapters of Ephesians and list some doctrines Paul mentioned. List doctrines under *What?* Now write *So What?* on the chalkboard. Explain that today's lesson will help explain what difference the doctrine makes.

Ask members to look at 4:1–6. Ask, What qualities (v. 2) did Paul suggest believers ought to have if they are to "walk worthy"? How does the world look at these characteristics?

Ask members to look at verses 5 and 6. On a chalkboard write (omit italicized responses):

Oneness in Christ

Marks of Oneness	Scripture Reference
Body	2:16
Spirit	2:18
Hope	1:18
Lord	1:2
Faith	2:8
Baptism	–
God and Father	1:3

Ask, What marks of oneness did Paul suggest believers should have? List these on the chalkboard. Then add the Scripture references and ask members to look them up to see how these marks are a development of Paul's earlier statements.

Ask members to look at 4:7–12. Ask: Who has been given spiritual gifts? (Every believer.) Who gave the gifts? (Christ.)

DISCUSS: Why do you think Paul listed gifted people instead of gifts in verse 12?

Use the material in "Studying the Bible" to explain how removing the commas in verse 12 makes the text say something quite different. (With commas, the verse means that God gave the pastor/staff to do the work of perfecting, ministry, edifying; without the commas, it means God gave the pastor/staff to perfect the saints so they can do the work of ministry and build up the body of Christ.) Ask: Which interpretation is more biblical? Why? Which one does our church follow?

Ask members to look at verses 13–16 and find the goal of church growth (unity) and the means of achieving that goal (maturity). Ask: What is required for believers to mature? What indicates that we are immature (v. 14b)? What does verse 15 suggest is the evidence that we have matured?

Read all six of the "Summary of Bible Truths."

Give the Truth a Personal Focus

Use number 5, "When Does the Service Begin?" in "Applying the Bible" to close the lesson.

---

1. Vern McLessan, *Quips, Quotes, and Quests* (Eugene, Oregon: Harvest House Publishers, 1982), 40.

Called to Responsible Living

Background Passage: Ephesians 5:1–6:4

Focal Passages: Ephesians 5:1–5, 21–29; 6:1–4

Ephesians 5:1–6:4 is the heart of Paul's ethical exhortations in chapters 4–6. Living worthy of their calling as Christians meant living as Christians in a non-Christian society. This kind of responsible Christian living applied especially to Christian families.

Study Aim: *To summarize the responsibilities of each member of a Christian family.*

STUDYING THE BIBLE

OUTLINE AND SUMMARY

- **I. Christian Conduct in a Sinful World (Eph. 5:1–20)**
  - **1. Love versus lust (5:1–7)**
  - **2. Light versus darkness (5:8–14)**
  - **3. Wisdom versus folly (5:15–20)**
- **II. Christian Family Relationships (Eph. 5:21–6:4)**
  - **1. Wives and husbands (5:21–33)**
  - **2. Children and parents (6:1–4)**

Children of God are to live in self-giving love and to avoid sexual immorality in deed and word (5:1–7). They are to live as children of light and avoid works of darkness (5:8–14). They are to live wisely, avoiding the foolish ways of sinful society (5:15–20). Christian marriage involves voluntary submission by wives to husbands who practice self-giving love (5:21–33). Children are to honor their parents, who in turn are to raise the children to be Christians (6:1–4).

I. Christian Conduct in a Sinful World (Eph. 5:1–20)

1. Love versus lust (5:1–7)

1 Be ye therefore followers of God, as dear children;

2 And walk in love, as Christ also hath loved us, and hath given himself for us an offering and a sacrifice to God for a sweetsmelling savour.

"Followers" means "imitators." "Dear" translates a word meaning "beloved." Thus, Paul called Christians to live godly lives because of the love the Father has for His children.

"Therefore" ties chapter 5 to chapter 4. Paul had just instructed believers to avoid any form of anger and hatred toward one another (4:31). Instead they were to forgive one another as God in Christ had forgiven them (4:32). This connection is clear in 5:2. Christians are to "walk in love." The word for "love" is the self-giving love of God in sending His Son (John 3:16). This is the love shown by the Son's giving Himself for the salvation of sinners in obedience to the will of God.

3 But fornication, and all uncleanness, or covetousness, let it not be once named among you, as becometh saints;

4 Neither filthiness, nor foolish talking, nor jesting, which are not convenient: but rather giving of thanks.

5 For this ye know, that no whoremonger, nor unclean person, nor covetous man, who is an idolater, hath any inheritance in the kingdom of Christ and of God.

First-century society was notoriously immoral. "Fornication" includes any sexual relations outside the one-flesh union of marriage. "Uncleanness" describes the moral filthiness of such sins. "Covetousness" means wanting something someone else has. Usually, it refers to greed and envy over material possessions. That may be its meaning here, for greed is a serious sin. However, many Bible scholars believe that its inclusion in this list of sexual sins indicates that the word referred here to unbridled sexual lust.

"Not be named" may mean "not mentioned"; but don't preachers, teachers, and parents need to mention such sins to warn against them? Thus, "let it not be once named" probably means not to let it be mentioned as something of which a Christian was guilty. Such sins are totally inappropriate for any Christian.

Verse 4 includes not only actions but words that deal with sexual immorality. "Filthiness" is a word that includes both obscene deeds and words. "Foolish talking" is a literal translation of the meaning of the word. "Jesting" does not refer to joking in general, but to dirty jokes and stories. "Not convenient" means "not fit." Instead of these and other sins of the tongue (see 4:25, 29, 31), Christians are to use their voices to express gratitude to God.

Verse 5 sternly warns that people who practice these sins will not inherit God's kingdom. "Whoremonger" is "one who commits fornication."

2. Light versus darkness (5:8–14)

As children of light, Christians are to bear the fruit of the Spirit, not the works of darkness (5:8–11a). Instead of practicing or condoning such sins, Christians are to reprove them by bringing these sins into the light (5:11b–13). Christians are to live in the daytime of God's light, not in the darkness of sin (5:14).

3. Wisdom versus folly (5:15–20)

Wisdom calls for careful walking, taking advantage of opportunities, and doing God's will (5:15–17). They are to be intoxicated with the fullness of God's Spirit, not with wine (5:18). They are to sing and give thanks to God (5:19, 20).

II. Christian Family Relationships (Eph. 5:21–6:4)

1. Wives and husbands (5:21–33)

21 Submitting yourselves one to another in the fear of God.

22 Wives, submit yourselves unto your own husbands, as unto the Lord.

23 For the husband is the head of the wife, even as Christ is the head of the church: and he is the saviour of the body.

24 Therefore as the church is subject unto Christ, so let the wives be to their own husbands in every thing.

Verse 21 sets forth a principle that applies to all Christians—whether in the church or in the family. This is the principle of voluntary mutual submission to one another. Each believer is to look not to his own interests only but also to the interests of others. This is an important aspect of Christian humility and love, as we saw in studying Philippians 2:1–4.

The Christian wife is to practice this principle of voluntary submission to her husband. Later in verse 25, the husband is told to practice Christian love toward his wife; but his responsibility is stated as self-giving love. Verses 22 and 25 are inseparable in terms of an ideal Christian marriage relationship. The relation is founded on a common commitment to the Lord Jesus and to the practice of Christlike love: for the wife, this is voluntary submission; for the husband, this is sacrificial, self-giving love.

"As unto the Lord" does not mean that the wife is to treat her husband as a lord comparable to the Lord they both worship and serve. Colossians 3:18 clarifies the meaning, "Wives, submit yourselves unto your own husbands, as it is fit in the Lord."

One of the things that makes Ephesians 5:21–33 so difficult is that Paul compared the union of husband and wife to the relation between Christ and the church. They are alike in some ways, but not in others. Verse 23, for example, compares Christ as head of the church and the husband as head of the wife. But the verse also mentions that Christ is "saviour of the body." A husband has a head-of-the-home responsibility, but he is not the Lord and Savior of his wife or of his children.

The Bible says for wives to submit themselves voluntarily to their husbands, but it never says for the husband to subject his wife to himself. This is her decision and responsibility.

25 Husbands, love your wives, even as Christ also loved the church, and gave himself for it;

26 That he might sanctify and cleanse it with the washing of water by the word,

27 That he might present it to himself a glorious church, not having spot, or wrinkle, or any such thing; but that it should be holy and without blemish.

28 So ought men to love their wives as their own bodies. He that loveth his wife loveth himself.

29 For no man ever yet hated his own flesh; but nourisheth and cherisheth it, even as the Lord the church.

Paul did not endorse all the aspects of first-century marriages. In pagan marriages, the man was head of the house in such a way that he could treat his wife and children as he chose. Often, husbands were harsh. Many saw their wives only as homemakers and mothers of their children. They had mistresses for their pleasure. Paul obviously set forth a view of Christian marriage that called for lifetime faithfulness and lifetime self-giving love.

Verses 26 and 27 apply to Christ and the church, with no direct lessons that apply to marriage. Indirectly, the implication is that husbands will want and seek the best for their wives. Only Christ can wash, cleanse, and sanctify anyone. He does this for the church, men and women alike.

Verses 28 and 29 raise this question: What did Paul mean by "bodies" and "flesh"? Paul wrote that men ought to love their wives "as their own bodies." He wrote of a man's concern for "his own flesh." Some Bible translators and scholars assume Paul was referring to the man's physical body. However, does it not make better sense to define "flesh" in light of the one-flesh union?

In fact, Paul immediately referred to the church as the body of Christ in verse 30; and he quoted Genesis 2:24 in verse 31. Thus, Paul wasn't saying that a husband ought to love his wife as he loves his own physical body and flesh; he was saying that a husband ought to love his wife because she and he constitute one body in their one-flesh union. In loving her, he is respecting the one-flesh union in which they both share.

2. Children and parents (6:1–4)

> **1 Children, obey your parents in the Lord: for this is right.**
>
> **2 Honour thy father and mother; which is the first commandment with promise;**
>
> **3 That it may be well with thee, and thou mayest live long on the earth.**

Paul used two words to describe children's responsibilities toward their parents: "obey" and "honour." As children are growing up, they are to honor and obey their father and mother. When children are grown, they are always to honor their parents. Jesus taught and exemplified obedience as a child and lifetime respect, honor, and care.

"In the Lord" is clarified in Colossians 3:20: "Children, obey your parents in all things: for this is well pleasing unto the Lord." Paul quoted the fourth commandment, and he told Gentile converts that this ancient Jewish commandment was an abiding part of Christian home life. Obeying and honoring parents is the Christian thing to do and the right thing to do.

The reference to the promise of long life shows that this is a basic foundation for a happy, healthy life. The family is the basic building block of human society as God intended it to be. Society is only as stable as its families. Honoring parents is a key.

> **4 And, ye fathers, provoke not your children to wrath: but bring them up in the nurture and admonition of the Lord.**

Fathers in ancient society often either ignored or mistreated their children. Thus, Paul addressed this problem head-on. Fathers were not to mistreat their children, nor were they to neglect them. A Christian father had a primary role not only in providing a living but also in raising the children. Christian fathers were to bring up their children in the nurture and admonition of the Lord. This meant consistent, loving discipline; but the main emphasis of the words is on raising children in the Lord. This requires instruction by word and especially by example. Instead of provoking their children to anger as pagan fathers did, they were to influence their children to follow the Lord.

Did Paul intend to exclude mothers? Probably not. He had included both parents in verse 2, and he probably assumed their involvement. He may have singled out fathers for two reasons: (1) They were the prime offenders in mistreating children, and (2) they needed to shoulder their responsibility to raise their children as Christians.

SUMMARY OF BIBLE TRUTHS

1. Christians are to practice self-giving love.
2. Christians are to avoid sexual immorality in deed and word.
3. Christian wives are to submit themselves to their husbands.
4. Christian husbands are to give of themselves for their wives.
5. Children are to obey and honor their parents.
6. Parents are to raise their children to be Christians.

APPLYING THE BIBLE

1. Governing immorality. Our culture's confusion over love and lust reached a new zenith in 1998 as the nation endured both the grief and shame of President Clinton's confessions of an "inappropriate relationship" with a White House aide, Monica Lewinsky. In a commentary on the moral dilemma faced by the nation, Terry Mattingly wrote, "It's hard to repent of sexual sins in your personal life when, in your political life, you're in charge of defending the sexual revolution."[1]

While this certainly is not an attempt to excuse the president for his immoral actions, it does call for a serious look at the spirit of toleration cultivated in America during the past fifty years. All need to recognize that the state of the nation and its leaders are in many ways reflective of an entire nation's drift away from a holy God.

2. Sad commentary on the family. "The United States in the 1980s may be the first society in history in which children are distinctly worse off than adults" (Daniel Patrick Moynihan).

3. Sending an important message. In a full-page advertisement sponsored by the Office of National Drug Control Policy and Partnership for a Drug-Free Tennessee and America, parents are urged to begin talking with their children at an early age about the dangers of drugs. The encouragement in the ad copy reminds parents that no matter how difficult, no matter how inexperienced a parent may feel, if a parent will simply try, their child will pick up a threefold message. This message tells children that you care about them, that you understand something about the conflicts they face, and that you are there when they need you.

This threefold message is basic. Every child in a Christian family should have this reassurance. Unfortunately, not every child in a Christian family does. Parents get distracted with urgent demands, not always by intention, but the results are the same. When children think parents are too busy to be concerned about them, the lure of drugs can become too strong to resist.

4. Influence: the signature of your life. Upon her installation as U.S. treasurer, Katherine D. Ortega said, "In the next year or so, my signature will appear on $60 billion of United States currency. More important to me, however, is the signature that appears on my life—the strong, proud, assertive handwriting of a loving father and mother."

Each of us has the opportunity to affix the signature of our lives on those whom we influence. Today's lesson speaks to the demand for Christian influence in the home between husbands and wives and between parents and children.

5. First things first. In a Christian family, you cannot be the parent your children need until you are the partner your spouse needs, and you cannot be the partner your spouse needs until you are the person God calls you to be.

6. Quotes on the family:

"There is just as much authority in the family today as there ever was, only now, the children exercise it."

"Mankind owes to the child the best it has to give" (opening words of the United Nations' Declaration of the Rights of the Child).

TEACHING THE BIBLE

- *Main Idea:* All family members have responsibilities to one another.
- *Suggested Teaching Aim:* To lead adults to identify the responsibilities of each family member.

A TEACHING OUTLINE

1. *Christian Conduct in a Sinful World (Eph. 5:1–20)*
2. *Christian Family Relationships (Eph. 5:21—6:4)*

Introduce the Bible Study

Use number 5, "First Things First," in "Applying the Bible" to introduce the lesson.

Search for Biblical Truth

IN ADVANCE, make two strip posters of the two points in "A Teaching Outline."

Ask members to open their Bibles to Ephesians 5:1. Place the first strip poster on the wall. Ask, What word in verse 1 ties this material to the earlier discussion? ("Therefore.") Write on a chalkboard or a large sheet of paper:

Ask members to look at verses 3 and 4 and identify the six lifestyles believers must avoid if they are to walk in love. After listing the six negatives, ask them to suggest six positive steps that are opposite the negative ones.

Walk in Love

Avoid	Practice
Fornication	
Uncleanness	
Covetousness	
Filthiness	
Foolish talking	
Jesting	

Place the second strip poster on the wall. Suggest that a second way we can live responsibly as Christians is to have proper relationships in our families. Write on a chalkboard (omit italicized phrases):

Christian Family Relationships

Instead of	Do
Opposing each other	Submit to each other

Lecture briefly covering the following points:

1. The principle of submission applies to all Christians.
2. The wife's obedience is voluntary—it cannot be demanded.
3. The husband must practice self-giving love—it cannot be demanded.
4. The wife should put her husband first as both put Christ first.
5. The pattern for both is Christ.
6. The husband should love his wife because she and he constitute one body in their flesh union.

Ask members to look at 6:1–4 and then complete the following chart:

Christian Family Relationships

Instead of	Do
Disobeying parents	Obey parents
Dishonoring parents	Honor parents
Provoking children to wrath	Bring them up in the Lord

DISCUSS: How can parents instruct their children about the Lord? Use No. 3, "Sending an Important Message," in "Applying the Bible."

Read the following six statements and ask members if they agree or disagree and why. Then ask the follow-up questions.

1. Christians are to practice self-giving love. Ask, How did you practice self-giving love this past week?
2. Christians are to avoid sexual immorality in deed or word. Ask, How has your language this past week violated this principle?
3. Christian wives are to submit themselves to their husbands. Ask: Can you think of a wife who has a beautiful relationship with her

husband? How would you describe her in relationship to this principle?

4. Christian husbands are to give of themselves for their wives. Ask: Can you think of a husband who has a beautiful relationship with his wife? How would you describe him in relationship to this principle?
5. Children are to obey and honor their parents. Ask: How can a child honor a parent who is not worthy of honor? Does Scripture teach that children should honor dishonorable parents?
6. Parents are to raise their children to be Christians. Ask, How far can parents go in raising their children to be Christians before they have to let the children's responsibility take over?

Give the Truth a Personal Focus

Close in prayer that members will be responsible members of the Christian family.

---

1. Terry Mattingly, "Clinton & That Loaded Word 'Sin'," Washington Bureau: Scripps Howard News Service, Aug. 26, 1998.

Called to Stand Firm

July
30
2000

Background Passage: Ephesians 6:10–24
Focal Passage: Ephesians 6:10–20

The Bible has a lot to say about overcoming temptation. Ephesians 6:10–20 is one of the helpful passages on the subject.

Study Aim: *To identify biblical guidelines for overcoming temptation.*

STUDYING THE BIBLE

OUTLINE AND SUMMARY

I. The Call to Stand (Eph. 6:10–12)
  1. Strong in the Lord (6:10)
  2. Stand against the devil (6:11, 12)
II. Equipment to Stand (Eph. 6:13–17)
  1. Whole armor of God (6:13)
  2. Parts of the armor (6:14–17)
III. Importance of Prayer (Eph. 6:18–24)
  1. Characteristics of prayer (6:18)
  2. Praying for Paul (6:19–24)

Paul called believers to be strong in the Lord (v. 10) in order to be able to stand against the devil's temptations (vv. 11, 12). He told them to stand in the whole armor of God (v. 13), which he identified piece by piece by comparing Christian characteristics with the equipment of a Roman soldier (vv. 14–17). He called them to pray for all Christians (v. 18), including him—asking that they pray that he would have boldness to speak for the Lord (vv. 19–24).

I. The Call to Stand (Eph. 6:10–12)

1. Strong in the Lord (v. 10)

10 Finally, my brethren, be strong in the Lord, and in the power of his might.

In Paul's opening prayer, he had asked that the Lord would show believers "the exceeding greatness of his power to us-ward who believe, according to the working of his mighty power" (Eph. 1:19). Ephesians 6:10 contains two of the same words: "power" and "might." "Be strong" is a verb form from the word for "power." Obviously Paul wanted to impress Christians with the divine power available to them. Notice especially the words "in the Lord." Christians' strength comes from our relationship in Christ.

2. Stand against the devil (vv. 11, 12)

11 Put on the whole armour of God, that ye may be able to stand against the wiles of the devil.

12 For we wrestle not against flesh and blood, but against principalities, against powers, against the rulers of the darkness of this world, against spiritual wickedness in high places.

"Put on the whole armour of God" was Paul's prescription for how to "be strong in the Lord." In verses 14–17, Paul listed the specific parts of the soldier's equipment; however, Paul wanted to emphasize that this is "of God." We cannot overcome our crafty enemy in our own strength, only by being "strong in the Lord."

"Stand against" in the context of warfare refers to a soldier taking a stand and holding a position against the onslaughts of a powerful and cunning enemy. Our enemy is the devil, meaning "the slanderer." The evil one slanders God and God's people. He is the sworn enemy of both.

"Wiles" refers to the deceitful devices and tricky schemes of Satan. Jesus said that "he is a liar and the father of lies" (John 8:44, NIV). Paul warned that he "masquerades as an angel of light" (2 Cor. 11:14, NIV).

"Wrestle" refers to a contest or struggle in which one throws down an opponent. As Christians, we sometimes struggle with evil human beings; but back of them stands our real opponent, the devil. Our day-by-day internal conflict is with the spiritual forces of darkness. Many of the words Paul used in verse 12 at times were used of evil people in positions of power ("principalities," "powers," "rulers," "high places"), but Paul made it clear that he was warning here of Satan and his allies. He emphasized that "we wrestle not against flesh and blood." He also used the word *spiritual* to describe "wickedness in high places."

II. Equipment to Stand (Eph. 6:13–17)

1. Whole armor of God (v. 13)

13 Wherefore take unto you the whole armour of God, that ye may be able to withstand in the evil day, and having done all, to stand.

Paul repeated the challenge about putting on "the whole armour of God." "Be able" translates a word for empowerment, in this case empowerment from God and the armor He provides. "Withstand" is a combination of the Greek prefix meaning "against" with the word meaning "stand." He had already made this point with the words "stand against" in verse 11 and "wrestle . . . against" in verse 12. The word from verse 13 is found in James 4:7 and 1 Peter 5:8, 9—two other important passages about overcoming the devil's temptations.

"The evil day" may refer to a future time of Satanic power. More likely, however, it refers to those times in each life when evil threatens most. When the smoke of this spiritual combat has cleared, Christians—clothed in the whole armor of God and strong in the Lord—will still be standing.

2. Parts of the armor (vv. 14–17)

14 Stand therefore, having your loins girt about with truth, and having on the breastplate of righteousness;

15 And your feet shod with the preparation of the gospel of peace;

16 Above all, taking the shield of faith, wherewith ye shall be able to quench all the fiery darts of the wicked.

17 And take the helmet of salvation, and the sword of the Spirit, which is the word of God.

"Stand" is obviously a key word in the passage. The word in some form appears four times in this passage. The way to stand is to put on the whole armor of God, which Paul now proceeds to list by comparing the combat equipment of Christians to the equipment of a Roman soldier.

Paul had two sources for this comparison. One was the presence of a Roman soldier guarding him. The other is the use in the Old Testament of this kind of comparison (Isa. 11:5; 59:17).

"Loins girt about with truth" compares the belt of a soldier to truth. Paul may have had in mind the truth of the gospel message to which Christians bore witness; however, he probably had in mind the fact that Christians were people of truth. They spoke and lived the truth (Eph. 4:15; 5:9). Nothing is so potent a defense against the father of lies, the devil.

"The breastplate" was crucial in protecting the vital organs of a soldier against damage from the blows of the enemy. "Righteousness" is comparable in protecting a Christian against evil. The word may refer to justification, in which God declares sinners right with Him through Christ's death and the faith of the justified person. However, justification is inseparable from sanctification—the process of becoming righteous by the power of God's Spirit.

Any soldier in any age can testify to the importance of footwear. Roman soldiers needed footwear that enabled them to march great distances and also to maintain firm footing for hand-to-hand combat. The Roman soldier needed to be able to plant his feet and know that he would not slip and fall. "Feet shod with the preparation of the gospel of peace" can be interpreted in two ways: (1) "Preparation" can mean readiness to take the good news to those who need to hear it; (2) "preparation" can also mean readiness to stand against the onslaughts of the enemy.

Choosing between these two interpretations isn't easy. Both are New Testament teachings. Both lead to actions that upset the devil. Both thwart his attempts to win a victory for evil. The context seems to favor the first interpretation; however, if Paul was thinking of Isaiah 52:7, he may have had the other one in mind.

A Roman soldier was virtually defenseless without an adequate shield. "Adequate" meant that it could deflect blows from an enemy's sword in hand-to-hand combat or the arrows fired from a distance. At times, arrows were dipped in pitch and set on fire. The shields were made of bronze and often covered in oxhide. These shields would deflect the arrows and help quench the arrows set on fire. Paul obviously had such a shield in mind when he described "the shield of faith, wherewith ye shall be able to quench all the fiery darts of the wicked." "Faith" involves a personal relationship with and total reliance on the Lord. A person without such faith is like a Roman soldier going into battle without a shield—totally helpless before the enemy.

Head wounds are often fatal and always serious. A Roman soldier's helmet protected his brain and to some degree his eyes. Paul—no doubt influenced by Isaiah 59:17—compared the helmet to "salvation." A person without salvation is vulnerable to the devil's temptations. Paul spoke of salvation as a past experience of deliverance from sin's penalty, as a present experience of power over sin, and as a future removal of any presence of sin.

The Roman soldier's sword was used in both defensive and offensive actions against the enemy. Paul wrote of "the sword of the Spirit, which is the word of God." We can overcome the devil's temptations as we rely on the Spirit of the Lord. One of His best ways of helping us is through the Word of God. This Word was inspired by God's Spirit. He illumines our understanding of the Word. He uses this Word as a weapon against Satan. Jesus' use of Scripture in overcoming the devil's temptations is our example.

III. Importance of Prayer (Eph. 6:18–24)

1. Characteristics of prayer (v. 18)

18 Praying always with all prayer and supplication in the Spirit, and watching thereunto with all perseverance and supplication for all saints.

Although Paul did not compare prayer to a specific part of the whole armor of God, prayer is crucial in using all the parts of the armor. Verse 18 lists five characteristics of prayer:

1. "Praying always" means praying on all occasions. This surely means that Christians should develop the discipline of daily prayer.
2. "With all prayer and supplication" reminds us that all kinds of prayers are important.
3. "In the Spirit" emphasizes the Spirit's role in helping us to pray (Rom. 8:26, 27).
4. "Watching thereunto with all perseverance and supplication" reminds us that God uses our prayers in ways beyond our understanding. For example, He uses the prayers of His people in the cosmic warfare against the forces of darkness. Therefore, the devil does everything he can to keep us from praying. Paul challenges us to persevere in prayer.
5. "For all saints" means for all Christians. We are to pray not just for ourselves and those close to us; we also are to pray for all God's people. This includes missionaries and believers in others lands. It includes Christians of all denominations.

2. Praying for Paul (vv. 19–24)

19 And for me, that utterance may be given unto me, that I may open my mouth boldly, to make known the mystery of the gospel,

20 For which I am an ambassador in bonds: that therein I may speak boldly, as I ought to speak.

Paul wanted to be remembered in prayer. He was far from them, but he believed that God would use their prayers to help him fulfill his mission as a prisoner in Rome. Although he was in chains, Paul considered himself the Lord's ambassador to the Roman guards and other people with whom he had contact.

Notice that he did not ask them to pray for his release from prison but for boldness to speak for Christ while he was in prison. Paul was not superhuman. He was tempted at times to remain silent. He wanted courage always to "speak boldly" for the Lord Jesus.

Paul closed by referring them to Tychicus for information about him (vv. 21, 22) and with a final benediction (vv. 23, 24).

PRONUNCIATION GUIDE

Tychicus [TIK ih kuhs]

SUMMARY OF BIBLE TRUTHS

1. Rely on God's power.
2. Resist the temptations of the devil.
3. Live a consistent Christian life.
4. Take a firm stand.
5. Use the Word of God.
6. Persevere in prayer.

APPLYING THE BIBLE

1. Avoiding temptation. When interviewed by *Time* magazine several years ago, Billy Graham was asked his opinion about the "fall" of certain television evangelists in the 1980s. Instead of speculating on the subjects in question, the veteran evangelist shared his convictions that Satan attacks God's servants in the areas of sex, money, and pride. After being told by a mentor to be cautious in these areas, Dr. Graham said, "From that moment on I never rode in a car with a woman alone. I never have eaten a meal with my secretary alone or ridden in a car with her alone. If we sit in here and I dictate something to her, the door is open."[1]

Standing firm is made possible when we are careful not to put ourselves in situations where we can be tempted.

2. Compromise. The dictionary defines compromise as "a settlement of differences in which each side makes concessions."

Temptation is a form of compromise. It is a settlement rather than a stand. It is always detrimental. The "whole armor" is designed to enable the child of God to avoid compromise. Consider the various pieces of armor listed in the text today and identify how each one can be particularly helpful in avoiding a specific area of compromise.

3. Taking a stand. The third stanza of the hymn "Stand Up, Stand Up for Jesus" is based on today's text.

Stand up, stand up for Jesus, Stand in His strength alone.
The arm of flesh will fail you, Ye dare not trust your own:
Put on the gospel armor, Each piece put on with pray'r;
Where duty calls, or danger, Be never wanting there.[2]

4. Scriptural armor for temptation. Using the word *armor* for an acrostic, the following mnemonic can be easily recalled for help in times of temptation.

A ***Ask*** **for help.** "And this is the confidence that we have in him, that, if we **ask** any thing according to his will, he heareth us" (1 John 5:14).

R ***Resist*** **the Devil.** "Submit yourselves therefore to God. **Resist** the devil, and he will flee from you" (James 4:7).

M **God will** ***make*** **a way.** "There hath no temptation taken you but such as is common to man: but God *is* faithful, who will not suffer you to be tempted above that ye are able; but will with the temptation also **make** a **way** to escape, that ye may be able to bear *it*" (1 Cor. 10:13).

O ***Obey*** **God, not lust.** "Let not sin therefore reign in your mortal body, that ye should **obey** it in the lusts thereof" (Rom. 6:12).

R ***Run*** **from temptation if necessary.** "She [Potiphar's wife] caught him by his garment, saying, Lie with me: But he left his garment in her hand, and fled, and got him out" (Gen. 39:12).

5. Fleeing temptation. "When you flee from temptation, be sure you don't leave a forwarding address."[3]

6. Prayer can't hurt. When Henry M. Stanley was sent to find missionary David Livingston in Africa, he observed, "On all my expeditions prayer made me stronger than my non-praying companions. It did not blind my eyes or dull my mind or close my ears, but on the contrary it gave me confidence; it did more, it gave me joy and pride in my work and lifted me beautifully over the 1,500 miles of forest tracks, eager to face the day's perils and fatigue."[4]

7. Physical beneifts proven. Several studies have concluded that patients with strong religious faith have better recovery rates than non-believers, and many doctors agree. As one researcher noted, there are really only three options:

- Prayer is a placebo and does nothing beneficial.
- Prayer is intrinsically harmful and offers false hope.
- Prayer is intrinsically helpful because God answers prayer.[5]

More and more evidence is supporting the third view.

Paul knew what research studies are discovering. God answers prayer. It would be true for the Ephesians when facing temptation, and it would be true for his ministry as believers prayed for him.

TEACHING THE BIBLE

- *Main Idea:* God has given us some biblical guidelines to overcome temptation.
- *Suggested Teaching Aim:* To lead adults to identify biblical guidelines to overcoming temptation.

A TEACHING OUTLINE

1. *The Call to Stand (Eph. 6:10–12)*
2. *Equipment to Stand (Eph. 6:13–17)*
3. *Importance of Prayer (Eph. 6:18–24)*

Introduce the Bible Study

Use number 4, " Scriptural Armor for Temptation," in "Applying the Bible" to introduce the lesson.

Search for Biblical Truth

IN ADVANCE:

- Make three strip posters of the three points in "A Teaching Outline" on the previous page.
- Copy these two sets of questions to give to two groups.

Group 1: Read Ephesians 6:10–12, answer these questions, and choose someone to report the results of your study to the group.

1. What two significant words appear in Ephesians 1:9 and 6:10?
2. How does our relationship with Christ give us strength for the battle?
3. Which piece of the armor is most important? least?
4. What happens when Christians take a "stand against the wiles of the devil"?
5. How does combating a spiritual opponent require a different approach than combating a physical one?

Group 2: Read Ephesians 6:13–17, answer these questions, and select someone to present to the whole group the results of your study.

1. What are some examples of "evil days" against which we need to take a stand?
2. List each of the parts of the physical armor with its spiritual counterpart. Do you think that the spiritual counterpart is a good choice? Why? Would there be other parts of the armor if Paul wrote today and what would be their spiritual counterpart?
3. How do we put on each piece of armor?
4. Explain how each piece defends us against temptation.

Organize the class into two groups. Give each group a set of the above questions. Allow about ten minutes for study.

Place the first outline point on the wall. Define the following words based on "Studying the Bible": principalities, powers, ruler of darkness, spiritual wickedness.

Call on Group 1 for their report. Add any information from "Studying the Bible" that would help members understand the Scriptures.

Place the second outline point on the wall. Define the following words based on "Studying the Bible": be able, evil day. Call on Group 2 to report. Add any information that would be helpful from "Studying the Bible" about the meaning of the terms used for the spiritual armor.

Place the third outline point on the wall. Read aloud Ephesians 6:18 and 19. Using the material in "Studying the Bible," describe the five characteristics of prayer in verse 18.

Read the first statement in "Summary of Bible Truths." Ask members if they can share an example of how doing this helped them overcome temptation. Follow this procedure with the other five statements.

Give the Truth a Personal Focus

Use number 6, "Prayer Can't Hurt," in "Applying the Bible" to close the lesson. Close in prayer that members will use the armor God has given each of us to oppose temptation.

---

1. David Aikman, "Preachers, Politics and Temptation," *Time,* May 28, 1990, 12.
2. *The Baptist Hymnal,* Hymn 485 (Convention Press, 1991).
3. Vern McLellan, *Quips, Quotes, and Quests* (Eugene, Oregon: Harvest House Publishers, 1982), 12.
4. Wallace Friday, *Adults at Worship* (New York: Abingdon Press, 1969).
5. Gary Thomas, "Doctors Who Pray: How the Medical Community Is Discovering the Power of Prayer," *Christianity Today,* Jan. 6, 1997, 20.

The Supremacy of Christ

August

6

2000

Background Passage: Colossians 1:1–28

Focal Passage: Colossians 1:15–28

Colossians 1 is among the most powerful and deep passages in the New Testament. Its description of Christ reminds us of John 1:1–18; Philippians 2:6–11; and Hebrews 1:1–4. It emphasizes the supremacy of Christ and appropriate responses to Him.

Study Aim: *To identify marks of Christ's supremacy and appropriate personal responses.*

STUDYING THE BIBLE

OUTLINE AND SUMMARY

I. Christ, Paul, and the Colossians (Col. 1:1–14)
  1. Greetings from Christ's apostle (1:1, 2)
  2. Gratitude for their response to the gospel (1:3–8)
  3. Paul's prayer for them (1:9–14)

II. The Preeminent Christ (Col. 1:15–29)
  1. Lord of creation (1:15–17)
  2. Lord of the new creation (1:18–20)
  3. Preeminent among the Colossians (1:21–23)
  4. Preeminent in Paul's ministry (1:24–29)

After greeting the Colossians (vv 1, 2), Paul expressed gratitude for them (vv. 3, 8) and prayed for them (vv. 9–14). He exalted Christ as Lord of creation (vv. 15–17) and Lord of the new creation (vv. 18–20). He wrote of what Christ had done, was doing, and would do among the Colossians (vv. 21–23). He testified of his own ministry in the gospel (vv. 24–29).

I. Christ, Paul, and the Colossians (Col. 1:1–14)

1. Greetings from Christ's apostle (vv. 1, 2)

One of Paul's four Prison Letters was sent to Colosse, a town in the Roman province of Asia. Paul described himself as Christ's apostle and addressed them as saints and faithful brothers. He invoked God's grace and peace on them.

2. Gratitude for their response to the gospel (vv. 3–8)

Paul thanked God for their faith in Christ, love for other Christians, and hope of heaven (vv. 3–5). Paul had heard this from Epaphras, who had taken the gospel to Colosse (vv. 6–8).

3. Paul's prayer for them (vv. 9–14)

Paul asked God to give them the knowledge of His will in order that they might live worthy and fruitful lives (vv. 9, 10). He prayed that God would give them power so they could endure with joy (v. 11). Paul wanted the Colossians to express thanks for their deliverance through Christ's blood from the power of darkness to God's kingdom of light (vv. 12–14).

August

6

2000

OUTLINE OF COLOSSIANS

I. Introduction (1:1–14)
   1. Greetings (1:1, 2)
   2. Gratitude (1:3–8)
   3. Intercession (1:9–14)

II. The Preeminent Christ (1:15–29)
   1. Lord of creation and new creation (1:15–20)
   2. Christ's work among the Colossians (1:21–23)
   3. Paul's ministry in the gospel (1:24–29)

III. Warning against False Teachers (2:1–23)
   1. Paul's personal appeal (2:1–7)
   2. Warning against false doctrine (2:8–15)
   3. Warning against false practices (2:16–23)

IV. New Life in Christ (3:1–4:6)
   1. Risen with Christ (3:1–4)
   2. The old life (3:5–11)
   3. The new life (3:12–17)
   4. A Christian household (3:18–4:1)
   5. Prayer and influence (4:2–7)

V. Final Greetings (4:8–18)

II. The Preeminent Christ (Col. 1:15–29)

1. Lord of creation (vv. 15–17)

15 Who is the image of the invisible God, the firstborn of every creature:

16 For by him were all things created, that are in heaven, and that are in earth, visible and invisible, whether they be thrones, or dominions, or principalities, or powers: all things were created by him, and for him:

17 And he is before all things, and by him all things consist.

Many Bible scholars believe that Colossians 1:15–20 was an early hymn. Although these verses are filled with heavy theological words, they do have a lyrical flow.

"The image of the invisible God" points to Christ as the presence of God in human form. The word translated "image" can mean a symbol of something or the reality it depicts. Christ is not just a symbol of God; He is the Son of God Himself. During Old Testament times, people were warned that no one could see God and live. Yet in His incarnate Son, God has enabled humans to see as much of God as we are capable of seeing (John 1:14, 18; 14:9).

"Firstborn" could mean the first son to be born, but it also came to emphasize priority without any reference to birth. Some false teachers claimed that Christ was a created being, not the eternal Word of God who became flesh. This is totally inconsistent with New Testament teachings about Christ's preexistence. Verse 16 clearly shows that "firstborn of every creature" refers to first in importance, not first in time.

Far from being a created being Himself, "by him were all things created." He created "all things" "in heaven" and "in earth, visible and invisible." Paul especially focused on "thrones, or dominions, or principalities, or powers." These words could refer to earthly powers, but Paul generally used them of spiritual beings (Rom. 8:38; Eph. 1:21; 6:12; Col. 2:10, 15). Since he refers to angel worship in Colossians 2:18, Paul made clear that Christ created the angels. He alone, not they, is worthy of worship.

Paul stressed that "all things were created by him, and for him." He is not only the Creator but also the goal of creation.

Christ "is before all things." "Before" refers to being before them in time and being superior to them. "Consist" means to "hold together." Christ not only created all things, but He also sustains and upholds the created universe.

2. Lord of the new creation (vv. 18–20)

18 And he is the head of the body, the church: who is the beginning, the firstborn from the dead; that in all things he might have the preeminence.

19 For it pleased the Father that in him should all fulness dwell;

20 And, having made peace through the blood of the cross, by him to reconcile all things unto himself; by him, I say, whether they be things in earth, or things in heaven.

Christ is Lord not only of the creation but of the new creation. The primary focus of Christ's reconciliation is sinful humanity. The outcome of that reconciliation is "the church." In Ephesians 1:22 and 23, Paul emphasized the church as Christ's body and Christ as head of the church. Colossians emphasizes the head of the body more than the body itself, while Ephesians emphasized the body.

Other words in verse 18 shed light on Christ as head of the church. He is "the beginning." That is, Christ created the church, called it into being as part of the new creation. Christ is "firstborn from the dead." Notice again the word *firstborn.* Christ was not the first to return from the dead; however, Christ was the first to conquer death (Rom. 6:9). Only He can say, "Because I live, ye shall live also" (John 14:19).

Christ is the only head of the church. The church is His body. It belongs to Him, not to those who are members of the body, even to those whom Christ has called as pastors of His body. Many mistakes in church life are made because we forget this basic truth.

"Fulness" was apparently an issue in the false teachings at Colosse. Colossians 2:9 declares that in Christ "dwelleth all the fulness of the Godhead bodily." The false teachers implied that Christ was not fully God and not fully adequate. Paul insisted that He was. This should call forth our full faith in Him in whom God was pleased that all fullness dwell.

Verse 20 says that Christ's death avails for the reconciliation of all things, not just people. Sin spread its effects not only to human beings but also to the entire creation. Thus, Christ, who created "all things," is at work "to reconcile all things unto himself."

We cannot know for sure if Colossians 1:15–20 was a hymn of praise, but these inspired words of holy Scripture surely call us to praise the Lord of creation and the new creation.

3. Preeminent among the Colossians (vv. 21–23)

21 And you, that were sometime alienated and enemies in your mind by wicked works, yet now hath he reconciled

22 In the body of his flesh through death, to present you holy and unblameable and unreproveable in his sight:

23 If ye continue in the faith grounded and settled, and be not moved away from the hope of the gospel, which ye have heard, and which was preached to every creature which is under heaven; whereof I Paul am made a minister.

Before the coming of the gospel, the Colossians had been "alienated" from God and even "enemies" of God because of a sinful "mind" and "wicked works." Sin separates from God because sin is basically a turning away from God and also because sin is an offense to a holy God. The Father yearns to reconcile sinners and gave His Son to make that possible.

The "body of his flesh" refers to the incarnate Christ, who is "the image of the invisible God" in verse 15. "Through death" is the "blood of his cross" of verse 20. The death of Christ was the means of alienated sinners being "reconciled" to God.

Those who are reconciled are set apart by God and for God. That is the meaning of the word *holy.* Christ works in the lives of sinners to enable them to be set right with God or justified. The words "in his sight" imply justification. However, justified sinners are set apart or sanctified for a new life. Only in glory will any believer be perfectly "unblameable and unreproveable," but the process of moral transformation is at work now.

The first part of verse 23 sounds as if Paul were basing his assurance on their ability to "continue in the faith." He was not saying that if you continue in the faith, you will earn your way to heaven. He was saying that if you continue in the faith, you show that your faith is genuine. People who allow false teachers to move them "away from the hope of the gospel" need to reexamine their faith. Even genuine Christians falter at times, but they are "grounded and settled" enough to be held by the hope of the gospel.

4. Preeminent in Paul's ministry (vv. 24–29)

24 Who now rejoice in my sufferings for you, and fill up that which is behind of the afflictions of Christ in my flesh for his body's sake, which is the church:

25 Whereof I am made a minister, according to the dispensation of God which is given to me for you, to fulfill the word of God;

26 Even the mystery which hath been hid from ages and from generations, but now is made manifest to his saints:

27 To whom God would make known what is the riches of the glory of this mystery among the Gentiles; which is Christ in you, the hope of glory:

28 Whom we preach, warning every man, and teaching every man in all wisdom; that we may present every man perfect in Christ Jesus:

Paul's mention of the gospel in verse 23 led into a discussion of his own ministry. The meaning of most of verses 24–28 is fairly self-evident. He wrote of his calling as a minister "to fulfill the word of God" (v. 25); of his mission to the Gentiles (vv. 26, 27); of his methods of preaching, warning, and teaching (v. 28a); and of his goal of maturity for each believer (v. 28b).

The hardest part of this passage is verse 24. Paul wrote that his sufferings served to "fill up that which is behind [lacking] of the afflictions of Christ." What was lacking in Christ's afflictions, and how did Paul's sufferings fill it up? First of all, we can rule out any question that Christ's sufferings on the cross were not a full and adequate atonement for our sins. Paul surely did not mean that his own sufferings were in any way redemptive.

On the Damascus Road, Paul learned that in persecuting Christians, he had persecuted Christ Himself (Acts 9:4, 5). Christ so identifies with His people that when they suffer, so does He. Paul thus emphasized that his sufferings were for the Colossians and for the body of Christ. In this sense, Paul was sharing in and helping to fulfill Christ's concern for His people.

The word *mystery* meant something different to Paul than it does in its English translation. He was referring to something that is unknown until God reveals it. The mystery of which Paul wrote was the revelation that God's plan is to include all people in His kingdom, Gentiles as well as Jews. The only condition is that a person know Christ. Thus, the Colossians' "hope of glory" was that Christ was in and among them as Lord and Savior.

PRONUNCIATION GUIDE

Colosse	[koh LAHS ee]
Epaphras	[EP uh frass]

SUMMARY OF BIBLE TRUTHS

1. Christ is Lord of creation and of the new creation.
2. He is worthy of our full faith and praise.
3. Sinners need to be reconciled to God.
4. Christians have been set apart to live holy lives.
5. Christians share in Christ's sufferings when we give ourselves for His body the church.
6. The basis for Christian hope is Christ in us.

APPLYING THE BIBLE

1. The Creator can fix it. An old story tells of a man who bought a new Ford Model T. He was quite proud of his new possession, and he took it out in the country for a Sunday drive. He began to have problems with the car, and eventually it quit. He parked it beside the road and raised the hood. He looked hopelessly at the strange elements under the hood. He had absolutely no idea what to do.

As he stood wondering what to do, a car pulled up behind him, and a well-dressed man got out and asked if he could help. The owner described the problem, and the man went to his car and got some tools. In just a few minutes, he had the car fixed.

The owner had watched in amazement that anyone would know how to make the repairs in this complicated piece of machinery. He thanked the stranger and offered to pay him. The stranger refused.

"How did you know how to fix this car?" the owner asked.

The stranger replied, "My name is Henry Ford. I built this car."

2. What does an invisible God look like? A young boy was drawing a picture one day. Art Linkletter asked, "What are you drawing?" The boy replied, "A picture of God." Linkletter told the young boy, "No one knows what God looks like." The boy replied with great confidence, "They will when I get through."

Jesus is the image of the invisible God. The incarnation was God's way of saying, "This is what I look like." The writer of Hebrews said that God revealed Himself ultimately in Christ (Heb. 1:1–3). Paul said the same thing in this passage.

3. Characteristics of an invisible God. In his excellent commentary on 1 Corinthians 13: 4–8, John MacArthur says that Paul is painting a portrait of love and Jesus is sitting for the portrait. A good reminder of the characteristics of God can be found by reading the text of 1 Corinthians 13:4–8 and substituting the name of Christ for the word "love" each time it appears. Using the Phillips translation, the passage would read as follows:

"This Jesus of which I speak is slow to lose patience—He looks for a way of being constructive. He is not possessive: Jesus is neither anxious to impress nor does He cherish inflated ideas of His own importance. Jesus has good manners and does not pursue selfish advantage. He is not touchy. He does not keep account of evil or gloat over the wickedness of other people. On the contrary, Jesus shares the joy of those who live by the truth. Jesus knows no limit to His endurance, no end to His trust, no fading of His hope: Jesus can outlast anything. Jesus Christ never fails."

4. Making the most out of a prototype. Prototypes are designed to reassure people and to learn what works and what doesn't. There are three methods of prototyping in the computer industry. (1) First there is the possibilities method. This is what you do when you interview clients to see what they are looking for in a new product. (2) Second is the feasibility method. This is where you try to see if your client will be able to connect with a new product. (3) Finally, there is the improvement method. This is where you seek to incrementally add new features to an existing product.[1]

Colossians 1:15 says Jesus is the firstborn of every creature. "Firstborn" comes from a Greek word that sounds like prototype (the word is *prototokos*). Ask members of your class to brainstorm this truth. Some possible answers could be: (1) God knew what we needed . . . forgiveness from sin. (2) God made it feasible for us to connect . . . what the law could not do, Christ has done for us. (3) God fulfilled the promise of the new covenant, an improvement based on a faith relationship where His laws are written on our hearts.

5. Hope. The word *hope* is found three times in the first chapter of Colossians. Hope is defined as a joyful and confident expectation of eternal salvation. Hope is a defining characteristic of the believer. Discuss the following two quotes regarding "hope" to see how those in your class understand the meaning and the promise behind the word.

"Disappointment should always be taken as a stimulant, and never viewed as a discouragement."[2]

"Curiosity is simply another word for hope."[3]

6. Deliverance. Colossians 1:13 reminds us that we have been delivered from the domain of darkness. People in darkness are driven to find answers to the following questions.

- Is it possible that the poor could find food and shelter?
- That the lonely could find companionship?
- That the bereaved could find comfort?
- That the frightened could find peace?
- That the sick could find health?
- That the hopeless could find hope?

The answer to all these questions finds their "yes" in the person of Jesus.

7. Chance. Bertrand Russell said, "Human life, its growth, its hopes, fears, loves, et cetera, are the results of accidents." He could not be more wrong. Colossians 1:16 and 17 reminds us that our Savior is also our Creator. Paul continues by saying Jesus is also our sustainer. (In him all things hold together.) Among the wonderful truths found in today's lesson, one thing stands out clearly: There is a creative, intentional process to life, orchestrated, directed, and carried out from the throne of glory! Life is not a series of accidents; it is a series of divine appointments!

8. Christ, our leader. Napoleon Bonaparte said, "A leader is a dealer in hope." The general was correct, even though he was probably not thinking about spiritual truth. Jesus, the firstborn from the dead, deals exclusively in hope.

- The hope for a new beginning is found in forgiveness.
- The hope for daily living is found in His ability to hold all things together.
- The hope for the church is found in His position as head over the body.
- The hope for a right standing before God is found in what Jesus has already done on our behalf; His death reconciled us to God and makes us holy and blameless.

9. Quotes on hope:

"The miserable have no other medicine but only hope" (William Shakespeare).

"Where there is no future before a people, there is no hope" (Edward Wilmot Blyden).

TEACHING THE BIBLE

- *Main Idea:* Christ's supremacy calls for an appropriate response from us.
- *Suggested Teaching Aim:* To lead adults to affirm Christ's supremacy and to respond personally to Him.

A TEACHING OUTLINE

1. *Lord of Creation (Col. 1:15–17)*
2. *Lord of the New Creation (Col. 1:18–20)*
3. *Preeminent Among the Colossians (Col. 1:21–23)*
4. *Preeminent in Paul's Ministry (Col. 1:24–29)*

Introduce the Bible Study

Use number 1, "The Creator Can Fix It," in "Applying the Bible" to introduce the lesson. Point out that Jesus is the Creator who knows how to fix us and provide for our needs.

Search for Biblical Truth

IN ADVANCE:

- Make four outline strip posters of the four points in "A Teaching Outline."
- Provide paper and pencils for each person.
- Enlist two members to read alternately the Scripture passage when called on.
- Copy the six "Summary of Bible Truths" statements on a large sheet of paper.

Briefly summarize the information in "Studying the Bible" under "I. Christ, Paul, and the Colossians" to set the context for the study.

Distribute paper and pencils to all members. Ask half the class to listen for phrases and statements in the biblical text and study that describe who Christ is. Ask the other half to listen for phrases and statements in the biblical text and study that describe what Christ does/did.

Place the first outline strip poster on the wall. Ask the first reader to read Colossians 1:15–17. Lecture briefly on these points: (1) Many Bible scholars believe that 1:15–20 was an early hymn. (2) "Image" can be a symbol of something or the reality it depicts. (3) "Firstborn" could mean the first son born, but it also emphasizes priority without regard to birth. (4) Christ created all things—including angels—and therefore is worthy of worship; He is "before all things." (5) By virtue of His power as Creator, Christ holds everything together. Ask, Why is Jesus more worthy of worship than angels? According to verse 16, what did Jesus create?

DISCUSS: If these words are true, what happens if we do not accept this Creator as our Savior?

Place the second outline strip poster on the wall. Ask the second reader to read verses 18–20. Lecture briefly on these points: (1) Christ is the "head of the body," the church. (2) He is "the beginning" who created the church and called it into being. (3) He is the "firstborn from the dead"—the first to conquer death. (4) This gives Christ "preeminence" over all creation since He created it and then bought it back with His death. (5) Jesus is fully God, not just partially God. (6) He made peace between all things and reconciled all things by His death.

DISCUSS: What are some examples of how Jesus' death reconciled "all things"—human and nonhuman?

Place the third outline strip poster on the wall. Ask the first reader to read verses 21–23. Lecture briefly on these points: (1) Christ reconciled the Colossians who were alienated from God. (2) He presents us in God's presence as holy. (3) We have a responsibility to "continue in the faith" as a part of Christ's presenting us to God.

Place the fourth outline strip poster on the wall. Ask the second reader to read aloud verses 24–28. Lecture briefly on these points: (1) Paul described how Christ was preeminent in his (Paul's) ministry. (2) Christ identifies so closely with His people that when they suffer, Christ suffers. (3) Paul was sharing in and helping to fulfill Christ's concern for His people. (4) The "mystery" of which Paul spoke was something unknown to humans until God decided to reveal it: namely, God planned to include all people in His kingdom, Gentiles as well as Jews. (5) Christ is our hope of glory.

DISCUSS: How do we complete what is lacking in Christ's sufferings for the sake of the church?

Display the six "Summary of Bible Truths" statements. Read them aloud and then read the "Main Idea" of the lesson: Christ's supremacy calls for an appropriate response from us.

Give the Truth a Personal Focus

Ask members to form groups of three or four individuals. Distribute paper and pencils and ask them to take the statements in the six "Summary of Bible Truths" and write a hymn to a familiar hymn tune such as "All Hail the Power of Jesus' Name," the "Doxology," or "Joyful, Joyful, We Adore Thee," or any other tune they wish. Allow six to eight minutes and ask volunteers to share their hymns. Close in a prayer of adoration for Christ's preeminence.

---

1. Christine Comaford, "Mission Critical: Making the Most Out of Design Prototypes," *PC Week*, Dec. 28, 1992, 46.
2. Vern McLellan, *Quips, Quotes and Quests* (Eugene, Oregon: Harvest House Publishers, 1982), 43.
3. Ibid., 19.

August

13

2000

A Complete Life in Christ

Background Passage: Colossians 2:6–19

Focal Passage: Colossians 2:6–19

Epaphras told Paul good things about the Colossians (1:3–8). Epaphras was probably also Paul's source of information (4:12) that they were being beguiled with enticing words by false teachers (2:4). Bible scholars debate the exact nature of the false teaching. Whatever it was, Paul magnified Christ as fully adequate to reveal God, to save from sin, and to provide a complete life.

Study Aim: *To contrast Christ and His way with the false teachings at Colosse.*

STUDYING THE BIBLE

OUTLINE AND SUMMARY

I. Continue to Walk in Christ (Col. 2:6, 7)

II. Beware of Non-Christian Teachings (Col. 2:8)

III. Christ Is All You Need (Col. 2:9–15)

1. Christ, the fullness of God, makes you full (2:9, 10)

2. Christ fully saves from sin (2:11–14)

3. Christ triumphed over evil (2:15)

IV. False Practices Deny Christ (Col. 2:16–19)

1. They replace Christ with old covenant ways (2:16, 17)

2. They forsake Christ (2:18, 19)

Continue to live and grow in Christ (vv. 6, 7). Beware of deceptive, non-Christian teachings (v. 8). Christ is fully God and makes us full (vv. 9, 10). Christ forgives sin and enables us to die to sin and live a new life (vv. 11–14). Christ triumphed over Satan and his allies (v. 15). Don't let anyone judge you about such things as food laws and keeping special days and seasons (vv. 16, 17). Don't be fooled into false worship (vv. 18, 19).

I. Continue to Walk in Christ (Col. 2:6, 7)

6 As ye have therefore received Christ Jesus the Lord, so walk ye in him:

7 Rooted and built up in him, and stablished in the faith, as ye have been taught, abounding therein with thanksgiving.

Paul made a strong personal appeal for the Colossians to continue in the Christian faith and life. They had "received Christ Jesus the Lord," not just some teachings about Him and His way.

Because true faith is personal, believers "walk in him." People who walk with the Lord have a growing relationship with Him and become more like Him. "Walk in him," Paul's basic appeal in verses 6 and 7, was described in three ways: (1) They were to grow like plants deeply "rooted" in good soil and like a structure "built up" on a solid foundation; (2) they were to continue in the stability and strength ("stablished") of what had "been taught"; and (3) they were to continue to abound "with thanksgiving."

II. Beware of Non-Christian Teachings (Col. 2:8)

8 Beware lest any man spoil you through philosophy and vain deceit. after the tradition of men, after the rudiments of the world, and not after Christ.

In Colossians 2:4, Paul had mentioned the danger when he wrote, "lest any man should beguile you with enticing words." Verse 8 does two things: It issues a strong warning of the danger, and it also gives the first explicit clues of the nature of the false teachings.

Verse 8 begins with the word *beware.* "Spoil" translates a word meaning "enslave." The false teachings sounded captivating, but they would make captives of those who believed such words. Paul was not condemning the academic discipline of "philosophy," but the kind of thinking that overlooks realities seen only through faith in divine revelation. "Vain deceit" refers to empty lies.

What were the false teachings? Paul gave three ways to characterize them. (1) Paul said that the false teachings were based on "tradition of men," not revelation from God; (2) he said that they were either elementary or pagan, depending on which of two meanings of "rudiments of the world" you prefer; and (3) he said they were "not after Christ," non-Christian.

The Greek for "rudiments of the world" can refer to elementary things, or it can refer to the elemental spirits of the universe. If it was the former, Paul's point was that they had exchanged the deep truths of God for kindergarten truths. If it was the latter, Paul was warning against their fascination with spirit beings.

III. Christ Is All You Need (Col. 2:9–15)

1. Christ, the fullness of God, makes you full (vv. 9, 10)

9 For in him dwelleth all the fulness of the Godhead bodily.

10 And ye are complete in him, which is the head of all principality and power.

Judging from Paul's affirmations, *fulness* was probably a key word for the false teachers in Colosse. Paul had used the word in Colossians 1:19. He used it again in 2:9. In fact, he also used the verb form in 2:10. "Are complete" is literally "have been made full." Very likely, the false teachers were denying the two basic Christian truths that Paul strongly affirmed in verses 9 and 10.

Paul asserted that "in him dwelleth all the fulness of the Godhead bodily." Christ was not one part of many beings, the sum total of which equaled fullness. Christ and Christ alone constitutes divine fullness. The word *bodily* may refer to His incarnate body, but it probably refers to His glorified body.

Second, Paul asserted that "ye are complete in him." Christ, the fullness of God, has filled us and made us full and complete in every way. We do not need any of the beliefs in spirit beings, for Christ is "the head of all principality and power." Christ alone offers all we need. He gives us life: real, abundant, eternal.

2. Christ fully saves from sin (vv. 11–14)

11 In whom also ye are circumcised with the circumcision made without hands, in putting off the body of the sins of the flesh by the circumcision of Christ:

12 Buried with him in baptism, wherein also ye are risen with him through the faith of the operation of God, who hath raised him from the dead.

13 And you, being dead in your sins and the uncircumcision of your flesh, hath he quickened together with him, having forgiven you all trespasses;

14 Blotting out the handwriting of ordinances that was against us, which was contrary to us, and took it out of the way, nailing it to his cross.

The false teachers probably advocated "the circumcision made" with "hands." Paul had often done battle with people who made circumcision necessary for salvation. In such cases, circumcision was combined with works of the Jewish Law. Colossians 2:14, 16–18, 21–23 strongly imply that legalism was part of the false doctrine at Colosse.

Paul said that "the circumcision of Christ" makes physical circumcision unnecessary for religious purposes. Paul used spiritual circumcision as a way of describing "putting off the body of the sins of the flesh." Paul characteristically used "flesh" not to describe the physical body, but the total person given over to a life of sin. Paul enables believers to put off this old life (see further in Col. 3:5–9).

Paul used baptism to signify the same reality he had just described as "the circumcision of Christ." Baptism signifies the death and burial of the old life of sin and the resurrection to a new life in Christ. This is possible only "with him," not in our own strength. We were "buried with him in baptism" and "quickened [made alive] together with him."

At the end of verse 13, Paul mentioned all trespasses being forgiven. Verse 14 elaborates on this familiar teaching in an unusual way. Our guilt is depicted as "handwriting of ordinances . . . against us." In Greek, these words described a written instrument of indebtedness. In this case, their indebtedness was related to "ordinances," a word describing laws and rules. Some people tried to attain righteousness by perfectly obeying the ordinances. Paul had tried that and found that his best efforts failed. Thus, the very law that was supposed to be the instrument of his salvation became the instrument of his condemnation (Rom. 7).

Paul also had found that Christ can do what the law could not do; Christ forgave his sins and empowered him to live a new life (Rom. 8:1–4). Paul described this forgiveness in connection with Christ and His cross. Christ blotted out or canceled that debt document of sins against sinners. He took away the guilt. In a sense, Paul said that Christ had nailed that list of accusations to the cross.

3. Christ triumphed over evil (v. 15)

15 And having spoiled principalities and powers, he made a shew of them openly, triumphing over them in it.

When a Roman general won a great victory, he was honored with a victory parade. He and his officers and soldiers were followed by the prisoners, usually in chains. This was called a Roman triumph. This seems to have been in the back of Paul's mind when he wrote verse 15.

Paul compared Christ to the victorious general. He had triumphed over "principalities and powers." We have noted how often Paul used these terms in Colossians, and we have noted that he used these terms to describe spiritual beings. Some of these spiritual beings are evil. Ephesians 6:12 used these terms to describe Satan and his evil forces. Christ defeated Satan and his spiritual allies. This teaching is familiar from John 12:31 and Hebrews 2:14, 15. Colossians 2:15 makes the same point in its own way.

Three terms in verse 15 support the view that Paul was comparing Christ's victory to a Roman triumph. "Having spoiled" is not the same word used in verse 8. The word in verse 15 means "disgrace." "Made a shew of them openly" means that Christ exposed them to open shame in their defeat. "Triumphing over them" contains the Greek word for a Roman triumph.

IV. False Practices Deny Christ (Col. 2:16–19)

1. They replace Christ with old covenant ways (vv. 16, 17)

16 Let no man therefore judge you in meat, or in drink, or in respect of an holyday, or of the new moon, or of the sabbath days:

17 Which are a shadow of things to come; but the body is of Christ.

One of the emphases of the false teachers at Colosse was the observance of laws about food and about special religious days and seasons. Since Paul referred to these as "a shadow of things to come," these likely were Old Testament practices, like observing the clean and unclean food laws and special days and feasts.

Paul was tolerant of sincere Christians who held on to such practices (Rom. 14:1–15:7), but he had no patience with people who substituted such legalism as a means of salvation (Gal. 4:9–11). Paul warned the Colossians that putting their trust in such practices was retreating from the reality of Christ into the shadows of past practices that no longer served any good purpose.

2. They forsake Christ (vv. 18, 19)

18 Let no man beguile you of your reward in a voluntary humility and worshipping of angels, intruding into those things which he hath not seen, vainly puffed up by his fleshly mind,

19 And not holding the Head, from which all the body by joints and bands having nourishment ministered, and knit together, increaseth with the increase of God.

These are difficult verses to translate and understand, but one thing is obvious: The false teachers were trying to beguile the Colossians into practices that would result in forsaking Christ. Verse 18 warned of the danger of substituting the worship of angels for the worship of Christ. This verse helps appreciate all the previous affirmations of Christ's superiority to spirit beings. The false teachers seem to have worshiped a hierarchy of supernatural beings, of which Christ was only one among many.

Verse 19 warns that this is a denial of the head of the church, who alone holds all things together. A church without Christ as its head ceases to be the church.

SUMMARY OF BIBLE TRUTHS

1. Remain loyal to Christ.
2. Beware of deceptive teachings that are non-Christian.
3. Only in Christ are we made complete.
4. Only Christ forgives and transforms.
5. Avoid practices that substitute for Christ.
6. Don't be fooled into worshiping anything but God revealed in Christ.

APPLYING THE BIBLE

1. Beware of non-Christian teachings. Elizabeth Clare Prophet, spiritual leader of the Church Universal and Triumphant, warned in the 1980s that a nuclear holocaust was coming. She convinced members of her New Age sect to relocate from California to Montana, where construction of a survivalist complex took place in what had been a peaceful, mountain community. A bomb-shelter style complex was buried under seven acres and stocked with food, water, and weapons that Prophet said would be needed for survival. She predicted that a nuclear war would destroy civilization in March 1990.

Heeding Mrs. Prophet's warnings, sect members ignored the staggering cost of the shelter. Many church members helped pay for it by taking out large personal loans and mortgaging their homes. In their view, based on Prophet's teachings, all debt would be obliterated by the coming holocaust. They thought they had nothing to lose.

Today, disillusionment replaces the fervor that once held many members. March 1990 came, but the predicted calamity didn't materialize. Left with a deep sense of emptiness, many have left the church which blended Eastern and Western religions offering karma, reincarnation, communal living, and the promise of survival.

All this shows the attractiveness of being a part of something new, something that purports to offer answers, something that appeals to a need to be needed and involved. Paul's warning is still appropriate today. Christians should beware of non-Christian teachings, and should be aware of the teachings of cults and sects that depart from biblical revelation.

2. Don't be so gullible. A student at Eagle Rock Junior High School won first prize at a science fair. He was attempting to show how conditioned we have become to alarmists practicing junk science and spreading fear of everything in our environment. In his project he urged people to sign a petition demanding strict control or total elimination of the chemical "dihydrogen monoxide."

His petition listed these dangers of the chemical: It can cause excessive sweating and vomiting, it is a major component in acid rain, it can cause severe burns in its gaseous state, accidental inhalation can kill you, it contributes to erosion, it decreases effectiveness of automobile brakes, and it has been found in tumors of terminal cancer patients.

He asked fifty people if they supported a ban of the chemical. Forty-three said yes, six were undecided, and only one knew that the chemical was water.

The title of his prize-winning project: "How Gullible Are We?"

3. Check everything by Scripture. Three former (excommunicated) members of a polygamist church have sued the sect, claiming its leader never delivered on a promised face-to-face meeting with Jesus Christ. Over the years, these same individuals turned over all of their money and possessions to the self-proclaimed prophet of The True and Living Church of Jesus Christ of Saints of the Last Days. The church, with about three hundred members, has its roots in Mormonism and teaches that the world will soon end with only its members being saved. They also believe their leader is a reincarnated Joseph Smith and that members can meet Jesus Christ if they consecrate all they have to the church.

False teachings are everywhere. Yet they can clearly be avoided by checking all their promises against the truth of God's Word. None of the false promises offered by the leaders of The True and Living Church of Jesus Christ of Saints of the Last Days is found in God's Word.

4. Quotes about truth:

"Jesus saith unto him, 'I am the way, the truth, and the life: no one cometh unto the Father, but by me'" (John 14:6).

"Falsehoods not only disagree with truths, but usually quarrel among themselves" (Daniel Webster).

"Truth, like surgery, may hurt, but it cures" (Han Suyin).

"Truth exists, only falsehood has to be invented" (Georges Braque).

"Truth is what God says about a thing."

"The truth shall make you free" (John 8:32).

5. Forgiveness. Christ can forgive any trespass, but He can overlook none.

6. Christ makes you full. New home owners in England cleaned out an old storage shed on the property they purchased earlier in the year. They discovered among the old lumber and rusty farm equipment a five-foot-tall painting of Apollo and Daphne by the seventeenth-century artist Lorenzo Lippi. Investigations revealed the painting to be authentic, and it later sold for $144,000 at a Christie's auction in London. The painting had been removed from a house during renovations in the mid seventies, when the previous home owners had a wall removed. Once the wall was gone, the painting had been forgotten.[1]

The painting was discovered in a storage shed with other discards and disposables. What seemed like simple canvas and lumber became valuable because of the signature of the artist. It was just a painting until experts researched the signature. Suddenly, what had been forgotten became a treasure of great value. This is exactly what happens to us when we give our lives to Christ. Our value is not in and of ourselves, but wholly and completely in Him.

TEACHING THE BIBLE

- *Main Idea:* Christ's way is superior to all other teachings.
- *Suggested Teaching Aim:* To lead adults to contrast Christ and His way with the false teachings at Colosse.

A TEACHING OUTLINE

1. *Continue to Walk in Christ (Col. 2:6, 7)*
2. *Beware of Non-Christian Teachings (Col. 2:8)*
3. *Christ Is All You Need (Col. 2:9–15)*
4. *False Practices Deny Christ (Col. 2:16–19)*

Introduce the Bible Study

Use number 1, "Beware of Non-Christian Teachings," in "Applying the Bible" to introduce the lesson.

Search for Biblical Truth

IN ADVANCE:

- Enlist a member to take the seven statements in "Outline and Summary" and put them in a paragraph that would read as though Paul were telling us what this section is about.
- Enlist a person to read the Scripture passages when called on.
- Copy on small slips of paper the explanations under "II. Beware of Non-Christian Teachings (Col. 2:8)" of (1) "beguile you," (2) the three characterizations of the false teachings, and (3) the two meanings of the "rudiments of the world." Give these to three members to share in the class session.

Call for the class member you enlisted to read the summary of the passage. Write the following on a chalkboard or large sheet of paper (omit italicized statements):

False Teaching	True Teaching
Do not follow Christ	Walk in Christ
"Philosophy"	Only Christ contains God's fullness
Human tradition	In Christ we are made complete
Elementary or pagan	True circumcision
Non-Christian	Baptism
Fullness	Forgiveness
Human circumcision	Christ triumphed over all enemies
Obey certain food laws	Christ alone is the Head of all things

False Teaching	True Teaching
Observe special religious days	He holds all things together
Worshiped angels	
Practiced false humility	

Ask the Scripture reader to read Colossians 2:6 and 7. Point out that true teaching is to walk in Christ or follow Him. This can be done in three ways: (1) grow like plants deeply rooted in good soil and like a structure built on a solid foundation; (2) continue to be strong in what they had been taught; (3) be grateful. False teaching is the opposite.

DISCUSS: What is the relationship between gratitude and the mature Christian life?

Ask the Scripture reader to read verse 8. Call for the three enlisted members to share their three explanations of (1) "beguile you," (2) the three characterizations of the false teachings, and (3) the two meanings of the "rudiments of the world." Under *False Teaching* write: "philosophy," human tradition, elementary or pagan, non-Christian.

Ask the Scripture reader to read verses 9 and 10. Explain: (1) the false teaching taught that their teaching had the "fullness"; (2) Paul taught that only Christ contains God's fullness; (3) in Christ we are made complete. Add these to the chart.

DISCUSS: Have you received the genuine fullness of life from Christ: real, abundant, eternal?

Ask the Scripture reader to read verses 11–15. Explain: (1) the false teachers advocated human circumcision as a way to salvation; (2) Paul taught that true circumcision was removing sins from our bodies; (3) baptism symbolized that removal of sins; (4) all of this came about because Christ had forgiven us. Write these on the chart.

DISCUSS: Describe your joy over knowing that all your sins have been nailed to the cross.

Ask the Scripture reader to read verse 15. Explain: (1) the Roman victory celebration behind this verse; (2) Christ defeated Satan and his spiritual allies. Add this to the chart.

Ask the Scripture reader to read verses 16 and 17. Explain: (1) the false teachers taught believers must obey certain food laws and observe special religious days. Add these to the chart.

Ask the Scripture reader to read verses 18 and 19. Explain: (1) the false teachers worshiped angels and practiced false humility; (2) Paul taught that Christ alone is the Head of all things; He holds all things together.

Give the Truth a Personal Focus

Use number 2, "Don't Be So Gullible," in "Applying the Bible" to close the lesson.

---

1. "Painting Out of Shed Fetches $144,000," *Las Vegas Review Journal.*

August

20

2000

The Way to Righteousness

Background Passage: Colossians 3:1–17
Focal Passages: Colossians 3:1–3, 5–17

In Colossians, as in most of Paul's letters, he dealt first with doctrine; then he moved to ethical exhortations. Colossians 3:1–17 is a concise statement of people's lives before and after becoming Christians.

Study Aim: *To contrast Paul's descriptions of the new life in Christ with the old life of sin.*

STUDYING THE BIBLE

OUTLINE AND SUMMARY

I. Living It Up (Col. 3:1–4)

II. Old and New Kinds of People (Col. 3:5–11)
- **1. Sins of the old life (3:5–9)**
- **2. New life in Christ (3:10, 11)**

III. God's New People (Col. 3:12–17)
- **1. Christlike living (3:12–14)**
- **2. Life in the church (3:15–17)**

Christians are to focus on living the upward life (vv. 1–4). They are to avoid the sins of the old life (vv. 5–9). They are to be re-created into a fellowship of one new humanity (vv. 10, 11). As God's new people, they are to live Christlike lives (vv. 12–14). The church is to be a model of peace and gratitude that is expressed in teaching and singing, all in the name of Jesus (vv. 15–17).

I. Living It Up (Col. 3:1–4)

1 If ye then be risen with Christ, seek those things which are above, where Christ sitteth on the right hand of God.

2 Set your affection on things above, not on things on the earth.

3 For ye are dead, and your life is hid with Christ in God.

"Above" means "up" or "upward." Christians are to "seek those things which are above," or make heavenly standards and values their priority. "Set your affection" means to set their desires on heavenly things. This is the basis for the heading, "Living It Up."

These two exhortations are based on the fact that Christians have died (literal meaning of "are dead") and have been raised "with Christ." Paul was repeating a point he had made in Colossians 2:12 and 13. The old life of sin has been crucified, dead, and buried; and believers have been raised to walk in newness of life (Rom. 6:3, 4).

"Hid" probably refers to the fact that the world fails to perceive any of this. Only "when Christ, who is our life, shall appear, then shall" Christians "appear with him in glory" (v. 4).

II. Old and New Kinds of People (Col. 3:5–11)

1. Sins of the old life (vv. 5–9)

5 Mortify therefore your members which are upon the earth; fornication, uncleanness, inordinate affection, evil concupiscence, and covetousness, which is idolatry:

6 For which things' sake the wrath of God cometh on the children of disobedience:

7 In the which ye also walked sometime, when ye lived in them.

8 But now ye also put off all these; anger, wrath, malice, blasphemy, filthy communication out of your mouth.

9 Lie not one to another, seeing that ye have put off the old man with his deeds.

Paul listed eleven sins of the old life. "Mortify" means "put to death." Paul had already said that the old life had died and been buried (2:12, 13; 3:1–3). Why do Christians need to keep putting their sins to death? Christian salvation and living has a once-for-all quality and a day-by-day quality. Conversion takes place in a moment, but overcoming temptation is a lifetime endeavor.

Paul listed five sins in verse 5. The first four are sexual sins. "Fornication" referred to any sexual act not done within the one-flesh union of marriage. "Uncleanness" described the filthiness in God's eyes of all such sins and perversions. The other two sexual sins refer to uncontrolled and evil sexual lusts.

"Covetousness" is the fifth sin listed. Since one aspect of this sin is the insatiable desire for more and more of something, especially something that belongs to another person, some Bible scholars believe Paul used "covetousness" here exclusively of sexual desires. The tenth commandment does specifically forbid coveting a neighbor's wife, but most of the other things refer to material possessions. Jesus used "covetousness" in this way in Luke 12:13–21. Paul said that covetousness "is idolatry." Jesus warned that no one can serve God and mammon (Matt. 6:24).

The sins in verse 5 were the normal way of living for "children of disobedience," on whom "the wrath of God cometh." Many Gentile believers in the first century had once lived in just such sins, but they had been cleansed and set apart to live for God (see 1 Cor. 6:9–11). Therefore, they were to put such sins to death daily.

Verse 8 uses another analogy. Take off the garments that have become dirty because of sins and take off the sins with them. Verse 8 lists five more sins. Three are "anger, wrath, malice." These words describe a state of anger, temper tantrums, and inward hostility. These words describe living on the edge, filled with hatred and anger, ready to explode at the slightest provocation.

Verse 8 warned against two sins of speech, which in this context probably refer to sins of speech directed against others. "Blasphemy" can be directed against God, or it can be slander or gossip directed against others. "Filthy communication" can mean dirty talking or verbal abuse, probably the latter here.

Lying is mentioned separately in verse 9, but it really is a third sin of speech that harms other people. No human relationships can withstand lying. Lasting relations must include trust, and this requires honesty in all things, especially in speech.

2. New life in Christ (vv. 10, 11)

10 And have put on the new man, which is renewed in knowledge after the image of him that created him:

11 Where there is neither Greek nor Jew, circumcision nor uncircumcision, Barbarian, Scythian, bond nor free: but Christ is all, and in all.

The "new man" is not just an individual, but a new humanity or new people of God. God made humans in His own image, but sin spoiled the image of God in people. God's new creation is a renewing of His original intention for us to be in His image.

The end result of this is described in idealistic terms in verse 11, a verse that has much in common with Ephesians 2:11–22. One of the bitter fruits of sin is the alienation and hatred of one group of people against other groups. God's plan is ultimately to have a fellowship in which all the human barriers and hostilities have been removed: between Gentiles and Jews, between civilized and uncivilized people (represented by "Barbarian" and "Scythian"), between masters and slaves. Even now the Christian congregation should be a fellowship in which these old barriers come down and the old hatreds and prejudices die. This is possible only when "Christ is all, and in all."

III. God's New People (Col. 3:12–17)

1. Christlike living (vv. 12–14)

12 Put on therefore, as the elect of God, holy and beloved, bowels of mercies, kindness, humbleness of mind, meekness, longsuffering;

13 Forbearing one another, and forgiving one another, if any man have a quarrel against any: even as Christ forgave you, so also do ye.

14 And above all these things put on charity, which is the bond of perfectness.

"Elect" means "chosen." The same terms used of the chosen people of the old covenant described the chosen people of the new covenant: "holy and beloved." Israelites were the chosen of the old covenant; verse 11 describes the all-encompassing definition of the new covenant chosen people.

Verse 12 lists five qualities of the new people of God. These qualities, which have to do with human relations, are the opposites of the sins of verse 8. God's new people are to be merciful (compassionate), kind, humble, meek (gentle), and "longsuffering."

When these qualities are put into practice, they are often expressed by forbearance and/or forgiveness. Notice the words *one another*. The New

Testament uses a variety of words before "one another." None is more important than "forbearing one another, and forgiving one another." Forbearance refers to putting up with the petty annoyances that result from different kinds of people trying to get along. It is crucial in a church, where people sometimes rub one another the wrong way.

Forgiveness has to do with the real hurts that sometimes happen in human relationships. Paul said, "if any man have a quarrel against any." He was writing about quarrels arising out of real or imagined hurts, for which the only cure is forgiveness. When a Christian has been hurt, "even as Christ forgave you, so also do ye." Since Christ has forgiven us much worse sins and hurts against God, we must allow His Spirit to enable us to bear the pain in order to offer forgiveness.

Verses 12 and 13 name things that are manifestations of agape love ("charity"). Verse 14, like 1 Corinthians 13, names agape (Godlike, self-giving love) as the supreme Christian virtue. Such love binds all the other Christian virtues together.

2. Life in the church (vv. 15–17)

> **15 And let the peace of God rule in your hearts, to the which also ye are called in one body; and be ye thankful.**
>
> **16 Let the word of Christ dwell in you richly in all wisdom; teaching and admonishing one another in psalms and hymns and spiritual songs, singing with grace in your hearts to the Lord.**
>
> **17 And whatsoever ye do in word or deed, do all in the name of the Lord Jesus, giving thanks to God and the Father by him.**

"Peace of God" refers to peace with God, inner peace, or peace with one another. The words "ye are called in one body" show that Paul had the latter meaning in mind. It is "of God" because only a right relationship with God opens our lives to this peace. It is not just the absence of conflict in a church; it is the rich, positive kind of fellowship reflected in verse 16.

Notice that Paul again wrote, "And be ye thankful." The apostle mentioned thanksgiving in Colossians 1:12 and 2:7, no doubt because gratitude to God is the heart of a church's life.

Verse 16 is an inspiring one-verse summary of life in the body of Christ. Because the church is the body of Christ and He is our head, "the word of Christ" must have priority. This includes the good news of salvation in Christ as well as the words and teachings of Jesus. This word must "dwell in" us "richly."

This word is expressed in a variety of ways. Paul focused on "teaching and admonishing one another." Notice again "one another." A church has some people with the gift and office of teacher; but verse 16 says that in a larger sense, all of us are to teach one another and thus learn from one another.

Paul seems to tie the teaching to "singing with grace in your hearts to the Lord." He mentioned "psalms and hymns and spiritual songs," which implies a variety of kinds of music and singing. Singing can be praise directed "to the Lord" and/or teaching and testimony directed to one another. In either case, it must be done with "grace in" our "hearts."

Verse 17 is a kind of all-inclusive guideline for everything God's new people do together or individually. Paul included "word or deed" in this guideline. "Do all in the name of the Lord Jesus." To act or speak in His name is to do so in His Spirit's power and in a way consistent with "the word of Christ" (v. 16).

Notice again the emphasis on "giving thanks to God and the Father by him." This reminds us that we come to God only in and through Jesus Christ.

PRONUNCIATION GUIDE

Barbarian	[bahr BEAR ih uhn]
Scythian	[SITH ih uhn]

SUMMARY OF BIBLE TRUTHS

1. Christians are to live by the standards of heaven.
2. Sins of the old life are to be put to death.
3. God's ideal for His new people is to include all kinds.
4. Christlike qualities are to be lived by Christians.
5. Life in the church is based on living by the Word of Christ.
6. Singing and thanksgiving are normal parts of church life.

APPLYING THE BIBLE

1. Christ is all. The hymn writer understood the truth of today's lesson and illustrated it well in the hymn "All That Thrills My Soul." Stanzas 2 and 3 speak clearly to the miracle of rebirth and cleansing that believers experience in coming to Christ.

Love of Christ so freely given, Grace of God beyond degree,
Mercy higher than the heaven, Deeper than the deepest sea.
What a wonderful redemption never can a mortal know.
How my sin tho red like crimson, Can be whiter than the snow.
All that thrills my soul is Jesus, He is more than life to me.
And the fairest of ten thousand, in my blessed Lord I see.

2. Maybe we're lucky. One of my on-line devotional sources recently ran the following devotion. The original author is unknown.

"The following notice was spotted in the lost-and-found section of the newspaper: Lost dog. $50 reward. Black and tan dog of poodle and German shepherd descent. Flea-bitten, left hind leg missing, no hair on rump, blind, and recently neutered. Answers to the name of *Lucky*.

"Some of us are a lot like Lucky. Of mixed ancestry, not much to look at, and in pretty bad shape, we still answer to the name of Lucky. We are indeed fortunate, for like the dog, we have Someone who cares enough about us to look for us, to pursue us, to pay to get us back. And our Master did pay to get us back. It cost Him the life of His only Son. That dog is lucky, and so are we—lucky that our Master would love us so much."

3. The cross as an accessory. In an interview on the subject of celebrities and others wearing cross jewelry, a pastor said, "The cross is not an accessory. It's a powerful symbol of our faith." Julie Brown agrees. "I'm a big believer," she says. "When somebody sees you wearing a beautiful cross, they know that you have good things going on inside."[1]

4. Characteristics of the crucified life. The cross is not just a piece of jewelry. It is a statement of belief. The characteristics of one being crucified can be observed as follows:

- They are looking only one way.
- They have surrendered all available options.
- They have no plans of their own.

5. The crucified life. "After crosses and losses, men grow humbler and wiser" (Benjamin Franklin).

6. New life in Christ is actually good for your health. Going to church and reading the Bible regularly may do more than save your soul—they may extend your life. Duke University researchers recently found that people 65 or older who regularly participated in religious activities were 40 percent less likely to have high blood pressure. Religion also may provide the faithful with comfort or a loving community in their golden years, thereby lowering stress and blood pressure, researchers said; and churchgoers may be able to cope with stress better than the less religious.[2]

7. Faith and obedience. "The Bible recognizes no faith that does not lead to obedience, nor does it recognize any obedience that does not spring from faith. The two are at opposite sides of the same coin" (A. W. Tozer).

TEACHING THE BIBLE

- *Main Idea:* Believers are called to turn from the old life of sin and walk in the new life with Christ.
- *Suggested Teaching Aim:* To lead adults to contrast Paul's descriptions of the new life in Christ with the old life of sin.

A TEACHING OUTLINE

1. *Living It Up (Col. 3:1–4)*
2. *Old and New Kinds of People (Col. 3:5–11)*
3. *God's New People (Col. 3:12–17)*

Introduce the Bible Study

Use number 2, "Maybe We're Lucky," in "Applying the Bible" to introduce the lesson.

Search for Biblical Truth

IN ADVANCE:

- On large sheets of paper, copy the five Scripture references for the five outline subpoints. Tape these at random around the room.
- Be sure every person has a Bible to use in the Scripture search.

➧ Bring several newspapers from this week.

Read the five summary statements from "Outline and Summary" and ask members to match them with the appropriate verses taped to the wall from Colossians 3:1–17.

On a chalkboard or a large sheet of paper write:

The Old Life	The New Life

Ask members to open their Bibles to Colossians 3:1–17. Ask half the class to find references to the old life of sin and the other half to find references to the new life in Christ as you move through the lesson.

Ask members to read silently verses 1–3 and find descriptions of the old life and new life. (Seek, set, dead, life is hid.)

Ask members to read silently verses 5–9 and find descriptions of the old life (fornication, uncleanness, inordinate affections, evil concupiscence, covetousness, anger, wrath, malice, blasphemy, filthy communication, lying) and new life (put off). Distribute newspapers and ask members to find examples of the eleven sins Paul mentioned here.

Ask members to read silently verses 10 and 11 and find descriptions of the old life and new life. (Put on new man, Christ is all in all.)

DISCUSS: How good a job does our church do in ignoring racial (Greek nor Jew), religious (circumcision nor uncircumcision), cultural (Barbarian, Scythian), or social (bond nor free) differences? What can we do to make some of these old prejudices die?

Ask members to read silently verses 12 and 13 and find descriptions of the old and new life. (Elect of God, holy, beloved, bowels of mercies, kindness, humbleness, meekness, longsuffering, forbearance, forgiveness, love.)

DISCUSS: Which one of these qualities do you most like to be the recipient of? Which quality do you most like to practice?

Ask members to read silently verses 15–17 and find descriptions of the old and new life. (Peace, thankfulness, one body, word of Christ dwelling in us, wisdom, teaching and admonishing, singing with psalms, hymns and spiritual songs, doing all in the name of Christ, thanking God.)

DISCUSS: How do you use your gratitude ("be ye thankful" v. 15) as a way of encouraging others in the body of Christ? wisdom? teaching?

Read aloud the five summary statements on the wall to summarize the lesson.

Give the Truth a Personal Focus

Use No. 1, "Christ Is All," in "Applying the Bible" to close the session. If practical, sing "All That Thrills My Soul Is Jesus."

---

1. Michael Neill, *People Weekly,* Aug. 18, 1997, 68.
2. Published in *The Orlando Sentinel,* Aug. 29, 1998.

Welcoming Others in Christ

Background Passage: Philemon 1–25
Focal Passage: Philemon 4–21

Paul's letter to Philemon is a personal letter in which Paul asked a lot of a fellow Christian. He made an earnest plea that Philemon welcome back his runaway slave Onesimus and treat him as a Christian brother, not as a slave.

Study Aim: *To describe what is involved in welcoming fellow Christians in spite of past sins and differences.*

STUDYING THE BIBLE

OUTLINE AND SUMMARY

I. Paul's Friendship with Philemon (Philem. 1–7)
  1. Personal greeting (vv. 1–3)
  2. Gratitude and prayer for Philemon (vv. 4–7)

II. Paul's Appeal to Philemon for Onesimus (Philem. 8–25)
  1. An appeal for love's sake (vv. 8, 9)
  2. An appeal for Onesimus (vv. 10–14)
  3. An appeal to welcome Onesimus as a brother (vv. 15–19)
  4. Paul's confidence in Philemon (vv. 20–22)
  5. Greetings to Philemon from those with Paul (vv. 23–25)

Paul greeted his friend Philemon (vv. 1–3). He told Philemon that he prayed for him and gave thanks for him (vv. 4–7). He based his appeal to Philemon on love (vv. 8, 9). He appealed for Onesimus, his son in the faith (vv. 10–14). He asked Philemon to welcome Onesimus as a brother in Christ (vv. 15–19). Paul was confident that Philemon would do more than Paul asked (vv. 20–22). He sent greetings from those with him (vv. 23–25).

I. Paul's Friendship with Philemon (Philem. 1–7)

1. Personal greeting (vv. 1–3)

Paul greeted Philemon as "our dearly beloved, and fellowlabourer" (v. 1). Paul also greeted Apphia (probably Philemon's wife), Archippus (probably his son), and the church meeting in Philemon's house (v. 2). He greeted them with his usual words of grace and peace in Christ (v. 3).

2. Gratitude and prayer for Philemon (vv. 4–7)

4 I thank my God, making mention of thee always in my prayers,

5 Hearing of thy love and faith, which thou hast toward the Lord Jesus, and toward all saints;

6 That the communication of thy faith may become effectual by the acknowledging of every good thing which is in you in Christ Jesus.

7 For we have great joy and consolation in thy love, because the bowels of the saints are refreshed by thee, brother.

Paul prayed for Philemon; and when he did, he expressed gratitude for his friend. He was grateful for Philemon's faith in the Lord and for his love for all the saints (all fellow believers).

"Communication" translates a word that emphasizes the oneness of Christians because of their common relationship with the Lord. "Acknowledging" translates a word that emphasizes learning through personal experience. "Bowels" was an ancient way of describing the emotions; we use the word "heart."

Verse 6 is Paul's prayer for Philemon. He prayed that his friend would express the oneness of his faith in fellowship with other Christians. He also prayed that Philemon would grow in his personal experience of all the good things believers have in Christ.

Verse 7 is another word of commendation and thanksgiving for Philemon. Paul was filled with joy and encouragement because Philemon was so faithful in refreshing the saints.

II. Paul's Appeal to Philemon for Onesimus (Philem. 8–25)

1. An appeal for love's sake (vv. 8, 9)

8 Wherefore, though I might be much bold in Christ to enjoin thee that which is convenient,

9 Yet for love's sake I rather beseech thee, being such an one as Paul the aged, and now also a prisoner of Jesus Christ.

"Enjoin" means "command." "Convenient" means doing what is right and proper. Paul said that he could have boldly commanded Philemon to do the right thing. However, rather than command his friend as an apostle, Paul fervently appealed to him to act for love's sake.

In making this appeal, Paul reminded Philemon what he personally was doing for love's sake. He pictured himself as an old man who was in prison for Christ's sake.

2. An appeal for Onesimus (vv. 10–14)

10 I beseech thee for my son Onesimus, whom I have begotten in my bonds:

11 Which in time past was to thee unprofitable, but now profitable to thee and to me:

12 Whom I have sent again: thou therefore receive him, that is, mine own bowels:

13 Whom I would have retained with me, that in thy stead he might have ministered unto me in the bonds of the gospel:

14 But without thy mind would I do nothing; that thy benefit should not be as it were of necessity, but willingly.

Paul did everything he could to encourage Philemon to do the right thing. In verse 10, the apostle referred to Onesimus as his son, whom he had begotten while in prison. This probably means that Onesimus had come to Rome and been won to faith in Christ by Paul.

The name "Onesimus" means "profitable" or "useful." Onesimus had not lived up to his name, but Paul told Philemon that the formerly useless one would now be useful to Philemon and to Paul.

"Sent again" implies that Onesimus had run away from Philemon. In verse 16, Onesimus is called a "servant," which translates the word "slave." Thus, it seems that Onesimus was a runaway slave.

Onesimus must have been willing to go back to Philemon and to hope for the best. He was not under guard, so he could have run away from Paul or on the way home. Based on a comparison with Colossians 4:7–9, Tychicus and Onesimus traveled together to Colosse in order to deliver the letter to the Colossian church and the letter to Philemon.

Paul made clear to Philemon how he personally felt about his son in the faith. "Mine own bowels" means "my own heart." In sending Onesimus back, Paul was sending one who was dear to him.

Paul's preference would have been to keep Onesimus with him. Onesimus "might have ministered unto" Paul during his confinement. "In thy stead" means that Onesimus could have helped Paul in a way that Philemon would have done if he had been with Paul. "Without thy mind" means "without your decision." Paul would have liked to keep Onesimus with him as a helper, but he did not want to do this without Philemon's decision that it be done.

3. An appeal to welcome Onesimus as a brother (vv. 15–19)

> **15 For perhaps he therefore departed for a season, that thou shouldest receive him for ever;**
>
> **16 Not now as a servant, but above a servant, a brother beloved, specially to me, but how much more unto thee, both in the flesh, and in the Lord?**
>
> **17 If thou count me therefore a partner, receive him as myself.**

Paul's point in verse 15 is that God could bring good out of a bad situation if Philemon would receive Onesimus. He had left for a short time, but now Philemon might have him back forever. Paul implied that God had been at work to bring something good out of something bad (Gen. 50:20; Rom. 8:28).

The words *receive* and *brother* are key words in verses 15–17 and in the letter as a whole. The word *receive* in verse 15 means to "have back." This is a different word from the Greek word translated "receive" in verse 17. The word in verse 17 means "accept" or "welcome." Paul used that word in Romans 14:1 and 15:7 of welcoming fellow Christians with whom one group of Christians had had disagreements. Paul's appeal to Philemon was to welcome back Onesimus in spite of the fact that he had run away.

Verse 16 is the heart of the letter because Paul appealed that Philemon welcome Onesimus as a "brother." Onesimus was a "servant," which means not a hired servant but a slave. Onesimus belonged to Philemon. He had run away; and as we shall see when we look at verses 17 and 18, he had probably stolen from Philemon. He had been to Rome, where Paul won him to Christ. Now he was back carrying this letter of appeal from Paul. Ordinarily in first-century society, runaway slaves were either killed or branded on the forehead. Paul, however, asked Philemon to welcome Onesimus as a Christian brother.

Paul used the word *partner* to describe his relation to Philemon. They shared a common faith in the Lord; they had been fellow workers for the same Lord. Paul asked his partner in the Lord to receive Onesimus as he would receive Paul himself.

> **18 If he hath wronged thee, or oweth thee ought, put that on mine account;**
>
> **19 I Paul have written it with mine own hand, I will repay it: albeit I do not say to thee how thou owest unto me even thine own self besides.**

The word *forgiveness* is not found in the letter to Philemon, but the idea is clearly implied in many ways. One meaning of forgiveness is canceling a debt. Onesimus owed Philemon something. Since his service was worth something, Onesimus had robbed his master of his service while he was away. However, Onesimus probably also had stolen some money. How else could he have made the long journey to Rome without money?

"Put that on mine account" was a business term meaning "charge it to me." Paul promised Philemon that he personally would pay anything that Onesimus owed his master. Ordinarily, Paul only dictated his letters; and someone else wrote down the words. However, at this point Paul himself wrote, "I will repay it."

As Paul made this promise, Paul reminded Philemon of a debt that Philemon owed Paul. He owed himself to Paul. This probably means that Paul had won Philemon to the Lord.

4. Paul's confidence in Philemon (vv. 20–22)

> **20 Yea, brother, let me have joy of thee in the Lord: refresh my bowels in the Lord.**
>
> **21 Having confidence in thy obedience I wrote unto thee, knowing that thou wilt also do more than I say.**

Paul asked Philemon to bring joy to his heart by forgiving Onesimus and treating him as a Christian brother. Paul expressed confidence that Philemon would do even more than Paul had asked. What did Paul mean when he wrote, "Thou wilt also do more than I say"? Paul had asked Philemon to welcome Onesimus as a brother, not as a slave. What more did Paul expect Philemon to do?

Was Paul implying that Philemon give Onesimus his freedom? This is possible; however, Paul elsewhere did not attack the institution of slavery or advocate emancipation of slaves. Colossians 3:22–4:1 is typical of his instructions to Christian slaves and masters. He told slaves to obey their masters, but to do it as believers whose real master was Christ. He also reminded slave owners to remember they would give account to their master. Nothing is said about setting slaves free; however, the implication of such passages and especially of verses like Colossians 3:11 eventually ended slavery in lands influenced by Christianity.

Paul never spelled out for Philemon exactly what he was to do in treating his runaway slave as a brother. Paul left Philemon to struggle with the implications of the appeal in verse 16.

Verse 22 is another evidence of Paul's confidence that Philemon would do the right thing. Paul asked his friend to provide him a place to stay when he came for a visit.

5. Greetings to Philemon from those with Paul (vv. 23–25)

Paul sent greetings from Epaphras and several others who were with him.

PRONUNCIATION GUIDE

Apphia	[AF ih uh]
Archippus	[ahr KIP uhs]
Epaphras	[EP uh frass]
Onesimus	[oh NESS ih muhs]
Philemon	[figh LEE muhn]
Tychicus	[TIK ih kuhs]

SUMMARY OF BIBLE TRUTHS

1. Christians can pray for and commend one another.
2. Christians should do the right thing for love's sake.
3. Christians can witness to and sometimes win the lost.
4. Christians ought to welcome fellow believers in spite of past sins and differences.
5. Christians can encourage one another to welcome those who have wronged them.
6. Love motivates believers to do more than the minimum.

APPLYING THE BIBLE

1. An impossible task. Imagine how Onesimus must have felt following his conversion when he realized he had to return to Philemon. Had he turned to a modern-day "how-to" guide, he might have come across the following words of advice: "People who become well-known and well-liked at work usually are good at talking and getting along well with people. Ways to get along well with people include knowing personal details, selectively complimenting people and telling short, funny stories. Listening is the best quality."[1]

2. The art of subtle schmooze. Adele Scheele, director of the Career Center at California State University at Northridge and author of *Skills for Success,* says you need to know how to schmooze—gab, chat, flatter, and back-scratch your way into people's hearts. She offers the following suggestions which she calls "The Art of Subtle Schmoozing":

- Stock up on specifics.
- Be selective and sincere.
- Stealth schmooze.
- Respect private moments.
- Listen.[2]

Onesimus did not have to do any of these things to get back on track with Philemon because he had a friend like Paul. Paul didn't schmooze Philemon either; he simply appealed to him on the basis of their friendship and the Christian ethic.

If you were Onesimus, imagine how thankful you would be that someone like Paul had taken an interest in your plight. Is there an Onesimus/Philemon situation somewhere on your horizon? If so, what steps can you take to assist in a reconciliation?

3. True repentance. A man who stole a canoe repented of his deed some twenty-five years later and sent $150 to the owner. Dale Wagner of Bradgate, Iowa, the canoe's original owner, remembered the theft when he read the letter of apology and simply said, "I've forgiven him."

The letter and cash were found in an unaddressed letter left for the postmaster of the town. In the words of the repentant canoe thief the letter stated, "I take no pride in what I did . . . but pray that in some small way I have righted the wrong I committed so many years ago. Please use the money for the town unless someone can identify the person I stole the canoe from."

4. Taking the next step. The example above shows how a request for forgiveness is supposed to be given: (1) It shows remorse, (2) it seeks to set right a wrong committed, (3) it accepts responsibility without making excuses, and (4) it calls the action "wrong."

You can almost hear Paul reminding Onesimus of the proper way to state his apology to Philemon. Think of a wrong you have committed that needs to be made right. Consider writing out the request for forgiveness and reconciliation word for word. Select your words carefully by showing remorse, seeking to set right the wrong committed, accepting responsibility without making an excuse, and referring to what you did as wrong. Practice saying it a few times. Now, be like Onesimus and do the right thing!

5. Forgiveness defined. Forgiveness is agreeing to live with the consequences of another person's sin. Philemon received Onesimus back at great personal cost. For Philemon to forgive Onesimus, he had to place himself in a vulnerable position with every other slave on his estate. To receive Onesimus back could send a message to the other slaves that the penalty for running away was no longer enforced. Make no mistake about it: forgiveness is expensive and Philemon had to pay a great price.[3]

6. Steps to forgiveness. Neil Anderson has helped thousands with the issue of forgiveness. His counsel rings true for those who find themselves feeling like Philemon. Try these four steps if you are having a difficult time forgiving someone who has hurt you in the past.

- Acknowledge the hurt and the hate.
- Let God bring the pain to the surface so He can deal with it.

- Decide that you will bear the burden of their offenses by not using the information about their offenses against them in the future.
- Don't wait to forgive until you feel like forgiving.[4]

7. Great truths of Philemon:

- Redemption relates all men in Christ. Paul the apostle, Philemon the slave owner, and Onesimus the runaway are all brothers in Christ through redeeming grace.
- Christian grace often obligates the greater to the lesser. Paul obligates himself to Philemon, even though Philemon owes everything to Paul. Paul appeals to Philemon to obligate himself to Onesimus, a new brother in Christ.
- Love goes far beyond bare necessity; it gives and goes as far as it can to aid another.[5]

TEACHING THE BIBLE

- *Main Idea:* God asks us to forgive those He has forgiven and accept them as fellow brothers and sisters in Christ.
- *Suggested Teaching Aim:* To lead adults to describe what is involved in welcoming fellow Christians in spite of past sins and differences.

A TEACHING OUTLINE

1. *Paul's Friendship with Philemon (Philem. 1–7)*
2. *Paul's Appeal to Philemon for Onesimus (Philem. 8–25)*

Introduce the Bible Study

Use number 3, "True Repentance," in "Applying the Bible" to introduce the lesson.

Search for Biblical Truth

IN ADVANCE:

- Place this list on the focal wall:

List of Characters	
Philemon	the owner of Onesimus, a runaway slave
Apphia	possibly Philemon's wife
Archippus	possibly Philemon's son
Onesimus	runaway slave converted by Paul
Paul	letter writer who is in jail

- Provide paper and pencils for all members.
- Enlist a good reader to read Philemon from a more recent translation.
- Copy the letter and place it in an envelope. Read it as though it were a letter recently received.

Share this life situation: Bob (Bobbi) had made some unkind and untrue statements about Bill (Billie) years earlier that had resulted in a ruined reputation and even financial loss for Bill (Billie). Bob (Bobbi) had left town and hadn't been heard from in years. One day he (she) showed up at Bill's (Billie's) door, explained that he (she) had become a Christian recently, and wanted to apologize for what he (she) had said and do what he (she) could to make things right. Bill (Billie) said . . . Ask several members to complete what they think Bill (Billie) said.

Place the "List of Characters" on the wall and identify them.

Ask members to look at verses 4–7. Ask: What one word do you think sums up Paul's feelings toward Philemon? (Gratitude or some similar feeling.)

Ask members to look at verses 8 and 9. Ask, What did Paul say he could have done? (Commanded Philemon.) Why do you think Paul did not do this? How did he describe his own situation? (Old and in jail.) Do you think this had any influence on Philemon?

Ask members to look at verses 10–14. Ask, What does verse 10 tell us had happened to Onesimus? (Saved.) Ask members to identify those things Paul did to encourage Philemon to do the right thing for Onesimus. List these on a chalkboard. Ask: Why did Paul want to keep Onesimus? Why was it important for both Onesimus and Philemon for Onesimus to return home?

Ask members to look at verses 15–19. Ask: How could Romans 8:28 apply to Philemon 15? (God can bring good out of evil.) What word did Paul use to refer to Onesimus in verse 16? (Brother.) How did Paul want Philemon to accept Onesimus? (As he would accept Paul.) What did Paul say about what Onesimus had stolen from Philemon? (Paul would pay him back.)

Ask members to look at verses 20 and 21. Ask: What did Paul mean by "Thou wilt also do more than I say"? (See "Studying the Bible.") Why do you think Paul never spelled out exactly for Philemon what he was to do in treating his runaway slave as a brother?

Read aloud the six "Summary of Bible Truths" statements.

Give the Truth a Personal Focus

Distribute paper and pencils. Use number 4, "Taking the Next Step," in "Applying the Bible" to close the session. Ask members to identify a situation in their lives that needs to be set right and write out their request for forgiveness and reconciliation. Assure them that you will not see the papers. Close in prayer that members will be able to forgive and turn something bad into something good.

---

1. Amanda Weiss, "The New Secret to Winning Friends and Influencing People," *Redbook,* March 1997, 45.
2. Cited by Weiss.
3. Neil Anderson, *The Bondage Breaker* (Eugene, Oregon: Harvest House Publishers) 1990.
4. Ibid.
5. William Deal, *Baker's Pictorial Introduction to the Bible* (New York: Bonnza, 1967), 38.

Index

The following index gives the lesson date on which a particular passage of Scripture has been treated in *Broadman Comments* from September 1994 through August 2000. Since the International Bible Lessons, Uniform Series, are planned in six-year cycles, the lessons during any six consecutive years include the better-known books and passages on central teachings. Thus, anyone who has access to the 1994-2000 volumes of *Comments* can use this index to find a discussion of almost any part of the Bible he or she may be interested in studying.

* Denotes Sanctity of Human Life emphasis.

Judges

Ruth

1 Samuel

2 Samuel

1 Kings

2 Kings

1 Chronicles

2 Chronicles

Ezra

Nehemiah

Esther

Job

Psalms

Proverbs

Luke

John

Acts

Romans

1 Corinthians